The Birth of Modern Britain 1780–1914

Eric J. Evans

LONGMAN

Contents

Part Three: Democracy, empire and welfare, 1867–1914

Editorial introduction

This aim of this book is to give you as clear a picture as possible of the events and developments in the period you are studying. You may well be using this book to prepare for an examination and the book has several special features, listed below, to help you in this. Most of all, we hope it will help you to develop a critical awareness about, and a continuing interest in, the past.

FOCUS: Each chapter has a main focus, listed in the contents. These are the main issues and 'concepts', like cause and consequence, the evaluation of evidence, the role of the individual, key themes, historical controversies or interpretations and so on. All of these are important in studying and understanding history. Identifying a focus does not mean that the chapter only looks at the past in one way; rather that you are encouraged to find out about topics from a different slant.

TIME CHARTS: Most chapters begin with a time chart. It helps you follow the chronology. Some time charts develop a basic point which is not in the main text. You should also find that the charts provide you with a handy reference point.

KEY TERMS: There are some words or phrases which it is important to know in order to understand a wider topic. These have been highlighted in the text so that you can easily look up what they mean. Sometimes quite simple ideas appear in unfamiliar form or in jargon. Decoding these should help you to make sense of the wider ideas to which the terms relate. Towards the end of the book you will find a separate index of the key terms.

PROFILES: There is not space in a book like this to provide full biographies of the people you will meet. The profiles give you the information you need to understand why an individual is important and what his or her main achievements were. Like the time charts, you might want to use these for reference. As with 'key terms', there is a separate index of people who are the subject of profiles.

TASKS and ACTIVITIES: Nearly all the chapters end with some suggestions for follow-up work and further study. These include:

- guidance on how, and why, to take notes
- suggestions for class discussion and debate

- help on how to use historical evidence of different types
- tips on answering source questions
- hints on planning and writing essays
- specimen examination questions so that you can prepare for assessment.

FURTHER READING: You will find that you need more help on certain topics than can be provided in a book like this. The further reading guides you to some more detailed or specialist texts. The reading is listed with the most immediately obvious supporting texts placed first, followed by others – some of which may be considerably more detailed – and ending with articles and other shorter pieces, where these are appropriate.

INDEX: Many individuals, issues and themes are mentioned in more than one chapter. The index is designed to help you find what you are looking for quickly and easily by showing you how to collect together information which is spread about. Get practice in using an index; it will save you a lot of time.

The historian's job is to recreate the past. On one level, this is obviously an impossible task. There is far too much of it to put into one book while at the same time much of the information we need has been long since lost. Most of it can never be recovered. It is because there is so much of it that the historian has to impose his or her priorities by selecting. It is because so much more has been lost that he or she has to try to fill in the gaps and supply answers which other people can challenge. The processes of **Selection** and **Interpretation** are the key tasks of the historian and they help to make the subject endlessly fascinating. Every time a historian makes a decision about what to put in and what to leave out that decision implies a judgement which others might challenge. Historians try to get as close to the truth as they can, in the knowledge that others may disagree with which they say. Don't be surprised, then, to find a number of personal views or 'interpretations'. Some of these will make comparisons between the present and the period you are studying. These personal views have not been included in order to persuade you to agree with them. We aim to make you *think* about what you are reading and not always to accept everything at face value. If this book helps you to tell the difference between fact and opinion while keeping up your interest in the past, it will have served its purpose.

Christopher Culpin
Eric Evans
Series Editors

Part One

The old order challenged, 1780–1832

INTRODUCTION

1 Britain at the end of the eighteenth century

Numbers and places

This book begins with a brief look at Britain more than 200 years ago. How different were things then? A time traveller from our own day who was able to visit Britain in 1780 would be struck by the differences between the country then and now. Firstly, late eighteenth-century Britain contained far fewer people; many parts of it would seem to us almost empty. We have no official population figures until the first census was taken in 1801 but contemporary estimates and a great deal of recent research make us fairly confident in stating that the combined populations of England and Wales in 1781 totalled about 7.5 million (see Figure 1.1), compared with some 52 million today.

Secondly, that population was distributed very differently from today's. Some things, however, were the same. London was the capital and much the biggest city in England; about 10 per cent of the population lived there. The main centres of Britain's population nowadays – London and its neighbourhood, the West Midlands, Lancashire, South and West Yorkshire, the North-East (around Newcastle and Sunderland) and central Scotland – were all highly populated in 1780.

Beyond this, however, the main emphasis is on change. Almost 80 per cent of the population nowadays lives in large towns. Most British people in 1780 lived in villages; only about 20 per cent of Britain's population were in towns of 10,000 people or more. Liverpool had not yet taken

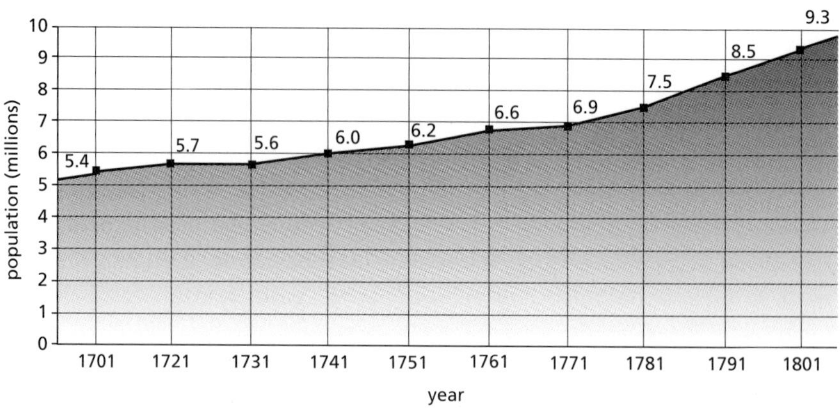

Figure 1.1 The growth in population of England and Wales, 1700–1800

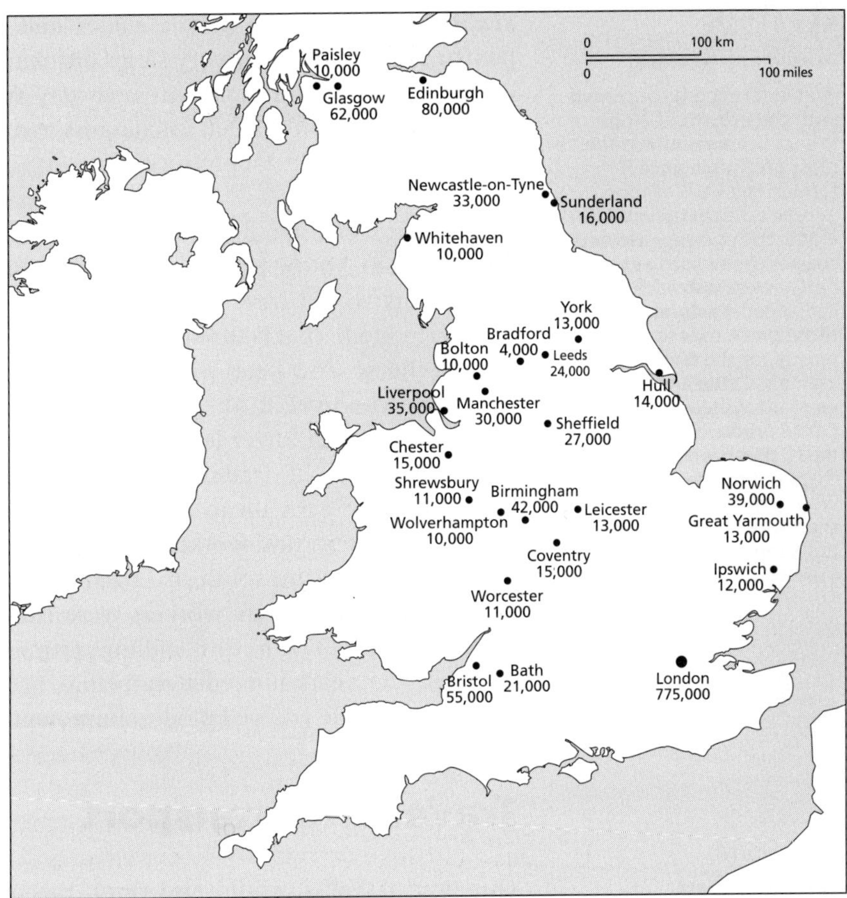

Figure 1.2 *Map of Britain in the eighteenth century*

over from Bristol as the biggest port. In 1780, Norwich was the fourth largest town in England, its wealth deriving from the prosperous wool trade. It has now been greatly outstripped by industrial towns like Manchester, Leeds, Newcastle and Sheffield. Places which are now little more than villages, such as Melksham and Trowbridge in Wiltshire, were in 1780 leading towns for the manufacture of woollen cloth.

The restless cotton mills of Lancashire and Lanarkshire, on which so much of Britain's nineteenth-century industrial might would be built (see chapters 3 and 4), were in 1780 still in their infancy. Some of the leading cotton towns, Blackburn, Bolton, Paisley and Stockport were small towns with populations between 5,000 and 12,000. The present capital of Wales, Cardiff, hardly existed in 1780; Barrow-in-Furness and Middlesborough were still towns of the future, and would not be found on an eighteenth-century map.

Britain in 1780 was predominantly a rural country, producing almost all of its own food. The south and east of England was the main centre of

KEY TERMS:

Arable and pastoral

Arable farming is concerned with the growth of crops. Wheat production was the most profitable since it formed the basis of the people's diet in the late eighteenth century. However, coarser grains such as oats and barley were also widely consumed. **Pastoral** areas are those given over to grass, mostly for the feeding of animals. Cattle and sheep were nourished on grass. Cattle produced milk and meat; sheep were bred for meat but mostly for their wool. The humble sheep therefore provided a vital link between agriculture and industry.

arable farming; the generally hillier and wetter north and west was **pastoral**. Britain had a very large number of towns in the eighteenth century but a visitor from our own day would not recognise them as such. Many had only 2,000 inhabitants at most and functioned largely as markets for agricultural produce.

Our time traveller would also notice that people were not always paid in money. Many young people who worked for **tenant farmers** as domestic servants would have very little money to spend. Their wages were mostly 'in kind', that is to say their employers provided lodging and food. Bread, cheese and beer was also frequently provided for agricultural labourers who lived in their own cottages. Both wages and prices were also at very much lower levels than we are used to. A skilled craftsman who had learned his trade via **apprenticeship** and whose skills were in demand might earn up to 30 shillings (£1.50) per week, but this was exceptional. Few rural workers would earn more than 12 shillings (60p) per week and in the south of England, where by the end of the eighteenth century too many workers were chasing too few permanent jobs, wages of 7s 6d (37½ p) or 8 shillings (40p) were common. Nevertheless, prices in the years immediately before 1780 had been relatively stable and many people enjoyed modest improvements in their living standards.

Travel and transport

KEY TERM:

Tenant farmers

Tenant farmers did not own their own land. They rented it from landowners and were responsible for keeping it productive. The tenant farmer would pay an agreed sum for a lease from the landlord which gave him the right to farm the land. During the eighteenth century, leases often gave precise instructions about how the land was to be farmed. The tenant aimed to make a profit from his business arrangement with the landlord. Tenant farmers were particularly important agents of change in eighteenth-century society precisely because their aim was profit. Small landowners who worked the land solely (or mainly) to feed themselves and their families (**subsistence** farmers or **peasants**) do not have such an incentive to change and develop.

Our time traveller would also think that the pace of life in 1780 was much slower than today. Trains hauled by James Watt's new steam-engine, developed in the 1780s, were almost 50 years away. Much money had already been invested in canals, and a further 'canal boom' would take place in the 1790s. Canals made the transport of bulky goods, such as coal and heavy metals, both easier and cheaper. When the famous Worsley canal, built with money provided by the Duke of Bridgewater, was completed in the early 1760s its widespread use lowered transport costs so much that the price of coal in Manchester was halved.

Most heavy goods were transported by water because so many roads were of very bad quality. During wet winters, they became literally impassable for months at a time. Important improvements had been made during the eighteenth century, largely by the creation of metal roads. These were called 'turnpike' roads and people were required to pay tolls to travel on them. Almost 20,000 miles of turnpike roads existed at the end of the eighteenth century linking most of the major centres of trade and industry. They were still desperately slow. It took about 20 hours to travel the 190 miles from London to York, for example, and 36 hours to get the 270 miles to Newcastle. Cargoes moving long distances from one part of Britain to another in 1780 were much more likely to be carried around the coast rather than over land.

Movement across England from east to west was very difficult because of the natural barrier presented by the Pennine range of hills from Derbyshire up to the Scottish border. Much of Wales is mountainous and effective north–south communications across the Principality elude transport systems to this day. Scotland was called by one of its composers in the early twentieth century 'The Land of the Mountain and the Flood'. In the eighteenth century, its spectacular scenery attracted few tourists and Scotland's peaks and lochs were seen as a barrier to change and progress. Almost 90 per cent of Scotland's population became concentrated in a narrow area between the mountains known as the Southern Uplands and the Grampians. This process was speeded up by the so-called 'Highland Clearances' of the late eighteenth and early nineteenth centuries. These cleared large numbers of crofters and peasants off their smallholdings. Landlords like the wealthy Duke of Sutherland knew that sheep would make them more money than labourers would. It is no accident that the Scots, as well as the Irish whose numbers were so pitiably reduced by a great famine in the years 1845–7, featured disproportionately frequently as emigrants to a new and, they hoped, better life in Canada, Australia or New Zealand during the nineteenth century.

KEY TERM:

Apprenticeship

Apprenticeship was a legally enforceable arrangement by which young people (mostly men) worked with established craftsmen to learn a trade such as masonry, shoemaking and metal working. Apprenticeships were usually for a period of seven years and a young man could obtain a thorough mastery of the craft during this time. Most apprentices worked in towns. Successful apprentices would expect to be able to make a good living from the skill they had acquired. Many also enjoyed a measure of independence and modest prosperity. Apprenticeship could also operate as a rationing device which restricted entry to the trade only to the able and skilful. Good-quality workmanship could therefore be guaranteed. Buyers of goods made in well-known workshops would expect to pay well for high-quality work. Early in the nineteenth century, when the pace of industrial change increased very rapidly, apprenticeship came under increasing attack. It was seen as too restrictive and an obstacle to new ideas. In 1813 and 1814, workers lost the legally enforceable right to restrict employment in a trade to those who could prove that they had served an apprenticeship.

Change and development

So far our imaginary time traveller has picked up a picture of late eighteenth-century Britain as under-developed and, in places, primitive. Yet how did Britain compare with its European neighbours? If we move from imaginary time travel to what real visitors from Europe thought about late eighteenth-century Britain, a very different picture emerges. These visitors were impressed by Britain's wealth and its new opportunities. Being an island gave Britain enormous advantages in the development of overseas trade. Trade outside Europe grew at a very rapid rate throughout the eighteenth century and Britain was better placed than any of its competitors to exploit new opportunities in the Americas, India and Asia.

Britain, as an island, had always needed to give special priority to its navy as a means of defence. During the eighteenth century, Britain's shipping was important both for defence and for the expansion of trade overseas. The main nations of Europe, including Britain, were frequently at war at this time. Britain had no territory of its own to defend in mainland Europe whereas France, Spain and the Dutch – its main trading rivals – did. These nations needed to give priority to mainland Europe while Britain could afford to concentrate more on its colonial interests outside

Europe. This was one reason why, by 1780, Britain had outdistanced its main rivals both in the search for new markets and in the development of colonies, especially in the Americas. Colonies were important for defence and as suppliers of raw materials and consumers of manufactured goods.

The opening up of the Americas explains why Britain's west-coast ports, Liverpool, Glasgow, Bristol and the rest, were so dynamic. By the early 1770s, the value of exports to the Americas stood at about £4 million, from a total of just over £10 million. Seventy years earlier, the Americas had realised barely £½ million in a total of £4½ million. On the eve of the American War of Independence, which began in 1775, the 13 colonies which were rebelling against Britain had a combined population of approximately 2 million people and represented a huge market for British manufactured goods. The loss of this market was feared by many when the colonies gained their independence in 1783. However, the new 'United States' found that there was mutual benefit in trade with Britain. Trading links between the two countries expanded even more rapidly. Much of the raw cotton which flooded into the textile mills of Lanarkshire and Lancashire was grown in the southern states of the USA.

Overseas trade was one major reason for increases in Britain's overall wealth. Advanced agriculture was another. Much experimental work had been done during the eighteenth century to improve crop yields and to make animals capable of yielding more milk and better meat. More scientific principles were applied to farming generally and journals like *Annals of Agriculture* appeared to spread the word throughout the land. A regular contributor to this journal early in the nineteenth century was John Ellman (1753–1852), from the Sussex village of Glynde. Ellman was steward of a large agricultural estate near Lewes. He was also a notable breeder of local Southdown sheep and was involved in numerous other improvement schemes. He thought it extremely important to publicise his findings and thus to encourage other farmers to experiment. The legacy of a century of agricultural improvement associated with great pioneers like 'Turnip' Townshend, Coke of Holkham, Jethro Tull and Robert Bakewell, the Leicestershire sheep breeder, was thus carried on.

Though Britain's population almost doubled during the course of the century, the country remained a net exporter of food until the end of the 1780s. Britain – the remoter highland regions apart – was a nation largely without peasants. Tenant farmers' need to produce for the market, rather than for domestic self-sufficiency, contributed much towards making agriculture one of the most dynamic sectors in the British economy.

Eighteenth-century Britain did not have many large factories but manufacturing nevertheless flourished. Many of the famous inventions which

Figure 1.3 *James Hargreaves's Spinning Jenny*

helped the textile industry to grow so rapidly – such as Kay's Flying Shuttle (1733), Hargreaves's Spinning Jenny (1766) and Crompton's Water Mule (1786) – were designed to be used in the home. Improved methods of iron production developed by the Darby family in Coalbrookdale (Shropshire) enabled the metal industries to expand. The need for heat to generate power provided an important stimulus for coal production in many parts of Britain. The development of Henry Cort's new 'puddling and rolling' process in 1783–4 eliminated charcoal from the production of wrought iron. This led to dramatic price reductions and a consequent rapid expansion of the iron industry. Some landowners, like the Earl of Balcarres on the Haigh estate near Wigan (Lancashire), and Sir James Lowther, who invested half a million pounds in West Cumberland in the first half of the eighteenth century, considered coal more important to their fortunes than land itself. Men, women and children all contributed to the manufacture of woollen cloth, either in small workshops or in the home. When he visited the West Riding of Yorkshire in the early 1720s during a tour of Britain the author Daniel Defoe marvelled at the extent of industry being carried on in and around the town of Halifax.

Foreign visitors frequently remarked on the relative prosperity of ordinary folk in Britain. They had small surpluses of income which they used to buy consumer goods. They might, of course, choose to spend too much on drink. Well-known pictures, notably by William Hogarth, portray London almost as one vast unlicensed alehouse which befuddled the senses and debauched the morals of young and old alike. The mid-eighteenth-century phrase 'Drunk for a penny, dead drunk for twopence' was literally true for some. Throughout the century, moralising Christians were calling for 'a reformation of manners' by rich and poor alike. **Evangelicals** thought that much was wrong with the state of Britain, criticising particularly an upper class whose gambling, lavish parties and extravagant debts provided a thoroughly bad example to the poor.

KEY TERM:

Evangelicals

Evangelical Christians believed in the importance of direct religious experience, often by 'conversion'. Many were active preachers, calling for sober behaviour and observance of proper religious duty. One of the most famous preachers of all time, John Wesley (1703–91), founder of the Methodist movement, laid particular stress on direct religious experience. At the end of the eighteenth century leading evangelicals such as William Wilberforce and Zachary Macaulay were calling for the abolition of the trade in slaves, on which the wealth of many overseas traders depended. Others like Hannah More set up schools to teach children of the poor good behaviour and obedience to authority.

What evangelicals and others had to contend with was that Britain had a freer society than almost all its European rivals. People with money and property could choose how to use them and the state, though eager to defend the property of wealthy citizens, saw no need for a professional police force. Most justice was administered locally by country squires and, increasingly, by clergymen of the Church of England. Though these men frequently had strong ideas about poaching and petty theft, they were not representatives of a police state or a centralised, authoritarian regime. Propertied Englishmen thought that they lived in a society which cherished liberty and did not prescribe narrow channels of behaviour for all of their fellow citizens to follow.

Assumptions about Britain as a society of shared values and open opportunity can be challenged but, in comparison with the rest of Europe in the last quarter of the eighteenth century, Britain was relatively free and relatively prosperous. The diversity of its manufactures, the extent of its overseas trade and the ability of many of its citizens to buy cheap manufactured goods were all putting distance between Britain and its main competitors. Britain in 1780 was the most advanced nation on earth.

Task

This chapter has given you some of the evidence on which to come to a conclusion about how advanced a nation Britain was in 1780. Form yourselves into small groups to consider the following questions:

a As a 'time traveller' would you be more impressed by the evidence of backwardness given in this chapter, or by the evidence of progress?

b Why do you think many contemporaries placed so much emphasis on overseas trade when they were looking for evidence of Britain's advance during the eighteenth century?

c The map of Britain (Figure 1.2) shows most of the leading towns and gives estimates of their population. How would you explain the distribution and extent of the main urban centres at this time?

Further reading

R. Porter, *English Society in the Eighteenth Century* (Penguin, 1982) is quite brief, very lively and expresses strong opinions.

G. E. Mingay, *Land and Society in England, 1750–1980* (Addison Wesley Longman, 1994).

The following two books provide up-to-date surveys:

J. Rule, *The Vital Century: England's Developing Economy, 1714–1815* (Addison Wesley Longman, 1992).

J. Rule, *Albion's People: English Society, 1714–1815* (Addison Wesley Longman, 1992).

P. Corfield, *The Impact of English Towns, 1700–1800* (Oxford University Press, 1982) – good for explaining why towns were important as more than centres of trade and manufactures.

THEMATIC

2 Who were the British and how were they governed in the late eighteenth century?

Time chart

1688–9: 'Glorious Revolution' gets rid of Catholic monarch and sets some formal limits to royal power through the 'Bill of Rights'

1701: Act of Settlement requires the monarch to be a Protestant and not to marry a Catholic

1714: Death of Queen Anne sees the end of the Stuart monarchy. George I becomes the first Hanoverian monarch, preserving the Protestant succession

1760: George III becomes King and attempts to make more direct use of some of the powers of the monarchy. Frequent government instability in the 1760s as George clashes with Whig ministers

1780–83: Government crisis during later stages of American war threatens George III's position

1783: Treaty of Versailles confirms independence of the 13 American colonies. This is widely seen as a national humiliation for Britain

1783–4: William Pitt the Younger appointed Prime Minister (December 1783) and wins general election (March 1784) which restores government stability. This represents a victory for the King and a defeat for his Whig opponents, led by Charles James Fox

1785: Pitt attempts modest reform of Parliament by removing some very small boroughs and transferring seats to the counties. Bill defeated by 74 votes and Pitt never proposes parliamentary reform again

Britons?

Britain in 1780 was both one nation and three. England had been a united nation since the ninth century and had not been successfully invaded since the Norman Conquest of 1066. In medieval times, however, England had frequently been in conflict with both Wales and Scotland. Fierce Welsh resistance to English supremacy had finally been subdued by King Edward I (1272–1307) and after 1282 Wales was ruled by English kings. The unification of the states was formally effected during the reign of Henry VIII (1509–47) by statutes passed in 1536 and 1543. These declared that Wales was 'incorporated, united and annexed' to England. Separate authorities called 'Marcher Lordships' were abolished and Wales was divided into 13 counties governed, like England's, by sheriffs and justices of the peace. English common law applied also to the whole of Wales, and English language was also declared to be the official language, which all agents of government must speak.

Scotland proved a tougher nut for medieval English monarchs to crack. Had the warlike Edward I lived a few years longer he might have managed it but his son, Edward II (1307–27), suffered a humiliating defeat at the Battle of Bannockburn in 1314, after which the fires of separate Scottish national identity burned ever more brightly. Raids across the border from Scotland were a frequent feature in the fourteenth, fifteenth and sixteenth centuries. Many were eagerly reciprocated by Englishmen anxious for revenge and booty. States of war between the two nations were not uncommon until the middle of the sixteenth century. Readers who know the north-east coast of England will know that Northumberland contains some of Britain's most spectacular castles. Bamburgh, Alnwick and the rest were built to such a high standard because they were needed for fortification against a hostile northern neighbour.

Relations only improved in the seventeenth century when James Stuart (King James VI of Scotland since 1567) became King James I of England on the death of Queen Elizabeth I in 1603. The unification of the Crowns, however, did little to reduce mutual suspicion between the two nations. Formal political Union was effected in 1707, in the face of much hostility. It would probably not have come about at all had politically influential Scottish merchants not feared the long-term consequences of being cut out of the increasingly profitable English overseas trade. This group, at least, was richly rewarded during the eighteenth century for its combination of business sense and political wisdom. For its part, England was glad during a long war against the French to be finally rid of the threat of 'the auld alliance' between Scotland and France. Anglo–Scottish union was in no sense full assimilation. In 1707 the Scots gave up their own parliament but they retained their separate legal and educational systems and have continued to assert (with varying degrees of plausibility) the superiority of both over their English counterparts from that day to this.

As always, Ireland was different. After the Reformation the only reliably

Catholic part of the British Isles, the country was usually treated by the British (with the Scots especially eager participants – witness the colonisation of much of Ulster by Presbyterians in the seventeenth century) with a mixture of brutality and contempt. Anti-Catholicism fuelled much of the brutality and Oliver Cromwell's excesses there in 1649–51 were justified not only on the grounds of putting down rebels who had defied the parliamentary army but also of reducing the Catholic threat. In 1780 Ireland was about to enjoy a brief period of greater freedom with a Parliament which had some independence. However, British control of Ireland through the 'Protestant Ascendancy' remained tight, and forced political union on Britain's terms was always an option, as we shall see (chapter 8).

KEY TERM:

Aristocracy

Aristocracy is a Greek word meaning literally 'the government of a state by its best citizens'. In the period covered by this book, aristocracies are titled families whose wealth, and social prestige, are passed down the generations by inheritance. A very small number of families, about 200 or so, controlled most of the nation's land and dominated its political and social leadership. The magazine *Pall Mall Gazette* as late as 1865 referred approvingly to an aristocratic system of government as one in which 'distinguished birth, inherited wealth, and education, are the chief titles to political power'.

Rule from Westminster

England, therefore, was but the dominant element in a greater Britain comprising other nations which harboured varying degrees of resentment at the political domination exercised from London. In each of the constituent countries, however, both social and political leadership was provided by a landowning **aristocracy**. Marriage between members of great families across national borders provided an important element of mixing which reduced the sense of difference between the elites. It is no accident, for example, that many Scottish peers ceased to speak with Scottish accents. This development, however, made many ordinary Scots resentful that 'their' social leaders were watering down their Scottish origins.

Most European states at the time were **autocracies**; Britain was not. During the seventeenth century, the Stuart kings often came into conflict with Parliament over a number of issues, particularly money and religion. Though the Stuarts often ruled either without Parliament or by dictating terms to it, the so-called 'Glorious Revolution' of 1688–9 helped to redefine the relationship between King and Parliament. In effect the Catholic king, James II, was forced off the throne by opposition from leading landowners and churchmen. He was replaced by the husband-and-wife team of Mary II (James's elder daughter) and William III, a Dutch Calvinist.

KEY TERM:

Autocracies

Autocracy literally means 'self-sustaining power'. Forms of government where power is concentrated in the hands of one person are often referred to as autocracies. In the seventeenth and eighteenth centuries, such regimes were frequently called 'absolute monarchies' because kings, or emperors, wielded 'absolute' power. They might take advice – all autocracies included powerful government advisers – but decision-making was ultimately their sole responsibility.

The so-called 'Bill of Rights' of 1689 produced a kind of contract. It was drawn up by Parliament and specified what the king could not do 'without consent of Parliament'. One of the key things which the king could not do was to levy money without its consent. Since the arrival of William III committed Britain to long wars with France, and since those wars required huge amounts of money, Parliament from the end of the seventeenth century became a permanent and irreplaceable part of the

Figure 2.1 The House of Commons in 1793

constitution. Since the 1690s, no year has gone by without a meeting of Parliament. The arrival in 1714 of a German dynasty – the Hanoverians – only served to strengthen the perception that monarchy was only one element in the British political system, and not necessarily the most important or powerful one.

It would be quite wrong to think that Hanoverian monarchies exercised no power. George III (1760–1820) frequently used his powers in the first half of his reign to appoint and dismiss ministers. His choice of **William Pitt the Younger** as prime minister proved to be of immense political importance. Pitt was a very able prime minister whose policies in the 1780s helped to restore national finances and national morale after the demoralising loss of the American colonies. Pitt controlled Parliament with few serious challenges to his authority from 1783 to 1801. Nevertheless, he held power not because he headed a major political party but because he was the King's choice. One of the things which attracted Pitt to the King, in fact, was that he was not a 'party man'. When Pitt disagreed with the King on a matter George III considered of vital importance, as he did over giving more political liberties to Roman Catholics in Ireland in 1801, he was dismissed – again not because he had lost the confidence of Parliament, but because the King required him to

PROFILE: *William Pitt the Younger*

William Pitt the Younger was born in 1759, the son of the then prime minister William Pitt, later Earl of Chatham. He entered Parliament at the age of 21. After a brief spell as Chancellor of the Exchequer, he was appointed Prime Minister at the age of 24 – much the youngest ever – as George III tried to solve one of many crises during the first part of his reign arising from the fact that politicians who agreed with him often could not command a majority in the House of Commons.

Pitt was prime minister continuously from 1783 to 1801 and then from 1804 to January 1806. His early death was probably precipitated by a combination of overwork and excessive drinking – then a particularly common vice among politicians. Pitt's career as prime minister can be divided into two phases. Between December 1783 and February 1793 Britain was at peace and Pitt introduced a number of important taxation and financial reforms. Many high-profile taxes, such as those on servants and windows, proved unpopular, raised little money and were withdrawn. Nevertheless, generally careful husbanding of national resources helped to reduce debt. A government financial deficit of about £12 million in the early 1780s was turned into a surplus of about £5 million 10 years later. Pitt's administrative reforms made government more cost-conscious and efficient. Pitt also attempted to reduce the often very high import duties levied on goods entering the country and helped to negotiate trade treaties with France and Ireland in which both sides agreed to reduce duties. This policy was ended by the outbreak of war in 1793.

Pitt's work as a peacetime prime minister has received widespread praise from historians. About his leadership in the wars against France opinion is much more divided. Some see him as slavishly following policies which his father had adopted with success during an earlier war (1756–63), but in different, and less favourable, circumstances and blame him for lack of foresight. Others have noted that in concentrating Britain's direct involvement outside Europe, Pitt was seeking to support Britain's main long-term objectives in trade and commercial supremacy over European rivals.

KEY TERM:

Oligarchy

In an **oligarchy** government is in the hands of a small, privileged group or elite. Britain in the late eighteenth century was dominated by a number of landowners, many of whom were extremely wealthy. They used part of their wealth to influence the restricted number of electors in most parliamentary constituencies to support candidates of their own choice. In this way, groups of politicians owing allegiance to an aristocratic family grew up, often vying for supremacy and sometimes cooperating to secure advantage either against other great families or against the Crown. While 'aristocracy' was considered an appropriate form of government, the use of 'oligarchy' usually implies criticism.

go. The monarchy undoubtedly lost influence during the eighteenth century but George III showed that it could still exercise considerable direct power – especially over the choice of ministers. Ironically, it was Pitt's administrative reforms (see profile) which cut away much of the monarch's patronage. This meant that more and more power became concentrated in Parliament. George III was mentally unstable in the last years of his reign and was replaced by his eldest son as Prince Regent from 1811. Prince George (later George IV, 1820–30) was a vain, posturing and politically inept man who found that he could not assert his will over a prime minister he disagreed with. By the early nineteenth century the independent power of the monarchy was in irreversible decline.

Then as now, Parliament consists of two houses – the Lords and the Commons. In 1780, many of the most powerful men in the country were peers of the realm and thus sat in the Lords. By this time, however, it was clear that the more important house was the Commons, not least because it controlled legislation concerned with raising money. Since Britain is often described at this time as an **oligarchy**, it might at first seem strange to notice that some of the most powerful men in the land sat in the less powerful house. The paradox is easily explained. Most great landowners had great political influence – or 'patronage' – because they could determine who sat in the House of Commons. Throughout the late eighteenth and early nineteenth centuries, in fact, the largest social category in the House of Commons was sons or other near relatives of peers.

Influence in the House of Commons was possible on an extensive scale because so many Members of Parliament were selected by a very small numbers of electors. A huge number of different rules governed who was entitled to vote in different types of parliamentary seat. In the so-called 'county seats', anyone who owned property worth 40 shillings (£2) a year could vote and many electorates, not least those in the most populated counties such as Lancashire, Yorkshire, Warwickshire or Middlesex, were very large. Likewise in a handful of 'borough' seats, the right to vote was drawn so widely that most adult males who had lived in the place for a year or more could vote. Northampton, Coventry and Westminster were examples of very large electorates. In large constituencies it was very difficult for anyone to buy control and something close to a genuine test of male public opinion was possible when seats came up for election.

Most seats were not like this. In many boroughs (and more than 80 per cent of England's parliamentary seats were boroughs), the number of electors was fewer than 100, and sometimes fewer than a dozen. These seats tended be under the control of one great landowning patron or another. Actual elections in such seats were relatively rare, since electors had been persuaded, or straightforwardly bribed, to support the candidate of the great landowner's, or the Crown's (for the Crown owned much parliamentary patronage too) choice.

Which places qualified to be parliamentary boroughs was a matter more of history than of current economic or commercial significance. What were once places of considerable significance, particularly fishing villages and small ports, were by 1780 in decline, if not actually decrepit. Most of the borough of Dunwich (Suffolk) which continued to send two MPs to Parliament until 1832 had long since submitted to coastal erosion; most of it no longer existed. The remote south-western county of Cornwall sent a total of 44 MPs to Parliament when rapidly developing Lancashire sent only 13 and the whole of Scotland 45. Manchester, Sheffield, Leeds and Birmingham, with a combined population of more than 120,000 in 1780, did not have a single MP between them.

As the recent work of Professor Frank O'Gorman has shown, people without the vote could, and frequently did, hold strong opinions. When those opinions were effectively marshalled, levels of debate and political awareness could be high and MPs owed at least some degree of accountability to wider opinion than that represented by often pitifully small numbers of voters. The political nation was therefore much broader than the 400,000 or so actual voters. Furthermore, it was not only respectable middle classes, large tenant farmers and landowners who participated. In the larger boroughs, especially, the opinions of artisans and other skilled workers could be of importance.

Nor did the House of Commons comprise only well-connected landowners, although landowners were in a substantial majority overall. As defenders of the old system frequently pointed out, lack of parliamentary reform was no bar to 'new' interests finding their way into the House of Commons. Certainly, the interests of overseas traders with the Americas did not lack powerful voices there and the 'sugar interest' was a powerful one. Likewise men of talent from relatively humble backgrounds did not find it difficult to attract an influential patron and, through him, a parliamentary seat. The House of Commons did not lack for doctors, clever lawyers and sometimes not-so-clever retired army or navy officers. A reasonable representation of propertied interests was not only possible but regularly achieved in the unreformed House of Commons. Big money talked in the eighteenth century as in any other century, and large estates were the securest basis for a successful career, but these were not the only voices to be heard. Though a very long way from being democratic (an idea which almost all MPs abominated), Parliament in 1780 was more representative than the standard recital of '**rotten boroughs**', bribery and corruption would suggest. In political, as much as in social, structures Britain was relatively advanced.

KEY TERM:

Rotten boroughs

The term **rotten boroughs** was used somewhat ironically to describe parliamentary boroughs which had very few electors. Places like Old Sarum, just outside Salisbury in Wiltshire, and East and West Looe in Cornwall had a dozen or so electors. They were thus easy for a 'patron' to control, almost as a piece of individual property. Because it was so rarely possible to hold an election in such places at all, let alone use the contest as a test of public opinion, the borough was said to be 'rotten', implying corruption.

Figure 2.2 *This clock tower is one of many features added to Wallington Hall by Sir Walter Blackett, MP. It was built in 1754. Blackett was a leading Newcastle businessman and used business money to adorn his country estate, about 20 miles north of Newcastle. This is one of many examples of great wealth being put at the service of architectural beauty. There was a political point to this also. Such buildings symbolised local power. Men of wealth built lavishly not only for aesthetic reasons but also to mark themselves off from ordinary folk.*

In the localities

Too many textbooks fail to mention that the story of how Britain was governed at the end of the eighteenth century cannot be told exclusively from Westminster. The matters which directly concerned central government were relatively restricted: raising money, signing treaties and keeping a watchful eye on defence were the normal limits. Yet Parliament spent much time considering what we would nowadays call 'private members' bills' – *i.e.* those proposals which were the responsibility of an ordinary MP rather than the government. Very often when an MP raised an issue in Parliament – about proposals to enclose a village and restrict common rights over land, for example – he was acting on behalf of powerful local interests. Both the 'government' and the justice which ordinary folk saw in operation was much more likely to be that provided by local landowners. The great peers of the realm, the Duke of Northumberland at Alnwick or the Duke of Devonshire at Chatsworth in Derbyshire, were expected to control local affairs through an extensive network of relatives and stewards. Far humbler landowners, however, were equally expected to give a lead to their communities.

'A landed proprietor is especially in a responsible position. He is the natural head of a parish or district – in which he should be looked up to as the bond of union between classes. To him the poor man should look up for protection; those in doubt or difficulty for advice; the ill-disposed for reproof [correction] or punishment; the deserving, of all classes, for consideration and hospitality, and all for a dignified, honourable and Christian example.'

The Victorian architect Sir George Gilbert Scott (1811–78) was best known for designing St Pancras Station and the Albert Memorial in Kensington. He also planned many landowners' houses and, as this statement shows, was well aware of the power and responsibilities of landownership well into the nineteenth century. The quotation is found in M. Girouard, *The Victorian Country House* (1971).

Formally, English and Welsh counties were controlled by non-elected Lords Lieutenant, Sheriffs and Justices of the Peace. The main criterion for appointment was importance in the community. Importance in practice meant landed wealth. Both in counties and towns, unelected elites dispensed justice and administration in assemblies with quaint and curious names, recalling medieval times and practices: 'court leet', 'court baron' or 'select vestry'. Probably, the most old-fashioned government structures in late eighteenth-century Britain were local rather than central. Not until 1835 were some of Britain's greatest towns and cities directly elected by ratepayers (see chapter 11) rather than controlled by small, unrepresentative groups often linked to a church which the majority of citizens never attended, and whose authority it rejected.

Further reading

All of the following are textbooks which will give you more detail about the workings of eighteenth-century politics if you need it.

E. J. Evans, *The Forging of the Modern State: Early Industrial Britain, 1783–1870* (Addison Wesley Longman, second edition, 1996) – a modern textbook.

W. A. Speck, *A Concise History of Britain, 1707–1975* (Cambridge University Press, 1993) – shorter than the rest but a survey by one of the leading authorities on eighteenth-century England.

I. R. Christie, *Wars and Revolutions, 1760–1815* (Arnold, 1982).

G. Holmes and D. Szechi, *The Age of Oligarchy: Pre-Industrial Britain, 1722–83* (Addison Wesley Longman, 1993).

CAUSATION

3 Why was Britain the first nation to have an industrial revolution?

Time chart

1733: John Kay's 'Flying Shuttle' invented; it increases the speed of textile weaving machines

1767: James Hargreaves's 'Spinning Jenny' invented; it greatly increases the output per person

1769: Richard Arkwright's 'Water Frame' (see profile of Arkwright on page 24)

1779: Samuel Crompton takes out a patent for spinning by 'mule'

1780s: 477 inventors' patents registered (in the 1710s there had been only 38)
Value of exports from Britain (mostly manufactured goods) top £10 million for the first time (in the 1700s they had been less than £5 million)

1782: James Watt's rotary steam-engine invented; it enabled concentration of power away from fast-flowing streams and thus aided growth of industrial towns

1783–4: Henry Cort's 'puddling' process allowed coal, rather than charcoal, to be the main fuel used in iron refining

1786: Edmund Cartwright's power loom invented; it promises to increase speed of weaving, but is not widely introduced to textile areas until 1820s

1802: The value of exports of cotton goods exceeds those of woollen ones for the first time

The necessary link between political and social history

Until recently, most nineteenth-century history syllabuses for sixth formers were overwhelmingly political in their emphasis. What leading politicians were up to, and particularly how they handled relations with other countries, was considered the stuff of History. Such considerations have an important place, as they will do later in this book. However, history is just as much about how ordinary people earn a living, how they organise their lives and what factors influence their opportunities as it is about the doings of the great. The great themselves did not think that they lived in an isolated, and supremely privileged, vacuum, however ostentatious their lifestyles and however sumptuous the palladian mansions in which they lived during the summer months when Parliament was not sitting. These men usually had a well-developed awareness – especially before the political system contained any elements of democracy – that they were discharging a trust on behalf of those who were not directly represented. They could not afford to act out of pure selfishness or greed. This was not necessarily a matter of priggishness or high-mindedness.

Nineteenth-century politicians were keenly aware of the dangers of public-order breakdown and even of the threat of revolution. They were so because they were presiding over a society which was changing at breakneck speed, and was ever threatening to career out of their control. This happened because of the industrial revolution. The single most important fact about Britain in the nineteenth century was that it became the world's first industrial nation. This fact gave it huge advantages over all other nations until the 1870s. It also set much of the agenda for political debate, at least from the so-called 'decade of reform' in the 1830s (see chapter 12). This chapter focuses, therefore, on two crucial aspects of the early industrial revolution: the different definitions which might lead us to decide what an industrial revolution *is*; and why Britain experienced industrial revolution before any other nation.

Industrial revolution: definitions

The industrial revolution cannot be easily defined. It cannot be turned simply into a 'key term' which can be briefly, and reasonably uncontroversially, explained like so many others in this book. Historians disagree about what it means. Two generations of detailed research has offered three different models:

1 We might consider an industrial revolution as a process which utterly changes certain important sectors of the economy in a relatively short period of time. If we accept this definition, then we should concentrate on what happened to Britain's cotton industry, and perhaps also to its iron industry, between about 1780 and 1830. Both industries were dramatically changed by technological innovation. In the cotton industry, more machines were driven by steam power provided by the technological breakthrough of James Watt, whose separate steam condenser engines enabled the harnessing of water power in much more efficient ways. Watt engines could only be used in large work spaces and the

KEY TERMS:

Primary, secondary and tertiary sectors of the economy

These terms may sound intimidating but they can easily be explained. They relate to different forms of economic activity, with reference to the provision of goods and services which all societies need. **Primary** production is concerned with food gathering and growing, normally agriculture and fisheries. **Secondary** production relates to manufacturing industry and to the mining of minerals (mostly coal) which was so crucial to providing power for the manufacturing process. **Tertiary** activity is concerned with the provision of services. These may themselves be usefully divided into two: specific material services such as shops and the retailing industry and wider professional services of the kind which a rich, diverse and developed society needs more of than an under-developed one. Education, the Law and Medicine are the obvious examples. People 'buying' these services, either directly or indirectly through taxes, are paying for specialist expertise. Professional organisations try to restrict access to their 'trade' in order to guarantee quality service and also to keep up their fees. Some are much more successful at this than others!

cotton industry also saw revolutionary development of factory production. Many factories brought large numbers of workers together (two-thirds of them typically women and children) and required revolutionary changes in the organisation of work itself.

2 Alternatively, we might take a broader view of what an industrial revolution meant. This definition would place the emphasis upon the changing nature of employment. Put simply, a non-industrialised nation is one in which the majority of the population is engaged in so-called '**primary** activities', whereas an industrial nation has the majority of the population working in manufacturing – '**secondary** activities'. As an industrial society becomes more mature, so it develops a greater need for '**tertiary**' or service-sector occupations. Such transformations take very long periods of time. In Britain's case, the transition from primary to secondary occupations took well over a century from 1700 to 1850 or 1860, while the main expansion of the service (or tertiary) sector has taken place during the course of the twentieth century.

3 A third definition is associated with the theory of the US economic historian, W. W. Rostow. In the 1960s he made use of the phrase 'take-off'. Had he made use of the language of space exploration in vogue at that time, he might have used 'lift-off' to describe the dramatic complex of changes which he believed took place in the 1780s. According to this idea, the transformation of Britain's cotton industry was so dramatic that it sucked into a process of change most other sectors of the economy. Most sectors thus participated in what he called a 'self-sustaining growth process'. Once take-off, or lift-off, had been achieved, the process was irreversible. Nations were destined for an industrialised future.

The first two of these definitions are still widely used by economic historians, who are now very careful to distinguish between them. The third has gone out of fashion, perhaps unjustifiably. Much detailed research has failed to substantiate the so-called 'linkages' which, according to Rostow, enabled other industries to emulate cotton's technological innovation. It has also been pointed out that, at least until 1850, older forms of domestic textile production remained extensive and, on the whole, profitable, while industrialised cotton production was concentrated only in south-east Lancashire and west-central Scotland. In defence of Rostow, however, it can be argued that the cotton industry's voracious need for overseas markets emphasised the *difference* between Britain and most other nations by 1850 and fostered revolutionary changes in the country's pattern of trade. If the cotton industry, Britain's 'leading sector' which generated more than 70 per cent of the value of all its exports by the 1830s, did not 'cause' a wider industrial revolution, it certainly contributed mightily to making Britain the workshop of the nineteenth-century world.

Why was Britain first?

Economic historians are agreed about very little in this area, but on one point there is unanimity. No one reason by itself explains why Britain, a fairly remote group of islands in the north-west corner of Europe, became the world's first industrial nation. There is increasing agreement, also, that the human dimension is of critical importance. No infallible model has been devised by development economists to serve as a blue-print for industrial development. Had it been, many of the appalling problems of the developing world would have been lessened, if not eliminated. It is increasingly recognised that the nature of a given country's society is critical. Industrial change is produced by real people, not by theory or by abstract models of growth.

Historians must attempt to explain, even when the variables are so diverse, and sometimes so complex, that convincing analysis is next to impossible. Those seeking to understand why the pace of Britain's industrial life quickened so much in the last quarter of the eighteenth century should know about the following factors, though other 'explanations of industrialism' have been offered. To help you come to your own conclusions, some critical questions are posed which relate to each one:

1 *Geography*: Britain is a small country with many navigable rivers, good mineral deposits and relatively few huge natural obstacles to movement of trade and people. Water power, crucial for technological development, is abundant.
Question: Though these favourable factors are difficult to dispute, how can they be used to explain the timing of the industrial revolution? Fast-flowing streams were not created in the last quarter of the eighteenth century!

2 *Diversity*: Britain has a diverse climate, enabling good-quality wheat to be grown in the south and east and animals to be nourished in lush western pastures. Diversity aids growing specialisation in agriculture, while Lancashire's famously mild and wet climate was conducive to the processing of raw cotton.
Question: Are there any other European countries which have similar diversity, and do not some have more extensive natural advantages in agriculture?

3 *Earlier economic development*: The eighteenth century had seen remarkable advances in both trade and industry, resulting in rising incomes and the capacity for many people to consume manufactured goods.
Question: Can we confidently say that rising domestic demand offered

KEY TERM:

Entrepreneurs

The French origin of this word might suggest that **entrepreneurs** were 'go-betweens'. In one sense this is true, since the provider of goods operated 'in between' raw materials and their consumption in different form. Entrepreneurs were businessmen who took risks in pursuit of profit by selling goods and services. The entrepreneurs looked out for market opportunities which arose, for example, from turning imported raw cotton into cheap and reliable garments for which there was a market both at home and abroad.

sufficient incentive for **entrepreneurs** to invest in new plant and machinery, and do people anyway consume according to any predetermined model?

4 *Rising population growth*: Britain's population almost doubled in the course of the eighteenth century and the growth was most marked towards the end of the century. More people in society mean more opportunities for production and consumption.
Questions: Other European nations experienced rapid population growth; why, then, did they not industrialise at the same time? Also, might not more mouths to feed be more of a burden than an opportunity? Limiting population growth is a key objective for most nations in the developing world at the end of the twentieth century.

5 *The profitability of overseas trade*: Britain had a healthy lead over European competitors in overseas trade, particularly in India and the Americas. Successes in war up to 1763 had extended this advantage.
Questions: How can it be shown that commercial opportunity outside Europe linked up with decisions about forms of industrial production within Britain? Why did the pace of industrial growth quicken at the very time (1775–84) when the value of imports and exports actually declined for the first time in the century?

6 *The role of government*: Strategic considerations induced eighteenth-century governments to involve themselves in wars which had substantial commercial advantage. The frequent wars of the period 1689–1815 gave periodic boosts to the iron industry because of the need for armaments. Soldiers also need uniforms, which helps the textile industry. British governments nearly always gave high priority to naval expenditure and a fighting navy could form useful protection for overseas traders. During the late eighteenth and early nineteenth centuries, furthermore, governments were less and less likely to uphold apprenticeship regulations and other restrictions on the free movement of labour. At a time of rapid economic expansion, this was important.
Questions: Could governments do more than provide unintended support for a phenomenon – industrial growth – which was not yet understood? How could government 'cause' the vital spark to ignite an industrial revolution?

7 *Britain as an inventive society*: Britain generated a huge number of innovative ideas during the eighteenth century. The famous industrial innovations – the Water Frame, Power Loom and the rest – were symptomatic of a much wider commitment to experiment, from which society benefited. Also new institutions, such as the Royal Society of Arts (1754), promoted innovation and diffusion of scientific and technological

Figure 3.1 A Watt rotary steam-engine

ideas. The development of transport networks helped to spread such ideas in the second half of the century. So did the increased availability of newspapers and magazines. Provincial newspapers had begun to appear in England at the beginning of the eighteenth century. By 1750, most towns of any size had at least one journal including a mixture of local affairs, national and international 'intelligence'.

Questions: How many of these busy innovations were of any practical use? The London Patent Office was stacked high with ingenious but impractical contraptions. Was Britain anyway uniquely inventive? Much high-quality scientific enquiry was being pursued in other European countries. Britain enjoyed no obvious lead in scientific understanding. Was not the opportunity to discuss change and relate it to specific business opportunity more important?

8 *Britain's advantage as a Protestant country and the role of dissenters*: This explanation has its origins in the views of the German sociologist Max Weber who argued that Protestant values and lifestyles were more conducive to thrift, hard work and accumulations of money than were Catholic ones. Furthermore, Protestant dissenters were often discriminated against in English society, being excluded from elite social and educational networks, including universities. Dissenters could not attend Oxford and Cambridge until the 1870s. In response to this, English dissenters developed their own networks, placing an emphasis on business, trade and commerce. If land was the dominant form of property, dissenters sought distinction via a different route.

Questions: Does not the evidence suggest that the majority of successful businessmen in Britain were members of the established Church

(Anglicans) and not dissenters? Dissenters were only a little more likely to become very wealthy than Anglicans. The alternative networks do not seem to have produced a decisive advantage for religious outsiders. Also, if Protestantism spurs capitalism, why did Catholic Belgium industrialise in the nineteenth century ahead of Protestant Holland?

9 *Britain as an 'open society'*: Some social historians, notably Professor Harold Perkin, have laid particular stress upon the unique nature of British society. He sees a society open to talent in which the ablest can rise to wealth, influence and power. Also Britain's aristocracy was not a closed caste; younger sons often married the heiresses of bankers and overseas traders, while very successful entrepreneurs from humble backgrounds, like Robert Peel senior and **Richard Arkwright**, could use their fortunes to buy landed estates, some even acquiring peerages. Landed society was thus continually renewed. Landowners were able to

PROFILE: *Richard Arkwright*

Richard Arkwright was born at Preston in 1732, the youngest of 13 children. The family was reasonably poor. He was apprenticed to a barber. After working for several years in Bolton where he was engaged in wig manufacture, he devoted his attention to mechanical inventions associated with textile spinning. He settled in Nottingham, a centre of the stocking industry, and from there in 1769 he took out a patent on a new type of spinning frame. Its principal innovation lay in spinning by four pairs of rollers.

Arkwright's business interests were usually enhanced by working in close cooperation with others. He worked in the 1760s with John Kay, the inventor of the Flying Shuttle, and later went into partnership with Jedediah Strutt of Derby. This partnership enabled him to establish mills using water power at Cromford in Derbyshire in 1771 and these eventually made his fortune. Further mills followed and Arkwright estimated in the early 1780s that he employed about 5,000 people in industrial plant worth more than £200,000. Arkwright was a pioneer of textile mills based on having individuals work ceaselessly at specific tasks ('division of labour'). His management technique was based on setting high standards for his workers, attention to detail and sometimes fierce discipline. As with several other spectacularly successful entrepreneurs, he used his wealth to buy himself into established society. He was knighted in 1786 and became High Sheriff of Derbyshire in 1787. In the last years of his life he bought the manor of Cromford and began to build Willersley Castle as a private residence for himself. He died in 1792.

enjoy the profits of coal found underneath their land, whereas in most European countries these were considered 'royalties' and thus the property of the monarch. Thus, the connection between land and industry was closer in Britain and helped to foster a landowning elite with entrepreneurial attitudes and ambitions.

Questions: Was Britain in reality such an 'open society'? Peerages were more difficult to obtain for outsiders between 1714 and 1780 than before or after. Is too much being made of a few, highly atypical, success stories? Do British businessmen behave in a significantly different way from their counterparts in other European countries? The evidence suggests that the British were not unusual and that existing business elites, often from families which went back generations, were as likely to be found in Holland, France and Germany. Do not traditional landed values, rather than thrusting entrepreneurial ones, characterise dominant behaviour in late eighteenth-century Britain?

Tasks

a Look at the list of factors above which historians have used to explain Britain's early industrial lead:

  i Put the factors in your own order of importance, giving your reasons.

  ii Do you think this list helps you to explain the precise timing of the industrial revolution? Explain your answer.

  iii These factors have been deliberately separated. Do you think that convincing explanations of the industrial revolution need to stress how factors acted together, rather than separately? Explain your answer.

b Why do you think that this chapter shows that different definitions of the industrial revolution have been attempted? Do you think any one definition more useful than another in making sense of this topic? Explain your answer.

c Can you work out from this chapter what kinds of evidence historians rely on when they give reasons for the industrial revolution?

Further reading

P. Mathias, *The First Industrial Nation* (Routledge, second edition, 1983) – good for explaining developments in the economy.

H. Perkin, *The Origins of Modern English Society, 1780–1880* (Routledge, 1969) – a study in social history which emphasises changes in social groups and their values.

C. More, *The Industrial Age: Economy and Society in Britain, 1750–1985* (Addison Wesley Longman, 1989).

P. Hudson, *The Industrial Revolution* (Arnold, 1992) – a modern study which emphasises the importance of the various regions of Britain.

M. Berg, *The Age of Manufacturers: Industry, Innovation and Work in Britain, 1700–1820* (Routledge, second edition, 1994) – particularly valuable if you want to find out about women's contribution to the change in industry.

CHANGE

4 How much change did the industrial revolution bring to early nineteenth-century Britain?

'Liverpool, which is now regarded as the largest commercial town in Great Britain after London, is probably, in respect of extent and population, one of the most important in the whole world. Its commerce has in a space of 15 to 20 years so noticeably increased that whereas Bristol, whose trade may now be somewhat in decline, formerly had twice as much commerce as Liverpool, the proportions are now said to be reversed. This is attributed partly to the position, which is very advantageous for overseas trade, for communications with Ireland, and for the commission and transportation business with the large inland manufacturing towns; and in part it is seen as a consequence of the generally recognised industry, mode of living and thrift of the inhabitants. The harbour here, which is good in itself, has been made more convenient in recent times by means of docks and landing stages, and one only needs to be there a short time to get an approximate idea of the quantity of goods loaded and unloaded, of the numbers of arriving and departing ships, and of the value of the enormous stocks which are in the warehouse near the harbour ...

Some years ago some business people and persons of rank had agreed upon the establishment of a literary society on approximately the same plan as that at Newcastle. To that end a subscription was opened, in which within a short time 500 persons with 20 guineas each had joined for the first foundation of the institution ... Besides newspapers and journals in all languages ... the works of the best authors in the sciences and fine arts are to be found in the libraries and besides that, what one does not always find in large libraries, a crowd of readers.

The town has been adorned in recent years with several new and fine buildings, and they are now engaged in laying out whole streets and market places. Outside the town I saw some beautiful country houses, which for the most part had been built by the people of Liverpool.

... I travelled to Manchester ... this town, which in respect of population and manufactures has long since been one of the most important in

England, has extended extraordinarily, especially in the last 15 years, through its cotton manufactures. The number of its inhabitants is calculated at 70,000 to 80,000, who for the most part are engaged on this work. Several circumstances have united here to favour this branch of industry, among which the general use of the fine, white and light cotton fabric, which has almost supplanted the silk throughout Europe, may deserve the first place. Next to this comes the invention of the spinning machines, which first became common in Manchester, and are not only there brought to the greatest perfection, but also housed with an outward magnificence which is otherwise not so common in the English factories. As proof of this a spinning mill may serve, where the building itself is of brick, and in good style, also the inside, which is otherwise normally of wood, is made either of dressed stone or iron, to say nothing of some others in and outside the town, whose fine installations and buildings enrich and adorn the same. Almost all these spinning machines are driven by steam-engines, and in order to carry away the coal smoke, which could during finishing and packing of the goods take away from them something of the dazzling whiteness given to them by the bleaching, the chimneys at most of the mills are taken up high above the roofs, and in some places arrangements are made to burn up the smoke during the heating.'

Svedenstierna's Tour of Great Britain, 1802–3 (1973).

From the Travel Diary of Eric T. Svedenstierna, on tour in England in 1802–3. Svedenstierna was a Swedish metallurgist who came to England to learn about new techniques of iron production. During his tour, he also commented on leading ports and on the textile trade.

Views of three industrial enterprises by John Byng (1743–1813)

John Byng was a diarist and traveller.

'Neath, 6 August 1787:
Sir Herbert Mackworth must be one of the most extraordinary and enterprising geniuses in this kingdom; ever employ'd and in the greatest works; here, he surveys, beneath, and around him, the wonderful works of his own indefatigableness: colliers digging – copper works smoking – a domain of parkish ground, cultivated from barrenness to rich fertility – woods of extent and beauty – and about 300 men in daily pay . . . He has 6 coal pits in his park, at full work whence 50 tons of coal are daily

to his copper works, and several others that have been overflow'd but are now draining by fire engines . . . Sir H M has glass houses, collieries etc. etc. in other counties; has establish'd 3 banking houses in Wales; keeps all his own accounts; drives around the kingdom with a night cap in his pocket; and to all his followers has diffused a spirit of zeal and confidence.

Derby, 19 June 1789:
The silk mills quite bewildered me; such rattlings and twistings! Such heat and stinks! that I was glad to get out: we shou'd be full as happy, if silk worms had never been.

Stoke on Trent, 28 June 1792:
Now I enquired for Etruria, the grand pottery establish'd by Mr Wedgwood; and putting up my horses at the adjacent inn, sent up my name and compliments to Mr W with a desire to view his manufactory. . . I was shewn about the several workshops of this great pottery, wherein are employ'd 300 men; but this is a dull observation for any person who has seen China manufactories. The painting business – perform'd by females, is an hot, unwholesome employ; the work to be painted is allways lifted up in the left hand – Except some Irishmen . . . I did not find any persons had attempted to carry off the secrets of the art.'

C. Bruyn Andrews (ed.), *The Torrington Diaries*, vols 1–4 (1936).

Figure 4.1 *A watercolour of 'Mackworth's Works at Neath' drawn by John Byng*

This chapter is concerned with change. The very use of the word 'revolution' implies rapid and sustained change. Although the term 'industrial revolution' is not known to have been used before 1848, and was not in widespread use until the 1890s, contemporaries seemed well aware that they were living through a period of unprecedented change. Svedenstierna's evidence, quoted above, is one example among many which associates the changes described with progress. The general assumption is that Britain changed with enormous rapidity in the late eighteenth and early nineteenth centuries.

How much did the economy grow?

It is possible, however, to emphasise continuity rather than change. In recent years, historians have begun to re-examine this period and some have wondered whether we should rather be discussing an 'industrial evolution' than a revolution. Professor Crafts, in particular, has challenged Rostow's view that something decisively new took place in the 1780s and 1790s. Crafts stresses the gradualness of the process. He does not deny that growth rates both for industry and for the economy as a whole went up between 1700 and 1830, but he stresses this as a continuous development rather than one with a revolutionary break at the end of the eighteenth century.

Figure 4.2 *Crafts's estimates of economic growth, 1700–1860 (the figures give rates of growth each year during the given periods)*

Period	*Industrial output per cent*	*Whole economy per cent*
1700–60:	0.7	0.7
1760–80:	1.5	0.7
1780–1801:	2.1	1.3
1801–31:	3.0	2.0
1831–60	3.3	2.5

N. F. R. Crafts, 'The industrial revolution: economic growth in Britain, 1700–1860', *ReFresh*, York University, no. 4, 1986.

Notice how the estimates suggest that the rate of growth in the economy is *greater* in the first half of the nineteenth century than during Rostow's famous 'take-off' period. Nevertheless, even on Crafts's figures, it might be suggested that something very important is happening in the 1780s and 1790s. Growth rates in the whole economy almost double compared with the previous 20-year period and the rates of increase are never so rapid again. Perhaps we might still be allowed to call this a period of 'industrial revolution', as Professor P. Hudson has done in her recent book.

Factories and workshops

Nevertheless, Crafts is surely right to stress that industrial output is not just about cotton and iron – the so-called 'leading sectors' of growth at the end of the eighteenth century. In the main industrial areas, large factories grew up in a very short space of time. These factories required new forms of work, with an emphasis on time – clocking in, fines for lateness and many other regulations – all of which suggested that people were being required to work to the rhythm of the new machines. Cotton manufacture in Lanarkshire and Lancashire grew with unprecedented rapidity. By 1835, 304,000 people were working in cotton factories; 28 per cent of these were 18 years of age or under and no fewer than 40 per cent were adult females. Some previously insignificant places became substantial centres of industry in a couple of generations. Oldham had fewer than 5,000 people living in it in the early 1780s; by 1851, its population was 53,000. Salford, just north of Manchester, grew from 8,000 to 64,000 in the same period. The woollen industry was slightly slower to adopt new forms of factory production than was cotton. When the change came, however, it was every bit as rapid – if not more so. Bradford became the world's centre for the manufacture of worsted cloth and its population grew by more than 50 per cent in every decade from 1811 to 1851. The town's population had been a mere 4,000 in 1781; in 1851 it stood at an astonishing 104,000.

Similarly, centres of iron production took off in what can only be called revolutionary ways in the early nineteenth century. South Wales was totally transformed by coal and iron between 1790 and 1820. The great ironworks of Dowlais, Cyfarthfa, Plymouth and Penydarren dominated the scene and the ironmasters Richard Crawshay, Thomas Guest, Jeremiah Homfray and Joseph Bailey (who transplanted himself very successfully from Yorkshire) became hugely wealthy. There were 113 iron furnaces in South Wales by 1830. In 1796 there had been only 26. Pig iron production in the area exceeded 200,000 tons during the 1820s, when South Wales was producing 40 per cent of Britain's entire output. Not surprisingly, similar rates of urbanisation were seen here as in Lancashire and Yorkshire. Merthyr Tydfil and Dowlais each increased their populations by more than 40 per cent a decade during the first half of the nineteenth century. Merthyr's population was 8,000 in 1801 and 46,000 in 1851.

In these areas, then, change was massive, and expanded opportunities for work brought with them new kinds of crisis: over-long hours, some exploitation, industrial accidents and sharper social divisions between workers and employers. In the 1960s, Edward Thompson and Harold

Perkin were both clear in their conclusions that the first half of the nineteenth century witnessed the making of a British working class which defined itself in opposition to an antagonistic, employing industrial middle class.

More recently, historians have become much more cautious. We tend to know more about the areas which changed most, because they used to be most studied, but we are now much more aware that change took place at very different rates. Consequently, generalisations which hold that 'Britain became a class society' because of its industrial revolution have been treated with increasing scepticism. In many places, old forms of work and social organisation retained a tenacious hold. Factories were characteristic only of the textile industry. Even in Lancashire and Yorkshire the typical size of factories was not particularly large. A survey of 973 cotton factories in Lancashire in 1841 revealed that only 23 (3 per cent) employed more than 1,000 people. The most common category was of factories employing fewer than 100 people; in 1841, 423 were in this category, 43 per cent of the total. It is necessary to correct the image that Britain became a country dominated by huge factories during the first half of the nineteenth century. In textiles, also, large numbers of workers continued to work either from home or in smaller workshops. It was not always cheaper for entrepreneurs to invest heavily in factory machinery; labour – especially female labour – was plentiful and relatively cheap. Much work continued to be done from home and in conjunction with farming, as the design of houses in the moorlands on the Lancashire/Yorkshire border confirms.

Elsewhere, production expanded but without revolutionary change in the kind of work being done. This was particularly true of London, whose manufacturing remained based on small workshops, and the great metals centres of the West Midlands and South Yorkshire, Birmingham – 'the city of a thousand trades' – and Sheffield. The absence of revolutionary change hardly affected comparative rates of population growth in the large cities, however. London had three-quarters of a million people in 1781 and more than 2¼ million in 1851. At the same time, Birmingham and Sheffield's populations both went up approximately six-fold, to totals of 233,000 and 135,000 respectively. In the metals industry, fewer opportunities presented themselves for women's work since much heavy labour was required. Men who worked up a thirst making chains, say, in Lye or Cradley Heath in the Staffordshire 'Black Country' would slake it in the beer shop after work. It was not considered respectable for women to be seen in such places. The culture of male-dominated work is characteristic of metals and mining areas, such as Staffordshire and South Yorkshire.

Regression?

We have seen that change operated at very different rates in different industries. It is worth noting, finally, that some change during the early industrial period was in the direction of decline. Newer forms of production in textiles and iron inevitably squeezed out some older ones. Broadly speaking, the early stages of the industrial revolution moved the heart of manufacturing wealth creation from the south to the north. The largest fortunes still tended to be earned in the south of England, because these were either inherited, via land, or earned from finance capital, and London was the world's financial centre by 1850. However, manufacturing gains in Lanarkshire, Lancashire, Yorkshire and Glamorgan tended to be at the expense of older established enterprises in the south and east. In woollen textiles, the West Riding of Yorkshire's gain was Norfolk's loss. For most of the sixteenth and seventeenth centuries, Norwich was the second city of England, largely because it was the centre of quality wool production. Now it was in relative decline. Its population went up, of course, between 1781 and 1851 but it did not quite double, and thus grew less than the average rate of population growth in England at the time. In many of the smaller industrial communities, things were worse. The exciting implications for the iron industry of the innovations of Abraham Darby and Henry Cort passed Sussex and the Weald of Kent by. Previously flourishing iron, glass and timber works in these counties either marked time or fell into actual decline. Similarly, the textile industries of Gloucestershire and Wiltshire could not, by the early nineteenth century, compete with the advanced production methods and increasingly aggressive sales techniques of the successful entrepreneurs of Lancashire.

The years 1780–1850, then, were ones of enormous change in Britain. In this period, the country was irrevocably set on the path of full industrialisation and urbanisation. For many, the means of wealth creation were revolutionised. We should not conclude, however, that change happened at the same pace throughout the country, or that industrial progress was inevitably associated with huge factories or massive metal works. Industrial Lancashire, Yorkshire, central Scotland and South Wales were highly *atypical* of Britain as a whole. In some parts of Britain, furthermore, their success was at the expense of decline elsewhere. Even in the most successful parts of the country, industrial failure was at least as likely as industrial success. Entrepreneurship was a highly risky business. Those who study the trade directories, which list the names of businesses in particular towns, for the first time are frequently surprised to discover how great is the turnover. A very large number of businessmen are either forced to sell up, or go bust. Since many leave few, if any, records, it is very difficult for historians to be sure what has happened. However, the clear inference must be that business enterprise during the early years of the nineteenth century was no guarantee of riches and success. For huge numbers of people caught up in the early years of the industrial revolution, change certainly did not equal progress.

Tasks related to sources

a What can you infer from Svedenstierna's diary about his opinion of the development of Liverpool and Manchester?

b In what ways might Svedenstierna's motives for visiting England have influenced what he wrote about the development of its industry and cities?

c Do you think that John Byng is more impressed with evidence of Britain's manufacturing activities than Svedenstierna? Explain your answer.

d How useful are the eyewitness accounts of observers, such as these, to a student of Britain's industrial development in the 1780s and 1790s? You should use your own knowledge of these developments in your answer, as well as making use of both sources.

Follow-up work

If you live in, or near, a large town with a good public library, go to the local history section and ask to consult trade directories for the 1820s and 1830s. Take a part of your town and note down the names of firms for a particular year. Then look for the same part of the town in a later directory – say 10–12 years later. Work out how many businesses appear to be owned by the same people. Summarise your conclusions.

Further reading

P. Mathias, *The First Industrial Nation* (Routledge, second edition, 1983).

N. F. R. Crafts, *British Industrial Growth during the Industrial Revolution* (Oxford University Press, 1985) – argues against the idea of a rapid industrial 'take-off' in the 1780s.

P. Hudson, *The Industrial Revolution* (Arnold, 1992).

W. W. Rostow, *The Stages of Economic Growth* (Cambridge University Press, 1960).

E. P. Thompson, *The Making of the English Working Class* (Penguin, 1968) – a very big book in every way, and one to dip into. It will tell you a great deal about the culture and the political concerns of working people in the early nineteenth century.

H. J. Perkin, *The Origins of Modern English Society* (Routledge, 1969).

THEMATIC AND HISTORICAL CONTROVERSY

5 Rural society and poverty

Time chart

1760–1810: Main period of **parliamentary enclosure**, with particular concentrations in 1770s and 1790s

1782: Gilbert's Act passed. It encouraged local parishes to band together to build workhouses for the aged and infirm. Relief for the able-bodied should be largely provided outside workhouses. Few parishes adopted this legislation

1783–5: Annual cost for poor relief calculated at about £2 million

1793–1813: During French wars, price of bread rises sharply. It falls rapidly in the later 1810s and during the 1820s

1795: During a period of rising costs and unemployment, the magistrates of Speenhamland (Berkshire) established a sliding scale for supplementing wages to the level at which bread could be bought. The amount to which a family was entitled depended not only on its size but also on the price of bread at the time. The idea of wage supplementation was widely adopted elsewhere but there was no national legislation

1798: Thomas Malthus's *Essay on the Principle of Population* published

1801: Price of bread rises to new peak of 119s 6d (£4.97½)

1803: Cost of relieving the poor rises to about £4.3 million

1812: Price of bread reaches its highest nineteenth-century point of 126s 6d (£5.32½)

1816: Episodes of rick-burning and threatening letters in East Anglia

1817: David Ricardo's book *Principles of Political Economy and Taxation* published. It includes a savage attack on the old poor law

1818: Cost of relieving the poor reaches its peak (£7.8 million) before reform of the old system. This level was not reached again until 1871, when the population of England and Wales was almost exactly twice the 1818 figure

1821–3: Parliamentary Select Committee appointed to consider causes of agricultural distress

1830–31: 'Swing Riots' – named after a mythical leader, Captain Swing – break out and affect much of south-east England and East Anglia

KEY TERM:

Parliamentary enclosure

Enclosure was the means whereby land was held in separate blocs with clear and defined ownership. Parcels of land were separated by fences, hedges or ditches. Enclosure was of two kinds: enclosure of 'open fields' and of 'waste'. Over a long period from the sixteenth century onwards, land which had previously been held in strips alongside one another in 'open fields' was enclosed. Much of this enclosure had been with the agreement of all landowners, though the influence of the more wealthy members of a village would often be decisive. In the period 1760–1820 about 4,000 'parliamentary enclosures' were passed, affecting land particularly in the Midlands and East Anglia. These rearrangements of land were defined by an Act of Parliament which prescribed who owned land in a village and where it would be. **Parliamentary enclosures** were accompanied by legally enforceable apportionments and a map showing the new arrangements. Open-field enclosure represented a very heavy investment by landowners. They hoped for profitable returns since they were now able to farm in more efficient and cost-effective ways. Enclosure of waste was generally less controversial and involved bringing land of limited fertility into cultivation which had either lain entirely waste or had been used for rough grazing.

Why were so many rural people poor?

One of the most famous quotations in the Bible comes from St John's Gospel, chapter 12. It reads: 'The poor always ye have with you'. British society, which was certainly Christian at the end of the eighteenth century, had always taken this message reasonably to heart and had made some provision. In addition to charity, each parish recognised a responsibility to look after those whose income was insufficient to maintain themselves and their families. Two laws passed in 1598 and 1601, at the end of the reign of Elizabeth I, had confirmed that parishes had this duty. Rates were levied on landowners, the amount paid depending on the amount of land held. Though few people actually enjoy paying rates or taxes, the old poor law, as it became known, worked pretty well for much of the seventeenth and eighteenth centuries. The combination of poor law and individual acts of charity (which were many and sometimes exceptionally generous) kept people from starving.

The system worked, however, because population levels were in reasonable balance. After considerable inflation both in prices and in the number of people during the sixteenth century, the seventeenth and early eighteenth centuries were times of surprising stability. Prices often fell between 1660 and 1700, for example, and it is now almost certainly established that something like a major influenza epidemic caused British population actually to fall for the last time during the 1720s.

After about 1740, however, things began to change, first slowly and manageably, later much more quickly and apparently uncontrollably. Population growth is not necessarily a bad thing, of course. It can create new supplies of labour and where that labour is in demand (as it was in Britain's growing industrial and urban areas – see chapter 4), it is valuable. More people with some money in their pockets, of course, will create demand for manufactured goods. The success of the industrial revolution owed much to this growing domestic demand.

As we have seen, however, Britain cannot be seen as one region. Industrial production and commercial activity were concentrated in particular areas. Population growth, on the other hand, was relatively uniform across the country until the early nineteenth century (Figure 5.1).

The South of England which, London apart, enjoyed least industrial and commercial advance continued to contain about 38–39 per cent of England and Wales's population in the first half of the nineteenth century. The Midlands and East Anglia had a declining share (35–31 per cent between 1801 and 1851) and the North of England an increasing one

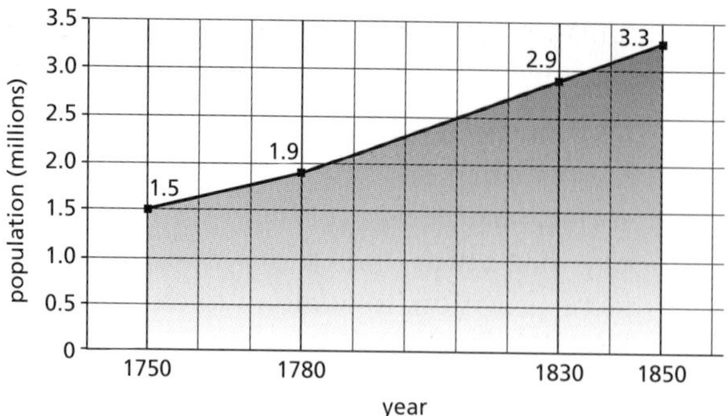

Figure 5.1 Population growth in the 15 counties in England and Wales least affected by industrial or commercial growth

(26–30 per cent during the same period). Where population rose and job opportunities did not, the result is what the economists – in their unlovely jargon – call 'a structural imbalance'. Put crudely, too many people chase too few jobs. The inevitable consequence is that wages are driven downwards and there is likely to be widespread unemployment.

1 The first, and much the most important, reason why rural poverty increased, therefore, is that the population increased more rapidly than job opportunities in much of the south and east.

2 Wages for agricultural workers were generally much lower in the south and east than they were in the north and west. By the end of the eighteenth century, agricultural labourers' wages in counties such as Hampshire and Wiltshire were as low as 6–7 shillings a week (30–35p), whereas in the far north-west, in Lancashire and Cumberland, they were regularly to be found in the range of 10–12 shillings (50–60p).

3 This wide discrepancy is largely explained by differing job opportunities outside agriculture. In the north and west, much agriculture was pastoral anyway (see chapter 1) and required more constant, if sometimes less intense, labour. Also, many new employment opportunities were being created in factories, in docks and in building. Both casual and permanent work was readily available in places like Manchester and Liverpool. In much of the south, the few alternative sources of labour were often being reduced by competition from more modern production methods in the industrial areas.

KEY TERM:

Capitalist methods of production

In the context of farming, **capitalist methods of production** relate to the use of investment to increase production and to sell at a profit in the market. The point of capitalism is to buy and sell for profit, perhaps using profits to reinvest and thus increase the size of the enterprise, with hope of still greater rewards. Eighteenth-century agriculture was increasingly capitalist in its organisation and tenant farmers (see chapter 1) took out leases in order to make a profit from what goods they sold.

4 The changing structure of employment in much of the south of England was also working to the disadvantage of rural labourers, whose numbers continued to increase until the middle of the nineteenth century. Increasingly, agriculture was converted to what might be called **capitalist methods of production**. Improvements in yield and productivity were achieved by investment and both landowners and tenants sought to ensure continued profits by making the most rational use of

KEY TERM:

Farm servant

A **farm servant** was distinguished from an agricultural labourer by the fact that he, or she, had been specifically hired (often at an annual hiring fair) for work during a period, usually a year or so. During that period, work was guaranteed. Farm servants often 'lived in' with the farmer, getting free board and lodging and receiving lower money wages in consequence. The advantage of being a farm servant was job security during the period of hire.

agricultural labour. Farmers made less use of **farm servants** and employed labourers only when they had work for them to do. Arable farming has obvious peaks and troughs during the farming year, with great need for labour at haymaking and harvest, and periods during the winter when there is little to do. Capitalist farming exploited these peaks and the surplus supplies of labour both to keep wages low and to employ an increasing proportion of workers only on a casual basis. Output per person increased since so many were now employed only at times of high demand. This added greatly to the extent of rural poverty, especially when bread prices went up, as they did during the wars with France at the end of the century. William Cobbett commented on the change in the 1820s:

> *'Why do not farmers now feed and lodge their workpeople, as they did formerly? Because they cannot keep them upon so little as they give them in wages . . . if the farmer now shuts his pantry against his labourers, and pays them wholly in money, is it not clear that he does it because he thereby gives them a living cheaper to him; that is to say a worse living than formerly?'*
>
> William Cobbett, *Rural Rides*, vols 1 and 2 (1825; Everyman edition, 1912).

5 During the period from about 1780 to 1815, agriculture was profitable and expanding. Although jobs may not have expanded sufficiently to keep pace with the growth in population, at least jobs *were* becoming more plentiful. The end of the French Wars, however, saw a sudden fall in food prices. The 1820s was a decade of low prices and, for many landowners and farmers as well as labourers, considerable distress. Some landowners had borrowed heavily during the 1790s to finance expansion and investment schemes and were still paying back high interest charges when the agricultural 'boom' came to an end.

> *That good old fame the farmers earnd of yore*
> *That made as equals not as slaves the poor*
> *That good old fame did in two sparks expire*
> *A shooting coxcomb and a hunting Squire*
> *And their old mansions that was dignified*
> *With things far better than the pomp of pride . . .*
> *Where master son and serving man and clown*
> *Without distinction daily sat them down*
> *These have all vanished like a dream of good*
>
> From John Clare's poem 'The Parish: A Satire'

6 Some historians have argued that parliamentary enclosure was a key factor in explaining rural poverty. This conclusion has been disputed by others. See below.

The attack on the old poor law

After two centuries of reasonably adequate service, the old poor law came under increasing attack from the late eighteenth century onwards. The reason was not far to seek. The system creaked under the increasing size of population, more 'efficient' systems of labour use and rising prices. The high prices of the 1790s provoked a surge of interest in alternative means of relieving the poor. The Speenhamland system was only one of many expedients (see time chart). The so-called 'Roundsman' system, for example, saw paupers sent round the parish to seek work at whatever wages the farmer was prepared to pay. The parish made up the difference between the inevitably inadequate payment and the cost needed to keep a labourer and his family alive.

Political economists, like **Malthus** and David Ricardo had a field day

PROFILE: *Thomas Malthus*

Thomas Malthus was born in 1766 at Dorking in Surrey. He was educated at Cambridge and became a clergyman in the Church of England in 1797. His opponents ironically referred to him as 'Parson Malthus', the irony residing in the belief that a clergyman should have more charitable views towards the poor. Malthus's *Essay on the Principle of Population*, published in two editions in 1798 and 1803, was extremely influential in converting educated opinion to the idea that the old system of poor relief was counterproductive. He argued that population had a natural tendency to rise, but would be 'checked' by natural means, such as famine or epidemic disease, when it became too high for a country's resources to sustain it. He wrote: 'It is undoubtedly a most disheartening reflection that the great obstacle in the way to any extraordinary improvement in society is of a nature which we can never hope to overcome.' The 'perpetual tendency' of mankind was 'to increase beyond the means of subsistence'. The old poor law, Malthus said, only made things worse because it transferred scarce resources to the poor who would only use what they were given to have more children. Malthus became Professor of Political Economy in the East India College in 1805. He wrote *Principles of Political Economy* in 1820, advocating free trade. Malthus died in 1834.

attacking what they saw as irrational solutions to the problem of poverty. They argued that misplaced charitable instincts only made the problems worse. If labourers knew that the parish would supplement whatever was paid by farmers, then no incentive existed either for labourers to seek work or for farmers to pay more than an absolute minimum. Also, if poor relief was given (as in the Speenhamland sliding scale) in proportion to the size of the family, would this not encourage the labourer to breed – thus making the problem even worse?

What lay behind these attacks on the poor law was the firm belief that a free market would work in the interests of society as a whole. What made the theory attractive to policy-makers was the prospect of reducing the ever increasing cost of poor relief. Farmers and politicians were convinced of the need for poor law reform (see chapter 14) not by economic logic but by the prospect of lower poor rates.

'The market price of labour is the price which is really paid for it, from the natural operation of the proportion of the supply and demand; labour is dear when it is scarce, and cheap when it is plentiful. However much the market price of labour may deviate from its natural price, it has, like commodities, a tendency to conform to it.

Like all other contracts, wages should be left to the fair and free competition of the market, and should never be controlled by the interference of the legislature.

The clear and direct tendency of the poor law, is in direct opposition to these obvious principles: it is not, as the legislature benevolently intended, to amend the condition of the poor, but to deteriorate the condition of both poor and rich; instead of making the poor rich, they are calculated to make the rich poor; and whilst the present laws are in force, it is quite in the natural order of things that the fund for the maintenance of the poor should progressively increase, till it has absorbed all the net revenue of the country, or at least so much of it as the state shall leave to us, after satisfying its own never failing demands for the public expenditure.'

D. Ricardo, *Principles of Political Economy and Taxation* (1817; Penguin, 1971).

During the long period of depression in much of the south and east of England after 1815, jobs became much scarcer as landowners and tenants sought to cut costs rather than go bankrupt. This development, linked to continued increases in population, made their labourers' condition even bleaker. One important consequence was the 'Swing Riots' of 1830–31. These riots should not be seen merely as an expression of deep despair. The work of the rioters was not random and suggested some planning and coordination. The targets of the rioters were various but all were rational. Some of the most important were:

- *Threshing machines*: These machines threatened to take away one of the few sources of work in wintertime. In many places the rioters managed to halt the introduction of this form of agricultural machinery for at least 30 years. The main period of mechanisation of agriculture did not occur until the 1850s and 1860s.

- *Poor law overseers*: Overseers had the job of administering poor relief and some were much meaner and harsher than others. These people tended to be singled out for hostility. Crude effigies of some were burnt in the village; others had their houses surrounded by rioters. This behaviour was intended to frighten and only rarely was physical violence involved.

- *Clergymen of the Church of England who acted as magistrates or who took high rates of tithe (the right to one-tenth of farming produce)*: Rural society seems to have been keenly aware of the sensitive position of the clergyman, who might be expected to offer charity and, where necessary, to mediate between farmers and labourers. Those clergy who were accused of harsh justice, or who were taking the farmers' side, often suffered the same treatment as mean overseers.

The impact of enclosure

Historians have frequently disagreed about the consequences of enclosure. The following views give you an opportunity to sample the debate. The time chart shows when parliamentary enclosure took place. Enclosure was highly controversial at the time and has remained so. Read the views below to see what different historians have made of the question.

View 1

'The governing class continued its policy of extinguishing the old village life and all the relationships and interests attached to it, with unsparing and unhesitating hand; and as its policy progressed there were displayed all the consequences predicted by its critics. Agriculture was revolutionised: rents leapt up: England seemed to be triumphing over the difficulties of a war with half the world. But it had one great permanent result which the rulers of England ignored. The anchorage of the poor was gone.

Enclosure was fatal to three classes: the small farmer, the cottager, and the squatter.'

J. L. and Barbara Hammond, *The Village Labourer* (1911).

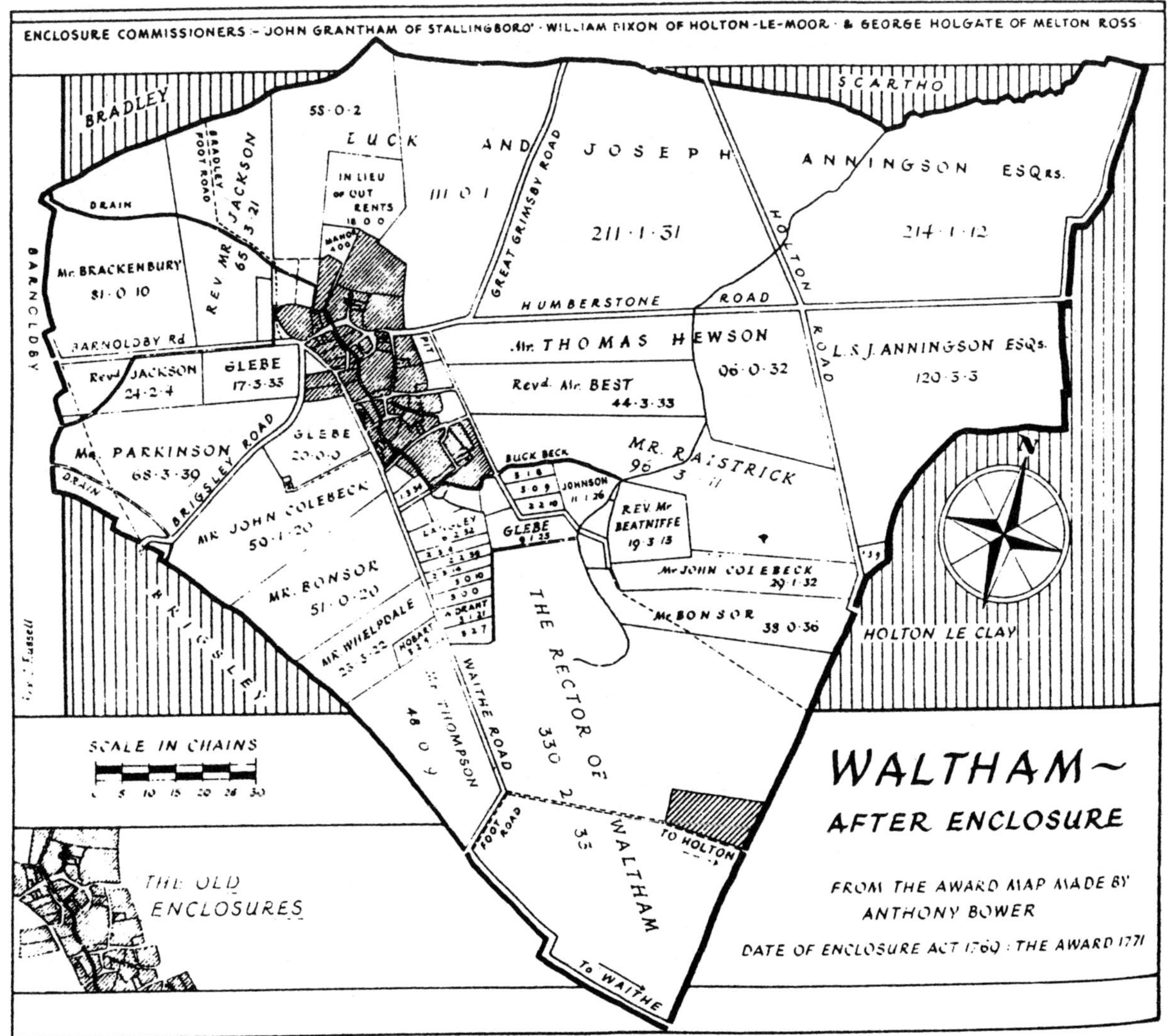

Figure 5.2 *The process of enclosure at Waltham (Lincolnshire)*

View 2

'The arguments of the enclosure propagandists were commonly phrased in terms of higher rental values and higher yield per acre. In village after village, enclosure destroyed the scratch-as-scratch-can subsistence economy of the poor – the cow or geese, fuel from the common, gleanings and all the rest. The cottager without legal proof of rights was rarely compensated. The cottager who was able to establish his claim was left with a parcel of land inadequate for subsistence and a disproportionate share of the very high enclosure costs ... In the enclosure of Barton-on-Humber [Lincolnshire] ... we find that out of nearly 6,000 acres, 63 per cent (3,733 acres) was divided between three people, while fifty-one

people were awarded between one and three acres ... Enclosure ... was a plain enough case of class robbery, played according to the fair rules of property and law laid down by a Parliament of property-owners and lawyers. The object of the operation (higher rents) was attained throughout the Napoleonic Wars.'

E. P. Thompson, *The Making of the English Working Class* (1968).

View 3

'It is [not] easy to generalise about the social consequences of enclosure. It can be said with some assurance that enclosure did not usually result in any sweeping change in the size of the farms, for it was usually difficult to find farmers with sufficient experience and capital to take on large concerns ... It is difficult to distinguish the overall effects of enclosure from those of other important changes that were going on at the same time ... Each village was in a sense unique... Consequently, it is simplistic to ascribe to enclosure changes, good or bad, which may well have arisen from quite other causes. The enclosures of the period, it must be remembered, affected considerably less than half the country and ... varied greatly in intensity from region to region, some districts experiencing little or none ... There were clear gains in the increased production of food and raw materials at a time of rising population and urban growth, and also in the improved efficiency of agriculture and its greater responsiveness to markets. There may have been a social loss in the possible decline of small owners and, more certainly, a deterioration in cottagers' standard of living. But progress can rarely, if ever, be achieved without some casualties, and it is evident that the old farming system could not have coped with the rapid growth of population ... So far as there was social deprivation, the fault must lie mainly with the landowners who usually, though not invariably, were the initiators of enclosure ... But, again, it is important to remind ourselves that enclosure was only one strand in the diverse web of rural social relations, and not necessarily the most common or most vital one. It is indeed highly significant that the riots of 1830 broke out in rural areas little affected by enclosure.'

G. E. Mingay, *Land and Society in England 1750–1980* (1994).

Task: questions on sources

Now answer the following questions. When you do so, make use of any information in this chapter together with any other information you have:

a Are views 1 and 2 agreed on the effects of enclosure? Explain your answer.

b **i** What differences do you detect in the way the authors present their opinions about enclosure?
ii 'View 3 directly contradicts views 1 and 2.' Do you agree? Explain your answer making use of all three sources.

c Notice the dates when each of these three views about enclosure was written. Do you think that students should rely on the most modern opinions? Explain your answer.

d **i** What do you think were the main reasons why so much enclosure took place between 1760 and 1820?
ii Which social groups would have had most cause to approve of parliamentary enclosure and why?

Further reading

G. E. Mingay, *Land and Society in England, 1750–1980* (Routledge, 1994) – a useful new general text.

K. D. M. Snell, *Annals of the Labouring Poor: Social Change and Agrarian England, 1600–1900* (Cambridge University Press, 1985) – a detailed, research-based study which views the plight of rural labourers very sympathetically.

M. E. Turner, *Enclosures in Britain*, Studies in Economic and Social History (Macmillan, 1984) – summarises the findings of research.

E. J. Hobsbawm and G. F. E. Rudé, *Captain Swing* (Penguin, 1969) – a fascinating and detailed study of the agricultural labourers' revolt of 1830–31.

W. A. Armstrong, *Farmworkers: A Social and Economic History* (Iowa State University Press, 1988).

EVALUATION OF EVIDENCE

6 Britain and the impact of the French Revolution, 1789–1815

Time chart

1789: Fall of the Bastille in Paris

1790: Edmund Burke's *Reflections on the Revolution in France* published; provides the first considered attack on the principles of the Revolution

1791: First part of Thomas Paine's *Rights of Ma*n published; the Priestley Riots see attacks on dissenters and reformers in Birmingham

1792: Foundation of the London Corresponding Society

1793: Trials of radical reformers in Scotland

1794: Government alarm at growth of radical activity: Pitt suspends Habeas Corpus Amendment Act. This suspension allowed the authorities to detain suspects, or merely nuisances against whom nothing could be proved, indefinitely without trial. Split within the Whig Party leads to the formation of a new Coalition government and the establishment of a new party of order. Some see this as the beginning of the modern Tory Party

1795: Peak year for radical protests. High food prices and discontent. Pitt introduces the Treasonable Practices Act, which makes more political activities treasonable, and the Seditious Meetings Act which restricts the ability to hold political meetings

1798: New taxes and greater regulation of newspapers introduced with the aim of stopping the poor from reading 'dangerous literature'

1799: Formal bans placed on radical societies such as the London Corresponding Society and the United Irishmen

1801: Year of social unrest and food riots. Habeas Corpus suspended again. William Pitt resigns over Catholic emancipation and is succeeded as Prime Minister by Henry Addington

1804: Addington resigns; Pitt the Younger becomes PM again

1806: Death of both Pitt and Fox. The Ministry of All the Talents briefly brings Whig politicians into government (falls in 1807)

1807: Duke of Portland becomes prime minister at head of anti-reform government

1809: Spencer Perceval takes over as PM; no change in policies

1811: In Nottinghamshire first Luddite attacks against new forms of machinery take place

1812: Economic distress stimulates revival of radical politics. Perceval assassinated; and Lord Liverpool becomes prime minister

KEY TERM:

Whig politician

The **Whigs** were the dominant political grouping in the eighteenth century. Most drew their beliefs from the Glorious Revolution of 1688, which had seen the overthrow of James II and the passing of the so-called 'Bill of Rights' (1689) which placed some restrictions on the power of the monarchy. Many Whigs supported ideas of liberty in politics, but no clear political doctrine covered them all. For much of the eighteenth century, they operated in smaller groups, clustered around one or more leading aristocrats. The groups competed for office and the political influence which went with it. Most Whig politicians were wealthy landowners, many with hereditary titles (see chapter 2).

'How much the greatest event it is that ever happened in the world, and how much the best!' This was the **Whig politician Charles James Fox's** reaction, expressed in a private letter to a friend, a fortnight after the fall of the Bastille. Fox's was an extreme example of enthusiasm but most politicians in Britain in 1789 cautiously approved a change which, they felt, would result in the non-violent establishment of a monarchy with limited powers. If this proved to be on similar lines to the British, so much the better. This chapter examines the main consequences of an event which almost all politicians at first misread.

PROFILE: *Charles James Fox*

Charles James Fox was born in London in 1749 at Holland House. He was the son of Henry Fox, Baron Holland, a leading Whig politician of the mid-eighteenth century. He was educated at Eton, always intended to make a career in politics and entered Parliament in 1768. He became attached to the Rockingham Whigs and was foreign secretary during the brief Rockingham government in 1782. Outmanoeuvred by the younger Pitt during the crisis of 1783–4, he was to spend almost all the remainder of his life in opposition. He supported greater political rights for religious dissenters in 1788–9. In the 1790s he disagreed with the majority of his party over the most appropriate response to the French Revolution. Fox stressed liberty over order; the majority of Whigs did not. Fox's Libel Act of 1792 enabled juries to decide whether alleged libels actually deserved to be described as such, rather than just whether the person accused was responsible. This reduced the scope allowed to judges and proved useful to several radical writers when they attacked the policies of government during the 1790s. Fox opposed Pitt's repressive policies in 1792–5. Notionally leader of the 'Foxite Whigs', who continued to argue that Whigs should defend the people's liberties, Fox was increasingly absent from Parliament during the 1790s. Just before his death, he supported the abolition of the slave trade and returned to office briefly as foreign secretary in the 'Ministry of All the Talents' (1806–7). He died in 1806, a few months after Pitt the Younger.

KEY TERMS:

Radicalism

Radicalism is a term which often causes confusion. Literally, it means a belief associated with getting to the root of something. It follows that radicals can hold very different views. What they have in common is a desire to institute significant change, quite possibly on the basis of belief in a particular political philosophy. Radicalism in this period is nearly always used to describe those – particularly outside Parliament – who wished for a fundamental change in the political system and the institution of a government based on principles of liberty and equality. Most took up ideas developed during the European Enlightenment of the eighteenth century and put into practice during the French Revolution. Many radicals were democrats, wanting to see free elections in which all citizens take part. Others wanted only an extension in the numbers of those entitled to vote.

Artisans

Artisans are often nowadays misleadingly contrasted with 'artists', implying that they are less creative and less talented. Artisans in late eighteenth- and nineteenth-century Britain were skilled workers, most of whom had served an apprenticeship. Most were in regular employment and earning above-average wages. They tended to be most numerous in non-factory towns like Sheffield, Norwich and, of course, London itself. Craft centres such as these were at the heart of radical politics in the 1790s and many historians refer to 'artisan radicalism', meaning the democratic beliefs held by many skilled literate workers at this time. Among the trades normally associated with radicalism were tailors, shoemakers and printers.

Within a year, however, Fox's great friend Edmund Burke had written a book denouncing the wild and speculative ideas of the revolutionaries and prophesying that the Revolution would lead on to disorder. Within three years, King Louis XVI had been arrested, the prospects for a limited monarchy in France had disappeared, revolutionary France was at war with the Austrian and Prussian monarchies and, partly in response to the challenge of war, the Revolution was about to enter its famous 'terror phase', with large numbers of arbitrary arrests and summary executions.

Within three years, also, societies had sprung up in Britain in support of the Revolution. The Sheffield Society for Constitutional Information, founded in 1791, and the London Corresponding Society were two of many organisations recruiting members to support democratic changes in Britain's political system. They called for the abolition of the monarchy, for proper representation and for each man to have a vote in free parliamentary elections. None of these proposals was new. Many middle-class nonconformists, writers and intellectuals had been discussing them for at least 20 years before the French Revolution. The novelty of 1790s **radicalism**, however, was the extent of support for these ideas now being shown by working people.

The key educator of the lower orders in attacks on established authority and support for republicanism and democracy was **Thomas Paine**. Paine's *The Rights of Man* has been called the 'Bible of British Radicalism'; it is a work of popularising genius. Paine simplified, and in some respects sharpened, the ideas of the European Enlightenment and made them both comprehensible and compellingly attractive to craftsmen, **artisans** and other working men with an interest in politics. Radical ideas spread like wildfire in the years 1792–5, especially since prices were rising and economic distress was rife. Time and again between 1789 and 1832, years of peak political agitation for change were also years of social discontent.

Paine offered a stiff challenge to the government. Debates about the nature of government which could be tolerated, even encouraged, among an educated elite were utterly unacceptable when they spread to the lower orders. Ordinary folk, most landowners believed, had neither the education nor the maturity to understand the great issues of the day. Pitt, who had supported modest parliamentary reform earlier in his career, now turned firmly against any political changes. Beginning in 1792, when Paine's book was banned, the government moved against the threat of radicalism. Government propaganda concentrated on the threat from 'Jacobins [the name given to the most extreme group in the French National Assembly] and Atheists'. New societies to defend the old order sprang up; some, like John Reeves's association movement, had government money. Prominent radicals in Scotland and in the London

PROFILE: *Thomas Paine*

Thomas Paine was born in Thetford (Norfolk) in 1737, the son of a corset manufacturer. He was apprenticed to this trade himself but left and was, by the early 1760s, an excise officer. He lost his job because he led a protest to government for excise officers to have more pay. He went to America in 1774 and there published his first important book, *Common Sense* (1776), which supported the colonists' claims for independence. He fought on the colonists' side during that war. His fame was made by the publication, in two parts, of *The Rights of Man* (1791 and 1792). The first part attacked Burke and called for democracy and republicanism throughout Europe. The second looked forward to a republican world which would have no need to spend taxes on defence because only the pride and arrogance of monarchs and emperors caused wars! The money saved could be usefully spent on a range of social benefits, including family allowances. Part II sold 200,000 copies in six months, making it the biggest seller of the age. Paine's ideas were not socialist but egalitarian. He believed in giving all an equal chance to improve themselves. This was immensely attractive to many skilled workers. Compelled to flee from Britain, Paine went to France where he became a member of the National Assembly, representing Calais. He opposed the execution of Louis XVI and was arrested during the Terror, narrowly escaping execution. He wrote *The Age of Reason* while in prison; it questioned orthodox Christianity, giving the British authorities further reasons to regard him as the essence of evil, who corrupted impressionable men's minds. He returned to America in 1802, where he died seven years later. His influence on radicalism in Britain was substantially greater than that of the German socialist revolutionary Karl Marx in the later nineteenth century.

Corresponding Society were arrested in 1793–4 and some were charged with treason.

The year in which radical agitation reached its peak was 1795 and it ended with two new repressive pieces of legislation on the statute book (see time chart). After 1795 radicalism lost much popular support and was driven underground. It did not disappear. The naval mutinies of 1797 (see chapter 7) had a strong democratic element and some attempts at armed revolution were also mounted between 1798 and 1801. None had much popular support and the government's spy network was always equal to the task of infiltrating secret societies. With some justification, many MPs were thoroughly alarmed by the new turn events outside Westminster took in the 1790s. The speed with which radical activity revived at the end of the French Wars, furthermore, indicates that many reformers were not frightened off by government policies in the 1790s, but merely awaiting their moment to return to the attack.

Some historians, notably E. P. Thompson, have argued that the main importance of the French Revolution for British politics was the awakening of radical ideas among the masses. More recently, Harry Dickinson has suggested that the French Revolution's main impact was to stimulate effective defence of the old order. Property owners throughout Britain were mobilised not only against the French but also to fight the dangerous contagion of democracy at home. Government propaganda was extensive and, in many areas, effective. The unlikely figure of George III, fat, decidedly unheroic and recently mentally unstable, was promoted as a symbol of common sense, decency and national unity. The wars against revolutionary France may have begun for commercial reasons (see chapter 7), but they induced in many across all classes a strong sense of patriotism and a hatred of 'new' and 'speculative' ideas. We cannot *know* if more working people were awakened to support for democracy by the French Revolution than were alarmed by fears of Jacobin excesses and old prejudices against the French. It is certain, however, that the French Revolution politicised the British nation as it had not been politicised since the English Revolution of the 1640s and 1650s.

Within the privileged world of Westminster, the French Revolution also had profound consequences. Impressed by the arguments of Burke, many of the more conservative Whigs, who had provided coherent opposition to Pitt before 1790, saw increasing need to develop a common front against the threat from 'French politics'. Few Whigs supported parliamentary reform after 1792. As William Windham, MP for Norwich, a town with increasing radical sympathies, pithily put it: 'Who would rebuild their house in a hurricane season?' Family connections and loyalties based on aristocratic leadership mattered to the Whigs. This would normally have kept old political alliances alive. But these were not normal times. The French Revolution posed the most uncomfortable and basic question of all for the Whigs: did they value their own traditions and their support for liberty and freedom over the new threat to order and civilised values represented by revolutionary sympathisers in Britain? The great majority now feared disorder more than they loved liberty. Led by the Duke of Portland, conservative Whigs formed an alliance with Pitt in 1794. This gave the Prime Minister huge majorities in the House of Commons. It also established a majority grouping which, apart from one brief and unsuccessful interval in 1806–7, would rule Britain until the end of 1830. By the early nineteenth century, most politicians called it 'Tory'. Pitt always fought shy of party connections and labels, saying that, though he was not a 'party man', he supported Whig principles. It was increasingly difficult to make such a claim convincing.

The new grouping had coherent conservative beliefs. It opposed 'French principles', supported government by a landed elite, saw property as the best guarantee of political stability and believed that, of the various forms of property, land carried most weight and authority.

The small group of 50–60 MPs which opposed this majority had no prospect of forming a government but it could at least assert that, in supporting reform and in looking for an honourable way out of the French war, it was sustaining old Whig values. The Whig opposition was, however, in a very sorry state. Charles James Fox was suspicious of many of the plans of men like Charles Grey (who proposed two Reform Bills during the 1790s), the playwright Richard Brinsley Sheridan and Samuel Whitbread, a representative of the wealthy brewing family. For his part, Grey distrusted Fox's political judgement. He was probably pleased that he absented himself from the House of Commons for much of the later 1790s. Enough money and established political connections remained to enable the small minority group to continue to function as a party. The parliamentary Whig opposition could trumpet its consistency with old party beliefs in liberty and toleration. Consistency, however, is rarely a virtue in politics. In the frenzied climate created by the French Revolution the opposition Whigs paid for their consistency with more than 40 years out of office.

Task: using visual sources

Visual material can often give us a much more vivid picture of events in the past than the written word. The 1790s was a great age for cartoonists. Journals and prints frequently commented on the main events of the day. Additionally, politicians were beginning to realise that they could influence opinion by the kinds of impressions they gave in their cartoons and drawings. Some of this material is an early attempt at what we would now call 'media manipulation'. Sources 1–3 give us a good idea about the political world in Britain immediately after the French Revolution.

Study the sources carefully. Your task is to write three or four paragraphs indicating what you are able to deduce about the period from this kind of material. What are the strengths of this kind of evidence for someone studying the controversy over reform at this time, and what possible weaknesses might such material have?

Use the following questions to help shape your answer. Don't think of them as examination questions, so much as a stimulus to *think* about the material.

1 What can you work out about the cartoonists' ideas and attitudes from the facial expressions shown in the pictures?

Source 1

Source 2

Source 3

2 Source 1 is a cartoon by James Gillray and shows one of the large political meetings held in the open air in London during the disturbed year 1795. Why does this source show a crowd listening to a political speech? What other things are people doing? What does the cartoonist want readers to think about the people in the crowd? What groups in society do they represent?

3 What attitude does Gillray, the cartoonist in Sources 1 and 2, have towards Britain and France in 1795–6? How can you tell?

4 Source 3 shows King George III pictured in a gilt frame. What impression of the King is the artist, Francis Bartolozzi, trying to convey? How can you tell? Which groups, or individuals, do you think would want to show the King looking like this? Is this portrait an example of 'media manipulation'?

5 Source 3 gives many other images than those of George III himself. Remember that the King was head of state during a time of war. Can you think of reasons why the picture uses so many other images? What do they represent?

6 Cartoonists always use visual tricks to give emphasis to their messages. What 'tricks' or symbols are being used in these three cartoons and for what purposes? Look at some cartoons drawn today. What comparisons and contrasts do you notice between the way present-day cartoonists represent public figures and the images used in cartoons in the 1790s? Can you think of reasons why the imagery is so different?

Further reading

H. Dickinson (ed.), *Britain and the French Revolution* (Macmillan, 1989) – a good collection of essays by leading scholars of the period. See particularly chapters 1, 2, 3, 5 and 10 by Dickinson, Derry, Stevenson and Emsley.

C. Emsley, *British Society and the French Wars* (Macmillan, 1979).

E. P. Thompson, *The Making of the English Working Class* Part 1 (Penguin edition, 1968).

A. Goodwin, *The Friends of Liberty* (Hutchinson, 1979) – concentrates on the radical political societies of the 1790s.

E. J. Evans, *Political Parties in Britain, 1783–1867,* Lancaster Pamphlet (Routledge, 1985) – explains how this period saw important political changes.

John Keane, *Tom Paine: A Political Life* (Little, 1995) – a research biography of the most influential British radical writer of the eighteenth or nineteenth century.

CAUSE AND CONSEQUENCE

7 The wars with France, 1793–1815

Time chart

1793: Britain and France go to war over French occupation of Belgian territories, which threatened Dutch and also British trade routes via the River Scheldt to northern Europe. Defeat of British army at Hondschoote (September)

1794: British navy occupies West Indian islands Martinique and St Lucia

1795: Unsuccessful British attempt to help French counter-revolutionaries in Brittany through expedition to Quiberon Bay. Ceylon captured from the Dutch

1797: Naval victory against Spain (Battle of St Vincent, February). Naval mutinies at Spithead and the Nore (April–May). Strong threat of French invasion. Admiral Duncan defeats Dutch fleet at Camperdown

1798: Nelson defeats French fleet in Aboukir Bay (Battle of the Nile, August) and frustrates Napoleon's progress in his Egyptian campaign

1800: Britain captures Malta. Its trading interests in northern Europe are threatened by the 'Armed Neutrality' involving Russia, Sweden, Denmark and Prussia

1801: British naval actions weaken the Armed Neutrality. Nelson wins Battle of Copenhagen against the Danes (April). Armed Neutrality breaks up (June)

1802: First phase of the war ends with Treaty of Amiens which sees Britain and France return most of their conquests. Britain retains Trinidad and Ceylon

1803: On resumption of war, Britain captures St Lucia, Tobago and Dutch Guiana

1804: Spain declares war on Britain after British attacks on silver convoys

1805: Napoleon's victories against the Austrians at Ulm (October) and against the Austrians and Russians at Austerlitz (December) confirm French domination of continental Europe. Nelson's victory against the French and Spanish fleet at Trafalgar (October) confirms British domination of the seas. Possibility of stalemate between Britain and France

1806: Napoleon issues the Berlin Decrees, thereby instituting a new phase of the war – the Continental System – by trying to deprive Britain of trade and thus to starve it into defeat

1807: Britain retaliates with a naval blockade against enemy trade. France invades Portugal, which refuses to participate in the Continental System

1808: British Expeditionary Force under Arthur Wellesley sent to Portugal – the Peninsula War begins

1809: Successes in the Peninsula at Oporto and Talavera but a major expedition to Walcheren (Netherlands) to help the Austrians fails

1810: Wellington's defensive action at Torres Vedras prevents France from capturing Lisbon. Britain captures Guadeloupe

1811: Wellington remains on the defensive in the Peninsula. Portugal defeated by the French. Java is occupied

1812: Victories in the Peninsula at Ciudad Rodrigo and Badajoz. Wellington enters Madrid (August). Napoleon begins his Russian campaign, defeats the Russians at Borodino (October) and enters Moscow. Napoleon's resources are overstretched; he is forced to begin a long and fateful retreat (December)

1813: Wellington wins a major victory at Vitoria and now controls all the Peninsula. Napoleon wins battles in the east at Lutzen and Bautzen (May) but suffers a major defeat at Leipzig (October). This forces the collapse of his coalition. In the same month, Wellington enters France across the Pyrenees

1814: Wellington captures Bordeaux and war seems to have ended when the allies enter Paris. Napoleon exiled

1815: Napoleon's return (March) begins his 'Hundred Days' campaign, when he threatens to overturn his earlier defeats. Wellington and the Prussian general Blücher defeat Napoleon at Waterloo (June), finally ending the war

The wars against Revolutionary and Napoleonic France were the most expensive that Britain had yet fought. The campaigns on sea and land produced some of the most celebrated victories in British history, won by some of our most distinguished commanders, particularly **Admiral Nelson** and the **Duke of Wellington**. The time chart and the maps (Figures 7.1 and 7.2) show where the major battles took place. This chapter is concerned with two key analytical questions about the wars:

1 Why did they last so long?

2 Why was Britain eventually able to defeat France when, militarily, the odds seemed stacked against it?

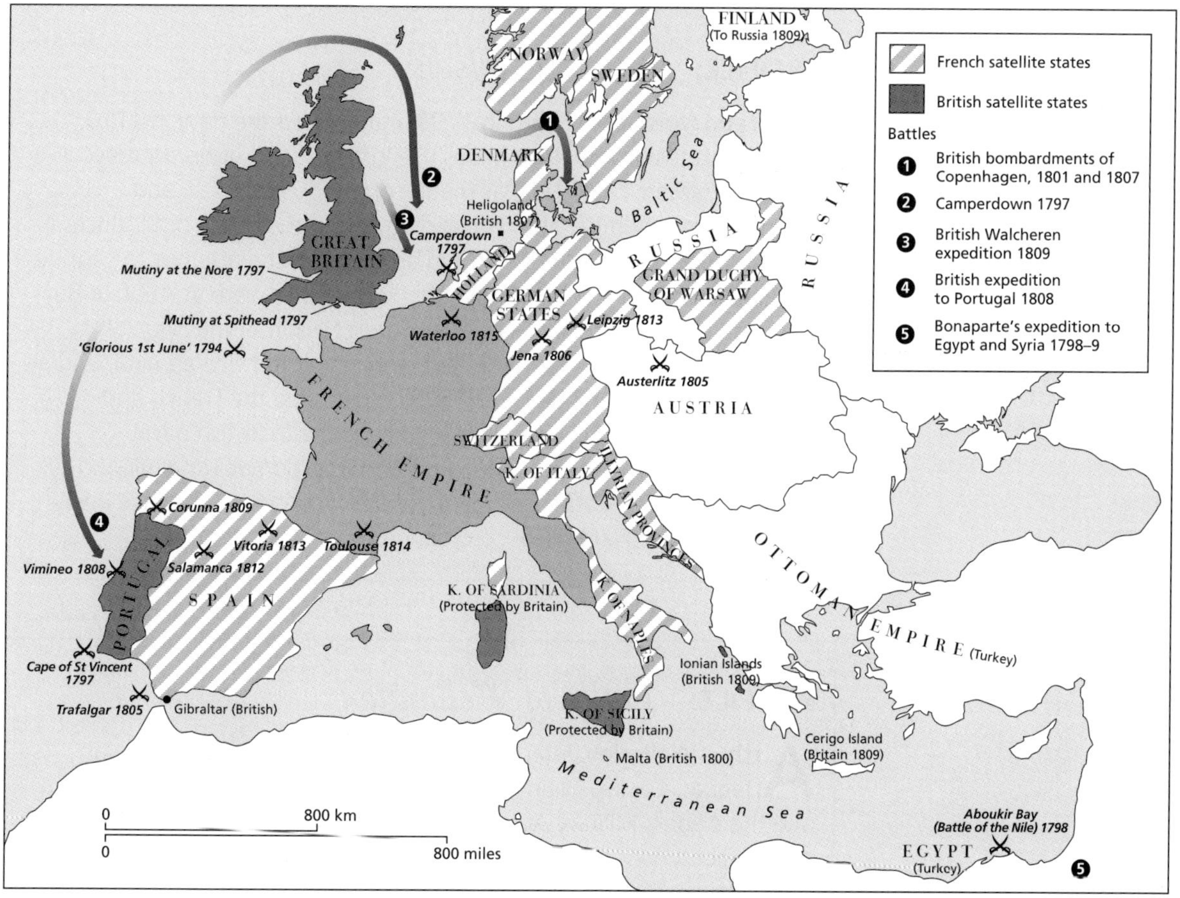

Figure 7.1 Major battles in the wars with France, 1793–1815

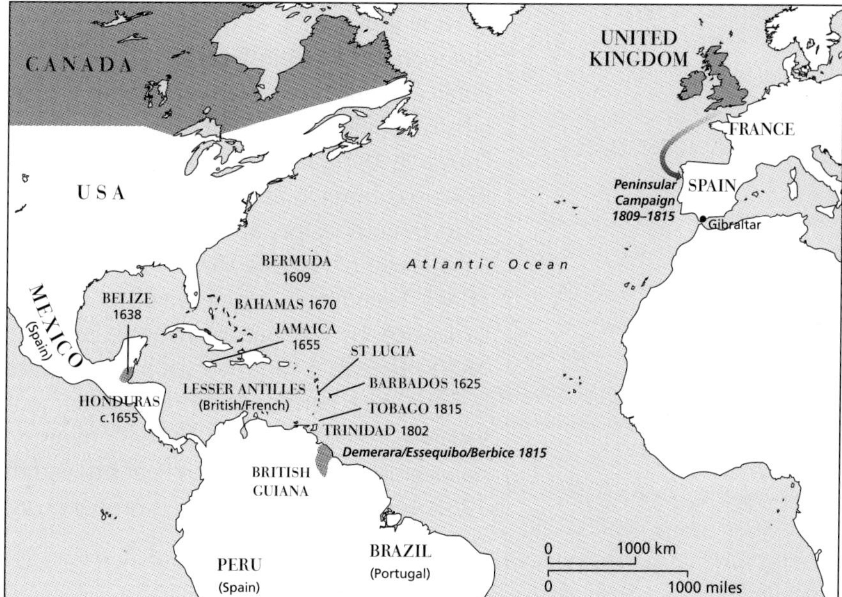

Figure 7.2 War in the West Indies

PROFILE: *Horatio Nelson*

Horatio Nelson was born in 1758 and entered the navy in 1770, serving first in the West Indies. He lost the sight of his right eye in a battle at Calvi in 1794. He was made commodore in 1796 and promoted rear-admiral after his leading role in the Battle of St Vincent. He lost his right arm in 1797 during an unsuccessful attempt to capture a Spanish treasure ship. His most famous victories were at Aboukir Bay in 1798 (after which he was created Baron Nelson of the Nile), at Copenhagen in 1801, shortly after being promoted vice-admiral, and at Trafalgar where on 21 October 1805 he defeated the French and Spanish fleets, effectively ending any challenge to British naval supremacy during the wars. He was killed in action at Trafalgar and buried in St Paul's Cathedral. He is generally considered to have been Britain's most brilliant naval commander.

PROFILE: *Duke of Wellington*

Arthur Wellesley, later first **Duke of Wellington**, was born at Dangan Castle, County Meath, in 1769. He was educated at Eton and the Angers Military Academy. He was an Irish MP from 1790–95 and, as lieutenant general, commanded a regiment in the Netherlands campaign, before seeing service in India from 1797 to 1804. He combined a political with a military career, entering the UK Parliament in 1806 and serving as Chief Secretary for Ireland in 1807–9. He was in command of the British forces in the Peninsula, where his attention to detail and ability to switch from defence to attack suggested military gifts of a high order. After taking the victorious British army through France in 1814, he was created Duke of Wellington. He returned to military command at the head of allied forces in 1815, winning his most famous victory at Waterloo against Napoleon on 18 June 1815. For the rest of his long life he was at, or near, the centre of political affairs, becoming a cabinet minister in 1818 as Master General of the Ordnance. He was heavily involved in foreign affairs throughout the 1820s. He was a controversial prime minister from 1828 to 1830, during which period he opposed parliamentary reform. He served briefly as foreign secretary in Peel's ministry of 1834–5 and was minister without portfolio in Peel's government of 1841–6. He died in 1852. His military reputation is probably unshakable, but his record in politics is more patchy.

Why was Britain at war for so long?

1 One important reason why the war lasted so long was that the British and the French had contrasting strengths which largely cancelled one another out. The British, though the navy had some early difficulties, could count on supremacy on the seas. The French, firstly through the revolutionary zeal of its conscripted forces, and later through the military genius of Napoleon Bonaparte, were dominant on the continent of Europe. Britain had no direct territorial ambitions on the continent of Europe and Napoleon could not gain control of the seas even for the brief period needed to transport his army across to Britain. Stalemate resulted.

2 The length of the war may also be partially explained by Britain's lack of preparation. Britain did not go to war to eliminate the heresies of the French Revolution and its poisonous political doctrines, but to defend its trade routes in northern Europe and to stop France developing a dominant influence there. The French threat blew up suddenly in 1792. Early that year Pitt had told Parliament: 'Unquestionably, there never was a time in the history of this country when, from the situation in Europe, we might reasonably expect 15 years of peace than at the present moment.' In early 1793 Britain had only 39,000 men recruited into the army, and 15,000 of them were serving abroad. By 1801, it had swollen to 150,000; by 1815, 264,000 British and colonial troops were under arms. The navy had been dreadfully run down during the years of peace from 1783 to 1793. At the outbreak of war only 15,000 sailors were in service, which increased to a maximum of 144,000 in 1810. It took a considerable time for Britain to punch its full weight.

3 Britain's war strategy depended to a considerable extent upon foreign allies who were supported by British subsidies. However, relations between Britain and its allies were frequently poor and Austrians, Prussians and Russians all considered that Britain was asking them to bear the brunt of the war while it indulged its separate trading interests in India and the Americas. Since the European allies usually had to fight highly trained and brilliantly led French forces, their frustration at Britain's limited, and usually unsuccessful, military assistance can be understood. Coalitions were frequent, but fell apart not only because of military defeat but also because of lack of trust and a perception that the allies' interests were different from Britain's. Only the last coalitions brought substantial success (see chart on page 58).

4 Perhaps the most important reason why the war lasted so long was that its outcome mattered so much to both sides while, at the same time, the ultimate objectives were so different. As with so many of its

British coalitions during the French Wars

1793: First coalition
Prussia (left in 1795); **Spain** (left in 1795); **Austria** (made a separate peace with **France** in 1797); **Holland** (defeated by France, 1795, and thereafter hostile to Britain as the Batavian Republic); **Sardinia** (left 1796)

1799: Second coalition
Russia (left in 1800); **Austria** (left in 1801); **Turkey**; **Portugal** (left in 1801); **Naples** (left in 1801)

1805: Third coalition (sometimes known as Treaty of St Petersburg)
Russia; **Austria** (left in December 1805 after its defeats by Napoleon)

1812: Treaty of Orebro
Russia and **Sweden**

1813: Treaty of Reichenbach
Russia and **Prussia**

1814: Treaty of Chaumont
Russia; **Prussia** and **Austria**: this coalition holds to secure victory against Napoleon

earlier wars, British objectives centred on trade and on securing a reasonable balance of power within Europe. When Henry Dundas was asked to explain why so much of Britain's military efforts were being expended in the West Indies rather than Europe, he said that conquests in the West Indies were 'of infinite moment, both in view of humbling the power of France, and with the view of enlarging our national wealth and security'. The West Indian strategy in the 1790s carried huge risks. Yellow Fever killed 40,000 troops and incapacitated as many more. However, the colonial strategy remained crucial for Britain. The French fought at first to preserve their Revolution. Had they been defeated in 1793 or 1794, then the Bourbon monarchy would have been restored and would doubtless have exercised unchecked autocratic powers. Later, under Napoleon, his own idiosyncratic interpretation of the French Revolution was imposed on a series of client states created by the success of his armies. It is only a minor oversimplification to say that the British fought for trade and commercial domination whereas the French fought for their Revolution.

5 The final stages of the war were also planned to last a long time. Having failed to invade Britain, Napoleon tried to starve Britain into defeat. The idea of laying siege to the most powerful trading nation in the world may seem bizarre but, given Napoleon's landed strength in Europe, it was probably his only prospect of an ultimately successful outcome. In the Middle Ages, sieges of individual towns or castles regularly took months. Laying siege to a nation is by definition a long-term strategy.

Why did Britain win the war?

1 Perhaps the most important reason for Britain's victory lay not in the quality of its commanders. No military commander could challenge Napoleon's strategic mastery. These wars were a long haul, calling at least as much for economic resources as for military or naval brilliance. Here Britain possessed a huge inbuilt advantage in its great and growing wealth. Britain could afford to pay allies to keep armies in the field and its credit in world money markets meant that it was able to raise loans more effectively than other nations. This was not done easily. National finances almost collapsed in 1797 when Pitt had to stop the Exchequer paying out gold, relying on notes (which the government could, of course, print) instead. The total cost of the war from 1793 to 1815 has been estimated at £1,039 million and no nation on earth could bear such a strain without dislocation and disruption. However, in a long war, it was not necessary for Britain to meet its bills easily, only for it to be able to keep going longer than its main rival. The French Wars may not have been won on the playing-fields of Eton, but they probably were in the iron foundries of south Wales and central Scotland, the cotton factories of Lancashire and the finance houses of the City of London. Britain was able to mobilise its financial advantages when it mattered. It is surely significant that the crucial coalition, fashioned in 1813, was supported by British subsidies totalling more than £26 million – and this at the end of a very long slog and determined efforts by Napoleon to crush the trading life out of the nation!

2 The British also proved good taxpayers. The income tax was levied for the first time in 1798 as a desperate war-time expedient. It proved unprecedentedly successful in raising money from property owners. It provided 28 per cent of the extra money raised for the war, and 80 per cent of money from the new taxes imposed by Pitt and his successors. Levels of existing taxes rose sharply and other new ones were introduced. The overall burden was formidable and only an unprecedentedly wealthy nation could have raised the sums required. It has been estimated that Britain raised taxes worth three times as much as France during the wars.

3 Obviously naval and military factors are important. Had Britain lost control of the seas even for a few hours in 1797, or in 1803–5, then Napoleon would have been able to transport his formidable army across to the Kent coast. Throughout the first 12 years of the war, the British navy continually frustrated French ambitions and commanders such as Howe, Duncan and Jervis are justly remembered. Nelson, of course, stands pre-eminent and it was his naval leadership which destroyed Napoleon's hopes of defeating Britain by force. The Battle of Trafalgar is of supreme significance. Between 21 October 1805 and 31 May 1916 –

the date of the Battle of Jutland during the First World War – no nation would challenge Britain's naval supremacy. This remained the rock upon which Britain's status as the world's leading power was to be secured.

4 Wellington's dour struggle in the Peninsula also contributed substantially to Britain's eventual success. The south-western corner of Europe was never entirely controlled by Napoleon and he committed 200,000 of his best troops in trying to drive the British out. Some have argued that Britain committed too much of its resources in one, relatively remote, place and that greater concentration in Belgium or the Netherlands in 1813–14 would have earned Britain swifter victory and greater rewards from the peace. Lord Grenville was a critic of the Peninsular strategy. However, it is far from clear that there was much more Britain would have wanted in terms of European settlement (see chapter 10), and the risk of Napoleon gaining complete control of Spain was substantial.

5 Ultimately Napoleon over-reached himself. He had control of almost the whole of Europe when he determined to take on Russia (which was, of course, almost limitless in territory and both a European and an Asiatic country) in 1812. The retreat from Moscow was both demoralising and debilitating for a previously all-conquering fighting force. It is surely significant that the coalitions which eventually *do* bring Napoleon to his knees and restore some kind of balance of power within Europe were forged in the aftermath of this defeat. After a 20-year slog, the collapse of France in 1813–14 came surprisingly quickly. Had Napoleon sustained his previous agreement with Tsar Alexander I, he could have continued to concentrate his efforts in central and western Europe with prospects of eventual success. Clearly, there is no one reason why Britain won and France lost in 1814–15. Whereas many older texts tended to place the emphasis squarely on campaigning strategies and military tactics, the emphasis has shifted in recent years away from military explanations to a concentration on national resources. It is for you to determine whether, from the factors given above and any others you know about, Wellington in Spain or the weaving sheds of Lancashire were ultimately more important in determining why it was Britain, rather than France, which emerged from the titanic struggles of 1793–1815 as the most powerful nation in the world.

Further reading

H. Dickinson (ed.), *Britain and the French Revolution, 1789–1815* (Macmillan, 1989). See chapters 6–9 by M. Duffy, P. Mackesy, P. O'Brien and F. Crouzet.

J. M. Sherwig, *Guineas and Gunpowder: British Foreign Aid in the Wars with France* (Cambridge, USA, 1969) – research study on how Britain spent money supporting its European allies.

P. Mackesy, *The War in the Mediterranean, 1803–10* (Addison Wesley Longman, 1957).

J. Weller, *Wellington in the Peninsula, 1808–14* (Addison Wesley Longman, 1962) – both Mackesy and Weller provide detailed analysis of war strategy.

CASE STUDY AND EXPLANATION

8 Why was Ireland a 'problem' for Britain?

Time chart

1620s and 1630s: Extensive settlement of lands in Ireland by the English and Scots

1652–3: After Cromwell's defeat of Irish supporting the royalists during the Civil Wars, Acts of Settlement confiscate much land and allocate it to English soldiers and adventurers. Irish to be resettled in the west of the country

1782: Catholic Relief Act enables Catholics to own land outside parliamentary boroughs; abolition of the Declaratory Act (1719) gives new powers to the Irish parliament ('Grattan's Parliament'). British Parliament could not amend legislation passed in the Irish parliament. Privy Council retains overall authority, however, and Irish legislation requires royal assent

1791: Formation of United Irishmen in Belfast – calling for links between Protestants and Catholics and democratic representation. Rejection of English influence

1792: Catholic Relief Act allows Roman Catholics to practise law in Ireland

1793: Relief Act allows Catholics to vote in parliamentary and municipal elections; most offices in Ireland open to them and, if property owners, they were entitled to bear arms

1798: Irish rebellion against British rule; limited French help, but rebellion defeated by end of the year. Many United Irishmen executed and transported. Between May 1798 and December 1799 more than 560 Irish rebels were executed and nearly 700 transported

1800: Act of Union ends separate Irish parliament

1803: Rebellion by Robert Emmet defeated

1822: Irish Constabulary Act sets up county police forces. Magistrates also to be paid

1823:	Foundation of the Catholic Association
1824:	Act establishing mutual free trade between Britain and Ireland
1828:	Election of Daniel O'Connell for County Clare begins crisis over Catholic emancipation
1829:	British government, fearing civil war in Ireland, grants Roman Catholic emancipation. Catholics could now enter Parliament and hold all civil and military offices. Qualification to vote in county seats raised from 40 shillings (£2) to £10. The effect was to reduce the electorate from about 216,000 to 37,000.

Ireland in the early nineteenth century

Many older British history textbooks used to refer lightly to 'the Irish problem'. In one sense this is a useful description, since relations between Ireland and Britain have rarely been harmonious and Irish issues destroyed some British governments during the nineteenth century and rocked several more. On another level, however, it represents a patronising simplification of a much more complex set of relationships. For a large number of Irishmen, their 'problem' was continued rule from Britain. Ireland was separated from Britain not just by the Irish Sea but by a huge cultural, religious and ethnic divide. Ireland was 80 per cent Catholic; England (after its idiosyncratic Anglican fashion) was Protestant, and Scotland more clearly so. Protestants had huge political advantages. At the time this book begins, Catholics, however wealthy, could not vote in local or central elections. The Anglican 'Church of Ireland' was the official church, not the dominant Catholic Church. In 1780 Britain was on the threshold of an industrial revolution and an increasing proportion of its population was living in towns. Ireland, apart from Dublin, its cosmopolitan and cultivated capital city, and Belfast, the centre of its linen industry, was overwhelmingly rural. Industrialisation would not come to Ireland during our period. Indeed, by 1840 about one Irish person in eight lived in a community of 2,000 people or more – a smaller proportion than in 1780. More than 75 per cent of adult males depended on agriculture alone for a living.

One thing Britain and Ireland *did* have in common between 1780 and 1840 was rapidly rising population. Ireland had a much larger population than either Wales or Scotland, and it more than doubled in this period (4 million–8.2 million). The *consequences* of this common population growth, however, were devastatingly different. Whereas Britain was able to use its huge economic growth to provide jobs for its swollen population and

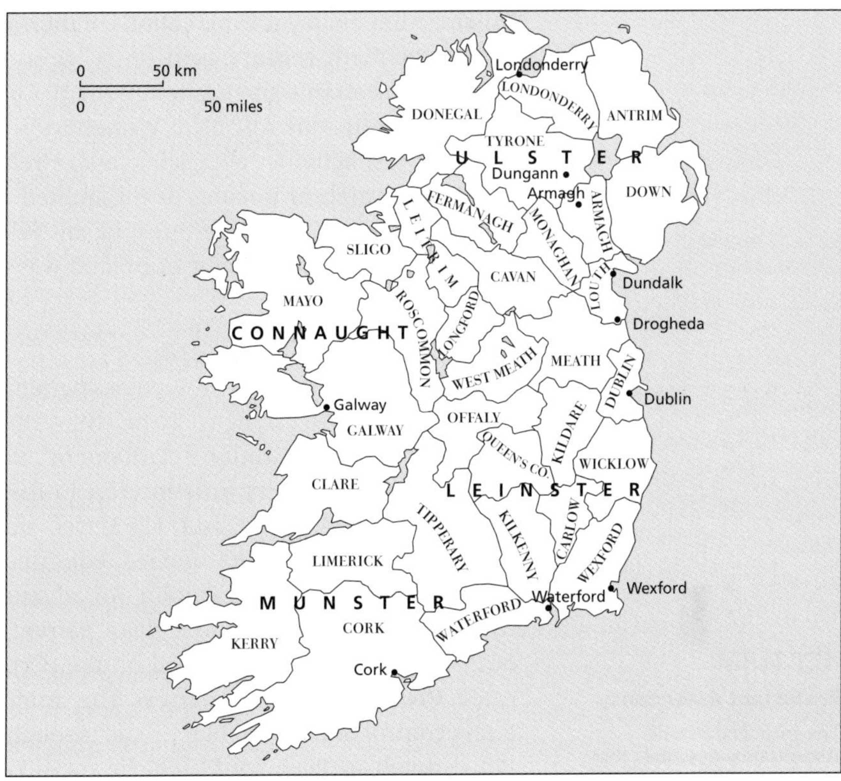

Figure 8.1 *Ireland in 1800*

at least to hold out the prospect of improved living standards, more and more Irish peasants remained dependent upon plots of land which became subdivided and could not sustain the increased numbers. A considerable proportion of Irish land was held in large units by about 150,000 owners who turned increasingly to grain production. The wheat, however, was for the British, not the Irish, market. The social gulf between substantial landowners and Irish peasants was immense. Peasants became increasingly dependent on the potato for subsistence. Local famines occurred in 1817, 1831 and 1835–7 causing considerable distress. These were early indications of the catastrophic famine of 1845–7 (see chapter 19). Well before this, young Irishmen were seeking work in Britain. Many did a variety of labouring jobs, sending back money to supplement inadequate family resources in Ireland. A fair number returned yearly but others became permanent migrants to Britain.

Problem factors

1 Religion

The simplified explanation of why Ireland was a problem for Britain would stress that Catholic Ireland resented domination from Protestant

Britain. After all, most explanations of the strife in Ireland in the last third of the twentieth century turn on religious hatred and mutual mistrust between Protestants and Catholics. Many Catholic peasants and labourers from the 1760s – the so-called 'Whiteboys' – were engaged in a wide variety of protest activities against excessive rents, paying tithes to the alien Anglican Church of Ireland, or the limited amount of land available for planting potatoes. However, most of this protest was dictated by hunger. The *political* nature of protest in Ireland was much more complicated.

2 Government

One reason why the British were so perplexed about Ireland was that it was the *British* government, rather than the Irish elite in Dublin, which called for reforms. 'Grattan's Parliament', while it existed between 1782 and 1801, showed very little interest in the Catholic majority. The concessions of 1782, 1792 and 1793 (see time chart) were imposed by Britain. In the early 1790s, indeed, educated Catholics learned to look to Westminster, rather than Dublin, for advancement of their civil liberties. Grattan and his friends had a clear 'Patriot' image of a separate Ireland, but it was one which depended on the perpetual domination of an educated **Protestant Ascendancy**. This minority secured its position by direct control of parliamentary seats through patronage. The British, from Pitt through to Peel, could see the merit of developing a Catholic elite loyal to the Crown. Before 1801 George III was separately King of Britain and of Ireland. However, day-to-day government in Ireland was discharged by wealthy Protestants who knew that their long-term interests were best served by a strong continued link with Britain. Men like John Beresford, Commissioner of Revenue from 1780, and John Fitzgibbon, Lord Chancellor after 1789, were both loyal and efficient servants of the Crown. Through men like this, the influence of the Crown in Irish affairs grew substantially after 1782.

KEY TERM:

Protestant Ascendancy

The term **Protestant Ascendancy** describes that minority of educated and mostly wealthy landowners and professionals who ruled Ireland from Dublin. It is particularly associated with the period 1782–1801 when the Dublin Parliament had a degree of independence from the British government, though not from the Crown, which appointed Irish ministers.

'... the gentlemen of Ireland [know] that the only security by which they hold their property, the only security they have for the present Constitution in Church and State, is the connection of the Irish Crown with, and its dependence upon, the Crown of England ... When we speak of the people of Ireland, it is a melancholy truth that we do not speak of the great body of the people ... The Act by which most of us hold our estates was an Act of violence – an Act subverting the principles of the Common Law in England and Ireland. I speak of the Act of Settlement.'

John Fitzgibbon, speaking in the Irish Parliament, 1789, quoted in E. M. Johnston, *Ireland in the Eighteenth Century* (1974).

The impact of the French Revolution on Ireland

KEY TERM:

Republicanism

Republicanism is the belief in government without emperors, kings or any hereditary rulers. Republicanism became a popular belief among educated elites in the second half of the eighteenth century, thanks to the influence of Enlightenment thinkers such as Rousseau. The creation of a republic in the United States of America in 1787 acted as a model for many republicans.

Just as the example of the American colonists seeking independence from Britain had inspired Protestant 'Patriots' and had resulted in the creation of 'Grattan's Parliament', so the French revolution gave many Irishmen visions of liberty and equality. For men like **Wolfe Tone**, one of the leaders of the United Irishmen, the objective was to achieve 'a cordial Union among ALL THE PEOPLE OF IRELAND . . . No reform is practicable . . . which does not include *Irishmen* of every religious persuasion'. Tone wanted democratic, **republican government** and his United Irishmen vigorously advocated the views of Thomas Paine (see chapter 6).

Most of the United Irish leadership was educated, middle class and Protestant, especially in Belfast. However, religious allegiance in Ireland meant that any mass support for political change in Ireland had to be largely Catholic. The reaction of the government to Irish radicalism polarised the political conflict into one between Protestant and Catholic. Radicals believed the concessions to Catholics in 1792 and 1793 hopelessly inadequate. Tone called them 'a disgrace to our constitution', and the Ascendancy in Dublin frustrated any more extensive plans for quietening

PROFILE: *Theobald Wolfe Tone*

Theobald Wolfe Tone was born in Dublin in 1763 and trained as a lawyer there. Influenced by the French Revolution and by enlightened ideas he helped to form the Society of United Irishmen. He forged links with the French revolutionaries from an early stage. In 1794 he wrote a memorandum in which he told them that 'In Ireland, a conquered, and oppressed and insulted country, the name of England and her power is equally odious, save with those who have an interest in maintaining it, such as the Government and its connections, the Church and its dependencies, the great landed property etc.'. His campaigns to bring democracy and separate nationhood to Ireland took him to France in 1795 and he accompanied the French attempts at invasion in 1796 and 1798. He was captured during a French attempt to land in Ireland off Donegal and committed suicide before he could be executed. He is remembered as one of the heroes of Irish nationalism. Tone was a clever and articulate man, but he failed to understand the importance of Roman Catholicism as a defining element in Irish identity. Like many radicals in the 1790s, he placed too much trust in the power of rational argument to bring substantial political change.

opposition which British politicians may have favoured. In any case, the likelihood after war broke out in 1793 that the French would seek to mount an invasion of Britain through Ireland's back door inclined the authorities to preference for the iron fist over the velvet glove.

Between 1793 and 1796 Protestant Yeomanries were created and Militia Acts passed with the aim of destroying radicalism. The United Irishmen were formally banned in 1794 and driven underground. From this time onwards, links between the radical Protestant elite and ordinary Catholic peasants and labourers grew closer. The Catholic 'Defenders', part agrarian saboteurs in defence of peasant rights and part nationalists, also made common cause with the United Irishmen. Not only were radicals and peasants alike affected by repressive legislation passed from Dublin but the economic crises of the 1790s brought higher rents and prices, widespread unemployment and dislocation of the linen industry. These magnified the grounds of discontent.

The Irish rebellion of 1798 was very poorly planned, badly coordinated and needed much more French assistance than it received. It was easily enough put down and reprisals exacted (see time chart). The rebellion, however, was crucially important. It politicised many Catholics and convinced them that no good would come from the Protestant Ascendancy. After 1798 most Catholics opposed English control. It also converted the few remaining United Irishmen to the view that political change could only come about if the Catholics were mobilised as an anti-British force. Protestantism had even more need of Britain. Westminster viewed the problem as one of national defence in time of war. The British government realised that a separate Dublin Parliament in the hands of wealthy Protestants was a dangerous indulgence. It could only alienate Catholics and radicals further. The fear of a fresh, better planned, French invasion increased the need for formal political union between the British and Irish Parliaments.

Most members of the Dublin Parliament hated the idea of Union and were persuaded to it only by a mixture of bribery and coercion. Many MPs were richly rewarded for their agreement to incorporation within the Westminster Parliament. The young Viscount Castlereagh was also able to negotiate some useful protection as a sweetener for Ulster linen manufacturers before full free trade between Britain and Ireland was established in the 1820s.

Many British politicians, led by Pitt himself, wanted to grant more political freedoms to Catholics. George III, however, regarded Catholic emancipation as a breach of his Coronation Oath and Pitt was forced to resign when he pressed the issue.

Main terms of the Act of Union 1800

1 Irish Parliament abolished and a new United Kingdom of Great Britain and Ireland came into effect on 1 January 1801.

2 One hundred Irish MPs added to the House of Commons at Westminster; 28 peers and four bishops represented Ireland in the House of Lords.

3 Many Irish boroughs disfranchised and their patrons compensated – at about £15,000 per seat.

4 The system of government and administration in Ireland largely retained, with a Chief Secretary (appointed by the Crown) as the Chief Executive.

5 Irish Exchequer to remain separate from the British in short term. The two exchequers were eventually amalgamated in 1816. Ireland to contribute about 12 per cent to United Kingdom budget.

6 Some tariffs remained, but the objective was to create a single free-trade area within the new United Kingdom.

'You know ... that it was always my opinion ... that the Union with Ireland would be a measure extremely incomplete and defective as to some of the most material benefits to be expected from it, unless immediate advantage were taken of it to attach the great body of Irish Catholics to the measure itself, and to the government as administered under the control of the United Parliament ... The removal of the remaining disqualifications from parliament, and from office, seemed to me to be one indispensable feature of such a system. Not so much from any positive and immediate effect which that removal would produce – for the number of Catholics whom it would introduce into parliament, or into office, would be very small – but because it was the best pledge that the United Parliament could give of its general good disposition towards the Catholic body, and because it was naturally regarded by the clergy, as a preliminary to their acceptance of the sort of provision which we wished to make for them, in order to render them more respectable in station, more independent of their flocks, and better disposed to support the established government.'

Lord Grenville to his brother, the Marquis of Buckingham, 2 February 1801, in *Memoirs of the Courts and Cabinets of George III* (1855).

'Those things which, if now liberally granted, might make the Irish a loyal people, will be of little avail when they are extorted [i.e. by the Irish] on a future day.'

Viscount Castlereagh, 1801, quoted in J. W. Derry, *Castlereagh* (1976).

From Union to emancipation

The worries of Pitt, Grenville and Castlereagh proved entirely justified. The Act of Union was seen by many Irish as political rape, forced on them by an alien authority and accepted by the hated Protestant minority only because they gained corrupt advantage from it. The Union would remain a symbol of Irish subservience throughout the nineteenth century.

In some respects, the Union changed little. The nature of government was not much altered by the absence of a Dublin Parliament. Sir Robert Peel, as Chief Secretary for Ireland, maintained staunch pro-Protestant policies administered with growing effectiveness. Agrarian outrages by 'Whiteboy' groups continued, especially during the economic depression of 1813–17. Prominently involved were skilled craftsmen, many with a better education than most peasants possessed and able to organise specific activities.

In other respects, however, things did change. One historian has notably called nineteenth-century Ireland a 'social laboratory'. Ministers did not neglect Ireland; they practised on it. Significantly, a paid police force appeared in Ireland seven years before Peel's famous 'Bobbies' began to patrol the streets of London.

The most important change, however, would substantially refocus Britain's perception of the 'problem' Ireland presented. From 1824 **Daniel O'Connell** refashioned the Catholic Association into an effective pressure group in support of Roman Catholic emancipation. His energy and powers of leadership enabled him to coordinate Catholic protest. He persuaded thousands of humble peasants to subscribe one penny a month to the campaign. Most of this money was raised locally by Catholic priests, who thus became linked with O'Connell's campaign. Several thousand pounds was raised in a few months and was used to fund national propaganda coordinated, of course, by O'Connell himself.

O'Connell capitalised upon the existence of the Catholic vote, not properly mobilised before. In the 1826 general election violence, intimidation

PROFILE: *Daniel O'Connell*

Daniel O'Connell was born into a gentry family in County Kerry in 1775. He was educated in London and France before being called to the Irish bar in 1798. He practised as a barrister. Unlike many educated Catholics he opposed the Union from the start and called for strenuous resistance to it. He helped to found the Catholic Association and then used it as a vehicle to mount unstoppable pressure for Catholic emancipation by coordinating agrarian activity within a political organisation. He was elected MP for County Clare in 1828, provoking the Emancipation Crisis. He was a substantial figure in UK politics throughout the 1830s and 1840s, helping to sustain Lord Melbourne's Whig government in office from 1835–41 via the Lichfield House Compact. In 1840 he founded the Repeal Association, to get rid of the Act of Union and became Lord Mayor of Dublin in 1841. He continued to organise activity against the Union until his death in 1847.

and propaganda by the priests all helped to get a pro-emancipation candidate returned at Waterford, a seat which (despite a strong potential Catholic majority) had obediently returned Tory, pro-Union candidates since 1801. O'Connell exploited the opportunity and put himself forward for a by-election at County Clare in 1828. Catholic priests in most parishes organised and held meetings in support of O'Connell. Since he could not legally take the seat the popular Catholic vote had won him, O'Connell's election provoked a constitutional crisis. It is significant that it was Robert Peel who persuaded a most reluctant Prime Minister, the Duke of Wellington, to concede the emancipation which allowed O'Connell to take his seat. While he was Chief Secretary Peel's nickname among educated Catholics was 'Orange Peel'. Orange was the colour used by the Protestant supporters of strong links with Britain.

Yoking an educated Catholic class obediently to the Union by emancipation in 1800 might have solved one of Britain's biggest problems in Ireland. The obstinacy of George III prevented it. As Castlereagh had feared, making a forced concession a generation later was not enough. Buoyed by success, the Catholic majority in Ireland now saw emancipation only as payment on account. The deliberate rigging of the franchise as part of the emancipation 'concession' (see time chart) infuriated them anyway, and it was to be but a small step from equality of political rights to pressure for national self-determination. From the 1820s onwards, there would always be enough Catholics ready to change the 'Irish question' again and again until – finally – they got something like the answer they wanted.

Taking notes

An important skill you need to acquire early in your sixth form course is note-taking.

Why make notes?

1 Notes will be shorter than the books you have read, and probably shorter than some of your class handouts as well.

2 Good notes help you to make coherent sense of a topic. Working on longer pieces of writing to produce shorter notes should help you to get your ideas in order.

3 Notes give you a chance to practise making your own selection of what is important from what is often a lot of detail. This is a valuable historical skill in its own right – and specially important at exam time.

4 Notes will be much easier to revise from when the time comes.

What makes good notes?

i Notes are for *you*. So devise a system which is for your benefit. People learn in different ways but notes should *always* be shorter than the source from which you are taking them.

ii You don't practise how to write essays in notes, so don't worry about complete sentences or even looking up how some words are spelled. Don't be afraid to use abbreviations, so long as you are sure that you will remember what they mean later. Try to simplify what you have read, but do remember that you may need to use them again in a year or more's time. Simplify in ways which will help you remember.

iii The way this book is organised should help you with your notes. It contains some big headings for you to follow. It also gives you specific factual information in the time charts. You will also find plenty of evidence in the form of sources. These are also intended to be used in your notes. You might want to jot down a key sentence or two.

iv It will probably be a good idea to stick with the main headings from the book, and then jot down notes which help you to understand why the heading is an important one.

v Don't forget that some themes are found in more than one chapter. The good note-taker will know that the **index** of a book is a useful way of finding out whether there are more references. The index in this book is in three parts and this should also help you. You will find reference to:

- the main content headings
- the **key terms** whose meaning you need to know
- the key people who are given brief **profiles** in the book.

You will find reference to the specific pages on which more information may be found. Become familiar with an index. A good index can provide numerous short-cuts to valuable ideas and information.

An example of note-taking

Getting started

Let us say that you want to take notes on the importance of the French Revolution on Ireland. You will see that there is a heading specifically on this, so that should be your starting-point. Look at that section very carefully. Your notes will probably follow the order of the section. You will also see that the section gives you references in bold type to a key term – Republicanism – and a key individual – Wolfe Tone. You will want to make use of these. You should also refer to the time chart. Look at the entries for 1791 and 1798, for example. After reading this section, you should see that specific information is given about the importance of the United Irishmen and the Irish rebellion.

Now look at the following example of notes on this section. The aim has been to shorten, to simplify and yet to give you sufficient information to help you when you come back to the topic – perhaps just before an examination:

Impact of Fr. Rev. on Ire.

1. Fr. Rev. gave Ire. examples of equality and democracy – one man one vote. In Ire. calls for change involved BOTH more votes (for Prots. and Caths.) and weakening power from Brit.
2. Wolfe Tone – leading rad. (remember: look up 'radical' in Index): close links with Fr. Rev. – showed Irish they were a nation, but also oppressed. Tried to unite the Irish to oppose British rule. Tone much influenced by Paine. Building up support for protest across Ireland. Tone came with troops on attempt. invasion from Fr.
3. Tone a Protestant but rich Prots. ruled Ireland and gt. maj. of Irish were Caths. So, most of the opposition in 1790s bound to be Cath. By end of 1790s, opp. was Cath. Ireland mostly divided between Caths. and Prots.

4 Not only Fr. Rev. which helped Irish radicals – 1790s high prices and higher rents. Poor Catholics worse off – much unemplymt.

5 Prots. organised into military force to combat radicals. Govt. has much more power on its side, Prots. wanting to keep Ireland linked to Britain.

6 Cath. discontent eventually helped to bring rebellion (1798), but Prot. rads. trying to get help from France – Tone trying to get French invasion. Rebell. finally convinced radical Prots. that they must cooperate with Caths. to get real change. Rebell. poorly organised; easily defeated.
(Remember *links* with other topics: Union of 1800; growth of Irish nationalism; radicalism in Britain)

Task: questions on sources

Look at the sources in this chapter and then answer the following:

a Which social group did Fitzgibbon have in mind when he spoke about 'the gentlemen of Ireland'?

b Noting its origins, and by reference to any other material you can find in this chapter, explain what reliance you would place upon Grenville's letter as evidence about the British government's views about the Catholics in Ireland in 1800.

c What can you infer about the reasons why Grenville and Castlereagh supported Catholic emancipation from the evidence given here?

d Why, despite these arguments, was Catholic emancipation not granted in 1800 or 1801?

e How likely was it that the Act of Union would bring the benefits hoped for by those who brought it into being? Explain your answer using these sources, the terms of the Act of Union and other information given in the chapter.

Further reading

R. Foster, *Modern Ireland, 1600–1972* (Macmillan, 1988) – now probably the most readable study of Irish history.

J. C. Beckett, *The Making of Modern Ireland, 1603–1923* (Faber, second edition, 1981).

K. T. Hoppen, *Ireland since 1800: Conflicts and Conformity* (Addison Wesley Longman, 1989) – looks sympathetically at society as well as Irish politics.

H. Dickinson (ed.), *Britain and the French Revolution* (Macmillan, 1989). See chapter 4, by Marianne Elliott – valuable on Ireland in the 1790s.

G. O'Tuathaigh, *Ireland before the Famine, 1798–1848* (Gill and Macmillan, 1972).

L. M. Cullen, *The Emergence of Modern Ireland, 1600–1923* (Gill and Macmillan, 1983).

EVALUATION OF EVIDENCE/ ROLE OF THE INDIVIDUAL

9 Stress and stability: Britain under Lord Liverpool, 1812–27

Time chart

1812: Lord Liverpool becomes Prime Minister, but the Prince Regent would have preferred Marquis Wellesley, Foreign Secretary and Wellington's elder brother, to have succeeded Perceval

1815: Government introduces a new corn law, which prohibits import of foreign corn when domestic price is less than 80 shillings (£4) a quarter (12.7 kg). Many considered this degree of protection excessive, since domestic prices were very rarely as high as 80 shillings before the French Wars

1816: Government fails to keep income tax in peacetime when Parliament votes against retaining it. State of government finances remain a worry. Radical protest meetings frequent

1817: Radical protests continue. 'March of the Blanketeers' to press for parliamentary reform. Government suspends Habeas Corpus and passes a new Seditious Meetings Bill

1818: General election confirms Liverpool in power, though the Whigs gain some seats. Improved economic conditions and less democratic agitation

1819: Return of poor economic conditions produces further pressure for reform. In Manchester a crowd assembled to hear speeches in favour of parliamentary reform is charged by the Manchester Yeomanry; 11 are killed: 'the Peterloo Massacre'. Government's Six Acts confirm policy of repression and restricted liberty in the face of radical challenges

1820: Death of George III. Prince Regent succeeds as George IV. His attempt to divorce his wife, Queen Caroline, produces further embarrassment for the government. Cato Street Conspiracy to murder the cabinet discovered and its leaders executed

1821: Restoration of government finances after the French Wars completed when Bank of England resumes cash payments (rather than relying on notes). With the return of better trading conditions and improved prosperity, support for parliamentary reform wanes

1822: Reshaping of the government after death of Castlereagh and resignation of Sidmouth and Vansittart. Promotions for ministers who institute economic and administrative reforms: Robinson, Huskisson and Peel

1823: Robinson and Huskisson begin to reduce protective duties in moves towards eventual adoption of free trade policies. Peel's reforms reduce the number of offences which carry the death penalty

1823–4: Gaols Acts rationalise prison administration and establish a system of inspection

1824–5: Repeal of Combination Acts makes trade unions legal but maintains firm restrictions on their activities

1826: General election preserves Liverpool's majority, but disputes within the party on whether to concede political emancipation to Roman Catholics threaten unity. Peel rationalises the criminal law on theft and other property offences

1827: Liverpool suffers a stroke and is forced to resign. Canning succeeds, but dies within months and is himself succeeded by Goderich

Liverpool was Prime Minister for a longer period than anyone else in the nineteenth or twentieth centuries. Only Sir Robert Walpole (1721–42) and the Younger Pitt (1783–1801; 1804–6) have held the office for longer. Liverpool was Prime Minister at the time of Britain's victories against the French, and the nation was both wealthier and much more prosperous at the end of his period in office than at the beginning. Yet his reputation, both among contemporaries and many historians, stands very low. Benjamin Disraeli's famous jibe that Liverpool was an 'arch-mediocrity' has been little challenged since. In this chapter we will look at the challenges Liverpool faced in office, how successfully he tackled them and whether his rather low reputation for political leadership is justified.

Coping with crisis

Liverpool became Prime Minister in the same year that Napoleon unwisely turned his forces on Russia. The defeats which this decision brought to Napoleon helped to stabilise Liverpool's leadership in the face of early criticism that a fussy, detail-driven man was not right for political leadership. Wellington's victories helped to keep Liverpool in power in the early years. After 1815, Liverpool's leadership of the Tory Party was secure and the Whigs were never strong, or united, enough to mount successful challenges.

PROFILE: *Lord Liverpool*

Robert Banks Jenkinson, second **Earl of Liverpool**, was born in 1770, the son of Charles Jenkinson, a political adviser to George III. He was educated at Oxford and became an MP in 1790. He served in minor office under Pitt, who was his political guide and whose policies he always followed, throughout the 1790s before becoming Foreign Secretary in Addington's government of 1801–4. When Pitt resumed office in 1804, he became Home Secretary, a post he also held under Portland (1807–9). He was secretary for the colonies under Spencer Perceval. Lord Liverpool was thus one of the most experienced ministers ever to become Prime Minister, when he was appointed in 1812. He is associated with supporting repressive measures against political radicals in Britain from 1815 to 1820 and against the Irish Catholic Association in the 1820s. He established good working relations with most of his cabinet, most of whom saw him as a much more attractive leader than any possible rival. He died in 1828.

The years 1815–21 were, however, troubled ones. The new corn law (see time chart) was defended by Liverpool as a way of ensuring that farmers kept producing much-needed wheat when prices fell after the long boom of the war years. Its many opponents saw matters differently, arguing that a parliament of landowners was feathering its own nest while the rest of society picked up the bill. The three sources below summarise the argument, but the 1815 corn law gave a considerable fillip to the reviving radical movement. From 1815 onwards, leaders like Henry Hunt, Thomas Sherwin and William Cobbett could portray their struggle as one between the 'productive' classes (i.e. those in the middle and working classes whose work and investments increased the nation's wealth) and the 'unproductive' (i.e. those landowners who had inherited their property, gained income from rent and whose selfish policies overtaxed the poor).

> *'The great object was the interest of the Consumer; and this ... would be effectually promoted by the present measure, the effect of which would be to render grain cheaper rather than dearer. The important point to attain was a steady and moderate price ... where the supply was fluctuating, a year of extraordinary cheapness of grain must necessarily be followed by one of dearness, unless measures were adopted to insure a regular domestic supply, and by this means a uniform steady and moderate price.'*
>
> Lord Liverpool, House of Lords, 15 March 1815.

'The landed interest want to have a law for raising the price of corn to double the amount of what it was before the war began.'

London Chronicle, 1815.

'[The Corn Bill is for] The benefit and aggrandisement of a few rapacious landholders ... at the cruel expense of the hitherto greatly oppressed community.'

Henry 'Orator' Hunt, the radical leader, in a speech made in 1815.

The government's failure to retain the income tax in peacetime, in the face of a backbench revolt, added to Liverpool's worries. The nation adjusted badly to peacetime conditions. The 300,000 or so discharged soldiers and sailors found it difficult to get civilian work, and glutted a labour market already swollen by the rapid increase in population. The sluggishness of the economy produced much discontent which radical leaders exploited. After 1815, much more pressure for parliamentary reform was coming from the new manufacturing districts as well as the old craft and workshop centres (see chapter 6). As Cobbett said in 1816: 'People everywhere [were] on the stir in the cause of parliamentary reform.' The response of Liverpool and his Home Secretary, **Viscount Sidmouth**, to increased discontent in 1815–17 was exactly the same as Pitt's had been in the 1790s. Leading radicals were temporarily locked up and legislation was passed making mass meetings more difficult to hold. Liverpool relied on property owners to rally to the cause of government by property owners who said they had the interests of the whole nation at heart. Some property owners, however, were beginning to wonder whether the old policies could be continued indefinitely. Sir Robert Peel, no friend to reform himself, captured the mood neatly in a private letter sent to a friend in 1820.

'Do not you think that the tone of England – of that great compound of folly, weakness, prejudice, wrong feeling, right feeling, obstinacy and newspaper paragraphs, which is called public opinion – is more liberal, to use an odious but intelligible phrase, than the policy of the government?'

Sir Robert Peel to John Wilson Croker, cited in N.Gash, *Mr Secretary Peel: The Life of Sir Robert Peel to 1830* (1985).

PROFILE: *Viscount Sidmouth*

In an egalitarian age, students are confused by the frequent changes of name which politicians undergo as they inherited, or are given, aristocratic titles. **Viscount Sidmouth** is a good example. Born in 1757 as **Henry Addington**, the son of a doctor, he was trained as a lawyer before becoming a politician. A snobbish age gave him the disrespectful nickname 'The Doctor' because of his social origins. He became an MP in 1784 and was Speaker of the House of Commons in the years 1789–1801 before, unexpectedly, taking over as Prime Minister in 1801 after Pitt resigned over the Catholic issue (see chapter 8). His ministry lasted until 1804 but was not successful in prosecuting the war. He was created Viscount Sidmouth in 1805 and served in Pitt's second ministry (1804–6) and in Spencer Perceval's (1809–12) as Lord President of the Council. As Home Secretary in the first part of Liverpool's government, he was associated with policies of repression against radicals, notably the 'Six Acts' of 1819. After resigning in 1822, he had a long retirement until his death in 1844.

By the end of 1820, the Liverpool government had coped with attempted revolutions and with the consequences of the so-called 'Peterloo Massacre' (see time chart). Expressions of popular discontent 'out of doors' (as extra-parliamentary agitation was often called) tended to unite landowners in Parliament in defence of their property but, as Peel saw, it was becoming more difficult to deny that Parliament was getting out of touch with public opinion. George IV's attempts to rid himself of his coarse and promiscuous wife during the so-called 'Queen Caroline Divorce Scandal' concentrated more unwelcome public attention on the misbehaviour of the rich; journalists and cartoonists gleefully pointed out that the new King was at least as guilty as his unloved wife. The King, who always sought to blame others for his substantial shortcomings, thought of dismissing Liverpool for his failure to 'fix' a divorce. It was the nearest he had come to losing office since 1815.

A report of the Peterloo Massacre

'The cloud which had for some time been darkening the political horizon, now broke into a fearful storm, the effects of which were felt for many subsequent months; Manchester, the focus of all the sedition and turbulence of England, had long been preparing for a decisive demonstration, and on the 16th of August, notwithstanding ... the prohibition of the authorities, a monster meeting took place in the neighbourhood, attended with more than the usual military marchings and revolutionary displays. The ostensible cause

Figure 9.1 Crowd assembled at St Peter's Fields, Manchester, in 1819 – prior to the Peterloo Massacre

was "Reform", but judging by the descriptions on the banners … the frequent display of the Cap of Liberty, was much more significant of the object, which was made more evident by the appearance of women in bands among the … masses – another feature from the French Revolution. "Let us die like men, and not be sold like slaves!" was inscribed on their red banner. On a black flag the words "Equal Representation or Death" were equally significant.

… At least 80,000 men in this formidable array, took up ground … Their chief leader Mr Orator Hunt, was so very earnest in the cause of Liberty, that he was making a grand attempt to divert taxation from the pockets of his multitudinous admirers, into his own, by substituting certain compounds, termed "Hunt's Herb Tea, and Tobacco" and "Roasted Corn", for those taxable but at least genuine luxuries, tea, tobacco and coffee. He had, however, scarcely commenced … to address his followers, when a detachment of sixty men of "the Manchester Yeomanry Cavalry" entered the field at a brisk trot. Scarcely had their horses become visible, when a panic seized the battalions … The cavalry drew their swords, and the candidates for martyrdom attempted to escape. The troop then advanced towards the waggons that contained Mr Hunt and his colleagues, surrounded the latter and took them into custody, seizing at the same time some of their treasonable flags.

Out of the 80,000, a few wedged closely round the waggons ventured on hostilities in the shape of a shower of brick-bats and heavy stones. A missile of the most formidable kind struck one of the yeomanry so heavily, that he dropped the reins, the horse fell, and his rider was thrown, fracturing his skull in the fall. This assault, from which many of the troop suffered to a less degree, may probably have given an additional impulse of their advance, for before the immense mob could be dispersed, four persons were killed and forty-four wounded – a few by the crush occasioned by the frantic efforts of such a mass to get out of the way of the cavalry.

A greater loss of life has more than once been occasioned by a panic in a theatre, when the stronger have crushed and trampled the weaker to death, while making their escape from real or imaginary danger.'

Duke of Buckingham and Chandos (ed.), *Memoirs of the Court of England during the Regency*, 2 vols (1856).

This account was compiled in the mid-1850s by the second Duke of Buckingham. The duke was born in 1797 and was elected MP for Buckingham in 1818. In 1832, as Marquis of Chandos, he introduced the famous clause into the Reform Act by which tenants could vote in county seats (see chapter 12). His account was published 'from original family documents'. Many members of the family were actively involved in politics at the time of the Peterloo Massacre, including his father who was Lord Lieutenant of Buckinghamshire.

Task on Buckingham's account of Peterloo

After reading both the source and the information given about it carefully, answer the following questions:

a What clues can you find within the source to the author's sympathies about the Peterloo Massacre?

b Find examples from the source which indicate what its author thought about Henry Hunt.

c Whom does the author blame for the Massacre?

d **i** How far can you rely on this account of the Massacre? Explain your answer.
ii Making use of the information given about the source, what use can it be for finding out about attitudes towards Peterloo?

Classwork task

a What is Cruikshank's attitude in Figure 9.2 towards 'the Six New Acts' and how is it shown in this cartoon?

b List the various ways in which Cruikshank comments on John Bull's plight in this cartoon. Use your knowledge of the period to link these images to specific government policies.

c Is it possible to tell from this cartoon what specific policies Cruikshank thought would improve John Bull's situation? Explain your answer.

With Queen Caroline out of the way and the economy at last on the turn, the early 1820s were generally much less troubled than the 1810s had been. The price of bread fell by about a third, making the staple diet of ordinary folk much more affordable. Unemployment in the textile and building industries declined, political protest receded and stomachs began

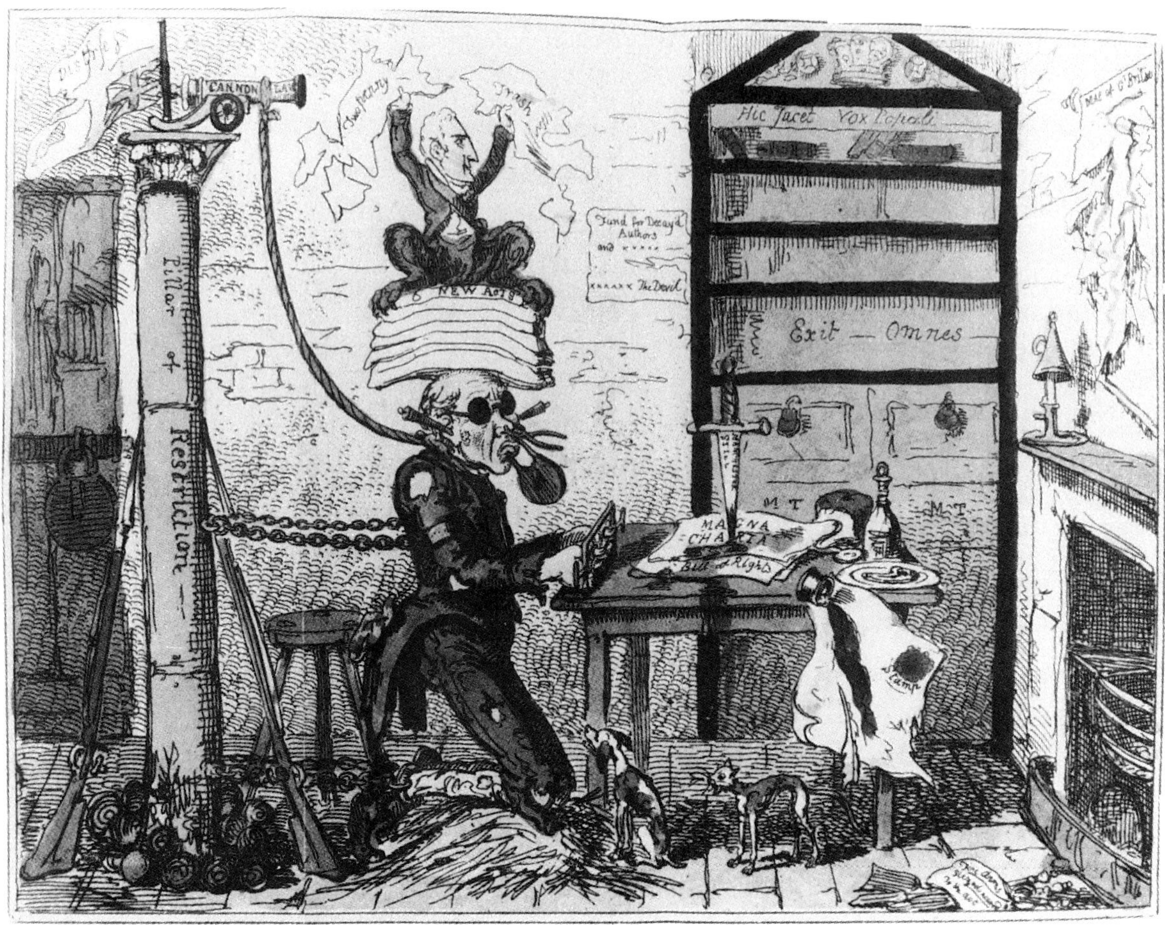

Figure 9.2 This cartoon by George Cruikshank, a genius with visual images, was published in January 1820. It shows John Bull, the traditional symbol not only of England but of Englishman's liberties, shackled and starved by the 'Six Acts'. Notice that John Bull is usually represented as a man of ample figure, symbolising his usual good health and prosperity.

to fill. Living standards for most sections of the community improved substantially during the 1820s. The government's finances also took a turn for the better. Debts declined and budgets began to balance. Despite substantial reductions in tariffs, trade expanded to such an extent that revenue from **customs** increased by 64 per cent in the years 1821–7, a much better outcome even than in William Pitt's 'National Revival' during the 1780s (chapter 2). In the years 1826–30, **excise** duties fell substantially, reflecting the reduced burden of taxation the government felt it necessary to impose during periods of prosperity.

Liberal Toryism?

The long Liverpool ministry can be divided into two phases. The first, from 1815 to about 1821, was characterised by distress as the nation struggled to adjust to peacetime conditions during times of economic uncertainty and discontent. The second, which lasted until illness forced

Liverpool to resign in February 1827, witnessed much greater prosperity. Since the two periods more or less coincide with changes in key ministries, it might be thought that this second phase represents a transition from repressive to **Liberal Toryism**. In 1941 the historian W. R. Brock published a book entitled *Lord Liverpool and Liberal Toryism*, and the phrase has stuck.

Figure 9.3 *Key ministers of the Liverpool government, 1812–27*

	Earlier	*Later*
Prime Minister	Liverpool	Liverpool
Home Secretary	Sidmouth (to 1822)	Peel (from 1822)
Chancellor of the Exchequer	Vansittart (to 1823)	Robinson (from 1823)
President of the Board of Trade	Robinson (1818–23)	Huskisson (from 1823)
Foreign Secretary	Castlereagh (to 1822)	Canning (from 1822)

The term Liberal Toryism has some use because the second phase of Liverpool's government was less fraught than the first. However, it should not be used to indicate that Liverpool underwent any kind of 'conversion' to reform in the early 1820s. The following points need to be borne in mind. Most of them might indicate that, during Liverpool's long ministry, continuity is a more important thread than change.

1 Liverpool's government remained firmly committed *against* parliamentary reform – the most important change for which radicals outside Parliament were clamouring.

2 Most of the supposedly 'new' men brought into high office by Liverpool in the early 1820s had served him in more minor posts before 1822. Peel, for example, had been Chief Secretary for Ireland between 1812 and 1818. Huskisson had been in the Department of Woods and Forests! They had not opposed the government line in its so-called 'repressive' phase. Their arrival in the offices for which they are best known resulted from promotion rather than the need to have 'new men for new policies'.

3 The financial policies of the 1820s had been developed well before Robinson became Chancellor of the Exchequer. Liverpool's government had established a Committee of Finance in 1819 which recommended resuming cash payments from the Bank of England in order to improve financial confidence. Cash payments had been stopped since the great crisis of 1797 (see chapter 7).

KEY TERMS:

Customs and excise

Customs and excise duties were the main sources of government revenue in the eighteenth and nineteenth centuries. Customs were taxes placed on goods coming into the country; excise, the taxes levied on goods produced at home. During the eighteenth century, the government received much more from excise than from customs. In the early 1780s, for example, excise produced 44 per cent of government revenue and customs 24 per cent (the remainder coming from taxes on land and from stamp duty). As overseas trade developed rapidly during the industrial revolution, so the value of customs as a proportion of income increased sharply. In the early 1820s, with world trade still affected by the consequences of war, customs were bringing in 22 per cent of revenue and excise 48 per cent. By the early 1840s, customs were worth 43 per cent and excise only 27 per cent.

Liberal Toryism

Liberal Toryism was not a term used by contemporaries and it has nothing to do with the Liberal Party. Contemporaries used the word 'liberal' to mean 'freedom'. Liberal policies were those which increased people's liberties. Some historians have used the phrase 'Liberal Toryism' to describe the second phase of Liverpool's government (1822–7) when Robinson and Huskisson were engaged in reducing customs and tariffs in the expectation that these would stimulate trade and prosperity, while Peel was introducing a number of important administrative and penal reforms from the Home Office (see time chart). At the same time, George Canning was championing the cause of nations breaking free from old empires. The whole package seemed reformist.

4 The policy of 'trade liberalisation', associated with Huskisson and Robinson's reduction of tariffs, was a continuation of the policy cautiously taken up by William Pitt in the 1780s but long suspended while much of Europe was at war. Small reductions in duties on imported corn in 1822 were part of the same long-term overall strategy.

5 Peel's important reforms at the Home Office (see time chart) were mainly administrative. They aimed to make the law work more speedily and efficiently. Juries had often refused to convict criminals convicted of relatively minor offences when they knew that these carried the death penalty. Peel worried about miscarriages of justice when juries felt accused persons to be guilty but of offences where the punishment did not fit the crime. His reforms, furthermore, could hardly have been promoted during times of massive radical agitation, such as 1815–20.

6 The contrast between the foreign policies of Castlereagh and Canning is in reality much more about style than substance, and about responding to changing external events (see chapter 10).

7 One possible area of reform which split the Tories concerned religion. By 1826, the cabinet was split between those who supported removing political disabilities from dissenters and allowing Catholics to sit in Parliament, and those who opposed it. Liverpool did not want to make a decision, since he knew that it would threaten party unity. Thus, the so-called 'Liberal Tories' were not as a whole 'liberal' on either political or religious reform.

We might, therefore, conclude that Liberal Toryism was more a response to changing circumstances than a commitment to reformist policies by a new generation of politicians.

Summing up: How good a prime minister was Lord Liverpool?

Liverpool's own status as a prime minister remains enigmatic. To survive in office for 15 years is an achievement in itself. Yet it was easier to do so in an age when general elections were not significant tests of public opinion and when, normally, they only occurred every six or seven years anyway. Also, like some other prime ministers in office for a long period, he was faced with an opposition which was uncertain of its direction and anyway divided. Many Whigs, for example, thought parliamentary reform likely to alienate more property owners than it attracted. Others thought it crucial for a party committed to the liberties of the people.

Liverpool was certainly no innovator and he never tried to provide dynamic leadership. In a sense, he carried on the policies of Pitt but circumstances dictated that he did so in reverse order. Whereas Pitt looked to financial and administrative reforms and to improve overseas trade at the beginning of his period in office, Liverpool did so at the end. What converted Pitt to repression and concern with public order from 1793 onwards was the French Wars. The early part of Liverpool's government likewise was dominated by war and its consequences. Liverpool's policies to deal with public discontent were almost a mirror image of Pitt's. He therefore, continued the policies of a much greater prime minister, and many of the reforming ideas of the 1820s came from able subordinates steeped in the new political economy. Some of them found Liverpool unduly cautious and unwilling to give a firm and decisive lead.

Does all of this make him Disraeli's 'arch-mediocrity'? Perhaps not. In terms of the offices held and his length of service, he was one of the best qualified of prime ministers when he was appointed. He used this experience not only to go with the grain of propertied public opinion against political reform but also to show steadfastness in riding out considerable hostility in the years of crisis from 1815–21. The ministerial promotions he made once he was secure in his job showed considerable judgement. The quality of Liverpool's ministerial team was much abler in 1827 than it had been in 1812. Once they were in office, he gave ministers considerable latitude to develop policies, backing his judgement on their capabilities. He was not often disappointed in his choices. He was not opposed to change on principle, as the last years of his prime ministership showed.

Liverpool also had one priceless quality which served the Tories well in the 1820s. He could get abler men to work reasonably harmoniously together under him. True, Tory unity was wearing thin on religious questions by 1826–7 but Liverpool's own authority was unchallengeable. Men like Huskisson, Peel and Canning were prepared to defer to him rather than squabble under an abler but less consensual leader. Perhaps the true measure of Liverpool's competent, if unexciting, leadership was the speed with which the Tory Party split once he left the scene. He probably deserves more credit for his achievements than has generally been given.

Further reading

E. J. Evans, *Britain before the Reform Act: Politics and Society, 1815–32,* Longman Seminar Studies (Addison Wesley Longman, 1989) – surveys all political, social, economic and foreign policy angles.

N. Gash, *Aristocracy and People, 1815–65* (Arnold, 1979) – good on politics at Westminster.

N. Gash, *Lord Liverpool* (Weidenfeld, 1984) – an important biography which offers a more sympathetic view of Liverpool than have most earlier writers.

J. E. Cookson, *Lord Liverpool's Administration, 1815–22* (Scottish Academic Press, 1975).

B. Hilton, *Corn, Cash, Commerce* (Oxford University Press, 1977).

THEMATIC AND ROLE OF THE INDIVIDUAL

10 Britain's changing world role: Castlereagh and Canning

KEY TERM:

Congress System

This was the name given to the agreement made by the allies who defeated France to meet regularly in 'Congresses' to discuss matters of mutual concern and to seek to settle disputes by agreement. Congresses were held from 1815 to 1825 (see time chart), but issues were rarely settled amicably and the system broke up. Many in Britain felt that the **Congress System** was being manipulated by the old empires, particularly Russia, to maintain established regimes and to oppose new ideas such as nationalism and representative government.

Time chart

1815: Congress of Vienna and Second Peace of Paris ends Napoleonic Wars

1818: Congress of Aix-la-Chapelle brings France into the **Congress System**. Britain refuses to strengthen alliances aimed at opposing revolutions in other states

1819: Stamford Raffles takes Singapore

1820: Congress of Troppau: Britain refuses to agree to intervention by great powers in case of revolutions. Castlereagh's *State Paper* (see below)

1821: Congress of Laibach. Greek struggle for independence from Turks begins

1822: Castlereagh commits suicide; Canning succeeds him as foreign secretary. Congress at Verona confirms splits in the Congress System. Britain withdraws from the system

1824: In Latin America, Canning recognises the independence of Buenos Aires, Mexico and Colombia

1825: Last Congress held at St Petersburg. Britain does not attend. Major disputes between Austria and Russia and the Congress is ineffective

1826: Canning despatches British troops to the River Tagus to defend Portugal against threat from Spain

1827: By Treaty of London, Britain, France and Russia support policy of self-government for Greece. Canning dies and is succeeded first by Earl Dudley and then (1828) by Aberdeen

1830: After war between Russia and Turkey, France, Russia and Britain agree to recognise the independence of Greece. The British government changes (November) and Palmerston becomes foreign secretary for the first time

1831: London Conference agrees on terms ('Protocols') for separation of an independent Belgium from Holland

The Congress System

In 1805, ten years before the wars with France finally ended and one year before he died, William Pitt looked ahead to peace. He concluded that the eventual peace would be of limited use unless it included 'a general Agreement and Guarantee for the mutual security and protection of the different Powers and for re-establishing a general System of Public Law in Europe'. It was to just such a system that the foreign secretary at the end of the wars, **Viscount Castlereagh**, committed Britain by Clause 4 of the Treaty of Vienna (see page 88). This was one of two aspects about the peace which some have found surprising.

PROFILE: *Viscount Castlereagh*

Robert Stewart, Viscount Castlereagh, was Irish and born in Dublin in 1769. His mother was related to the English aristocracy and his father was descended from Scottish Presbyterian settlers. Educated in Armagh and then Cambridge, he became a member of the Dublin Parliament in 1790 and the Westminster one in 1794. He became Chief Secretary for Ireland in 1797 and was responsible for policies against the Irish rebels in 1798. He became President of the Board of Control for India in 1801 and added the Secretaryship of War and the Colonies during Pitt's last administration of 1804–6. He became Foreign Secretary in February 1812, just before Spencer Perceval was assassinated. He kept the job under Liverpool and remained in the post continuously until his death by suicide in August 1822. Latterly, he combined the foreign secretaryship with leadership of the House of Commons. Overwork, the collapse of his plans for Congress diplomacy and fears about accusations of homosexuality all seem to have contributed to produce the mental imbalance which led to his suicide. Castlereagh was an extremely efficient administrator and had a clear grasp of Britain's national interests. He was, however, a poor speaker and an indifferent communicator outside a small group. He was hated by radical reformers and accused of preferring the company of European princes and diplomats to that of his own countrymen.

What was the attraction of 'Congress diplomacy'? Many in Britain were opposed to it for the reasons given by Castlereagh's great rival, **George Canning**, and by the diarist Charles Greville. Traditionally, Britain did not interfere with matters on the Continent, seeking rather a balance to prevent any one nation from becoming too powerful.

'[Canning] thinks the system of periodical meetings of the four great Powers, with a view to the general concerns of Europe, new, and of very questionable policy; that it will necessarily involve us deeply in all the politics of the Continent, whereas our true policy has always been not to interfere except in great emergencies, and then with a commanding force.'

Marquis of Londonderry (ed.), *Correspondence, Letters and Despatches of Lord Castlereagh*, 12 vols (1853).

'... we are mixed up in the affairs of the Continent in a manner which we never have been before, and which entails upon us endless negotiations and enormous expenses. We have associated ourselves with the Members of the Holy Alliance, and countenanced [tolerated] their acts of ambition and despotism in such a manner as to have drawn upon us the detestation of the nations of the Continent.'

Charles Greville, summarising in his *Diary*, 1815, the criticisms of the opposition to Castlereagh's Congress policy, quoted in C. J. Bartlett, *Castlereagh* (1976).

However, Castlereagh believed that Britain, as a great power, needed to be involved in European affairs, acting if possible as an arbitrator. The French Wars had strengthened Britain's reputation in world affairs. Britain had been the only power which had consistently stood up to France. However, Castlereagh knew that any attempt to humiliate France at the peace would be a source of instability in future years. Britain was also concerned at the growing power of Russia. Russia had been of great help in bringing down Napoleon. However, its Tsar, Alexander I, had big ambitions for his country. Castlereagh wished to keep these ambitions in check. In his judgement, there was now much greater need for Britain to participate fully in European discussions than before. He looked to maintain a reasonable balance of power between other nations while keeping a specially watchful eye on Russia.

The other apparently surprising aspect of the peace settlement is that Britain retained so little territory from its long and costly wartime endeavours. Why was this? Mostly, Britain already had the overseas territory it needed. The period of imperialist 'land-grabbing' almost as an end in itself lay ahead (see chapter 26). Britain's influence in the American continent was very great and the country had felt the benefits of this during the war. It was similarly dominant in India and was gaining key pieces of territory in the East. Within a few years, Britain would have gained extra territory in Singapore and Malaya. In both cases, the main purpose was not conquest but trade. Britain did not wish to antagonise

PROFILE: *George Canning*

George Canning (1770–1827) was the son of a rich merchant and, after being educated at Oxford, qualified as a lawyer. He became an MP in 1794 and was quickly given minor office by Pitt. He first came to prominence as editor of the government propaganda newspaper *Anti-Jacobin* and became Foreign Secretary in the Portland government of 1807–9. His rivalry with Castlereagh led to a duel between them in 1809. He did not return to office until 1816, when he accepted the post of president of the Board of Control, in charge of Indian affairs. He resigned in 1820 over the government's stance against his friend, Queen Caroline (see chapter 9), but came back to office as Foreign Secretary on Castlereagh's death. George IV, who hated him, tried to keep him out but Lord Liverpool won the battle of wills. As Foreign Secretary, Canning recognised the independence of Latin American states (see time chart) and gained the reputation of support for nationalism. He favoured Catholic emancipation (see chapter 8) and his succession to the prime ministership after Liverpool caused resignations among Tories who opposed this policy. Canning was extremely clever and a brilliant speaker in the House of Commons. He was also one of the first politicians in nineteenth-century Britain to recognise the importance of appealing to public opinion. He used the journalistic talents he acquired early in his career to great effect, frequently addressing his parliamentary constituents in Liverpool about the issues of the day. Like many with a genius for public relations, he often got on less well with his colleagues in private. Some envied his way with words, which he could use sarcastically. His words often hurt colleagues as well as political opponents. He was frequently criticised for excessive ambition. He died in office only a few months after becoming prime minister.

other powers by demanding more territory at a high-profile peace conference. It had no territorial demands in Europe and its interests were best served by a prolonged period of peace and stability. The historian Norman Gash thinks that Castlereagh's policies were sensible:

> *'The objects of [Britain's] diplomacy in 1815 were to obtain security in Europe, to safeguard its possessions overseas, and to promote freedom of commerce [trade] everywhere . . . The guiding principles followed by British policy were containment and order, not conquest and expansion.'*
>
> Norman Gash, *Aristocracy and People, 1815–65* (1979).

Britain and the peace with France, 1815: main terms

1. Army of occupation to stay in France for five years.
2. Britain retains Malta and Heligoland.
3. Victorious powers agree to act together to maintain the peace settlement if France tries to change it.
4. Meet regularly to discuss the working of the peace settlement: the Congress System. The participating states could consider any action which would promote the 'repose and prosperity of Nations and . . . the maintenance of the Peace of Europe'.
5. Britain establishes a protectorate over the Ionian islands (Greece).

As Castlereagh quickly realised, 'Congress diplomacy' meant different things to different powers. For Britain, it was about heading off conflict by international cooperation. For Austria and Russia, it was more a matter of using the new arrangements to crush nationalism and revolution. Tsar Alexander I wanted a 'Holy Alliance' to keep Europe safe for monarchy against threats from republicans and those smaller nations 'struggling to be free' and to claim their independence. Castlereagh did not personally attend any of the Congresses after 1818 and Britain's detachment from the system became rapidly apparent. In 1820 he wrote a famous *State Paper* in which he emphasised the British government's objection to 'the principle of one State interfering by force in the affairs of another, in order to enforce obedience to the governing authority'.

A case study: the Greek struggle for independence

In 1821, the Greeks mounted a rebellion against their Turkish rulers. Turkish power was declining and the nineteenth century would see a succession of challenges to its dwindling authority. Turkey would soon be known as the 'sick man of Europe'. How would Castlereagh react? On the one hand, he might be expected not to intervene in the internal affairs of other countries. He had been criticising members of the Holy Alliance for doing precisely this. On the other hand, three important considerations pointed towards involvement:

1 Most members of the government had been educated in classical languages and civilisation. They felt a special sympathy for the Greeks. Many artists and writers strongly supported Greek national identity.

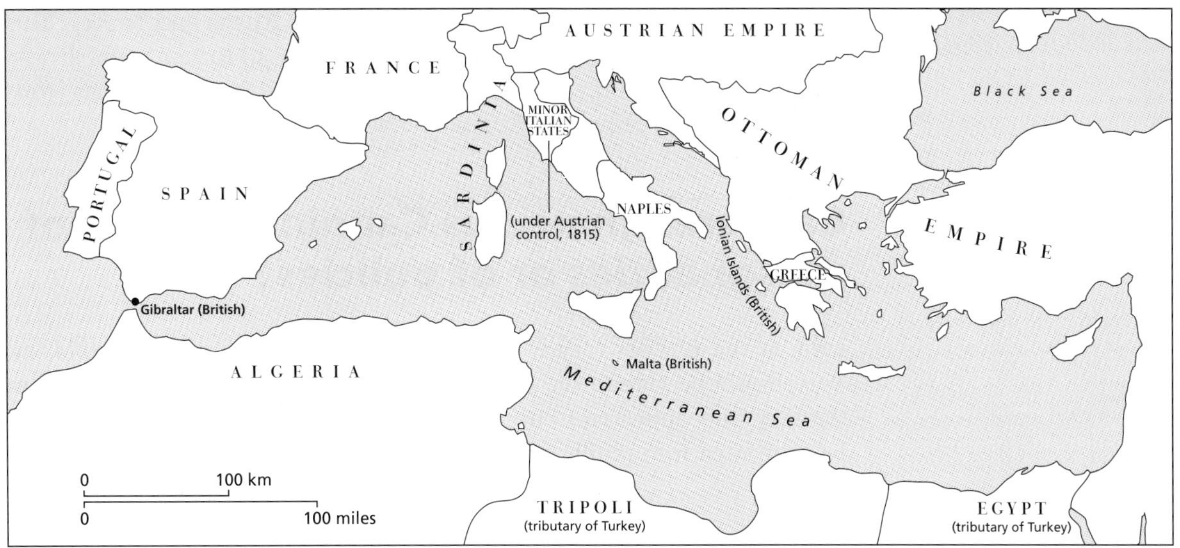

Figure 10.1 *Map of the Mediterranean in the 1820s*

2 Greece's position in the Mediterranean was of strategic importance. Britain wished to keep the Mediterranean safe for its trading vessels.

3 Other great powers would try to exploit Turkish weaknesses. Prime among these was Russia, an empire which was looking for just such an opportunity to expand its influence in the West. Though the Russians might pose as protectors of the Christian Greeks against threats from the Muslim Turks, Castlereagh was much more concerned about Russian activity in that part of the Mediterranean. A weak Turkey was much preferred to a strong Russia.

The response which Castlereagh adopted said much about perceptions of British national interest. Believing war to be the most damaging outcome for Britain, he negotiated with the Austrian minister Metternich to avoid war between Russia and the Turks. At the time of his suicide, he was working on a deal by which the Turks would agree to a limited amount of Greek self-government; he even harboured hopes that the Russians might back it. To this limited extent, Castlereagh still kept some faith in Congress dipomacy. After his death, Canning (who had far less) but who similarly wished to avoid war, negotiated an agreement with France and Russia for the three powers to arbitrate between the Turks and the Greeks. The Treaty of London (see time chart) represented a specific agreement between three powers; it was not part of any wider commitment to Congress diplomacy.

Unfortunately, it did not work. Soon after Canning's death, a British and French fleet destroyed a Turkish one at the Battle of Navarino (1827) when the Treaty of London failed to prevent further conflict between

Turks and Greeks. A brief war followed between Russia and Turkey. This produced increased Russian influence in the area, to Britain's embarrassment and frustration. After 1830, Britain would be increasingly concerned about the growth of Russian power and ambitions.

Castlereagh versus Canning: a clash of personalities or of policies?

Look at the profiles (pages 85 and 87) of these two foreign secretaries. You should be able to see obvious differences in their characters and in the way they appeared to the public. These personality differences might be translated into public affairs to show that the two men had different policies.

1. Castlereagh got on well with European leaders; Canning was more interested in appealing to British public opinion.
2. Castlereagh was in favour of the Congress System; Canning, from the beginning, was scornful of it.
3. Castlereagh was more sympathetic to the 'old world' of kings and emperors; Canning favoured the 'new' world of independent nations, especially in southern Europe and in the Americas.
4. Castlereagh was trying to *change* foreign policy traditions by committing Britain to a leading role in continental Europe; Canning stressed *continuity* by withdrawing from the Congress System and looking to the 'new' world.
5. Castlereagh was more interested in European diplomacy; Canning saw Britain's interests much more bound up in worldwide trade.

These conclusions might be *plausible*, and one historian has emphasised Castlereagh's overall grasp of policy, seeing his suicide as a tragedy for the policy of cooperation.

'Castlereagh's "new diplomacy" was by no means a bankrupt policy at the time of his suicide ... No vital British interests were sacrificed in the process, and. . .the only practical alternative to Castlereagh's policy would have been one of greater aloofness from European affairs. Such a policy would probably have so weakened Austria's position in Europe, and increased Russian and French freedom of action, that more positive British action would soon have been called for. Was not Canning driven to

> *work with Russia and France in 1826–7 [over Greece] as the best means of controlling them? Castlereagh preferred to try to anticipate such an eventuality by working with all the powers, and resorting to definite alignments [treaties favouring one power over another] only as a last resort . . . Castlereagh's course had the added merit of trying to keep the international temperature low, and of trying to prevent crises reaching flashpoint in the first place . . .*
>
> *Castlereagh's death, in so far as it is possible for an individual to influence the course of history, was a matter of profound international significance. In foreign affairs his suicide marked the end of an era, especially in foreign policy.'*
>
> C. Bartlett, *Castlereagh* (1966).

Most authorities nowadays emphasise continuity between Castlereagh and Canning. We should not read too much into the obvious differences of personality between the two men. Many of the apparent changes in policy actually owe more to changes abroad than to any desire by Canning to overturn all of Castlereagh's policies:

1 At the Congress of Verona in 1822, Wellington, the British representative, acting under direction from Canning, continued the process of detaching Britain from international alliance systems. Canning had a characteristically neat phrase to describe it: 'Every nation for itself, and God for us all.' However, Castlereagh in the last two years of his life had begun this policy, realising that his ambitions of 1814–15 for general European harmony were not going to work.

2 Canning was deeply involved in the Americas. He had two main objectives there:

- to increase British trade with Latin America
- to curb what he called the 'ambition and ascendancy of the United States of America'. Since the USA was dominant in the north of the continent, Canning wanted to use Britain's influence to expand trading opportunities in central and southern America.

> *'. . . the American questions are out of all proportion more important to us than the European . . . if we do not seize and turn them to our advantage in time, we shall rue the loss of an opportunity never, never to be recovered.'*
>
> Canning in a letter to Wellington, November 1822, quoted in W. Hinde, *Canning* (1973).

2 Canning's support for newly independent Latin American nations is well known (see time chart). The Duke of Wellington complained that Canning was delivering the continent up to 'revolutionary rascals and blackguards'. But was this policy really new? Canning was only emphasising long-standing British interest in opening up foreign trade across the globe. Castlereagh was not called upon to respond to these new nations. Had he been so, there is no reason to believe that he would have acted differently. And it is interesting to note that British trade to Latin America actually increased much more rapidly when Castlereagh was foreign secretary – in the decade *before* Colombia and the rest declared their independence. This had very little to do with Castlereagh personally, of course, but it could be cited as evidence of continuity in broad British interests, rather than change.

3 In 1826 Canning sent 4,000 troops to support an old ally, Portugal, against the threat of a Spanish takeover. He never considered referring his decision to any Congress of European powers. Perhaps Castlereagh might have done so. However, Portugal was not only an old ally. It was also a friendly power in south-west Europe which could support British trade in the Mediterranean. The Mediterranean was the gateway to the Middle East and beyond – where Britain had great ambitions. Portugal got British support because it was in Britain's interests to offer it.

Task: class discussion

1. Read this chapter carefully and then consider how important you think individuals are in making important changes in policy.
2. This chapter presents you with a case study of Castlereagh and Canning. Dr Bartlett's biography stresses the importance of Castlereagh. Do you think that the rest of this chapter supports his conclusions? Were the policy differences between Castlereagh and Canning more apparent than real?
3. Discuss the kinds of historical circumstances in which individuals really change things. Are any *general* conclusions possible about the importance of the individual in explaining change in history?

Further reading

M. Chamberlain, *Pax Britannica: British Foreign Policy, 1789–1914* (Addison Wesley Longman, 1988) – a good modern study of Britain's relations with European allies and rivals.

E. J. Evans, *Britain before the Reform Act: Politics and Society, 1815–32*, Longman Seminar Studies (Addison Wesley Longman, 1989) – a succinct treatment of both Castlereagh and Canning, with some documents.

P. J. Cain and A. G. Hopkins, *British Imperialism: Innovation and Expansion, 1688–1914* (Addison Wesley Longman, 1993) – an important, if in places difficult, book which offers a new interpretation of the importance of commerce and empire in the making of British foreign policy. It stresses Britain's world role.

N. Gash, *Aristocracy and People, 1815–65* (Arnold, 1979).

CAUSATION

11 Why was a parliamentary Reform Act passed in 1832?

Time chart

1827–8: Tory unity shatters after Lord Liverpool leaves office. Before his premature death, Canning's support for Catholic emancipation provokes resignations from his government. Goderich proves inept and resigns (January 1828)

1828: Wellington becomes Prime Minister and alienates liberal wing of the Tory Party. Huskisson, Aberdeen and Palmerston resign (May). Repeal of the Test and Corporation Acts enables dissenters to hold local and central government office. This legislation widens Tory splits

1829: Roman Catholic emancipation causes a further split between Wellington and Peel and the right-wing **ultras**. Birmingham Political Union founded by Thomas Attwood (December) in an attempt to unify middle-class and working-class pressure for parliamentary reform

1830: George IV dies and is succeeded by William IV. At the general election caused by the change of monarch, some anti-reformers lose their seats. Wellington's government resigns (November) and is replaced by a Whig administration, headed by Grey, which is pledged to introduce parliamentary reform

1831: First Reform Bill introduced (March); gains majority of one in Commons but is defeated in Committee. Whig government resigns; King grants a dissolution of Parliament. The resulting general election sees huge increase in support for Whigs. Second Reform Bill easily passes Commons (September) but is rejected by the Lords (October). Failure of the bill provokes rioting in Bristol and Nottingham

1832: Third Reform Bill passes Commons (March); Grey resigns in face of continued opposition in the Lords. Confusion results with Wellington unable to form a government. Grey resumes office and persuades the king to grant sufficient new peers to pass reform, if necessary. Reform Acts passed in June (England and Wales), Scotland (July) and Ireland (August).
General election (December) brings Whigs large majority

KEY TERM:

Ultras

Ultras or Ultra Tories were right-wing Tories who opposed any concessions to dissenters or Roman Catholics. Already alienated by the repeal of the Test and Corporation Acts, Ultras like the Marquis of Blandford were outraged by Roman Catholic emancipation. They regarded any concessions on religion as a direct attack on the Church of England, which they considered a crucial pillar of the state. Peel, in particular, was not forgiven for his 'betrayal' of Toryism. Some Ultras even supported parliamentary reform after 1829 because they believed that ordinary working people would vote against Catholics in elections.

The importance of reform

After many years of political prominence, parliamentary reform became overwhelmingly *the* issue of the early 1830s. For the first time since the medieval period, the government of the day – a Whig administration which came to power in November 1830 with **Earl Grey** as prime minister – proposed not only a thorough reshaping of the parliamentary constituencies of the United Kingdom but also a uniform and easily understood list of qualifications to vote in parliamentary elections.

PROFILE: *Charles Grey, Second Earl Grey*

Charles Grey was born at Fallodon in 1764 and educated at Eton and Winchester. He came from an established Whig landowning family. He was one of the leaders in Parliament of the campaign for parliamentary reform in the 1790s, introducing reform proposals in 1793 and 1797. As a Whig, most of his career was in opposition but he was first lord of the admiralty and foreign secretary during the brief Ministry of All the Talents (1806–7). He succeeded his father to the title of Earl Grey in 1807 and acted as leader of the Whig Party for most of the period between then and becoming prime minister in 1830. In the early part of that period, however, he shared leadership with Lord Grenville, who was considerably less keen on reform than he was. Frequently, Grey found opposition a frustrating job. He was prime minister 1830–34 and his reputation rests very largely on his being prime minister at the time of the 1832 Reform Act. He died in 1845.

Grey was an experienced politician of 58 when the Great Reform Act was passed. Soon after his death a large monument to him was erected in the centre of Newcastle-upon-Tyne, the nearest city to his family's extensive estates. The inscription (reproduced opposite) pays testimony to Grey's long-standing commitment to the cause of widening the franchise. We might think, therefore, that one reason why parliamentary reform was passed in 1832 was because of Grey's support during a period of over forty years and his determination to give more people the vote when he was finally in a position to do so.

In reality, the inscription on the monument is misleading. As so often with inscriptions and other pieces of evidence produced to honour an individual or celebrate a famous event, the concern to pay tribute outweighs the need to maintain strict historical accuracy. In the long years of opposition he frequently lamented what a difficult issue parliamentary

Inscription on the front of the Grey Monument, Newcastle-upon-Tyne

'Charles, Earl Grey KG who, during an active political career of nearly half a century, was the constant advocate of peace, and the fearless and consistent champion of civil and religious liberty. He first directed his efforts to the amendment of the representation of the people in 1792 and was the minister by whose advice, and under whose guidance, the great measure of parliamentary reform was, after an arduous and protracted struggle, safely and triumphantly achieved in the year 1832.'

Figure 11.2 *Monument to Earl Grey at the head of Grey Street, Newcastle-upon-Tyne*

reform was. Not all of his party supported it and many more thought it an irrelevance as a weapon with which to fight Lord Liverpool's Tory Party.

Furthermore, the precise wording of a reform bill would always be a source of dispute, even among those who supported the principle of giving more people the vote. How many was it safe to enfranchise? Were shopkeepers, for example, to be trusted to use a vote wisely? Very few Whigs supported the idea of giving all men the vote. Look at **Thomas Babington Macaulay**'s view, which appears as Document III (page 106).

PROFILE: *Thomas Babington Macaulay*

T. B. Macaulay, one of Britain's greatest historians, was born in 1800, the son of Zachary Macaulay, the wealthy anti-slavery campaigner, at Rothley Temple in Leicestershire. He was educated at Cambridge, becoming a Fellow of Trinity College there. He wrote many articles for the Whig *Edinburgh Review* before becoming an MP in 1830. He served as Secretary to the Board of Control for India in 1832 and went to India as a member of the Governor General's Council in 1834–8. He was Secretary at War at the end of Melbourne's government (1839–41). He is best known nowadays for his historical writings, including *Lays of Ancient Rome* and *A History of England*, which presents a brilliant, and brilliantly pro-Whig, version of the Glorious Revolution and the events leading up to it. He died in 1859.

There is a strong case for arguing that Grey adopted parliamentary reform when the Whigs finally returned to office not because of his old commitment to it, but because he saw it as the most effective means of quietening growing public discontent and perhaps even of staving off revolution. Much of Europe was beset by revolution, or attempted revolution, in 1830 and Grey did not want to see revolutionary virus infecting Britain and laying low the landed classes. Reform for both Macaulay and for Grey was a means not of hastening revolution (whatever their Tory opponents alleged), but of preventing it.

Explanations of how the Reform Act came to be passed fall into two categories: firstly as the result of pressure from outside Parliament and secondly because the previously strong alliance within Parliament against any kind of parliamentary reform crumbled with unexpected swiftness. The first explanation has long been the dominant one but recent work by political historians has laid greater emphasis on the collapse of the Tory Party after 1827.

1 Growing external pressures

KEY TERM:

Political Unions

Thomas Attwood, a banker from Birmingham, formed a 'General Political Union between the Lower and the Middle Classes of the People' there in the last days of 1829. Its title shows its purpose. The **Political Unions** were an attempt to coordinate political pressure outside Parliament by identifying the joint interests of different classes in a radical political reform. Political unions were formed in most British cities during 1830 and helped to focus attention on the lack of proper representation in the Commons. The unions were in fact less united in their specific objectives than might be thought, but the presence of large numbers of middle-class supporters in the pro-reform camp alarmed MPs. As the Whig Lord Holland put it: 'If the great mass of the middle class are bent upon that method of enforcing their views, there is not in the nature of society any real force that can prevent them.'

It is easy to point out that the old system of representation was out of tune with the nation's needs at a time of rapid urbanisation and the creation of new forms of wealth during the early stages of the industrial revolution. Cornwall, whose tin-mining industry was in severe decline and whose fishing was not flourishing either, nevertheless sent 44 MPs to Parliament before 1832, only one fewer than the whole of Scotland and 30 more than Lancashire, the cradle of the industrial revolution. Lancashire's second largest city, Manchester, did not have any MPs of its own.

Many of the urban middle classes did not have the vote before 1832. Evidence was mounting that small property owners were beginning to ally with the working classes to force the landowners into a change in qualifications for voting. A reform forced through by such an alliance would almost certainly be anti-aristocratic and a landowners' Parliament would be swept away. As Macaulay put it, in the unreformed parliamentary system 'we exclude from all share in government vast masses of property and intelligence – vast numbers of those who are most interested in preserving tranquillity, and who know best how to preserve it'. We can see, therefore, how pressures from outside Parliament eventually forced MPs to make concessions for fear of revolution if they did not.

The disturbances of 1830–32 increased the pressure substantially. The emergence of **Political Unions** was an important development in most British cities on the model of that devised by the Birmingham banker Thomas Attwood, who asserted a unity of interest between working people and the middle classes. Attwood's organisation declared that it was a 'General Political Union between the Lower and Middle Classes of the People', and its purpose was to agitate for parliamentary reform. Although the precise nature of the reform they wished to see remained unclear, the political unions, drawing on radical ideas from the 1790s (see chapter 6), served a vital function. They focused attention on the alleged evils of an unrepresentative constitution and made reform agitation more purely anti-aristocratic than ever before.

These unions now linked the 'productive classes' (*i.e.* those who, in one way or another, worked for their living) against the 'unproductive' (*i.e.* those who inherited their privileges and who lived on rent, the tribute of other people's labour).

Supported by an effective, and large-circulation, radical press and the oratorical skills of such veteran radicals as **Henry Hunt** and **William Cobbett**, the radical movement flourished to such an extent that the Whig government feared not only for its own security but also for the continuation of civilised society if reform failed to be passed. The first Reform Bill passed by a single vote (302–301) in March 1831, but failed to survive detailed scrutiny by parliamentary committee. The Whigs asked the King to dissolve Parliament and call fresh elections. Even from the old electorate, these produced an overwhelming majority in favour of reform. Reform could no longer be blocked in the Commons.

PROFILE: *Henry Hunt*

Henry Hunt was born into prosperous Wiltshire farming stock in 1773. In his youth a member of the local militia, Hunt took up radical causes after discussions with John Horne Tooke. He was imprisoned for assault in 1810 and here met William Cobbett. He gained a big reputation as a speaker and addressed mass meetings in London (especially the Spa Fields assembly in 1816) before giving the main address at St Peter's Fields, Manchester, in August 1819 on the occasion of the 'Peterloo Massacre' (see chapter 9). Hunt was arrested and spent two years in prison. He became MP for Preston in 1830 when he defeated Edward Stanley (later Earl of Derby) – the Tory, anti-reform candidate and future prime minister – in a high-profile contest. In Parliament he opposed the Whig bills as insufficiently radical. He lost his seat at Preston in 1833 and retired from political life. He died in 1835.

PROFILE: *William Cobbett*

William Cobbett was born in Hampshire in 1763, the son of a small-scale farmer and innkeeper. After a chequered early career which saw him work as a law clerk in London, enlist briefly in the army and settle for a few years in the United States, he settled to journalism in Britain. He adopted the pen-name Peter Porcupine, and his early political writings favoured the Tories. He was converted to radicalism, however, and became increasingly concerned with the weight of taxation which government imposed on the people. He published *Cobbett's Parliamentary Debates*, an unofficial record of parliamentary speeches before *Hansard*, the official journal, appeared. He became best known for his *Weekly Political Register* which was very widely read during the disturbed period after 1815 and its cheaper, untaxed sister, *Two-Penny Trash* which sold about 40,000 copies at its peak. His radicalism was not mainstream. As a farmer, he was much more concerned at the plight of rural labourers than most urban radicals and his *Rural Rides*, a journal of his journeys through the country in the early 1820s, painted the most vivid picture of rural distress. He tried to enter Parliament but was defeated in the general election of 1832. He finally became radical MP for the textile and engineering town of Oldham in the first general election held after the Reform Act. He was not, however, an effective performer in Parliament and he is best remembered for his journalism. He died in 1835.

When, however, the House of Lords rejected a second Reform Bill in October 1831, widespread rioting, notably in Derby, Nottingham and Bristol, followed. The main targets of hostility were the aristocracy and the Church of England, widely seen as the corrupt supporters of a still more corrupt system. Earl Grey wrote to the King's private secretary soon after these riots:

> *'These Unions have received a great impulse and extension from the rejection of the Reform Bill; and . . . many persons not otherwise disposed to do so, have been induced to join them for the purpose of promoting that measure. It is also undeniable that the middle classes, who have now shown so praiseworthy an alacrity in supporting the authority of the government (i.e. against the rioters) are actuated by an intense and almost unanimous feeling in favour of the measure of reform.'*
>
> Henry, Earl Grey (ed.), *Correspondence of Earl Grey and William IV*, 2 vols (1867).

Other factors heightened government alarm. The Swing Riots (see chapter 5) affected what was traditionally one of the most docile and least organised sections of the workforce. In Europe, 1830 saw much political disturbance, with nationalist activity in Belgium and Poland. Even more disturbing was the overthrow of the King of France, Charles X, who had reacted against the cautious reforms of his predecessor, Louis XVIII, suspended the National Assembly and introduced strict censorship. The role of the Parisian working class in manning the barricades and hastening the departure of the King was duly noted by politicians at Westminster.

KEY TERM:

Ruling elite

This term is used to describe the minority which exercises power. In Britain in the early nineteenth century it referred to a Parliament dominated by wealthy landowners and their clients.

On this line of reasoning, then, the 1832 Reform Act can be seen as a hasty concession by the **ruling elite** to preserve authority at a time of unprecedented opposition and social dislocation. A crucial element in this concession was the need to detach the middle classes from the recent alliance with working people. Put simply, the Reform Act was passed in 1832 because those in authority did not fear for their position any earlier. In the 1790s, and in the period 1815–20, reform could be overborne by government repression. In 1830–32 enough politicians feared that further repression would lead to revolution to secure government majorities for reform. Many of those who voted for reform in 1831–2 either still opposed it in principle but would not risk revolution or had fundamental reservations about the specific proposals before them.

2 The collapse of the Tories at Westminster

The second explanation for the passage of reform in 1832 has received less attention than it deserves. This concentrates on the sudden collapse of the anti-reform majority in the Commons between 1827 and 1831. The reason was not extra-parliamentary agitation but the divisive effects of the religious question on the Tory Party between 1827 and 1831.

Even before the stroke which removed Lord Liverpool from the premiership in February 1827, the Tory Party had been split into 'Catholic' and 'Protestant' factions over whether political emancipation should be given to Roman Catholics. The Protestant faction was strongly opposed to the idea. Liverpool's departure brought to the surface both personality clashes and division on issues of principle. Few 'Protestants' would serve under Liverpool's successor, George Canning, and when Canning died after only a few months as prime minister, his successor, **Viscount Goderich**, was unable to assert any kind of authority over the party.

Wellington's succession at the beginning of 1828 widened the split still further. His bluff, soldierly manner and his firm convictions soon antagonised Liberal-Canningite Tories. An alliance between them and the Whig opposition, which had begun during Canning's prime ministership, was

PROFILE: *Viscount Goderich*

Frederick Robinson, Viscount Goderich was born in 1782, the son of Baron Grantham, and educated at Eton and Cambridge. He became an MP in 1806 and grew to prominence as a loyal supporter of Lord Liverpool. He was appointed President of the Board of Trade in 1818, the first of a large number of ministerial appointments he filled in an active career which lasted until 1846. He was promoted to Chancellor of the Exchequer in 1823. In this office he was associated with policies designed to balance the national budget and increase freedom of trade. His successes here earned him the nickname 'Prosperity Robinson'. He proved disastrous as prime minister (1827–8) being quite unable to provide leadership. He was the only prime minister to resign without appearing in Parliament as holder of that office. He was not offered a post in Wellington's government and drifted closer to the Whigs. He served first as Colonial Secretary (1830–33) and then as Lord Privy Seal (1833–4). He was created Earl of Ripon in 1833. He returned to the Tory Party in late 1834 and served Peel as President of the Board of Trade (1841–3) and President of the Board of Control (1843–6). He remained a Peelite, though inactive, after 1846. He died in 1859.

significantly strengthened. Few of the Liberal Tories who resigned from Wellington's Tory government in May 1828 would serve in another one. Had William Huskisson, effectively the leader of this group, not become, in 1830, the very first civilian railway fatality, he might well have joined Grey's Whig government formed later that year. A younger, and ultimately much more famous, Liberal Tory, Viscount Palmerston, did so.

Wellington could ill afford to lose talented Liberal Tories, but a further split, this time with the right wing of the Tory Party, did still more damage. Strongly 'Protestant' Tories believed that, when Wellington took over as prime minister, all seditious nonsense over Roman Catholic emancipation (see chapter 8) would disappear. The 'Ultras', as they became known, swallowed the repeal of the Test and Corporation Acts with an ill grace in 1828. Although Wellington's Home Secretary, Robert Peel, advised him that the alternative to Catholic emancipation was civil war in Ireland, the Ultras could not stomach allowing Catholics into Parliament. They did not formally break with Wellington, but it was clear in 1828–30 that they no longer gave his government more than token support.

So, by the time that higher prices and economic hardship began to revive support for parliamentary reform 'out of doors' at the end of 1829, the Tory Party was split into three warring elements. What some historians have called the 'new Tory party' first came together in the Pitt–Portland 'Tory coalition' of 1794 to oppose reform (see chapter 6). While they were firmly in the saddle, as they were almost without a break from 1794 to 1830, under Pitt, then Portland, Perceval and Liverpool, parliamentary reform had almost no chance of success in the Commons. But the splintering of the anti-reformist party made parliamentary reform a practical political issue at Westminster for the first time in almost half a century. The Whig backbencher, Sir Robert Heron, pointed out the significance of Tory splits at the end of 1830: 'Two years ago, I thought Reform of Parliament almost hopeless. I now believe it to be certain and approaching.'

This explanation for the achievement of parliamentary reform in 1832 stresses the weakness of the anti-reformers in Parliament rather than the strength of reformers outside. Though parliamentary reform had greater and more vociferous public support between 1829 and 1832 than ever before, it is far from clear that this support would have been sufficient to move a united Tory Party to concessions. Tory leaders, though naturally well aware of public unrest in 1830–31, did not believe that its cause was the lack of a reformed Parliament. Only after the Wellington government fell in November 1830 did reform become *the* issue at Westminster. Grey, never the most assertive of political leaders, had not pushed his party's claims or made special efforts to attach disaffected Liberal Tories to the Whig side. The Tories would not have lost office had they not been so split over the religious question. Grey's public declaration that he was accepting office in order to bring in a reform bill concentrated attention decisively upon parliamentary reform for the first time in ten years.

The Reform Crisis, 1831–2

The general election held earlier in 1830, after the death of George IV, saw only small changes in the composition of the House of Commons, though some reformers won seats for the first time. The real swing of parliamentary opinion came with the general election which Grey called after the first Reform Bill had been wrecked by amendments. By the summer of 1831, public opinion had become massively reformist. Few MPs representing the larger constituencies – the only ones before 1832 in which public opinion could be reliably tested – survived a contested election if they had opposed reform earlier in the year.

Middle-class support for reform was undoubtedly cemented by the Lords' rejection of the second bill in October 1831, but even this was double-edged. Many shopkeepers and small entrepreneurs were outraged by the response of landowners 'who toil not neither do they spin'. Nevertheless, the riots to which the Lords' action gave rise made them at least as fearful for their own property. Grey and the Whigs knew that no section of society is more conservative and jealous of its property than those who have relatively little and who therefore see its conservation as their essential bastion against loss of hard-won status. The Great Reform Act was more about giving votes to the lower middle classes – clerks, shopkeepers, etc. – than the middle classes as a whole. It is too rarely noticed that the wealthier commercial, industrial and professional figures mostly had the vote before 1832, since they lived, or at least had property, in county constituencies usually through ownership of sufficient landed property to qualify under the now very low 'forty-shilling freehold'.

The Whigs did not have a consistent strategy for reform in 1830–32. A study of their private papers reveals deep divisions about where the new franchise lines should be drawn and which old parliamentary seats should disappear. Palmerston and Lansdowne were also much more concerned than Grey, Althorp and Durham that the new voting qualifications and the substantial increase in the numbers of large urban seats would reduce landed influence in government.

Two unifying factors, however, are worth stressing:

- The Whigs agreed that enfranchisement of the middle classes was both morally necessary and politically wise. As Grey put it, reform would enable 'a greater influence to be yielded to the middle classes who have made wonderful advances both in property and in intelligence, and this influence may be beneficially exerted upon the government'.
- The Whigs were perceptive enough to see that the anti-aristocratic alliance represented by the Political Unions was fragile and illogical. The commercial lower middle classes were at least as willing to be bought off by the ten-pound household franchise as the Whigs were to detach them from an improbable, but potentially fatal, alliance with the workers. Once **enfranchised**, they would prove the staunchest defenders of privilege against rude democratic assaults on the constitution, such as those mounted a few years later by the Chartists.

KEY TERM:

Enfranchised

Enfranchisement refers to the ability to vote. The **enfranchised** were those entitled to vote in parliamentary elections. Recent estimates suggest that about 440,000 adult men were able to vote before the Reform Act and about 650,000 after it.

A study of the circumstances surrounding the passage of the Great Reform Act should certainly stress the great state of public agitation and expectancy and also Whig anxiety to make concessions to the middle classes in order to reduce this agitation and to prevent revolution. As Althorp put it: 'The Plan for Reform . . . ought to be of such a scope and description as to satisfy all reasonable demands and remove at once, and for ever, all rational grounds of complaint from the minds of the intelligent and independent portion of the community.'

Three equally important factors, however, must not be overlooked:

- The reform agitation, though great between 1830 and 1832, remained dependent for mass support on short-term economic hardship. Politicians at Westminster probably exaggerated the potential for revolution in 1831–2.
- Events at Westminster contributed substantially to the heightened tension. Expectations of reform crystallised only with the shattering of Tory unity which had been built on resistance to reform.
- The shattering of the Tory majority in the Commons, that sure safeguard against reform since the 1790s, came about because of proposals not for political, but for religious, reform.

The student who wants to understand why the 1832 Reform Act was passed must enquire into Tory Party history between 1827 and 1830. Arguably, parliamentary reform was achieved more because the Tories, after a long period of dominance, failed than because the Whigs succeeded.

Source questions in examinations

Since this is the last chapter in the first section of the book, it seems a good idea to end it with some questions for you to try out which appear as they might in an examination paper.

Hints on answering the source questions below

1. Most source questions are designed to test your understanding of the material you are given. Very often this understanding will link to your own knowledge. You must get practice in tackling questions with a particular focus or emphasis.

2. When you have read through the sources, look at question **a**. It includes the phrase 'According to document I . . .'. This indicates that all you need to answer the question will be found in that document. The question is testing the skill of *comprehension*: can you understand why Lord John Russell thinks that his reform proposals are a compromise, and a compromise about what?

3. Question **b** asks you to draw *conclusions* from the speech of Sir Robert Inglis. It should be answered from the material within document II. However, the skill tested – *inference* – is different: can you work out a conclusion from material you are given? This is not the same skill as comprehension. It requires you to understand what is being said but, in addition, you have to work out (or 'infer') an attitude or position. You are being asked here to 'read between the lines'.

4. Question **c** requires you to make use of all three documents in order to come to a conclusion. The 'On what grounds' part

should give you a clue that you are first relying on comprehension. But 'for what reasons' requires more. The skill of *analysis* is being tested: can you work on different materials together before making your own judgement? All three sources offer relevant argument. However, you will find it useful to know who Lord John Russell and T. B. Macaulay *were* and what interests they represented. Such information can be introduced to support your answer. The profiles in this chapter will help you.

5 Question **d** is in two parts. The first asks 'in what ways' the sources 'help to explain'. You will again be working with the documents, but the clue word 'help' should suggest that your answer can be linked to your wider knowledge and understanding – in this case, of the attitudes of working-class radicals towards Members of Parliament. This is testing the skills of *source utility* and *historical judgement*: can you say how your sources (or documents) help you explain something? To do this you will need to rely on your wider knowledge – in this case of working-class *attitudes* towards those in Parliament.

The second part tests your wider knowledge of the source material. Not all examination papers include questions like this. When they do, they are not asking just for a list. The skill being tested is *knowledge and usefulness of sources*: do you know what sources are useful for a particular topic, explaining at the same time *in what ways*, or *why*, they are useful?

General hints in answering source or document questions

6 Always read your documents *slowly* and *carefully* at first to make sure that you understand them. When you start doing this, you may find the language unfamiliar. People in the past did not always speak or write as we do. You will get better at understanding as you gain experience and practice. Remember that part of your training as a student of history involves 'getting inside' the period you are studying. This includes getting familiar with the material which has been left behind from that period. Don't give up because some words, or phrases, are unfamiliar.

7 In answering document questions, you will almost certainly be asked not only to show understanding but also to draw conclusions. You may also be asked to comment on *how* the writer, or speaker (or perhaps cartoonist or artist) is putting the message across.

8 You will be given information about the *origins* of a source – its *provenance* to give it its technical name. This is designed to be used and can be as valuable to you as the material in the documents themselves. In the case of the questions below, it is useful to show awareness that all three documents are from speeches made in the House of Commons.

9 In examinations each sub-question will carry a maximum mark. The number of marks available is almost always a strong clue to how much you are expected to write. In many examinations, the number of marks 'builds up' so that the last question is worth most. Make sure that you have arranged your time so that you leave plenty of time for the questions with most marks. The example below has been given marks to help you.

10 In examinations, most candidates get more marks on document, or source, questions. Examiners more readily give maximum marks for an exercise marked out of 3 or 4 than they do for one out of 20 or 25. You can do yourself a lot of good by remembering the basic rules relating to document questions. Similarly, if you don't you will probably be throwing away marks on what most candidates consider the easier parts of the examination.

Examination question: Arguments about parliamentary reform, 1830–31

Read the following documents, and then answer questions **a** to **d** which follow.

Document I

'Sir, the object of my proposition is to improve the representation without doing injury to the Constitution. I wish to preserve the fundamentals of the Constitution, while I give to every individual his just rights. I consider my propositions are calculated to produce this effect . . . I . . . know no course I could pursue except that upon which I have decided.'

(Lord John Russell, speech in the House of Commons, 28 May 1830)

Document II

'The House of Commons, as it now exists, is the same, practically, as has existed since the [Glorious] Revolution [of 1688–9]; only *that it is more popular. It has adapted itself, almost like another work of nature, to our growth. How different is the county representation of England now from what it once was, how little are the country gentlemen now in this House like those a century ago; how have they grown with the growth of the country; how completely do they now reflect, in their own intelligence [knowledge], the mind of their constituents, as well as advocate their local wants! Such . . . as the House of Commons is now, such it has been for a long succession of years; it is the most complete representation of the interests of the people, which was ever assembled in any age or country. It . . . comprehends within itself those who can urge the wants and defend the claims of the landed, the commercial and the professional classes of the country.'*

(Sir Robert Inglis, a Tory MP, in a speech in the House of Commons, 2 March 1831)

Document III

'I do, sir, entertain great apprehension for the fate of my country ... Unless this measure, or some similar measure, be speedily adopted, great and terrible calamities will befall us ... I support this measure as a measure of Reform; but I support it still more as a measure of conservation ... We say, and we say justly, that it is not by mere numbers, but by property and intelligence, that the nation ought to be governed. Yet, saying this, we exclude from all share in the government vast masses of property and intelligence, vast numbers of those who are as interested in preserving tranquillity, and who know best how to preserve it. We do more. We drive over to the sin of revolution those whom we shut out from power.'

(Thomas Babington Macaulay, a Whig MP and writer, in a speech in the House of Commons, 2 March 1831)

Questions

a What, according to document I, is Lord John Russell's purpose in making his 'proposition' about reform? *3 marks*

b How can Sir Robert Inglis's attitude to parliamentary reform be inferred from his statements in document II about 'The House of Commons ... since the Revolution'? *5 marks*

c On what grounds, and for what reasons, might the speakers in documents I and III disagree with Inglis (document II) that 'The House of Commons' had become 'more popular'? *6 marks*

d **i** In what ways do these documents help to explain the hostility and suspicion of many working-class radicals towards MPs during the Reform Crisis? *6 marks*

ii On what other kinds of evidence produced at the time of this crisis might you draw to identify the attitudes of working-class radicals in 1830–32? *5 marks*

Total: 25 marks

Further reading

E. J. Evans, *The Great Reform Act of 1832*, Lancaster Pamphlet (Routledge, second edition, 1994) – shows that the old political system was not quite as corrupt and unrepresentative as was once thought.

M. Brock, *The Great Reform Act* (Hutchinson, 1973) – a detailed research study of the events of 1830–32 which is unlikely to be surpassed.

J. Cannon, *Parliamentary Reform, 1640–1832* (Cambridge University Press, second edition, 1980) – the last chapters deal with the reform crisis wittily and informatively.

Part Two Crisis and stability in mid-nineteenth-century Britain, 1832–67

CHANGE AND CONTINUITY

12 How much did the Great Reform Act Change?

Time chart

1832: First Reform Act (often called 'The Great Reform Act') becomes law
Whigs win huge majority in first general election held under new rules

1834: Tory leader Peel issues 'Tamworth Manifesto' asking directly for support in the country

1835: Peel gains a number of seats in the election, but Whigs stay in power with help of other anti-Tory groups

1837: William IV dies, necessitating a new general election. Whigs lose more support

1841: At general election, Tories defeat the Whigs: the first time that a party loses its majority to another party and forces change of government

1846: Peel forced to resign soon after passing the repeal of the corn laws. Two-thirds of his own party refuse to support him

Tory fears about reform

'It is not in my power to prevent the consequence of the mischief which has been done. The Government of England is destroyed. A Parliament will be returned, by means of which no set of men will be able to conduct the administration of affairs, and to protect the lives and properties of the King's subjects. I hear the worst accounts of the elections; indeed, I don't believe that gentlemen will be prevailed upon to offer themselves as candidates.'

Letter from the Duke of Wellington to the Duke of Buckingham, 23 June 1832.

In this chapter we investigate whether the Duke of Wellington's opinion, given a fortnight after the Reform Act passed into law, was justified. Prime Minister as recently as November 1830, Wellington had opposed parliamentary reform almost to the end. He, like most Tories, hated the idea of tinkering with Britain's beautiful constitution and prophesied that

KEY TERMS:

Boroughs and counties

Parliamentary **boroughs** were towns with the right to elect Members to Parliament. Until 1832, there was no standard qualification to vote. All English and Welsh **counties,** whatever their size, sent two members to Parliament before 1832. Most voters in counties were connected with agriculture; most borough voters had at least some connection with the towns they lived in.

the consequence would be chaos. He was not alone. A much more intellectual Tory, John Wilson Croker, said that 'The Reform Bill is a stepping stone in England to a republic. The Bill once passed, goodnight to the Monarchy and the Lords and the Church [of England].' The Tories did not believe the Whigs when they stated that the new Reform Bill, so far from destroying everything they held dear, would actually strengthen the old constitution. Who was right? The story of Britain in the 10 or 12 years after 1832 provides an excellent opportunity to understand that most major events not only produce change but can also be seen within a broad framework of continuity.

The changes made in 1832

The main changes brought about by the 1832 Reform Act are easy to summarise. The Act preserved the important distinction between '**borough**' and '**county**' seats, with different voting qualifications for both.

The Act clarified in statute for the first time that the privilege of voting was to be restricted to men only:

In county seats the following could vote:

- men who owned freehold property worth at least £2 a year
- men occupying copyhold land worth at least £10 a year
- men renting property worth at least £50 a year – the 'Chandos clause', passed because of a Tory amendment while the bill was going through Parliament.

In borough seats the following could vote:

- men owning, or occupying, property worth at least £10 a year, provided:
  a they had been in possession of it for at least one year, and were up to date with any taxes paid on the property
  b they had not needed to receive any poor relief during the previous year
- men who had been entitled to vote before 1832 if they lived within seven miles of the borough in which they were voting.

A register was to be compiled of all those who had successfully applied to vote. Only those on the register could vote.

The constituencies were, in many cases, dramatically changed. Fifty-six old boroughs lost the right to return two MPs and 30 more lost one. Famous rotten boroughs such as East Looe, Lostwithiel, Old Sarum and Winchilsea were swept away. It was the boldness of this Whig proposal which had most alarmed many Tories. Tories feared that property rights would be in danger and that this would weaken the constitution. They also feared that more electors from the towns would have less respect for the Church of England and for the other institutions of 'old England' which they held dear.

In all, the 405 old parliamentary boroughs were reduced by the Act to 260. To those which survived were added 63 new boroughs, mostly places of substantial population and growing rapidly during the economic expansion of the late eighteenth and early nineteenth centuries. For the first time, Manchester, Leeds and Birmingham received their own representation. Smaller, and often non-industrial, cities could also elect MPs for the first time. It is often forgotten that the 1832 Reform Act created the parliamentary boroughs of Cheltenham, Kendal and Whitby as well as those of Blackburn, Bradford and Sheffield.

Quite deliberately, however, the largest proportionate increase in parliamentary seats went to the counties. Here it was expected that landowners would remain the dominant influence. The number of English county seats was increased in 1832 from 80 to 144, and in Wales from 12 to 15.

The number of new voters created by the 1832 Reform Act was substantial. It has been calculated that almost 653,000 men had the right to vote in 1833 compared with 440,000 before the Act was passed, an increase of about 50 per cent. A larger proportion of new voters was created in the counties than the boroughs. Overall, however, the numbers of people entitled to vote after 1832 still remained modest. Fewer than one adult male in five was a voter in England in the late 1830s. In Scotland, Wales and Ireland the proportions were even lower. Most of the new voters were either tenant farmers, who tended to support their landlord's choice of candidate in elections, or what might loosely be termed the lower middle classes: shopkeepers, small-scale traders, some clerks and the like. The measure which so alarmed the Duke of Wellington in fact created an electorate of property owners. Most of the new electors were much more interested in conserving their own limited property and privileges than they were in agitating for more changes. To this extent, the Whigs had thus succeeded in greatly adding to the number of 'conservative' voters. These people did not necessarily vote Tory, but they would oppose further change.

The road to democracy? The case against

KEY TERM:

Democracy

Democracy is a system in which all citizens give their consent, usually by voting in elections, to the kind of government by which they are ruled. In 1832, very few people wanted 'universal manhood suffrage', which means the right of all *men* to vote. Very few MPs wanted to see democracy, or anything like it.

It is possible to see the 1832 Reform Act as the first step on Britain's road to **democracy**. Many historians writing in the late nineteenth and early twentieth centuries emphasised this aspect of the reform. J. R. M. Butler, who wrote a famously detailed study of reform in 1914, was in no doubt that this was a 'Great' Reform Act. Its passing 'showed that the fortress could be stormed ... it established a precedent of permanent force for enfranchising all classes when they should reach the stage of political consciousness and social power'. With the anti-reformers' defeat, 'the stage was cleared of political encumbrance for the working out of the destinies of Victorian England'. Even as late as 1938, E. L. Woodward, the author of a much-quoted textbook, admitted that 'neither side [reformers or anti-reformers] found the result as dramatic as it had expected' but he went on to assert: 'Yet the change was real and the Act of 1832 was a turning-point in modern English history.' Were these older historians correct in stressing change rather than continuity when they discussed the impact of the Reform Act?

It is easy to puncture some of the cruder interpretations which have passed out of the purview of history and into the general understanding of educated people who 'know a bit of history'. The last thing that the Whigs in 1831 and 1832 wanted to do was to pave the way for the coming of democracy. They agreed with Lord John Russell that 'universal suffrage and voting by ballot are measures that ... are incompatible with the Constitution of this country'. Macaulay believed democracy to be 'fatal to all the purposes for which government exists'. They saw the Reform Act as a means of staving off pressure for further, more radical, reform and – at least in the short term – they succeeded absolutely in this objective.

KEY TERM:

Middle classes

The **middle classes** are difficult to define. Broadly, they cover the ranks in society which did not do manual work and had at least some status. Many – the 'commercial' or 'industrial' middle classes – sought income by making profits from trade or industry. The 'professional middle classes', however, sold specialised services, as lawyers, doctors, writers or teachers. The numbers in the middle classes increased as society became more complicated and more wealthy.

Secondly, in no sense did the 1832 Reform Act 'give power' to the **middle classes** at Westminster.

Anyone studying the make-up of mid-nineteenth-century governments is struck by the apparent stranglehold on high office maintained by great landowners and their supporters. It is true that some such men came from non-aristocratic backgrounds. William Gladstone's family, for example, had made its fortune in Liverpool trade (including the slave trade) during the eighteenth century, but the family had bought land as the necessary route into local power and wider political influence. Anthony Trollope's fictional creation for his political novels, the Duke of Omnium, was a true enough representation of the kind of landed power-broker who operated well into the second half of the nineteenth century both among Whigs and Conservatives. Russell, Grey, Althorp, Palmerston, Stanley, Granville and Newcastle were among the names of great landowning families which dominated political life between the two Reform Acts and even for a time after the Second Reform Act of 1867.

Thirdly, the same political parties remained contenders for power. 'New' social groups sought assimilation within one or other of the Tory and Whig parties rather than determining to establish a new 'middle-class party' of their own. It is true that the commercial and industrial interests had a greater impact on the Whig Party, and were partly responsible for its transition into the 'Liberal Party' by the 1850s. No Liberal politician would want to alienate powerful industrial interests in Manchester or the Yorkshire's West Riding woollen towns. However, most political leadership from Westminster continued to be provided by the landed interest. The Tories underwent a change of name, usually associated with Peel's attempts to modernise his party. The 'Conservative' Party of Robert Peel in the 1830s and 1840s aimed to attract not just its traditional constituency of landowners, Anglican clergymen and some of the mercantile and banking interests in such established towns as London, Bristol and Liverpool but also a fair chunk of the newly enfranchised voters. Its roots, however, remained firmly landed.

Fourthly, the new voters seem to have exercised relatively little direct or independent influence. Few, even of the wealthier and more established middle classes, could contemplate a political career in a parliament where MPs received no salary and which was sitting for a larger proportion of the year than in the eighteenth century. Factory owners had businesses to manage and most felt the need to keep close eyes on the fortunes of their mills and workshops at a time of fierce competition and not infrequent trading slumps. Only when businesses were firmly established and a more modern-looking management hierarchy in place would many businessmen feel that they could afford to delegate sufficient responsibility to allow them to go into Parliament. The relatively slow expansion in the number of middle-class MPs is easily explained. The most prominent non-landed MPs remained, as they had been before 1832, from the professional, rather than the industrial, middle classes. Lawyers were both the best qualified and often the most influential politicians on the floor of the House of Commons.

Fifthly, the 1832 Reform Act did not abolish 'rotten' boroughs, though it greatly reduced their numbers. The historian Norman Gash calculated that about 70 seats after 1832 remained under the control of great landowners. At Huntingdon, for example, the Earl of Sandwich had been the patron of the unreformed borough and, after 1832, the Sandwich

PROFILE: *William Gladstone*

William Gladstone was born in 1809 into a wealthy Liverpool merchant's family. He was educated at Eton and soon sought a career in Parliament. He was elected MP for Newark in 1832 and was known as a strong anti-reforming Tory early on, writing extensively in defence of the Church of England. He was first Vice-President and then President of the Board of Trade under Peel (1841–6). He left office with Peel in 1846 and remained a 'Peelite', aloof from either political party, until 1859. While a Peelite, he served as Chancellor of the Exchequer in the Aberdeen Coalition (1853–5). He eventually joined the Liberal Party and served as Chancellor again under Palmerston and Russell (1859–66). He first became Prime Minister in December 1868, serving until defeated in the general election of 1874. He was Prime Minister three more times (1880–85, 1886 and 1892–4), and led the Liberals almost continuously from 1868 to 1894. His later reputation was as a reformer, especially in government and administration. Popular with many skilled working men he became known in his later career as 'the People's William'. His relationship with the Liberal Party was complex and frequently uneasy (see chapter 22). Some consider that his conversion to a policy of Irish Home Rule in 1885 set the Liberal Party on the long, slippery path to decline. He died in 1898.

family's preferences were still obediently attended to by the town's 390 or so electors.

By a nice irony, **William Gladstone**, later to be regarded as one of the great reforming prime ministers of the century, first became an MP at the election held shortly after the Reform Act was passed. Gladstone did not, however, seek to represent his native Liverpool or any of the new industrial centres in the North-West. He was selected, as a young man who had publicly opposed many of the main reforming initiatives of the day, by the fiercely conservative Duke of Newcastle and represented 'his' borough of Newark. Gladstone continued to believe in the value of boroughs which remained under electoral influence. As late as 1859 he asserted the value of getting young men into Parliament early, where they could learn their trade and then give the nation long and valued service. But, as he pointed out, very young politicians could not hope to be selected in constituencies where there was keen competition and where an established reputation in the community was of value:

> *'You cannot expect of large and populous constituencies that they return boys to Parliament; and yet, if you want a succession of men trained to take part in the government, you must have a great proportion of them returned to the House while they are boys.'*
>
> *English Historical Documents, 1832–74.*

His solution was to preserve boroughs in which members could be selected by men of influence, not elected by the constituency as a whole.

When elections *were* contested after 1832, many of them remained noisy, high-spirited and sometimes chaotic affairs more reminiscent of the famous scenes of drunkenness and 'treating' so vividly captured by the eighteenth-century artist William Hogarth. Some radicals had wanted voting to be in secret after 1832 but there was very little parliamentary support for the idea. Men cast their votes in the open after 1832 as before. Sometimes, the consequences were hilarious. In the 1830s, the novelist Charles Dickens was working as a reporter on the newspaper *Morning Chronicle.* His eye-witness reports of an election held in Northampton in 1835 might suggest how little things had changed.

The polling begins on Friday and then we shall have an incessant repetition of the sounds and sights of yesterday 'till the election is over – bells ringing, candidates speaking, drums sounding, a band of eight trombones (would you believe it?) blowing – men fighting, swearing, drinking and squabbling – all riotously excited, and all disgracing themselves.

16 December 1835

The noise and confusion here this morning – which is the first day of polling is so great that my head is actually splitting. There are about forty flags on either side, two tremendous bands, one hundred and fifty constables, and vehicles of every kind, sort and description. The last mentioned nuisances are constantly driving about and in and out and up [and] down the town, conveying voters to the Poll; and the voters themselves are drinking and guzzling and howling and roaring in every house of Entertainment there is . . .

18 December 1835

No artifice has been left untried, no influence has been withheld, no chicanery neglected by the Tory party; and the glorious result is, that Mr Maunsell is placed at the head of the poll, by the most ignorant, drunken and brutal electors in these Kingdoms, who have been treated and fed, and driven up to the poll the whole day, like herds of swine.

19 December 1835

From E. A. Smith (ed.), *Reform or Revolution: A Diary of Reform in England, 1830–32* (1992).

From the evidence above, we might conclude that 1832 produced far more elements of continuity than they did of change. Certainly, it will not do to see the Reform Act as the first step along a pre-determined route towards full adult suffrage conducted in secret and on principles designed to be as fair as possible. The Reform Act was a product of its own time and not some shining beacon to light the way forward to the representative democracy which, painfully and protractedly, Britain was eventually to become by a series of Acts passed between 1867 and 1969 – when 18-year-olds were allowed to vote.

The road to democracy? The case for

But has the pendulum swung too far? Having noticed important elements of continuity, might we not be justified in concluding that, nevertheless, the changes brought about by the Reform Act are more important? At least four reasons might be advanced for thinking so.

Firstly, the new electoral system required greater management. Not only were there new voters, but they needed to be placed upon a political register. What might be considered a bureaucratic activity was in fact a highly political one. By no means all new voters were well organised or absolutely determined to stake their claim to participate in elections. Many, then as now, had to be cajoled to vote. The Reform Act made local party organisation more important than ever before. Both political parties recognised the fact and established 'Registration Societies'. Their prime purpose was to see that as many of their own supporters were on the register as possible and that effective challenges were mounted to the claims of opponents. F. R. Bonham was the first professional party manager, advising Robert Peel while he was in opposition in the 1830s. Joseph Parkes, a Birmingham solicitor, performed a similar function for the Whigs. Political clubs – the Tory Carlton Club (1832) and the Whig Reform Club (1836) – were founded.

'There is a perfectly new element of political power – namely the registration of voters, a more powerful one than either the Sovereign or the House of Commons.

That party is the strongest in point of fact which has the existing register in its favour.'

There is little doubt that of the two parties, the Tories were the better organisers in the 1830s. Peel himself recognised the importance of the new procedures in his famous 'Register' speech of 1838 (left).

The changes brought about in the 1830s may be seen as the precursors of modern party activity and its attendant disciplines. As organisation became more professional, so the scope for the dilettante and the amateur in national politics was reduced. The advancement of political organisation stimulated the *second* important factor: growing party allegiance and discipline. It is certainly not true that political parties were brought into being because of the 1832 Reform Act. However, the Reform Act greatly accelerated their importance in national affairs. Before 1832, a significant number of MPs owed only limited, or fitful, party allegiance if any at all, arguing that their first duty was to represent their constituents at Westminster, not to follow any 'party line'. Such views became a luxury as party disciplines tightened. It has frequently been remarked that, in order to stabilise the constitution at a time of frighteningly rapid change, Peel urged his supporters to vote with the Whig government on important measures. It is equally important to note that MPs increasingly voted as a bloc. Party discipline both at Westminster and outside increased sharply after 1832.

Voters had two votes in most parliamentary seats, both before and after 1832. It was not unusual for such votes before 1832 to be split in the interests of local accord and harmony. After 1832, such agreements became much rarer. It has been calculated that in the different boroughs of Lewes (Sussex), Maidstone (Kent) and Northampton, whereas 'split voting' [*i.e.* between the parties] occurred in between 30 and 70 per cent of cases before 1832, at the election of 1841 fewer than 10 per cent of voters split their votes between parties in Northampton while only 1 per cent did so at Maidstone. It is difficult to escape the conclusion that the Reform Act contributed substantially to the polarisation of politics.

Thirdly, and linked to the earlier factors, the functions of general elections began to change. It is not commonly appreciated nowadays that the role of general elections in eighteenth- and early nineteenth-century Britain was not to elect a government but to return MPs. Between the Hanoverian succession of 1714 and the Reform Act of 1832 it cannot be said that any general election of itself changed a government. Much more commonly, as in 1784 with the Younger Pitt, they served as an opportunity for the electorate to confirm the monarch's choice of prime minister. With greater party organisation and an ever sharpening perception by voters about the choices before them after 1832, elections gradually developed into an overt struggle for power between two parties. Peel certainly saw the elections of 1835 and 1837 as an opportunity to appeal to the wider electorate for support and to claw back Tory losses made at the disastrous election of 1832. The 1841 election was the first occasion on which a government with a parliamentary majority was defeated in a single contest by an opposition party. It is true that not until 1868 did a serving prime minister – Disraeli – choose to offer his resignation *before* a newly elected Parliament had met, since he could be absolutely certain of his inability to command support there. However, as early as 1841 it had been established that general elections were taking on the central role in the distribution of power between political parties.

The fourth reason for suggesting that change, rather than continuity, deserves to have the main emphasis in discussions about the consequences of Reform is the most diffuse, but probably the most persuasive. The year 1832 initiated a climate of change with dramatic consequences over the next two decades. Many believed that extra-parliamentary pressure had been the decisive influence in the passing of the Reform Act. If such pressure were successful once, why not again – and perhaps in different areas of national life? It is significant that Robert Peel gave as the most important reason why he had opposed the Act not its specific terms but his inability to predict where it might lead. He was, he said, unwilling to open a door which he could see no prospect thereafter of closing. Despite Lord John Russell's assertion that 1832 represented 'the final solution of a great constitutional question', the Reform Act ushered in a decade of change and argument about change.

If 1832 did not give power to the middle classes at Westminster, the Municipal Corporations Act of 1835 made possible a whole series of power struggles between Whig and Tory, Liberal and Conservative – usually between contending groups from the middle classes – at local level about issues which were genuinely ones of life and death, including sewerage, lighting, burial grounds and other areas of public health. Chartists were spurred by the presumed slights of 1832 to seek more extensive reform (see chapter 16). The predominantly middle-class Anti-Corn Law League refined techniques of extra-parliamentary pressure in support of the economic changes they sought (see chapter 17). The 1830s as a whole have been seen by some as a 'decade of reform'. Whatever its precise consequences, the passage of the Reform Act altered the political process, creating a new 'psychology of change'. The dimensions of this are discussed in the chapters which follow.

Further reading

E. J. Evans, *The Great Reform Act of 1832,* Lancaster Pamphlet (Routledge, second edition, 1994) – surveys the arguments which stress both change and continuity arguments.

R. Stewart, *Party and Politics, 1830–52,* British History in Perspective (Macmillan, 1989) – a brief but clear summary grounded in detailed knowledge of the period.

J. Cannon, *Parliamentary Reform, 1640–1832* (Cambridge University Press, second edition, 1980).

M. Brock, *The Great Reform Act* (Hutchinson, 1973).

HISTORICAL CONTROVERSY/ ROLE OF THE INDIVIDUAL

13 Britain, 1830–50: the age of Peel?

Time chart

1830: Wellington's Tory government resigns

1834: William IV dismisses Melbourne's government and Peel forms a minority administration. He issues the 'Tamworth Manifesto' in which he promises to align his party behind support for moderate reform and 'the correction of proved grievances'. Some have seen this as the foundation of modern Conservatism

1835: 'Lichfield House Compact' – a coalition of Whigs, Irish and Radicals – forces Peel's resignation after general election increases Tory support

1835–41: In opposition, Peel and the Conservatives support a number of Whig reforms

1837: William IV dies and is succeeded by Victoria. At the subsequent general election, Tories further increase support. They now have about 310 seats, only 30 less than the government and its allies

1839: 'Bedchamber Crisis': Peel invited to form a government but refuses when Queen Victoria refuses to dismiss court servants – 'ladies of the bedchamber' – who were supporters of the Whig Party

1841: General election produces Tory majority of about 76. Peel becomes Prime Minister

1842: As part of wide-ranging plan to stabilise national finances, Peel introduces income tax for the first time in peace. The budget also announces major reductions in custom duties

1844: Bank Charter Act gives Bank of England new role in issuing banknotes and puts it on a more modern footing. A Factory Act restricts hours of work for women and children in factories

1845: Government gives increased aid to a Roman Catholic college at Maynooth (Ireland). This antagonises many right-wing Tories. Further moves towards free trade in the budget

1846: At the end of the Corn Law crisis, the corn laws are repealed but most of Peel's own party in the Commons vote against it. Peel resigns soon after and a Liberal government headed by Lord John Russell takes over

1847: General election sees the return of 90 supporters of Peel ('Peelites') who refuse to support either of the main parties. Russell has an overall majority of about 50

1849: Liberals further reduce customs and repeal the Navigation Act. Effectively, British economic policy is one of free trade

1850: Peel dies after a riding accident

Peel and his reputation

Sir Robert Peel is widely regarded as the dominant politician of his age. In the 1830s and 1840s, after a long and generally successful apprenticeship, he reached maturity. By 1834, he was leader of the Tory Party. His attempts to modernise it are usually associated with the change in name

PROFILE: *Sir Robert Peel*

Robert Peel was born in Bury in 1788, the son of a successful cotton manufacturer, Sir Robert Peel Snr, who also had a political career and was responsible for passing one of the first Factory Acts. Educated at Harrow and Oxford – where he was brilliantly successful – Peel was groomed by his father for politics. Peel Senior effectively bought Peel a parliamentary seat in 1809 when he represented the Irish constituency of Cashel, which had only about 20 voters. Within a year, he was Under-Secretary for War and the Colonies and from 1812 to 1818 Chief Secretary for Ireland. He first became prominent in public finance when he chaired a parliamentary committee to investigate returning the nation's currency to the gold standard in 1820. He was Home Secretary under Liverpool from 1822 to 1827, when he introduced a number of legal and administrative reforms, and under Wellington from 1828 to 1830 during which time he introduced the first professional police force – the 'Bobbies' or 'Peelers' – to the streets of London. This is the policy for which he is probably best remembered today. He persuaded Wellington to grant Roman Catholic emancipation in Ireland in 1829, earning himself the lasting hatred of many right-wing Tories. He refused to support the Great Reform Act, but during the 1830s generally supported moderate reforms proposed by the Whig government. He was prime minister from December 1834 to April 1835 and from August 1841 to June 1846. He was acknowledged by all as a brilliant administrator, a master of detail and an effective speaker in Parliament. He was, however, never fully trusted by many in his own party and his relationship with backbenchers was rarely close. He was accused of being more interested in 'statesmanship' than with the fortunes of the Conservative Party. Peel died in 1850.

from 'Tory' to 'Conservative'. The Conservatives' election victory gave Peel five years in power, during which he remodelled the nation's finances, apparently laying the foundations for the 'great Victorian boom' of the 1850s and 1860s based on peace, prosperity and free trade. He lost power only after his backbenchers refused to support the repeal of the corn laws. Getting rid of these laws Peel saw as essential not only to set Britain firmly on the road to free trade but also for removing social tensions. Giving working people cheap bread, he thought, was the surest way to remove the causes of their discontent. Radicalism (see chapters 6, 11 and 16) would therefore be much less of a threat to the ruling classes. Thoughout his term of office and again from 1846 to 1850, Peel's reputation as a statesman was very high. When he died in 1850, there was a great outpouring of public grief. Large numbers of public subscriptions were started, to which people from all social classes willingly contributed. The Peel parks and Peel statues, many of which survive to this day, represent the tribute of a grateful nation.

It might seem, therefore, that Peel richly earned his high reputation. Certainly, most historians have empathised with the feelings of those who crowded Tamworth railway station just before midnight on 5 July 1850 when his body made its last journey from London to his Staffordshire home. You will see the views of two of them below. One is from Peel's most famous biographer, Norman Gash. Gash goes even further in the title of a book of documents on the period 1828–50. He called it, simply, *The Age of Peel*.

View 1

'What Peel gave the Conservative opposition after 1832 was national leadership of a kind which they were not to see again for another generation ... national leadership is often more effective than party leadership. Peel may not have been a good party leader; there is a case for arguing that he was a great one.

Administrative skill, capacity for work, personal integrity, high standards, a sense of duty. To say that Peel had all these is to utter a commonplace. What is less often remarked on is his sheer intellectual power. It is this above all which enabled him to dominate his political contemporaries both in cabinet and in the House of Commons ...

The fundamental quality which Peel exhibited after 1841 was his desire to reunite the country ... By 1850, though Peel could not have known it as he lay dying at Whitehall Gardens, the larger problems of his time had been met and solved. The age of revolt was giving way to the age of stability; and of that age Peel had been the chief architect.'

Norman Gash, *Sir Robert Peel: The Life of Sir Robert Peel after 1830* (1986). [This is a small extract from a very long biography in two volumes.]

View 2

'[Peel] died the hero equally of the newly enfranchised, propertied middle classes, and of the unenfranchised, propertyless masses ... In troubled and changing times, he had satisfied the majority of British people of all classes that the reformed political system, under strong leadership, was capable of reacting purposefully to their needs.'

D. Read, *Peel and the Victorians* (1987). [This book attempts to explain Peel's reputation, and is concerned with events after Peel's death as much as before it.]

Disagreement and controversy are the life-blood of history. Either because new evidence comes to light or (and this is the more usual reason with widely studied figures such as Peel) existing evidence is reinterpreted, historians offer different opinions. In recent years, Peel has been viewed less favourably. In one sense, reinterpretation is long overdue. After all, Peel was a controversial figure in his own lifetime. He inspired respect, and even love, among the small number of administrative and governmental 'experts' whose company he sought out. Men like Aberdeen, Graham and Gladstone all venerated him. Gladstone called him 'My great Master and generous friend'. However, he was much disliked by many politicians. His personal relations were poor. The Duke of Wellington thought him 'crotchety' and difficult to get on with. The factory reformer Lord Ashley (later seventh **Earl of Shaftesbury**) called

KEY TERM:

Humanitarians

In the context of the industrial revolution, **humanitarians** – or humanitarian reformers – supported a range of causes intended to improve the conditions of working people. Central among these was limiting the length of the working day, but many humanitarians also wanted to see better education for workers. They were also alarmed at the inability of the Church of England to reach the poorer sections of society and called for more churches and clearer doctrine. Many humanitarians were members of the Tory Party, but few supported Peel's economic policies. Indeed, they criticised free trade as a doctrine which benefited only factory owners and profiteers. Some, like Ashley, opposed the Great Reform Act of 1832. They may have wanted to protect the poor, but they did not consider it right, or necessary, to give them equal political rights. The link between humanitarians and support for the landed interest was strong.

PROFILE: *Lord Shaftesbury*

The famous factory reformer, the seventh **Earl of Shaftesbury**, was born **Anthony Ashley Cooper** in London in 1801. He was educated at Harrow and Oxford and became an MP in 1826. He was a Tory and held minor office under Wellington and Peel in the governments of 1828–30 and 1834–5. He was most associated with policies commonly supported by Tories who were sceptical about the impact of the industrial revolution. They became known as '**humanitarians**'. Ashley felt that many factory owners were looking for opportunities to exploit their workforce, particularly women and children. Many, he felt, were unnecessarily cruel. He campaigned throughout the 1830s and 1840s for limitations on the maximum number of hours women and children could work. The Factory Acts of 1844 and 1847 owed much to his sponsorship and support. Ashley became Earl of Shaftesbury in 1851 and remained to the end of his life in 1885 an enthusiastic supporter of a range of social causes, including extended education for working people and the building of more him 'an iceberg with a slight thaw on the surface'. An important section of the Tory Party never trusted him after he 'ratted' on Catholic emancipation in 1829. Benjamin Disraeli, his great opponent in the Commons during the crisis over the corn laws in 1845–6, accused him of putting his own arrogant conception of 'the national interest' before party loyalty.

Below you will find three opinions of Peel which are much less favourable than those held by Gash and Read. Which does the evidence support? The rest of the chapter will give you an opportunity to make up your own mind on the basis of the evidence.

View 3

'Peel had only limited success in controlling his party and influencing its principles; his inability to convince his followers of the need for moderation forced him into fighting the 1841 election as the defender of existing ... privilege. What triumphed in those elections ... were not the Conservative principles of [the] Tamworth [Manifesto] but those aspects of Toryism which Tamworth sought to subvert [overthrow] ... Peel did not succeed, as he intended, in broadening the base of Conservative support ... He set out to build a party and instead split one, many of the materials of which were not of his making. Might this aspect of his career not be considered a study in failure?'

I. Newbould, 'Peel and the Conservative Party, 1832–41: A Study in Failure?', *English Historical Review* (1983). [*English Historical Review* is a journal written by, and mostly read by, professional historians. It publishes the findings of new research, mainly in political history.]

View 4

'Did Peel fashion, foresee, or merely respond to events? Was his fundamental outlook [as Gash says] ... executive and governmental? The verdicts differ but they all follow Disraeli's in assuming that Peel was a man who kept changing his mind. [I] suggest that Peel's economic policies, at least, were not flexible at all, but rather rigid; that though he may have been politically pragmatic, willing to bide his time for favourable moments in which to implement his ideas, the ideas themselves were usually held dogmatically ... Peel had little instinct for "the middle ground", since his opinions tended to harden away from compromise in a crisis.'

B. Hilton, 'Peel: A Reappraisal', *Historical Journal* (1979). [Like *English Historical Review*, this journal publishes the findings of new research.]

View 5

'Peel's conception of party may be criticised as both narrow and selfish. In the 1830s he had seen more clearly than most the implications of [the] 1832 [Reform Act] for political reorganisation in the constituencies. What he had not seen, or more likely had chosen to ignore, was that party was becoming a

dynamic factor whose importance in government would inevitably grow. The backbench case that Peel deserved his fate in 1846 is, at the least, a reasonable one. Between 1841 and 1845 Peel either ignored his followers' sensibilities or bludgeoned them into submission. He proved himself untrue to their Tory principles on Ireland, on religion, on commerce and, finally and fatally, on the landed interest itself.'

E. J. Evans, *Sir Robert Peel: Statesmanship, Power and Party* (1991). [A much shorter book than Gash's. It makes use of research, much of which was done after Gash's biography was published.]

When we try to make sense of contrasting viewpoints about an individual, it is important to bear in mind two points. First, interpretations rarely contradict one another. What they are much more likely to do is to stress different aspects of a problem – in this case the career of Peel. Different emphases lead to different interpretations and what matters is where the emphasis is placed. Secondly, when we study an individual, it might be interesting to read a biography and feel that we have 'got into the skin' of the person. However, historians very rarely think it sufficient to leave it at that. In order to evaluate the importance of Peel, we need to put him in his context. Did he really dominate the 1830s and 1840s to the extent that Gash's *Age of Peel* implies?

You can see from the points below how some selected aspects of Peel's career can be put in a favourable, or a less favourable, light depending upon where the emphasis is placed. Look at how A [unfavourable] tries to answer 1[favourable], B to answer 2, and so on. Historians are trained to look at both sides of a question, but also to come to an overall judgement. You should make your own mind up only after considering all the evidence in this chapter and any other information you have. Remember, though, that there is much more to be said. The more you *know*, the more valuable and the more securely founded your opinion is likely to be – provided that you can also *select* from a mass of detail.

Points to consider in a sympathetic picture of Peel and his achievement

1 Peel was a brilliant administrator who was a master of detail. For those topics he took an interest in, he made himself more knowledgeable than almost anyone. He could dominate the House of Commons with these skills.

2 He gave the Tories a philosophy fit for the modern industrial age. His *Tamworth Manifesto* projected a vision of a party which *would* react to need and would implement necessary change. It was a philosophy which appealed to the urban and industrial middle classes as well as to the landowners who had represented the bulk of the Tory Party to that point.

No man, it is probable, ever deserved better of a party than Sir Robert Peel did of his . . . Unassisted by the faculties, the temperate wisdom and the parliamentary tactics of their leader in the House of Commons, they could scarcely, it may be thought, have recovered with such steady rapidity, and with so few reverses, from the prostration in which the revolutionary struggle of 1831 and 1832 had left them.

Annual Register, 1839.

3 He led the Conservatives, as they were increasingly called, to a substantial victory at the general election of 1841. This was the first occasion on which a government with a majority in the Commons had been replaced at an election by a party which had a majority of its own. Most commentators thought Peel's contribution decisive.

4 He took over government when the nation's finances were at a low ebb. For the last two years of the Whig government, debts had been mounting and there was economic crisis. When Peel left office in 1846, debts had been reduced and investors had more confidence. It could be said that Peel's policies prepared the way for Victorian prosperity in the 1850s and 1860s and, in doing so, reduced social tension and political unrest. For this he was praised by working people.

Points to consider in a less favourable picture

A Peel's mastery of detail was at the cost of a loss of perspective. He was dominated by a single idea – achieving free trade – and was prepared to sacrifice almost everything to it. He was not a practical politician, therefore, but a man driven by his own vision. He often did not need to dominate the Commons because, when he was in opposition, he formed alliances with Whig leaders to pass reforms in the national interest. The Whig reforms of the poor law, education, local government and the Church were important, and the Whigs have not always been given the credit they deserve for piloting such a range of changes through parliament (see chapters 14 and 15). Peel's main target was not the Whig Party but radicals who had dangerous support outside Parliament.

B Peel entirely failed to sell his ideas about moderate and modernising Conservatism to his own supporters. Worse, he either misled or bullied them at crucial points. The Tories who campaigned in 1841 did so believing that the Whigs would destroy the corn laws which they saw as the main support to the landed interest and that they would preserve them. When in office, Peel refused to commit himself to any single item of policy. When his backbenchers opposed him on education policy or on trade regulations, he threatened to resign unless they backed down. Eventually, knowing what party opinion on the subject was, he repealed the corn laws. In doing so, he split his party. The Conservatives would not form a majority government again until 1874. His justification was that his was the best policy in the national interest.

C Though Peel saw the importance of getting supporters to register to vote under the new rules drawn up in 1832, others did much more of the detailed work than he. He also failed to attract large numbers of new voters in the biggest industrial and commercial constituencies. Peel's vision of a modernising Conservative Party was fundamentally at odds with the party he actually led. The Tories did best in the English county seats and in the smaller towns. They did worst in Ireland and Scotland and in the industrial north of England. The Conservative Party in 1841 had quite a narrow power base. It is also arguable, despite what contemporaries said, that support for a party opposed to rash reform would have occurred after 1832 anyway. The Whigs' alliance with various radical elements in the Lichfield House Compact (see time chart on page 118) alarmed many new voters who, having been given the vote, were mostly quite keen not to see it extended to less 'safe' lower orders.

D Was the revival of fortunes more to do with a natural upswing in the economy than with Peel's financial policies? From 1842 onwards there were substantial increases in domestic production in textiles, shipbuilding and transport. The 'Victorian economic miracle' was about much more than the financial capabilities of one leading politician.

Classwork task

a From the five views given on pages 120–123, identify the different aspects of Peel's career that they talk about.

b Are the authors all talking about the same elements of Peel's career? Explain your answer.

c In what ways, and to what extent, does the information you are given of the nature of the evidence about Peel affect your view?

d Do you think it likely that biographies will give more, or less, useful and reliable accounts of the importance of an individual than general histories?

e Why do you think historians disagree? Your answer should include specific reference to the views given above.

Further reading

P. Adelman, *Peel and the Conservative Party, 1830–50,* Longman Seminar Studies (Addison Wesley Longman, 1989) – has documents and provides a useful, orthodox account.

E. J. Evans, *Sir Robert Peel: Statesmanship, Power and Party,* Lancaster Pamphlets (Routledge, 1991) – takes a less favourable view of Peel than Gash does.

R. Stewart, *Party and Politics, 1830–52,* British History in Perspective (Macmillan, 1989).

I. Newbould, *Whiggery and Reform, 1830–41* (Macmillan, 1990) – the first detailed study for some time to look at the Whigs on their own terms and not as pale reflections thrown up in 'Peel's decade'.

D. Southgate (ed.), *The Conservative Leadership, 1832–1932* (Macmillan, 1974) – has a useful essay on Peel.

N. Gash, *Sir Robert Peel: The Life of Sir Robert Peel after 1830* (Addison Wesley Longman, 1986) – the definitive biography, now seen by some as too sympathetic to its subject.

EVALUATION OF EVIDENCE

14 Poverty and the new poor law

Time chart

1832: Whig government establishes a royal commission, chaired by the Bishop of London, to investigate the working of the unreformed poor law and recommend changes. It recommends getting rid of relief outside workhouses for those who were fit to work

1834: Poor Law Amendment Act passed

1842: Despite much opposition from Conservative backbenchers, the life of the Poor Law Commission is prolonged for five years

1844: Detailed improvements to the working of the new poor law are implemented

1846: Settlement Act gives the right for any person continuously resident in a parish for at least five years to apply for relief there and not to be taken away to the parish of original 'settlement'

1847: Poor Law Act replaced the Poor Law Commission with a Poor Law Board, headed by a president, who will be a member of the cabinet. Detailed parliamentary scrutiny of the workings of the poor law is increased

1852: Outdoor Regulation Relief Order finally recognised that able-bodied males might receive poor relief outside the workhouse in certain circumstances

1861: Settlement Act of 1846 amended so that right to relief is now guaranteed after three years

1865: Union Chargeability Act required a standard rate to be charged throughout a Poor Law Union. This corrects the problem caused in many parishes where poverty was extensive. Until this Act, wealthier parishes in the same Union were not obliged to offer any support to poorer ones. Also the length of time required to establish 'settlement' (see 1846 and 1861 above) is reduced to one year

1866: The poor law inspectorate now includes a doctor. Conditions in medical wards of workhouses now subject to regular inspection

KEY TERM:

Less eligibility

'Eligibility' means the power to choose. The idea of **less eligibility** as applied to the new system of poor law relief was that conditions for those applying to receive poor relief should be made worse than those experienced by the worst-off worker who could survive on wages alone. In this way, the poor would not 'choose' to apply for relief unless they really could not survive otherwise. Less eligibility would both save money for hard-pressed ratepayers and instil a new sense of respect in the poor by making them dependent on their own resources. Less eligibility therefore had a moral, as well as an economic, dimension.

The coming of a new system

The story of the new poor law used to be quite a simple one to tell. It went like this. Attacks on the old poor law (see chapter 5) proved too strong to resist. The royal commission of 1832 thoroughly condemned the old system and recommended radical changes. The aims were twofold: to save money and to improve efficiency. A new, central structure, called the Poor Law Commission, operated from London after 1834. 'Assistant Commissioners' were appointed to put the will of the central Commissioners into operation in each Poor Law Union, as the new local authorities for administering poor relief were to be called. The poor were forced to enter the workhouse to receive support (poor law relief) if they could not make ends meet. Conditions in workhouses were deliberately made as humiliating as possible so that people would not want to enter them. The principle of **less eligibility** ruled. Despite vigorous protests from working-class political leaders and humanitarian reformers, a harsh and degrading regime was put into operation and lasted for the rest of the nineteenth century.

The Poor Law Amendment Act of 1834

1 A Poor Law Commission established in London to regulate provision of poor law locally. Three Poor Law Commissioners appointed. Secretary of the Commission was **Edwin Chadwick**. (*The Poor Law Commission had recommended the abolition of outdoor relief for able-bodied,* i.e. *physically fit, adult males. The Act drew back from this commitment, leaving precise direction at the discretion of the Commissioners.*)

2 Assistant Commissioners worked under the guidance of the Poor Law Commissioners to supervise the implementation of the Act in the localities.

3 Poor Law Guardians were to be locally elected; they replaced the unelected 'Overseers of the Poor' whose work had been heavily criticised by the Poor Law Commission. Ratepayers were entitled to vote for Guardians; the more property they had, the larger the number of votes they could use.

4 Local magistrates (Justices of the Peace) continued to sit on the Board of Guardians.

5 Parishes were to be grouped together in Poor Law Unions to produce sufficiently large units to provide appropriate services and to build new workhouses if required. Each parish in a Union elected its own representatives separately, and each parish bore its own share of the cost (this changed in 1865 – see time chart).

PROFILE: *Edwin Chadwick*

Edwin Chadwick was born in humble circumstances near Manchester in 1800 and first worked in a solicitor's office before becoming a journalist. He wrote many articles on Britain's social problems and came to the attention of the influential theorist Jeremy Bentham. Under Bentham's influence, he worked first as an investigator for the Poor Law Commission and then played a major part in drafting its report. Somewhat to his annoyance – since he had wished to be a full Commissioner – he became Secretary to the Poor Law Commission in 1834, a post he held until 1846. He used his poor law position to investigate other social issues, particularly the state of public health and his *Report on the Sanitary Condition of the Labouring Poor*, published in 1842, was extremely influential in focusing attention on the need for state intervention to effect significant improvement. His always energetic lobbying also helped to secure a Public Health Act in 1848, but the Act contained fewer elements of compulsion than he would have liked. Chadwick was a much more impressive administrator than he was a politician and lobbyist. He might be called the first 'public service expert' but he frequently alienated opinion by his arrogant, opinionated ways. In consequence he frequently achieved less than he hoped. His long career in public service was eventually crowned with a knighthood in 1889 and he died in the following year.

KEY TERM:

Outdoor relief

This was the name for poor relief given to paupers who were not required to enter a workhouse. It could take very many forms. The most normal form was extra money to make inadequate wages up to a bare minimum necessary for survival, but it could take the form of clothing or medicine or extra support for a new baby. The opposite, '*indoor relief*', referred to relief offered in the workhouse. While such relief was often harsh and demeaning, as medical skills improved, some Poor Law Unions even took to treating non-paupers in workhouses. This was often a much more effective means of isolating infectious disease than trying to cope with it 'outdoors'.

As so often in history, the truth is by no means so simple. As a quick glance at the time chart will show you, the new poor law was subject to regular review and frequent change. Most historians nowadays stress its diversity rather than its uniformity: it worked in very different ways in different places. **Outdoor relief** not only continued; it was the main form of relief for most paupers. In 1855, for example, 121,000 paupers were recorded as having been given poor law relief in the workhouse and 776,000 outside. Few would claim either that the new system operated with ferocious hardness everywhere. Frequent differences of opinion between locally elected Poor Law Guardians and the central authority meant quite good conditions in some parishes and poor ones elsewhere. Plain inefficiency also meant that quite a bit of money continued to be wasted in lax administration. The evidence provided in the rest of this chapter will give you some of the information you need to answer the following key questions about the new poor law:

- How 'new' was it?
- From whom, and why, did it excite so much bitterness and opposition?
- Should it be seen as a key element in new controls being taken by a

KEY TERMS:

Benthamite and Utilitarian

Benthamite was the term used to describe followers of the philosopher Jeremy Bentham (1748–1832). Bentham had stated that the general objective of a well-run society was to create 'the greatest happiness of the greatest number', and his ideas were often described as **'Utilitarian'**. This meant that they should be judged by how useful they were to society. The terms Benthamite, Utilitarian and Benthamite Utilitarian are often used interchangeably. In the context of social policy, Benthamites believed that the greatest happiness of the greatest number could be achieved by letting wages and prices find their true level in a free market. In order to do this, however, they also felt that the state needed to take a firmer line by imposing centrally agreed standards to which institutions should adhere. So, local Poor Law Unions should be guided (and, if necessary, controlled) by a central authority – the Poor Law Commission. In this way, waste and inefficiency should be reduced while people were encouraged to 'stand on their own feet'. Benthamite Utilitarianism was popular with administrators and experts, of whom Chadwick was the best known. Many humanitarian reformers thought Benthamite solutions inappropriate, inflexible and destructive of local pride and local influence.

government anxious to create a more efficient system to deal with the much more complex problems thrown up by an industrial society?

When you are evaluating the source material which follows, you should also study the terms of the Act above and notice the following points:

1 The Act gave the Poor Law Commissioners fewer powers of compulsion than the **Benthamite** supporters of reform would have liked. The Commissioners did not even try to insist in the early years that every Union built a workhouse. Norwich, a town of more than 70,000 people in the late 1850s, did not have one until 1859.

2 However, after much early hostility had died down, the main principles of the Poor Law Amendment Act were put into effect in most places over the next 20 to 30 years.

3 Most MPs voted for a new poor law in 1834 not because they were beguiled by the arguments of Jeremy Bentham, still less Edwin Chadwick. Few MPs in any age are seriously interested in ideas or rational debate. They are more likely to respond to prejudice, **vested interest**, instinct or party loyalty. Those in 1834 were interested in saving ratepayers' money, and this the supporters of the new Act promised would happen. It seems that they were right. You can study the evidence for yourself below.

4 In many places, especially in the countryside, the arrival of Poor Law Guardians under the 1834 Act made little or no change to the structure of local power. Landowners or their representatives had acted as Poor Law Overseers before 1834; landowners or their representatives were elected as Poor Law Guardians. Whether by appointment or by election, the same social groups retained control.

5 Though the system was in theory more centralised, very wide varieties of practice survived. Though there were exceptions, workhouse regimes tended to improve as time went on. The famous 'Andover (Hampshire) Scandal' of 1845 followed the revelation that starving paupers were reduced to eating marrow from the bones supplied to the workhouse for crushing. From the 1870s workhouse inmates in South Shields (County Durham) were taken on trips to the local theatre, concerts and Punch-and-Judy shows.

6 The poor law was by no means the *only* response to problems of poverty. We know so much about the poor law because it generated so many records. The Victorian middle classes, however, were great charity-givers. Many charity payments were informal and casual and we

Figure 14.1 A poor law workhouse in London

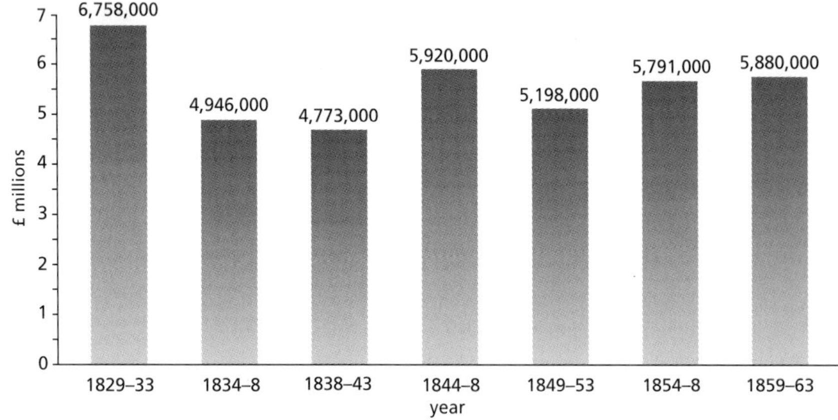

Figure 14.2 The changing cost of poor law relief: average expenditure on poor law relief, using averages calculated over five-year periods

cannot do much more than guess at them now. Both the formal agencies of charity and the evidence of wills and legacies, however, confirm that the rich often gave away enormous sums – usually to help the poor to help themselves. In 1869 some attempt was made to give charity payments a sharper and more rational focus with the establishment of the Charity Organisation Society. It is certain that the poor were given far more through the medium of charity than from the poor law.

KEY TERM:

Vested interest

Historians often use this term. It is a convenient shorthand way of suggesting that people are more likely to support measures which promise to advantage themselves, their families or their social group. This is not to say that people always behave selfishly, but that most people with power, wealth or influence are likely to consider whether that power, influence or wealth is likely to be threatened by a particular policy when deciding whether to support it or not. Turkeys might be said to have a vested interest in not voting for Christmas!

> *'The system of allowance is most mischievous and ruinous, and till it is abandoned the spirit of industry can never be revived ... Labourers are not as industrious [hardworking] as formerly ... If a system of allowances is adopted in a parish ... the whole of the labourers are made paupers ... One impoverished farmer turns off [makes redundant] all his labourers; the rest do the same, because they cannot employ their own shares and pay the rest in poor rates ... All grow poor together.'*
>
> S. and E. A. O. Checkland (eds), *The Poor Law Report of 1834* (1974).

'That we, the Radicals of Barnsley, have minutely discussed the leading features of the Poor Law Amendment Act, and also its cruel operations on the suffering poor; and we have come to the conclusion that a vote of censure . . . be passed upon the said Act, and the reformed parliament which enacted it; moreover we express an anxious wish that it be repealed, and that the 43rd of Elizabeth [the original Poor Law Act of 1601] be substituted in its place. We also call upon all good men to exert themselves in those encounters with the enemies of popular rights, which we, in union with the surrounding Radical Associations, are determined to enter upon.'

Notice printed in the *Leeds Times*, 5 March 1836, published in J. Knott, *Popular Opposition to the 1834 Poor Law* (1985).

'Gentlemen: Do for Gods sake take into consideration the sufferings of the poor of Lambeth workhouse ill used and half starved – the Master a perfect brute swearing at sick and aged, driving them to work when scarce able to stand – some of you I know to be men of feeling – my information I know is correct.

Yours respectfully,

A Parishioner

P.S. The food scarce fit for Hogs [pigs]'

Anonymous letter received by the Poor Law Commissioners, 1843, cited in A. Crowther, *The Workhouse System* (1981).

'When was the riot? – At the beginning of the formation of the [poor law] union in 1835.

What was the origin of the riot? – The origin was the change of the allowance system from money to bread, but the general feeling against the introduction of the law was another cause, the men being apprehensive of being shut up in the workhouse, and they stated to me most distinctly . . . that all they wanted was work; that was their constant cry . . .

Have you heard . . . that there is any improvement in the cultivation of the soil, arising from the greater employment of labourers? – I believe there is no doubt at all of that . . .

Do you perceive any difference . . . as between the employer and the employed? – . . . there can be no doubt whatever upon the subject . . . that those people now touch their hats to you as you pass; four years back ... they were always sulky, and now they are civil and polite.'

Evidence of Daniel Adey given to a parliamentary select committee on the poor laws, 1837–8, quoted in R. Brown, *Change and Continuity in British Society, 1800–1850*, Cambridge Topics in History (1987).

'When the overseers met in vestry, in November, for the purpose of making a rate for the winter half-year, it was found that, instead of a 5s [25p] or 6s [30p] book, as had hitherto been the case, a rate of 1s 6d [7.5p] would be amply sufficient ...

Here, then, was upwards of £1,000 left in the hands of the ratepayers, to meet the demands of such labourers as were willing to earn it; on the other hand, there were two houses for able-bodied men who were out of employment, with regular hours, regular diet, no beer, no tobacco, strict supervision, with the sedentary [non-active], and therefore to the agricultural labourer, irksome, employment of picking oakum.

The effect was almost magical: the ratepayers, who had been most violently opposed to the Union, now had substantial proofs in their own pockets of its advantages, and the labourers ... began to think, to use their own expression, that it was high time "to look out".'

Edwin Chadwick, 'An Article on the Principles and Progress of the Poor Law Amendment Act' (1837).

'It was said that the management of the New Poor Law was more economical than under the old; and with a view to prove this, Mr Weale, the Assistant Commissioner, stated that the average cost of the population of Aston is only 2s 8d [13p] while in Birmingham [still under the old system] it is 5s 5d [27.5p] a head. Now, this was extraordinary, but he should like to know how the parish of Aston could keep their poor at a cost of 2s 2d [11p] a head, that being the net cost of maintenance, exclusive of the other expenses ... He found, however, upon unquestionable authority, that the poor under the New Law, in 1836, amounted to £4,254,000, or a burden on each of the population of nearly 7s 7d [37.5p]. Where, then is this boasted economy under the new arrangement? It evaporated immediately the test was applied.'

From a speech made to Birmingham Town Council by J. H. Cutler, and reproduced in G. R. W. Baxter, *Book of Bastilles* (1841).

'With respect to the practice, lately commenced here, of giving a money grant in lieu of Tobacco and Snuff, we strongly recommend that this allowance of money should be at once discontinued, as the practice is found to lead to irregular and sometimes debasing habits in the recipients. With regard to premium upon earnings we recommend as a general rule that the present practice of giving one half of the total amount of these premiums weekly in money should be discontinued; and in lieu thereof that in every case where the premium exceeds three pence, only three pence of that gross sum shall be given to the paupers weekly, and the residue be retained by the Master for the use of the pauper when he may desire to leave the House, or if he die there, to cover the expenses of his funeral.'

Report of a Committee of Poor Law Guardians into the operation of the workhouse at Milnthorpe, near Kendal, 27 April 1842.

Task: class activity

Divide into four groups, each one representing people with different views about the new poor law. Each group has to use the evidence of this chapter to come up with reactions to the changes brought about in 1834. Remember to make use of the evidence contained in this chapter and any other information you may have. You are *not* allowed to make things up, or even to say how things 'must have been'! About the poor law, we have plenty of evidence about how things *were*. What makes the topic particularly interesting, of course, is that not all the evidence points in the same direction. Different people in the *same* group might have a different point of view.

a Landowners in southern England in the late 1830s

b Cotton workers in Lancashire thrown out of work during a trade depression in 1841

c Agricultural labourers in southern England in the late 1830s

d A working-class political leader living in Yorkshire in 1835–7.

Further reading

J. D. Marshall, *The Old Poor Law, 1795–1834,* Studies in Economic and Social History (Macmillan, second edition, 1985).

M. E. Rose, *The Relief of Poverty, 1834–1914,* Studies in Economic and Social History (Macmillan, second edition,1986) – both Marshall and Rose can be relied upon for useful brief introductions.

M. A. Crowther, *The Workhouse System, 1834–1929* (Batsford, 1981) – incorporates lots of detailed research which proves that not all workhouses were equally awful!

D. Fraser (ed.), *The New Poor Law in the Nineteenth Century* (Macmillan, 1976) – a collection of strong, research-based essays.

THEMATIC

15 Public health and education: a new role for the state?

Time chart

1831: Establishment of a central Board of Health and local boards to cope with an outbreak of cholera

1832: Cholera Act gives local boards of health powers to raise rates for the purpose of putting down cholera

1833: First Factory Act passed; creates an inspectorate. No child in textile factories to work under the age of 9; maximum 8-hour day for children between 9 and 13, who are also required to receive at least 2 hours' education per day
Government grant of £20,000 voted to aid churches to build school houses in England and Wales

1837: Civil registration of births, marriages and deaths provides the first official means of verifying children's ages, and thus their eligibility to work in textile factories

1839: First government administration connected with education for the poor. A 'Committee of the Privy Council' established to check on how grants were being spent. Government education inspectors appointed

1840: Vaccination Act introduces free vaccination against smallpox, administered through local medical officers and under agency of the new poor law

1842: Mines Act prohibits boys under the age of 10, and all women and children, from working underground. Edwin Chadwick's *Report on the Sanitary Condition of the Labouring Poor* published. His revelation that life expectancy was closely related to social class and environment increases pressure for public health legislation

1844: Factory Act reduces the maximum length of the working day for 9–13-year-olds to 6½ hours. They must also attend school for at least 3 hours a day. Women not allowed to work at nights
Following Chadwick's *Sanitary Report*, a Royal Commission on the Health of Towns was introduced. Its two Reports of 1844 and 1845 largely confirm Chadwick's findings and establish the connection between dirt, overcrowding and disease

1846: Government introduces pupil-teacher training, replacing untrained 'monitors' in schools supported by government grants

1847: Factory Act restricts women and young people of 13–18 years to a working day of 10 hours

1848: Public Health Act passed (for terms, see page 141)

1853: Further restrictions on starting and finishing times in textile factories in practice establishes a maximum 10-hour day for all Government attempts to make vaccination against smallpox compulsory, but many loopholes remain, and further legislation on the subject passed in 1858, 1867 and 1871

1858: Local Government Act and Public Health Act (see page 141)

1862: The government introduces a 'Revised Code' to save money by making grants dependent on satisfactory attendance and performance in tests before inspectors in reading, writing and arithmetic

1864: First of three Contagious Diseases Acts passed (others followed in 1866 and 1869). This aimed to stop the spread of venereal disease among the armed forces. Police could detain women in garrison towns suspected of being prostitutes and have them medically examined. If infected, they were kept in a locked hospital until cured

1866: Sanitary Act increases powers for local authorities and introduces elements of uniformity across authorities. Local authorities must remove 'nuisances' (rotting matter, excrement, etc.) to public health. For the first time, powers extended over domestic 'nuisances'

1867: New Factory Act extended the provisions previously governing textile factories to all factories. The Agricultural Gangs Act prohibited children under 8 years from working in the fields

1870: Elementary Education Act passed (for terms, see below)

An age of *laissez-faire*?

As the time chart above shows, much legislation was passed in the years 1830–70 to deal with what the Victorians called 'the social question'. This chapter asks why so much legislation was passed. Were the early Victorians humanitarians, anxious to spend money on a series of good legislative causes? Did they fear the consequences of doing nothing in a society which was rapidly changing and in which an increasing proportion of the population no longer lived in a village community under the watchful eyes of landowner and clergyman? Was reform motivated by **social control**?

KEY TERM:

Social control

This term has been used by historians who explain the relationship between classes in Victorian society in terms of one group (property owners) exercising power over another (labourers and ordinary workers). The idea is that the powerful were trying to 'control' the lower orders by channelling their energies into activities which were 'safe'. In this way, threats of revolution would be reduced and the British labour force would be less inclined to challenge the authority either of an employer or the government. Developments in education, for example, have been seen as a means of social control, since young people in a rapidly growing industrial town would be subject to all kinds of temptation unless they were given opportunities to go to school. There they would learn useful practical skills, like reading and writing. They would also be given firm moral lessons from the Bible and be taught the virtues of hard work and of saving. Other historians have seen **social control** as a less useful concept. They believe that the term implies too much direct manipulation of the lower orders by more powerful elements in society. They also challenge whether the values which the middle classes were trying to get the working classes to adopt were not present in important sections of working-class society anyway.

Apart from the poor law (see chapter 14), new legislation was probably most important in respect of factories, public health and education. However, these were by no means the only areas of life to come under regulation at this time. The mechanism of state intervention – central boards, local officials, regular reports to Parliament – was also extended to prisons and to the chemical industry via the Alkali Act of 1863. The Merchant Shipping Act of 1854 imposed new codes on ships and their crews, and was the first of five major pieces of legislation to be passed between then and 1876. There was even an inspectorate to guarantee the quality of lime juice. In 1869 it cost the taxpayer all of £2,000!

We might therefore be justified in suggesting that in this period government took massive new steps to regulate the lives of its citizens. Before we do so, however, we should be aware that many historians have seen this very period as one of ***laissez-faire***. Is this, then, not one of those **historical paradoxes** which writers of history books so delight in pointing out? On the one hand, the state is supposed to leave people alone, as never before; on the other, it inspects and regulates them, creating a new state bureaucracy as it does so in an attempt to ensure that regulations are not evaded. How are we to square this particular circle?

There are at least four ways to resolve the paradox of state intervention in 'an age of *laissez-faire*'. You may be able to think of others:

1 No state can ever abstain from 'intervention'. All governments need to raise taxes to pay for defence and all need legislation to administer law and order. It is interesting to notice that the great philosopher of *laissez-faire*, Adam Smith, also believed that an effective and civilised state needed to spend money on a proper education system.

2 The political economists, however, went much further than this. They recognised that while people did best when left to manage their own affairs not all were free agents. Notice how the legislation on factories related to women and children. Parliament recognised that they were not able to bargain for the best wages and conditions in the market place. The extent to which men could do so was, of course, extremely limited but Parliament was only prepared to take action to protect those who were unable to protect themselves.

3 Consider the *purpose* of the intervention. When you look at the examples of state intervention above, you will probably conclude that they were introduced to help an otherwise unregulated system work better. Children needed protection not only for reasons of humanity but also because exhausted workers were inefficient workers. Expanded education provision took thousands of children off the streets and made it less likely that young people in the sprawling towns and cities would turn to petty theft and, after that, to a life of crime. Edwin Chadwick's famous *Sanitary Report* argued strongly that state intervention in public health would greatly reduce what he called 'preventable disease'. This would save money and also help to provide a more efficient workforce.

4 Look again at the list of 'state interventions'. Notice how rarely *compulsory* powers are actually taken across the board. Either intervention is restricted to dealing with the problems of a specific and vulnerable group or the extent to which initiatives are taken depends on *local* initiatives. Between 1830 and 1870 the life chances of ordinary people in the growing towns usually depended much more on the attitudes of local authorities, and the priorities of the ratepayers who elected them, than they did on central government. Read the conclusion below from a historian who has made a study of the implementation of social legislation in two very different areas, Huddersfield (a leading woollen town in West Yorkshire) and the Isle of Wight (still rural and controlled by landowners). Throughout this period, local interests were zealously safeguarded, not least by backbench MPs who thought that their main job was to represent the constituencies they represented rather than formulate national policy. For these reasons **permissive legislation** was much more common than compulsory.

> *'The overall picture presented in this [book] is almost exactly the opposite of that painted by Chadwick, Simon and their biographers. Local Acts did some good, least was achieved under the Public Health Act, and the passage of the Local Government Act [of 1858 – see time chart] led to a rush of adoptions and . . . improvements. Clearly there was another England to that perceived by Chadwick and Simon.*
>
> J. Prest, *Liberty and Locality: Parliament, Permissive Legislation and Ratepayers' Democracies in the Mid-Nineteenth Century* (1990).

Overall, therefore, such state intervention as there was between 1830 and 1870 was restrictive and cautious, rather than confident and compulsory. The purpose was to regulate, when a water-tight case had been made, but very rarely to control.

There is, however, another way of looking at all of this. While it is crucial to recognise how limited state intervention was in this period and what an uphill battle 'centralisers' such as Edwin Chadwick had, the mechanism of state bureaucracy had inserted a slow-burning fuse into the system. Inspectors, paid by the state to investigate how new legislation is

KEY TERMS:

Laissez-faire

Laissez-faire is a term borrowed from the French language. Literally it means 'leave to do', but a better translation might be 'leave well alone'. In this period, it refers to policies designed to ensure that the state would have the least possible role in managing affairs. Believers in *laissez-faire* wanted customs and other trade regulations as low as possible, if not abolished completely. They wanted to see government expenditure kept low and they believed that businessmen and other risk-takers would flourish in a climate where the 'state was kept off their backs'. The abolition of the corn laws in 1846 (see chapters 13 and 17) and the repeal of the Navigation Acts in 1849 brought Britain extremely close to complete free trade. The few remaining duties on food were removed in stages down to 1874.

Historical paradox

A paradox is something which appears to be contradictory. **Historical paradoxes** often describe events which do not seem to follow one from another or in which apparently different beliefs or attitudes coexist. We might think it a historical paradox that later nineteenth-century Britain, overwhelmingly urban and industrial, was still ruled by governments in which landowners and aristocrats were numerically dominant. In reference to this chapter, you might think it a paradox that a state which was eagerly embracing *laissez-faire* policies and sought low taxation and maximum incentives for businessmen to invest, should nevertheless help to create elaborate mechanisms of state intervention in such areas as factories or education. One important task for a historian is to reconcile or 'resolve' these apparent contradictions.

KEY TERM:

Permissive legislation

Permissive legislation gives authorities powers which they *may* adopt but which they do not need to. A good example is the Public Health Act of 1848 (see page 141). Here the decision about whether to make use of its provisions rested with local ratepayers. Permissive Acts on social matters, and legislation which applied to specified places – such as the Rochdale Improvement Act of 1853, were much more common than compulsory ones until the last quarter of the nineteenth century.

being put into practice, are hardly likely to report that all is well. To do so would put them out of a job and civil servants rapidly develop high expertise in defending their own indispensability. There were 32,000 in post by 1861 and the administrative costs of government increased by about 50 per cent in the 20 years after 1848.

In any case, all was not well. Factory inspectors found it impossible to tell which children were really 9 years of age and which were not, and so which factory owners (and which parents) were conspiring to break the law. Civil registration was one response to this. Inspectors' reports were also full of further revelations which, they believed, the state should act upon. Inspectors always found reasons to advocate further intervention. So whether, as some historians believe, the new administration owed most to the ideas of Bentham and the Utilitarians (see chapter 14) or whether, as others assert, things developed their own momentum according to a largely unplanned 'pattern of government growth', the new initiatives produced their own legislative seeds which would germinate into more willing, and more extensive, state intervention after 1870 (see chapter 30).

Factory reform

In the 1830s and 1840s factory reform was a battleground between humanitarians and political economists. The former, led by **Richard Oastler**, Michael Thomas Sadler and the Earl of Shaftesbury, wished to

PROFILE: *Richard Oastler*

Richard Oastler was a Yorkshireman, born near Halifax in 1789. He was brought up as a Wesleyan Methodist and came into contact with factory workers in Leeds and Bradford. He came to prominence through his 'factory slavery' campaigns in 1830–32. Like his friend Michael Thomas Sadler, he was on the humanitarian wing of the Tory Party and consistently opposed Chadwick and his policies of centralisation. He helped to organise massive protests in Yorkshire against the introduction of the Poor Law Amendment Act and also formed anti-poor law associations. His journalistic skills were displayed in the *Fleet Papers*, published from prison in the early 1840s. Articles in this newspaper attacked the leaders of both the Whigs and Tories as promoters of centralisation. His hatred of free trade and the Anti-Corn Law League was a pronounced feature of the second half of his career. He died in 1861.

draw attention to the inhumanity of the factory system. Oastler in a letter to the *Leeds Mercury* in 1830 won a brilliant propaganda coup at a time when the government was moving towards the abolition of slavery in the British Empire. He drew unfavourable comparisons between the child 'factory slaves' of Yorkshire and the legal slaves in the West Indies.

Oastler's initiative led to the establishment of a parliamentary select committee in 1831. This was brilliantly manipulated by its Chairman, M. T. Sadler, to maximise its propaganda effect. A series of well-coached 'factory cripples' and well-meaning medical men were paraded before the committee to testify to the ills of the system. The political economists struck back arguing, with considerable justice, that Sadler had overstated his case. Enlightened employers had for many years seen the practical, as well as the humanitarian, value of treating children with care and consideration. As the leading thinker J. R. McCulloch said in an article in the magazine *Edinburgh Review* in 1835: 'Mr Sadler's famous Factory Report . . . contains more false statements, and exaggerated and fallacious [untrue] representations, than any other document of the kind laid before the Legislature.' Political economists called for much more modest legislation than Oastler, Sadler or Shaftesbury thought necessary, though they recognised that children needed some protection.

There is little doubt that the worst cases of factory exploitation took place at the end of the eighteenth century and in remoter water-powered mills away from prying eyes. As so often in politics, the result of the debate was a messy compromise but one from which the political economists took the greater comfort. The legislation of 1833 was limited. In particular, the factory reformers did not get their famous 'ten-hour day' for almost

Figure 15.1 *Bolton (Lancashire) in 1842*

another 20 years. Also, the operation of the legislation was restricted to textile factories until late 1867. As sympathetic observers increasingly complained, some of the worst abuses of workers took place in the smaller workshops or 'sweatshops', as they became known. Conditions for seamstresses and boxmakers in London's East End, for example, were notorious in the 1850s and 1860s because of long hours and low pay.

Public health

As we saw above, the study of public health is not just the history of Edwin Chadwick. Students are regularly too impressed both by Chadwick's overall impact on policy and by the significance of the 1848 Public Health Act. When you look at the terms of this Act, you will see that its powers were far less extensive than is often thought. Also, the mechanisms it put in place lasted only for 10 years. The 1858 Local Government and Public Health Acts were almost certainly more important in generating change, and numerous examples of local legislation more important to the conditions in which millions of ordinary English citizens actually lived than either.

Chadwick drew much of his inspiration for change from others. One of the first to demonstrate the appalling conjunction between dirt and disease was Dr James Kay, later much better known as the educational administrator **James Kay-Shuttleworth**. He also alerted his readers to the moral implications of squalor, a powerful incentive to reform:

> *'The state of the streets powerfully affects the health of their inhabitants. Sporadic cases of typhus chiefly appear in those which are narrow, ill ventilated, unpaved, or which contain heaps of refuse, or stagnant pools. The confined air and noxious exhalations, which abound in such places, depress the health of the people, and on this account contagious diseases are also most rapidly propagated [multiplied] there . . . The houses, in such situations, are uncleanly, ill provided with furniture; an air of discomfort if not of squalid and loathsome wretchedness pervades them, they are often dilapidated, badly drained, damp; and the habits of their tenants are gross – they are ill-fed, ill-clothed, and uneconomical – at once spendthrifts and destitute – denying themselves the comforts of life in order that they may wallow in the unrestrained licence of animal appetite . . . Want of cleanliness, of forethought, and economy, are found in almost invariable alliance with dissipation, reckless habits, and disease.'*
>
> J. Kay, *The Moral and Physical Condition of the Working Classes Employed in the Cotton Manufacture of Manchester* (1832).

The Public Health Act of 1848

1 Central Board of Health established, on lines of Poor Law Commission. It reports to Parliament.

2 If not less than 10 per cent of ratepayers require it, local boards of health set up. They report to the Central Board.

3 Authorities which had their own arrangements under separate legislation were not subject to central inspection. London did not come under its powers, nor did Scotland.

4 Compulsory establishment of local boards of health only where death rate exceeded 23 per thousand, compared with a national average of 21.

The Local Government Act and Public Health Act of 1858

1 The Board of Health wound up.

2 Powers of the Board transferred to a new Local Government Act Office.

3 A new medical department of the Privy Council set up.

4 Local initiatives in public health not so subject to central controls.

PROFILE: *Sir James Kay-Shuttleworth*

James Phillips Kay was born in Manchester in 1804 and trained as a doctor. He produced an influential report on the condition of Manchester in 1831–2. He moved into administration, making his reputation as the first Secretary of the Committee of the Privy Council on Education from 1839 to 1849. Much of his later career was devoted to education as a means of 'rescuing' children from the moral, as well as the material, consequences of poverty. He used the new poor law administration to develop ideas of training in practical skills for children of the poor. He helped to develop the pupil-teacher scheme which the government introduced in 1846 and favoured the introduction of a broad curriculum into schools receiving government grants. He opposed the introduction of what he saw as the restrictive Revised Code in 1862 (see time chart). He died in 1877.

Figure 15.2 *A Punch cartoon of 1858: 'Father Thames introducing his offspring (Diphtheria, Scrofula and Cholera) to the fair city of London'*

KEY TERMS:

Cholera and typhus

Cholera and **typhus** were two of nineteenth-century Britain's main killers. Cholera is an infection which affects the digestive system, producing frequent vomiting and diarrhoea. It was frequently fatal. Typhus, an acute infectious fever, also produced many fatalities but was found most commonly, as an Edinburgh doctor put it in the late 1830s, in 'the central and most crowded districts'.

Fear and self-interest proved the main spurs to public health reform. Parliament was more receptive to calls for legislation on public health during outbreaks of **cholera**. Those in 1831–2 and 1848–9 were specially significant (see time chart). Pressure in favour of a Public Health Act was undoubtedly increased because of an epidemic of cholera. This, a water-borne disease, was as likely to strike down the well-off as the poor. **Typhus**, on the other hand, was a disease much more commonly encountered in overcrowded districts. It was persistent especially in the tenement buildings of Glasgow and Edinburgh.

The Public Health Act had a brief, and chequered, history. In its first six years (1848–54), the General Board of Health supervised the implementation of local boards in about 300 towns containing, in all, about 2 million people, approximately 10 per cent of the population. However, Chadwick's heavy-handed manner offended many, especially those who continued to have severe reservations about the principle of centralisation. He was dismissed in 1854.

The most influential public health reformer after Chadwick was Sir John Simon. He was the first Medical Officer for the City of London from 1848 to 1855 when he resigned to take up a similar post at the Board of Health. As part of the administrative changes which saw the downfall of the Board in 1858 (see box on page 141), Simon was appointed Medical

Officer to the Privy Council. He used the position to lobby for further improvements. The Sanitary Act of 1866 (see time chart) introduced two important principles: identical obligations on local authorities for the removal of nuisances and an element of compulsion. These principles would be extended after 1870.

Chadwick's and Simon's campaigns for compulsion and uniformity met with only very limited success. Local initiatives could produce important advances in public health but the overall picture was bleak. Between 1848 and the early 1870s, the average death rate hardly altered. In the North-East in the early 1870s, three of the largest communities, Newcastle, Gateshead and Middlesbrough, all had death rates higher than those which had triggered the appearance of a compulsory Board of Health under the terms of the 1848 Act.

Education for the poor

No state system of education existed before 1870. Even the Elementary Education Act of that year (see box on page 146) only tried to fill up the gaps in provision for the children of the poor. The first state grant of £20,000 was made in 1833, on a vote in which a mere 76 MPs participated. The grant was to support school-building programmes under the supervision of the churches. The education inspectorate, which began its work in 1839, was serviced almost exclusively by clergymen until the 1870s. Since most church schools in England were run by the Anglican churches, many nonconformists opposed increases in grants unless schools were established without sectarian bias. There is little doubt that

Figure 15.3 *A National School for the children of the poor*

Kay-Shuttleworth was correct when he concluded that the conflict between Anglicans and Nonconformists hampered the development of a rational and effective programme of education for children of the poor.

An Anglican clergyman made the same point:

> *'Sooner or later, popular education must be an affair of the State ... not merely as making grants to different [religious] societies, and demanding the right to inspection over schools which receive such grants; but as establishing some system administered by an efficient and responsible board ... for providing masters to work on some well-matured plans, with books under a proper supervision, and paid, at least in great part, by the State ... The schoolmaster must become a public functionary, duly qualified for his office, and under due control.'*
>
> The Rvd W. H. Milman, 'The Education of the People', *Quarterly Review* vol. 78 (1846).

For the moment, however, education was too often a football between rival religious factions. Anglicans dominated the inspectorate; Nonconformists destroyed a Factory Reform Bill introduced by Peel's government in 1843 because they thought that the clauses relating to compulsory education of factory children unduly advantaged the Church of England. There was also no shortage of MPs who did not see why the children of the poor should acquire a range of skills which they would not use at work.

The ever-growing cost of state involvement was also highly controversial. The annual grant had grown to £30,000 by 1839, stood at £100,000 in 1847, a year after state support for teacher training began. By 1861, it exceeded £800,000. At that time, more than 1,600,000 pupils were being educated in church schools, compared with about 800,000 taught in a very wide range of private schools. In schools receiving grants, particularly in the larger cities, education inspectors regularly reported on dreadfully low standards. Approximately one-third of all children between the ages of 5 and 12 in England and Wales did not go to school at all.

The case for more systematic state involvement, supported by the massive evidence accumulated by a Royal Commission under the Duke of Newcastle (1858–61), was very strong. During the 1860s, the response was rationalisation and economy. The Vice-President of the Education Department, Robert Lowe, explained the basis of his so-called 'Revised Code' (see time chart) in stark terms. Kay-Shuttleworth, now out of the Education Department, produced a stinging rebuke.

'We propose to give no grant for the attendance of children at school, unless they can read [and] write ... but we do not say that they shall learn no more. We do not object to any amount of learning; the only question is, how much of that knowledge ought we to pay for ... It must never be forgotten that for whom this system is designed are the children of persons who are not able to pay for the teaching. We do not profess to give these children an education that will raise them above their station and business in life; that is not our object, but to give them an education that may fit them for that business.'

Robert Lowe, speech during a debate in the House of Commons, 13 February 1862.

'The last twenty-five years has witnessed a great municipal and religious revolution – the last fifteen years a still greater change in education ... [Teachers] had to struggle ... with the untamed brutishness of the wild or pauperised immigrant population – with the semi-barbarism of children from coarse sensual homes – with the utter want of consciousness in the population that humble learning could do their children any good ... with the late age at which children with no school-habits, savage, ignorant, incapable, wayward, or wild, came under their care ... To grapple with these evils, the Government resolved to create a new machinery of public education. This new machinery of apprenticed pupil-teachers has come into existence ... since 1847.

To give the people a worse education from motives of short-sighted economy, would be ... utterly inconsistent with all preceding national policy. The idea that an ignorant, brutish people is either more subordinate or more easily controlled than a people loyal by conviction and contented by experience and reason, is exploded.'

J. Kay-Shuttleworth, *Four Periods of Public Education* (1862).

Religious controversy dogged education developments right up to, and beyond, the Elementary Education Act. After the 1867 Reform Act had produced working-class majorities in many urban constituencies the case for increased educational provision became overwhelming. Nonconformists worked hard to remove the influence of the Church of England from the education of the poor, but such a policy was never practicable in a Parliament still dominated by Anglican landowners. More education there had to be, but on the basis of filling up the gaps left by the existing, church-dominated, voluntary system. It remained to be seen whether the new Board Schools could mount an effective challenge to the churches.

The Elementary Education Act of 1870

1 Establishment of local school boards, elected by local ratepayers. These boards would provide public 'elementary schools' to fill up gaps left by the voluntary church schools. The new schools quickly became known as 'Board Schools'.

2 These schools would charge fees, but local boards could pay them on behalf of individuals if they thought it necessary.

3 Women were entitled to vote for school boards and to sit on them.

4 Local boards could make attendance compulsory between the ages of 5 and 13, but this was optional.

5 'Board Schools' would not adopt education according to any specific religious denomination (Anglican, Catholic, etc.).

This Act did not *make elementary education compulsory. This did not happen until 1881.*

Tasks

1 This chapter can be used to make a list of those factors which suggest that government policy was moving in the direction of greater central control over social policy. Another list can be compiled which suggest the opposite. Working in two groups, one should produce the first list, another the second.

2 From the evidence given here, do you think that government involvement in social questions in this period was effective? What factors have helped you to make up your mind?

Further reading

O. MacDonagh, *Early Victorian Government, 1830–70* (Weidenfeld, 1977) – good at showing how government just grew under the pressure of facts and demands by inspectors for further reform.

F. B. Smith, *The People's Health, 1830–1910* (Croom Helm, 1979) – the best detailed research on the subject.

N. McCord, *British History, 1815–1906* (Oxford University Press, 1991), chapters 5 and 8 – refreshingly direct chapters on government intervention from a textbook which benefits from much detailed local knowledge.

G. Sutherland, *Elementary Education in the Nineteenth Century* (Historical Association Pamphlet, 1971) – still a very good introduction to the topic.

U. Henriques, *The Early Factory Acts and their Enforcement* (Historical Association Pamphlet, 1971).

EVALUATION OF EVIDENCE

16 Who were the Chartists and did they fail?

Time chart

1835: Working Men's and Radical Associations formed in Scotland and parts of the north of England

1836: London Working Men's Association formed

1837: East London Democratic Association formed. Various radical associations formed, especially in the textile districts of Lancashire and Yorkshire, to protest against the New Poor Law. First appearance of the most popular Chartist newspaper, *Northern Star*

1838: Publication of the People's Charter and the National Petition. Mass rallies and meetings

1839: First 'General Convention of the Industrious Classes' meets in London, then transfers to Birmingham. National Petition rejected by Commons (235 votes to 46). Demonstrations and mass meetings. An attempted rising of working people in Newport (Monmouthshire) is defeated (November). Arrests of leading Chartists follow over the next few months

1841: Support for Chartism builds up as trade depression has its effect but divisions are apparent between leaders and over tactics

1842: Second Chartist Petition defeated in Commons by 287 votes to 40 (May). Response of many Chartists is direct industrial action by sabotaging boilers – 'the Plug Plot' (August). Further arrest of Chartist leaders. Formation of the Complete Suffrage Movement by Joseph Sturge – an attempt to unite the interests of middle-class and working-class supporters of radical reform

1843: Trials of leading Chartists. Chartist Convention accepts a plan supported by Feargus O'Connor for land reform. This aims to buy up plots of land and settle Chartists on them in democratic communities

1845: Chartist Land Cooperative Society is established

1847: First Chartist land colony, 'O'Connorville', opened near Rickmansworth (Hertfordshire)

1848: Chartist Convention held in London and demonstration held on Kennington Common, south London (April). Authorities do not allow a petition to be presented by a large body of Chartists and, after threats of violence, the meeting breaks up peacefully

1850: Bronterre O'Brien's National Reform League founded. O'Connor's grip on Chartist leadership is weakened

1852: George Julian Harney and Ernest Jones gain control of Chartist movement, but support for it has very much reduced since 1848

1858: Last National Chartist Convention held

KEY TERM:

National Charter

The **National Charter** was drawn up in the form of a petition to Parliament calling for the establishment of a democratic system of government. It had six famous points, and these are listed, together with the date (in brackets) when the relevant 'point' became part of the British electoral system. A word of warning, however: students love to memorise these 'six points' and quote them in examination essays. This is rarely a good idea. It is much more important to understand:

- that these points were *not* new, most had been actively supported by radical politicians for at least 50 years;
- *why* so many working people supported what was, after all, a political programme at times of widespread economic distress.

Explaining the title of this chapter

Readers with some knowledge of Chartism might look at the title of this chapter and think that there is very little to say. Chartists supported the **National Charter**. The National Charter was not adopted by government, so the answer to the second part of the question is 'Yes'.

The six points of the National Charter

1 The vote for all adult males *(1918)*

2 Payment for Members of Parliament *(1911)*

3 Each parliamentary constituency should have roughly the same number of voters *(1885)*

4 Voting should be by secret ballot *(1872)*

5 MPs should not need to have a minimum amount of property before being allowed to take a seat in parliament *(1858)*

6 General elections to be held once a year *(not enacted – with good reason, you may think!)*

However, the answer to neither question is quite as obvious as it seems. If Chartism was Britain's first genuine working-class movement, why did delegates to the first Chartist convention include a Scottish landowner and Dr Arthur Wade, an Anglican clergyman from Nottinghamshire? If Chartism 'failed', why did so many political radicals and trade union leaders in the second half of the nineteenth century stress how much they owed to the movement? Why were five of the famous Chartist 'six points' eventually agreed to? Chartism was undoubtedly a short-term failure, but was it a longer-term success?

The general context

1 The peak Chartist years – 1838–9, 1841–2 and 1848 – coincided with years of economic depression and unemployment. This was normal for all radical protest in the first half of the nineteenth century.

2 Radical leaders drew on two main sources of *political* discontent also:

- frustration that the Great Reform Act had left so few working men with votes, while meeting virtually all of the needs of the middle classes (see chapter 12)
- anger that the Poor Law Amendment Act (see chapter 14) paid so little attention to working-class needs, particularly in the towns. The link between anti-poor law protest and Chartism is strong.

3 The six points had no real chance of being put into immediate effect – except by revolution, and that was unlikely too. It is very easy to explain why Chartism was a short-term failure:

- Both main political parties were firmly against further reform, and most MPs continued to fear democracy. Look at the time chart to see how few 'democratic' votes the Chartists could rely on in 1839 and 1842.
- Presenting a petition with six points on it leaves little room for compromise if the petition is rejected.
- Chartist leaders could not agree on the best strategy once the petitions had been rejected. Some historians have seen a division between **moral force** and **physical force Chartism**. Such a division is altogether too simple, but Chartist leaders often squabbled among themselves and **Feargus O'Connor's** high-profile leadership was resented by many others.
- The government had powerful weapons against Chartism. It could use the railways to transport troops speedily to places where there were disturbances. It had the support of almost all local magistrates in wanting to put an end to disorder. After 1839, also, the emergence of urban police forces gave the authorities more effective powers to break up demonstrations and head off trouble than before.
- The basis for alliance between the middle classes and the working classes was much weaker after the 1832 Reform Act. For most purposes, Chartists were isolated.
- Peel's government (see chapter 13) was working to remove the worst abuses. In doing so, it aimed to deprive Chartism of mass support. After 1842 it seemed to have succeeded. New factory reforms were enacted. Trade revived and Peel firmly believed that the repeal of the corn laws would give working people cheaper bread – as well as remove a major source of resentment (see chapter 9).

Historians have disagreed sharply about what Chartism represented. The political ideas underpinning Chartism had been around for a long time. They recalled struggles between 'useful' and 'useless' classes of society

KEY TERMS:

Moral force and physical force Chartism

These terms were coined by the first Chartist historian, R. G. Gammage, who wrote in the 1850s. He drew distinctions between the means favoured to achieve democratic change. **'Moral force'** Chartists believed in the power of argument and rational persuasion. Some felt that anything achieved by force would need to be held by the same means. **'Physical force'** Chartists, on the other hand, argued that reason had been tried, and found wanting. Force was the only method which was likely to bring results. The distinction was never a hard-and-fast one, partly because many 'physical force' Chartists preferred to use *threats* of violence rather than plan direct action, still less revolution. Nevertheless, moral force Chartism was more popular among artisan leaders like the cabinet-maker William Lovett and the poet and writer Thomas Cooper. They saw Chartism as a movement to educate working people to a sense of their own worth. Some became temperance reformers, believing that drink was an evil and that Chartism needed, as Robert Lowery put it, to be raised 'from the Pot House'. Physical force Chartists like Bronterre O'Brien and George Julian Harney were more likely to become supporters of socialism after Chartism collapsed.

PROFILE: *Feargus O'Connor*

Feargus O'Connor was born in 1794. He was not a working man, coming from a family of Irish landowners, and was educated in Dublin as a lawyer. He was MP for Cork from 1832 to 1835 and was a supporter of O'Connell. He emerged as the most powerful Chartist leader from the late 1830s, using the *Northern Star* to publish his views. His quarrelsome nature made him several enemies among other leading Chartists and historical opinion is divided as to the value of his contribution. He was a powerful orator and a formidable organiser but it has been claimed that his articles and speeches raised unrealistic expectations. O'Connor later championed the Land Plan (see time chart) which raised further controversy since others argued that Chartists should be more concerned with improving conditions of industrial workers than in romantic schemes to put them back on the land. He became the only Chartist MP when he was returned for Nottingham in the 1847 election, but was declared insane in 1852 and died in an asylum in 1855.

(chapters 6 and 9). Some historians have said that Chartism was not a 'new' movement of working people at all. It looked back to eighteenth-century political solutions instead of looking forward to the new industrial world and developing an analysis which stressed conflict between labourers and employers, capital and industry. Others think this is nonsense – yet another desperate attempt to explain something which is only of interest to Marxists: why Britain (the world's first industrial nation) failed to produce the world's first Communist revolution.

While some argue that Chartism was too political in its focus, others have suggested that it did represent the first working-class political movement in Britain. Some historians have pointed out:

- how little middle-class support Chartism attracted, particularly after the Newport Rising of 1839
- how bitter, yet precisely argued, was the Chartist case against the middle classes, who had 'sold out' in 1832 (see chapter 12)
- Chartists felt that the middle classes were now at least as much the enemy to working people as the old aristocracy had been before 1832.

No radical movement in British history has generated such an extensive variety of source material and so many conflicting interpretations. The sources and the questions which follow them help you to enquire into the strengths and weaknesses of Chartism.

Source-based enquiry

Source 1

1 To draw into one bond of unity the intelligent and influential portion of the working classes in town and country

2 To seek by every legal means to place all classes of society in possession of their equal political and social rights

3 To devise every possible means, and to use every exertion, to remove those cruel laws that prevent the free circulation of thought through the medium of a cheap and honest press

4 To promote, by all available means, the education of the rising generation, and the extirpation [rooting out] of those systems which tend to future slavery . . .

8 To form a library of reference and useful information; to maintain a place where [members] can associate for mental improvement, and where their brethren from the country can meet with kindred minds actuated by one great motive – that of benefiting politically, socially and morally, the useful classes.

Extracts from the Objectives of the London Working Men's Association, June 1836.

Source 2

'"Let their oppressors beware. The people were not bloodthirsty, they were patient and enduring; but though patient and enduring, they would not always remain so (Hear, Hear) . . . Rather than submit to the present system, and behold our countrymen crossing the Atlantic to find in other climes scope for their energies and remuneration [payment] for their labour, it would be better to put an end to it at any sacrifice." (On sitting down the speaker was cheered for several seconds. The speech, of which the above is necessarily a faint outline, was the most eloquent and effective that has been delivered during the sittings of the Convention. In the delivery it occupied upwards of two hours.)'

Report of a speech by Peter Murray McDouall, a Chartist lecturer, to the National Convention in 1839. It was reported in *The Chartist* on 16 March 1839. [McDouall was arrested in both 1839 and 1848.]

Source 3

'Should the Chartists accept help from the middle classes?

Mr James Ayr said, that he would suspect any man who proposed such a discussion [with the middle classes] of impure motives. The French working people had gained a revolution, and the middle classes came up and deprived them of the fruits. Such, he doubted not, was the intention of the middle classes in England.

Mr Mason said that Mr Ayr was mistaken as to matter of fact and history. The French Revolution was a revolution of the middle classes into which the people were merely brought as assistants. Therefore it was that the middle classes were able to take all the fruits under themselves. It would be very different in England.'

Debate at the Council of the Northern Political Union at Newcastle, April 1839, reprinted in D. Jones, *Chartism and the Chartists* (1975).

Source 4

A schedule of lectures planned to be given in southern Lancashire in early 1841

PLACES	Time of Meeting	January.					February.				March.			
		3	10	17	24	31	7	14	21	28	7	14	21	28
Tib-street, Manchester, Sunday	6	8	2	5	13	14	3	6	5	4	2	12	3	9
Brown-street, Do.	6	6	3	9	8	11	17	2	7	5	6	10	14	4
Salford, Do.	6½	2	7	17	10	6	8	3	9	2	4	5	6	11
Oldham, Do.	2	13	11	2	14	3	13	14	11	6	5	2	13	14
Do. Do.	6	12	14	2	11	3	12	11	13	6	5	2	12	15
Middleton, Do.	6	9	17	3	6	4	8	5	4	7	3	9	8	10
Ashton, Do.	2½	3	8	10	7	6	10	4	13	8	9	4	7	3
Newton Heath Do.	2½		1				6				8			
Do. Saturday	7				4				7				6	
Bolton, Monday Evening........	8	16	15	16	2	15	16	11	15	16	15	16	2	16
Mottram, Thursday Evening ...	8				3				2				11	
Droylsden, Tuesday	8	3	5	2	6	7	3	8	10	11	4	9	3	2
Failsworth, Sunday	6		1		9		17		14		10		5	
Rochdale, Do.	2	14	5	11	3	2	12	11	17	9	14	3	16	6
Do. Do.	6	14	5	11	3	2	12	11	17	9	14	3	16	6

LECTURERS

1. James Leech, Manchester
2. William Tillman, Do.
3. Charles Conner, Do.
4. Joseph Linney, Do.
5. Edward Curran, Do.
6. James Cartledge, Do.
7. William Shearer, Do.
8. John Campbell, Salford
9. William Bell, Do.
10. Richard Littler, Do.
11. James Greaves, Austerlands
12. John Greaves, Shaw
13. Francis Lowes, Oldham
14. Henry Smethurst, Do.
15. Richard Marsden, Bolton
16. John Gardiner, Do.
17. Edward Clark, Manchester

D. Jones, *Chartism and the Chartists* (1975).

Source 5

An analysis of occupations (3 instances and more) of those nominated to the Chartist General Council in 1841

Occupation	No.	Occupation	No.	Occupation	No.
Weaver	130	Block-printer	7	Mechanic	4
Shoe-maker	97	Boot-maker	7	Moulder	4
Tailor	58	Flax-dresser	6	Nailer	4
Framework knitter	33	Cabinet-maker	6	Needle-finisher	4
Cordwainer	30	Calico-printer	6	Warper	4
Labourer	19	Cloth-dresser	6	Watchmaker	4
Carpenter	18	Dyer	6	Baker	3
Joiner	17	Basket-maker	5	Boot-closer	3
Wool-comber	17	Bookseller	5	Bricklayer	3
Boot-and shoe-maker	13	Grocer	5	Brush-maker	3
Mason	12	Glover	5	Chair-maker	3
Hatter	12	Linen-weaver	5	Currier	3
Potter	11	Plasterer	5	Engineer	3
Printer	10	Schoolmaster	5	Hairdresser	3
Painter	10	Twister	5	Lace-maker	3
Spinner	10	Turner	5	Machine-maker	3
Newsagent	9	Button-maker	4	Plumber	3
Stonemason	9	Carder	4	Publican	3
Pitman	8	Cooper	4	Shipwright	3
Smith	8	Fustian-cutter	4	Tinman	3
Silk-worker	7	Gardener	4	Watch-and clock-maker	3

D. Jones, *Chartism and the Chartists* (1975).

Source 6

'Cooper, I am sick of the horrible vanity of our leaders! When in Scotland I have been ready to vomit at the little paltry jealousies of Collins and McDouall.'

From a letter from George White to Thomas Cooper, July 1842. It is reproduced in D. Thompson, *The Chartists* (1984).

Source 7

Punch cartoon 1848

A PHYSICAL FORCE CHARTIST ARMING FOR THE FIGHT.

Source 8

'We had arrayed against us, by our own folly, the very physical force to which we had appealed. The dread of general plunder and outrage by the savages of London, the national hatred of that French and Irish interference of which we had boasted, armed against us thousands of special constables, who had . . . little or no objection to our political opinions. The practical commonsense of England, whatever discontent it might feel with the existing system, refused to let it be hurled rudely down, on the mere chance of building up on its ruins something as yet untried, and even undefined ... The meeting which was to have been counted by hundreds of thousands, numbered hardly tens of thousands; and of them a frightful proportion were of those very rascal classes, against whom we ourselves had offered to be sworn in as special constables.'

From the novel *Alton Locke* by Charles Kingsley. [This novel was published in 1850 and in this extract the central character, Locke, tells the story of the events of April 1848.]

Source 9

'"What have we gained?" asked Julian Harney in 1848. "Is the reward proportionate to the toil expended?" Most would have said "Yes". It was Ernest Jones's proud boast that the Chartists had redefined the nature of democracy, and had challenged everything . . . which might oil the wheels of aristocratic monopoly and commercial expansion. They did not always succeed, of course, nor did they carry out their intentions to rewrite history and capture the cooperative working-class mind. In particular it was a matter of common regret that they had not paid more attention to the women and children who held the key to working-class progress. "The Charter will never become the law of the land", the ardent feminist Caroline Maria Williams had once said, "until we women are fully resolved that it shall be so". . . Chartists . . . prided themselves on being "practical men"; this was the message which they took to trade union and socialist meetings. Yet dreams stalk through the poetry which so many of them wrote. Each quiver abroad, each small victory at home, fired the imagination . . . The prodigious optimism of Chartist organisers . . . is difficult to explain, and the loyalty and sacrifices which they called forth. As the years passed, and the threat of violent change receded, people readjusted their hopes and strategy, but the faith remained. "The result IS certain – the numbers ARE coming – flow the tide DOES – and the future of the Charter is secure," wrote Ernest Jones in December 1852.

This conviction justified Chartist independence. The willingness of Chartists to rely on their own strength is the outstanding characteristic of the movement. At the local level, Chartism was often an integral part of the struggle for identity, dignity and improvement ... "Am I a man?" is a question which recurs in one form or another in Chartist speeches and poetry. Workmen, who were committed to education and self-help, had their own set of fears, values and objectives. In their support for Chartist schools, halls, churches, newspapers and estates; in their campaigns against capital punishment, army flogging and impressment; and in their belief that science and machinery should ultimately be harnessed to the benefit of all, we catch a glimpse of an alternative society – egalitarian, humane and harmonious ... Contemporaries were impressed by the initiative and independence shown by working men in the movements of this period. One suspects that some historians have underestimated the power, discretion and class feelings of ordinary Chartist members.'

From D. Jones, *Chartism and the Chartists* (1975).

KEY TERM:

Provenance

In general terms, **provenance** relates to origins. In the context of historical source material it also relates to origins. Provenance gives you the information you need to know, such as when a source was produced, what kind of source it is and, where appropriate, who wrote or said it. The provenance therefore can give vital clues to the value and reliability of a source for a particular purpose.

Tasks

1 Study sources 1, 3 and 4. Explain how you can use these sources to find out about the aims and priorities of the Chartists.

2 Study source 7. What impression does the *Punch* cartoonist intend to give of physical force Chartists? Explain your answer by detailed reference to the cartoon.

3 Do any other of these sources support this view of the Chartists? Explain your answer.

4 Choose *two* other sources which give a different impression of the Chartists. Explain in what ways the impressions are different.

5 Study source 8. Look at the **provenance** of this source. In the light of this, and of the information it contains, how useful do you think it is as evidence of the events of 10 April 1848?

6 Study all of the sources. Make a list of the weaknesses of Chartism to which these sources refer. As you make up your list, note which source gave you the information.

7 Study all of the sources. Do you think Chartism failed? Explain your answer by reference to these sources. You may make use of any further information you have on Chartism, either from this chapter or elsewhere. However, you should use this information to support, or to challenge, points made in the sources themselves.

Further reading

E. Royle, *Chartism* Longman Seminar Studies (Addison Wesley Longman, second edition, 1986) – the best introduction to the topic with short chapters and well-chosen sources.

J. T. Ward, *Chartism* (Batsford, 1973) – good for getting a detailed narrative.

A. Briggs (ed.), *Chartist Studies* (Macmillan, 1959) – a collection of regional essays which set new standards in Chartist scholarship for others to follow.

D. K. G. Thompson, *The Chartists* (Temple Smith, 1984) – the best detailed modern study which sees Chartism as a multi-faceted organisation.

F. C. Mather (ed.), *Chartism and Society* (Batsford, 1980) – an excellent collection of sources with some good commentary.

CAUSE AND CONSEQUENCE

17 The Anti-Corn Law League and the middle classes

Time chart

1815: Passage of corn law prohibits release of foreign corn on to the domestic market unless British price exceeds 80 shillings (£4) a quarter

1828: Corn law amended so that a sliding scale of duties introduced. Nominal rate of duty now applied when domestic price was 73 shillings (£3.65) a quarter

1838: Group of local radicals and businessmen form the Manchester Anti-Corn Law Association. Founders included J. B. Smith, Henry Ashworth, George Wilson and Archibald Prentice

1839: Anti-Corn Law League established (March) after Parliament had rejected the Manchester Association's petition for repeal of corn laws

1841: Candidates stand in the election specifically as opponents of the corn laws. They hope to make themselves a 'third party'. A series of high-profile by-elections are also fought by anti-corn law candidates. League funds also used to buy small plots of land to create more free-trade voters in county seats

1842: Revisions of the corn law to reduce overall level of duty: very heavy duty when price reached 51 shillings (£2.55), but light duty when domestic price reached 66 shillings (£3.30). Protectionist Duke of Buckingham resigned because he felt support for landed interest was now too limited

1843: The *Economist* newspaper was founded in order to publicise the case for free trade

1845: With support for the League declining, Peel announces his conversion to repeal of the corn laws

1846: Whig majority and Tory ministers combine to pass a bill repealing the corn laws

1849: Duties on import of foreign corn finally removed

Since they were organisations active at the same time, it used to be fashionable to contrast the 'success' of the Anti-Corn Law League with the 'failure' of the Chartists. The previous chapter showed that it is unwise to write the Chartists off as failures. In this chapter, we will cast a little cold water on the Anti-Corn Law League. Firstly, though, it might be useful to summarise some of the apparent advantages which the League had over the Chartists.

1 It had one great objective for which there was widespread support among the propertied classes, especially in the towns. The Chartists had six points which very few people with property supported.

2 The Anti-Corn Law League was widely trusted by urban businessmen, an increasingly influential section of the community. The Chartists were not.

3 The League was never short of cash. It made lavish donations to businessmen who gave up their time to the cause. The Chartists had far fewer resources.

4 The League had strong support in Parliament, particularly from the Whig-Liberal Party. The Chartists did not.

The Anti-Corn Law League: a failure?

Such a conclusion, however, does not tell anything like the whole truth. Chartism 'failed' only in the narrow sense of failing to achieve the six points. By the same token the Anti-Corn Law League 'succeeded' because the corn laws were repealed in 1846. Yet it is highly doubtful whether the corn laws were repealed *because* of Anti-Corn Law League pressure. Indeed, at the time Peel announced his conversion to corn law repeal, the Anti-Corn Law League was at its lowest ebb. Wheat prices had been dropping for some years. In 1845 they were about 30 shillings (£1.50) lower than the peak of 70 shillings (£3.50) a quarter reached in 1839. League speakers could no longer argue with confidence that the corn laws were keeping home prices artificially high. Some have even suggested that Peel waited until the strength was draining away from the League to announce his intentions on the corn laws. He was a traditional prime minister who hated the idea that his policies could have been influenced by pressure from outside Parliament (see chapter 13). Therefore, we might even say that the Anti-Corn Law League was a failure. It had been formed to bring such pressure on Westminster that politicians would be forced to abandon unpopular legislation. The pressure it was able to mount was substantial (see below). Yet it did not work. The government stood firm in the 1840s. Peel moved on the corn laws in his own time and, so far as the League was concerned, to his own agenda.

Why does the Anti-Corn Law League matter?

As so often in political life, what people at the time *thought* was very much more important than what historians 150 years later might conclude. Even had the corn laws not been repealed the League would be worth studying, for four main reasons:

1 *Radical symbols.* The League was taking up an issue which had been of central significance to political radicals for a generation. To economists, the 1815 corn law may have been just one more means of regulating supply of goods. To politicians of all persuasions, however, it was a powerful symbol. To radicals, it symbolised aristocratic predominance (see chapter 9). A Parliament of landowners had rigged the rules by passing legislation from which they, as a class, stood to benefit. Radicals characterised their struggle as one between the productive members of society, who worked hard for their living, and the unproductive, who idled and taxed their way to unmerited ease and luxury. So when the Manchester Anti-Corn Law Association declared its determination to be rid of the corn laws in 1838, it was doing more than opposing a trade regulation. It was challenging aristocratic predominance.

2 *Industrial heartland.* The League was founded in, and was always controlled from, Manchester – the cotton capital of the world. Cotton symbolised both new wealth and industrial progress. The founders of the League were all successful businessmen. J. B. Smith and Thomas Potter were both wealthy cotton dealers; the latter became Manchester's first Mayor. George Wilson, the League's President, was a starch and gum manufacturer. **Richard Cobden**, its organising genius, was a calico printer. In attacking the corn laws, they were attacking the aristocracy. It was very easy to characterise the Anti-Corn Law League as a struggle between industry and agriculture, middle classes against the aristocracy. Cobden and Bright both did so in their frequently class-based speeches. Certainly, those landowners who hastily organised 'Anti-Leagues' in rural counties like Suffolk and Sussex believed that they were fighting a class war on behalf of the traditional world against the vulgar pretensions of the 'business classes'.

> *'Corn and provision Laws are partial and unjust . . . they are calculated for the temporary enrichment of a small part of the community at the expense of the millions who subsist by honest industry.'*
>
> Richard Cobden in a letter challenging William Gladstone to a debate on the corn laws, 1841.

'Notwithstanding the hope that my Friend who has just addressed you has expressed, that it may not become a strife of classes, I am not sure that it has not already become such, and I doubt whether it can have any other character. I believe this to be a movement of the commercial and industrious classes against the lords and great proprietors of the soil . . . We have had landlord rule longer, far longer, than the life of the oldest man in this vast assembly, and I would ask you to look at the results of that rule . . . The landowners have had unlimited sway in Parliament and in the provinces . . . In all the great contests in which we have been engaged we have found that this ruling class have taken all the honours, while the people have taken all the scars . . . They sit down to make a law for the purpose of extorting from all the consumers of food a higher price than it is worth, that the extra price may find its way into the pockets of the proprietors of land, these proprietors being the very men by whom this infamous law is sustained.'

John Bright in a speech at Covent Garden, London, 19 December 1845.

PROFILE: *Richard Cobden*

Richard Cobden was born into a Sussex farming family in 1804, but made his money as a textile businessman. He rapidly assumed leadership of the Anti-Corn Law League and organised numerous campaigns to put pressure on the government. He was responsible for directing League activities towards the election of MPs who would not be 'party men' but would be single-mindedly concerned with the abolition of the corn laws. As he told Francis Place: '. . . we shall separate the question entirely from *party* politics and induce as many electors as possible to associate themselves together to form a body pledged only to the abolition of the corn law'. He represented the town of Stockport in Parliament from 1841 to 1847 and Yorkshire from 1847 to 1857. After defeat at the general election of 1857, he returned to Parliament in a by-election at Rochdale – John Bright's stamping ground. He remained a convinced free-trader all of his life and was the British representative in the 'Cobden–Chevalier' Treaty of 1860 which reduced tariffs on goods exported to and from France. Like many free-traders, he also hated war which he considered both barbaric and expensive. Though a fellow Liberal, he frequently criticised Palmerston for his aggressive foreign policy. He refused an offer of a cabinet post in Palmerston's government of 1859 and died in 1865.

KEY TERM:

Extra-parliamentary pressure group

As its name implies, **extra-parliamentary pressure groups** attempt to get political change by mobilising opinion outside Parliament. Successful groups usually have effective means of propaganda, which often involve appealing to people's sense of self-interest. Thus, the Anti-Corn Law League frequently employed emotive terms such as 'bread tax' in its propaganda, because it made a more direct impact than the rather distanced 'corn laws'. In the period before democracy, pressure groups aimed to make Parliament aware of abuses which they believed needed correcting. Some groups, like the League, had substantial representation in Parliament anyway, but nevertheless deserve the description 'extra-parliamentary' because the bulk of their work was done outside Parliament.

3 *Class politics?* If the Anti-Corn Law League thought its main opposition to be the idle aristocracy, there is no doubt that its working-class opponents thought that it represented a class enemy. Relations between Chartists and the League were extremely cool. It is not difficult to understand why. For Chartists, the Anti-Corn Law League symbolised middle-class betrayal in the 1832 Reform Act. Although a number of working-class groups were founded in places as diverse as Manchester, Carlisle and Leicester to press for the repeal of the corn laws, most Chartists remained resolute in their hatred of the League. Chartist heckling, scuffles and even violence at League meetings were all frequent. League lecturers hammered home their point time and time again: 'Repealing the corn laws will give working people cheap bread'. The Chartists had their answer ready: 'Cheap bread, they say, but they *mean* low wages'. We might conclude that the Anti-Corn Law League represented middle-class interests against those of both the aristocracy and the working classes.

4 *Propaganda.* The Anti-Corn Law League also matters because of the way it put its message across. It was not the first **extra-parliamentary pressure group**. A number of associations in the late eighteenth and early nineteenth centuries had attempted to convert reluctant MPs to the idea of parliamentary reform, for example (see chapter 6). In the range and sophistication of its methods, however, the League stands apart. It employed a number of articulate lecturers who toured the country banging the free-trade drum. It published a successful magazine, *The League*, and exerted powerful influence on a number of other newspapers and journals. The League's electoral strategy was ambitious and novel. Cobden's idea was to use League resources to build up a fund for fighting every by-election and also putting up a substantial number of League candidates in the most promising seats at general elections. This strategy has since been copied by many interest groups. Cobden was one of the first to appreciate that public attention can very much more effectively be concentrated on one issue at a by-election than in general elections. It has to be said, however, that Cobden's electoral ambitions ran a long way ahead of performance. In the boroughs the League followed up Peel's strategy by mounting a series of campaigns designed to ensure that as many supporters as possible were placed on the electoral register. In the counties the campaign to create 40-shilling freeholds had some initial success. However, far fewer seats were actually won than Cobden had hoped. **John Bright**, Cobden's great friend and political ally, warned him that the strategy was a waste even of the League's ample resources. Recent historians, indeed, have been a good deal more sceptical than earlier ones about the League's propaganda 'brilliance'. Nevertheless, the main purpose of propaganda is to gain attention – preferably favourable – for the cause. In our day, we might call such an exercise 'consciousness-

PROFILE: *John Bright*

John Bright was born into a Quaker cotton textile family in Rochdale in 1811, and was educated in a series of Quaker private schools until he was 15. He became associated with the Manchester Anti-Corn Law Association from its earliest days and then represented the Anti-Corn Law League in Rochdale. He became associated with Richard Cobden in 1841 and they formed one of the great political friendships of the nineteenth century. Bright's political ambitions were first met when he was elected MP for Durham City in 1843, representing it until elected one of Manchester's members in 1847. He served Manchester until his defeat at the general election of 1857. He then became MP for Birmingham. Here he established a reputation for fearless honesty and also as a supporter of the political aspirations of the working man. He consistently allied himself with radical Liberal causes, opposing the Crimean War and, in the late 1850s and 1860s, supporting further parliamentary reform. His long parliamentary career was characterised also by the quality of his oratory. He was one of the great platform speakers. Gladstone made him President of the Board of Trade in 1868 and he stayed in office until he suffered a breakdown in 1870, brought on by overwork and a sense that he was not mastering the administrative tasks required. He was also a minister under Gladstone in 1873–4 and 1880–82, but never again held departmental office. He resigned in protest against Gladstone's invasion of Egypt in 1882, and died in 1889.

raising'. Judged by this yardstick, Cobden and the League were very successful. Free trade became *the* issue of the day in the early 1840s.

Was the Anti-Corn Law League a united middle-class pressure group?

On one level, the answer is clearly 'Yes'. The overwhelming bulk of League support came from the middle classes. For a time it united the interests of the commercial middle classes, especially in cotton Lancashire, with the professional middle-class radicals (lecturers, teachers, lawyers and the like) who saw free trade as one of a number of highly desirable means of humbling an arrogant aristocracy.

Yet, when one looks beneath the surface confidence of League lecturers and business donations in 1841 or 1842, say, the famous League unity in support of free trade was built on shifting sands. League opponents were

KEY TERMS:

Secular education

Secular education was a policy supported by most nonconformists. 'Secular' means not being bound by religious rules. Nonconformists saw that the bulk of state support for educating the poor was being taken by the Church of England, which was using it – so they believed – to indoctrinate the children of the poor with Anglican propaganda. Those who supported secular education believed that the basic groundings should be taught without reference to any particular sect. Very few believers in secular education in Victorian Britain were nonbelievers. Secular education was an objective taken up in order to reduce the influence of the Church of England. Not surprisingly, most supporters of secular education were nonconformists. Atheists and agnostics were few in number and had little political influence.

not slow to pick up a crucial area of division. For some Leaguers, mostly the industrial businessmen, the abolition of the corn laws was indeed the issue, and the only issue. For others, including both of its most famous spokesmen, it was a central plank in a much bigger campaign – to pull the mighty aristocracy down from its seat of power. Many Leaguers were also prominent middle-class radicals, and middle-class radicals had an altogether wider agenda. The successful abolition of the corn laws was but a staging post (however important). Behind free trade came attacks on:

- *land laws*, which preserved aristocratic privileges by making it next to impossible to buy and sell hereditary land on the open market
- *game laws*, which gave the aristocracy a special privilege to kill wild animals for their own enjoyment and benefit
- the special *privileges of the Church of England*. Bright was only the most prominent of the nonconformists who believed that the established Church buttressed a corrupt aristocracy.

All of these items on the radical agenda could be rendered as legitimate extensions of free trade: free trade in land, free trade in those things nourished by the land, free trade in faith. The middle-class radical's kitbag also included other rationalist radical objectives such as **secular education** and republicanism.

Divisions appeared between those who saw the repeal of the corn laws as an end in itself and those who saw it as a means to an end. Peel was only one of many establishment politicians to see how the division could be exploited to the advantage of the old order. Timely abolition of the corn laws could preserve the rule of the aristocracy by taking the heat out of a potentially damaging campaign. It could reunite the interests of landed and commercial property. Just as Whig policy on political reform in 1832 had broken up a damaging alliance between working and middle classes, so Peel's initiative in 1845–6, damaging though it was to his own political party (see chapter 13), had similar benefits for the established order. It detached mere free-traders from that smaller, but politically more threatening, minority with a wider radical agenda. It also helped to heal the rifts between property owners. In the years after 1846, also, both Peel and the Whig government which followed him were able to point out that free trade did not have the damaging consequences which defensive landowners had predicted. No massive European surpluses were stacked in the North Sea waiting to flood the English market, carrying away a large proportion of the English aristocracy with it. It is a delicious irony that wheat prices in the free-trade 1850s were only a notch or two lower than they had been in the protected 1840s. During the 1850s and 1860s, against all the expectations of protectionists like the Dukes of Buckingham and Richmond, British agriculture entered a period of high investment and general profitability, often called 'High Farming'. The real free-trade reckoning would come later (see chapter 25).

Taking notes

This chapter has been mainly about the activities of the Anti-Corn Law League, but you will probably have noticed that it also raises some wider issues. If you are taking notes on this chapter, remember to refer back to the general guidance given at the end of chapter 8. In the case of this chapter you would probably find it useful to group your notes under particular headings. The following is an example. Though you may want to add more factual detail to this skeleton, remember that you are making notes for a purpose. It is always useful to have questions in mind as you do so. The headings here either *are* questions themselves, or should suggest questions to you about the significance of the Anti-Corn Law League.

- *Aims*. Getting rid of corn laws – est. of free trade in corn.
- *Why*. Free trade good for everyone? Reducing price of bread? Part of old programme of radical reform (remember to refer to ch. 6). Possibility of factory owners being able to pay lower wages and increase their profits (the Chartist belief)?
- *Methods*. Propaganda via meetings, lectures, well-supported publications; electoral strategy – registering more voters, putting up cands in high-profile by-elections.
- *Support from* many in middle classes, esp. Lancashire businessmen. Plenty in Parl. also wanted free trade (*NB* contrast with Chartists and democracy).
- *Remember also*. Free trade led on to other aims for some rads, like John Bright. These included: land reform, ending game laws, secular education.
- *Unity of ACLL*. Probably not as great as once thought. Divisions between 'one-issue' people and genuine radicals.
- *Opposed by*. Most Chartists (class hostility?); protectionist landowners who thought free trade would ruin them; gvt which hated pressure being put on MPs from outside Parl.
- *Success*. Corn Laws were repealed but when ACLL in decline. More credit to Peel than to Cobden. Is ACLL less successful than we used to think? Room for different interpretations.

Don't forget the purpose of the devices used in each chapter:

- The **time chart** gives you specific information arranged chronologically. Use it to pick out particular bits of information to link with general themes.
- **Profiles** highlight the careers of leading figures, material here relevant to the chapter, but other material from earlier, or later, in an individual's life. It might be useful to cross-refer (for example, material on Cobden's relationship with Palmerston from the profile in this chapter will be useful in chapters 18 and 20).
- **Key terms** help with phrases which you don't fully understand.

All of these devices should help you draw up your notes. Make full use of them. Get used to including them in your attempt to make sense of a new topic.

Further reading

Norman McCord, *The Anti-Corn Law League, 1838–46* (Allen and Unwin, 1958) – still the best detailed study.

D. Read, *Cobden and Bright: A Victorian Political Partnership* (Arnold, 1967).

D. A. Hamer, *The Politics of Electoral Pressure* (Hassocks, 1977). Chapter 5 is on the Anti-Corn Law League.

P. Adelman, *Victorian Radicalism: The Middle Class Experience, 1830–1914* (Addison Wesley Longman, 1984). Chapter 1 suggests that the League was the best example of a radical middle-class organisation.

THEMATIC

18 Did Britain really rule the waves? Power and foreign affairs

Time chart

1834: Quadruple Alliance of Britain, France, Spain and Portugal settles disputed succession questions in Spain and Portugal. Palmerston succeeds in stopping succession of absolutist rulers to the thrones of these countries

1839: Independence of Belgium confirmed, and the boundaries of Belgium and the Netherlands are settled

1840: The Treaty of London imposes settlement in war between Turkey (Ottoman Empire) and Egypt. British forces attack Acre and persuade Mehemet Ali, the Pasha (effectively ruler) of Egypt to come to terms

Treaty of Waitangi established British sovereignty in New Zealand

1841: Convention of the Straits settles affairs in the Middle East. Britain manages to check Russian and French ambitions as Ottoman Empire becomes weaker

Palmerston leaves office as Foreign Secretary after the Whigs lose the general election. Earl of Aberdeen takes over foreign affairs

1842: Treaty of Nanking ends the 'Opium War' with China (begun in 1839) to Britain's advantage. Britain gets access to Chinese ports and Hong Kong becomes a British colony

Webster–Ashburton Treaty settles territorial boundaries between the United States and the British colony of Canada

1846: Peel's government falls and Palmerston resumes as Foreign Secretary

1847–8: Palmerston suspected by the authorities in Austria of helping revolutionaries and also of supporting claims for Italian unification

1850: Palmerston asserts ('Don Pacifico' debate) that Britain will support the rights of British citizens abroad against attack from other powers. Palmerston takes opportunity to threaten the Greeks

1851: Palmerston dismissed as Foreign Secretary. Replaced by Earl Granville till 1852 then, during the Aberdeen coalition, first by Russell (1852–3) himself and then by the Earl of Clarendon (1853–5)

1854: After many years of suspicion, Britain and France sign an alliance designed to curb Russian threats of expansion in the eastern Mediterranean

1854–6: Crimean War against Russia: war eventually won but many criticisms made of the quality of the British army. The Treaty of Paris, which ended the war, sees Britain and Russia both guarantee Turkish independence but relations between these two powers remain cool

1855: Palmerston becomes Prime Minister during the Crimean War; Clarendon continues as Foreign Secretary

1856–60: Further wars with China, involving Britain, France and the United States, result in victories for the western powers. By Treaty of Peking (1860), more Chinese ports opened up to trade and more diplomatic activity. Chinese empire weakened

1857: Indian Mutiny breaks out, threatening British rule – 30,000 British troops sent out and the Mutiny put down, with considerable bloodshed, the following year

1858: Palmerston's government falls. Earl of Malmesbury briefly Foreign Secretary in Derby's minority government. When Palmerston returns to office in 1859, Russell takes over as Foreign Secretary

1859: Distrust of French ambitions inhibits support by Palmerston for the unification of Italy. Britain nevertheless happy to accept unification of southern and northern states when this is established in 1861

1861–5: Civil war in the United States; Britain remains neutral despite economic interests with the cotton states of the South, and considerable sympathy of many aristocratic politicians, including Palmerston, for the southern cause. Two disputes threatened neutrality: the North's capture of two southern politicians on the British ship *Trent* (1861) and northern grievance in 1862 that the government had not prevented a British-built ship, the *Alabama*, leaving Birkenhead to augment the Confederate (Southern) fleet. Palmerston avoids being dragged into war

1863: Palmerston refuses to support Polish revolt designed to secure independence from Russia

1863–4: British attempts to stop the duchies of Schleswig and Holstein (personally joined to the Crown of Denmark) being annexed by Prussia fail. Bismarck calls Palmerston's bluff. Major diplomatic defeat, not least because the King of Denmark's daughter, Princess Alexandra, had just married Edward, Prince of Wales

1865: After Palmerston's death, Russell becomes Prime Minister and Earl of Clarendon resumes as Foreign Secretary. He is succeeded (1866) by Lord Stanley, son of the incoming Tory Prime Minister, the Earl of Derby

1867: British North America Act creates 'Dominion Status' for Canada, effectively giving Britain's largest colony self-governing status in domestic affairs

In 1740 an obscure eighteenth-century British dramatist, James Thompson, composed the verses which became synonymous with British patriotism. In slightly amended form, they still provoke thousands of concert-goers to ostentatious, vulgar and anachronistic ritual at the last night of the annual Promenade concerts in London's Albert Hall:

> When Britain first, at heaven's command,
> Arose from out the azure main,
> This was the charter of the land
> And guardian angels sung this strain:
> 'Rule, Britannia, rule the waves;
> Britons never will be slaves.'

KEY TERM:

Gunboat diplomacy

A style of diplomacy associated with Viscount Palmerston. The term was coined to describe the kind of negotiations backed up by threats. Palmerston often said that other powers, especially smaller ones, usually wanted to avoid war with Britain. Gunboats carried medium-sized guns and were adept at manoeuvring in rivers. Therefore the threat 'to send a gunboat' usually achieved the results he wanted. Both Queen Victoria and many British politicians disliked Palmerston's bombastic approach, believing that Britain should use its strength in more orthodox and measured ways.

In the middle years of the nineteenth century, it seemed that Thompson's wishes had been granted. Naval supremacy after the Battle of Trafalgar (see chapter 7) was unchallengeable. Along with the country's ever-growing industrial might, it was one of the two pillars which supported Britain's elevated status as the most powerful nation in the world. It seemed to many patriotic Britons, also, that the nation had bred a statesman perfectly in tune with the times. **Viscount Palmerston**, it seemed, would never shrink from proclaiming Britain's greatness, or from teaching presumptuous foreigners a lesson. If British interests were threatened, Palmerston would always send a **gunboat** to sort the foreigners out.

The main theme of this chapter is the difference between image and reality. Three main questions will dominate the discussion:

1. Was Britain in reality the all-powerful state it appeared to be?
2. Was Palmerston's foreign policy as forthright, patriotic and aggressive as it appeared to be?

PROFILE: *Viscount Palmerston*

Henry Temple, third **Viscount Palmerston**, who was born in London in 1784, came from a Warwickshire family which had built up extensive landed interests in Ireland. The Palmerston family title was an Irish one, which meant that he could sit in the House of Commons. He entered the Commons for the rotten borough of Newport (Isle of Wight) in 1807, and was soon a junior minister. He served as Secretary at War continuously from 1809 to 1828. His early career was as a Tory, and he became associated with George Canning's more liberal wing, leaving office with Huskisson soon after Wellington became Prime Minister in 1828. He joined the Whigs in 1830, thus beginning a career as a senior Whig, or Liberal, minister which lasted until his death. He was Foreign Secretary 1830–34, 1835–41 and 1846–51. Though he had a brief spell as Home Secretary, with rather reformist policies, in the Aberdeen coalition (1852–5), his main interests were in foreign affairs. He became associated in the public imagination with aggressive policy, though an aggressive image often belied both more caution and more duplicity. Despite his very long period in office, he was frequently mistrusted by ministerial colleagues, who felt that he played far too much on his public reputation as a bluff, honest patriot. Some, like Gladstone, thought his colourful, and adulterous, private life shameful. He was Prime Minister for most of the last decade of his life (1855–8 and 1859–65) and died in office, soon after winning a general election in 1865, and just before his 81st birthday.

3 Was foreign policy in reality so different when it was not in Palmerston's hands?

As you consider these questions, you will find it useful to refer to the detail given in the time chart. This provides the chronology from which you can piece the story together.

The limits of British power

Britain did not seek world domination in any conventional sense. The country was no militant, aggressive state always on the prowl for new territory, though much was acquired in this period to support commercial activity. It *was*, however, a nation whose industry and trade were both expanding with unprecedented rapidity. Foreign policy aims were closely tied up with economic goals, and Britain relied heavily upon its navy to protect its ever-growing commercial activity. The value of British exports in the mid-1850s was more than seven times higher than in the 1780s. Almost as important was the worldwide cast of this activity. Exports to Asia were worth more than £20 million in the mid-1850s, compared with less than £2 million in the 1780s, while Africa, Australasia and Latin America all provided substantial markets.

The strategic weakness of all this was that it left British defences overstretched. The number of generally small new territories acquired between the 1830s and the 1870s included Gold Coast, Natal, Aden, Hong Kong, Burma and New Zealand, in addition to further acquisitions in Australia, Canada, India and South Africa. All needed defending. It is too often forgotten, since Britain found itself at war on the continent of Europe only once between 1815 and 1914, how often it was at war elsewhere. In this period, Britain was involved in wars, border disputes and colonial conflicts in China (twice), Afghanistan, Persia and India, in addition to the famous conflict in the Crimea. The government relied for the most part on the navy and on colonial forces to do the actual fighting. After 1815, with policy priorities usually requiring defence cuts, Britain was certainly nothing like a military machine. From the early 1820s until the outbreak of the Crimean War, the cost of the army and navy never

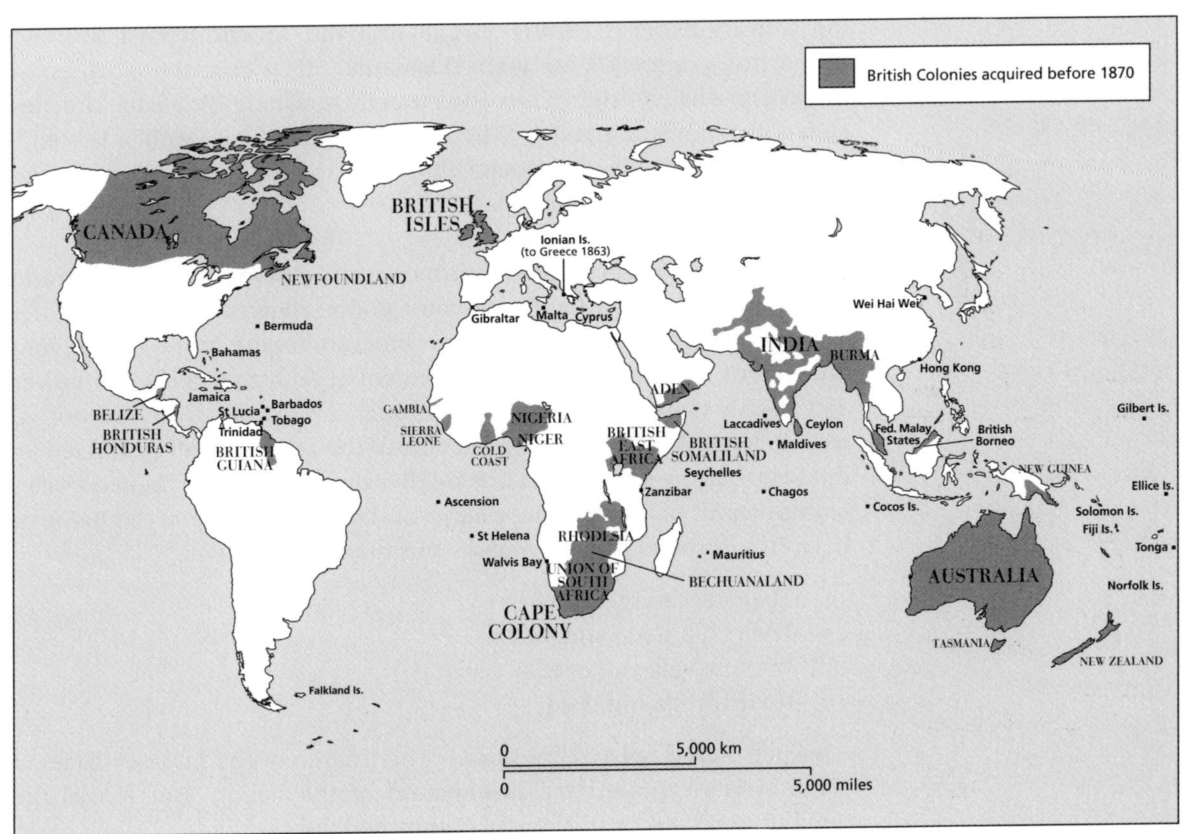

Figure 18.1 Map showing the British colonies, 1870

exceeded £18 million. During the last few years of the Napoleonic Wars, the army and navy had cost in excess of £60 million.

Within Europe, also, Britain's responses were determined by strategic considerations. It was vital to find a peaceful and permanent solution to the problem of Belgium's emergence as an independent nation, since Belgium was a crucial buffer against French, or possibly Prussian, expansion towards the North Sea. Palmerston was ambivalent about nationalism in Italy. In the late 1850s he wished to loosen Austria's grip in southern Italy, but sustain it in the north because he feared French expansion south of the Alps. As usual British ministers wished to preserve stable power blocs in Europe and Palmerston wanted Austria to continue as 'a great power in the centre of the Continent'. He was powerless, however, to prevent the degree of unification which had occurred by the end of 1861 and the Austrian humiliation which resulted. In Poland, where Britain had no obvious interests, Palmerston and Russell were not prepared to support a nationalist uprising in 1863 and rebuffed Napoleon III's approach that there should be an Anglo-French initiative in support of a nation struggling to be free.

In the 1860s, indeed, relatively little British diplomacy went right. True, the country avoided getting sucked into the American civil war but Palmerston's attempts to warn Bismarck off taking the duchies of Schleswig and Holstein into increasingly grasping Prussian clutches ended in humiliating failure. The Prussian general von Moltke brutally, but not inaccurately, concluded that 'England is as powerless on the Continent as she is presuming'.

The Crimean War did involve British interests. Aberdeen, Clarendon and Palmerston all agreed that Russia must not be allowed to profit from the ever more palpable weakness of the Ottoman Empire by expanding into the eastern Mediterranean, thus threatening both the balance of power and British trade routes. The war, though eventually won, did not go well. It demonstrated the consequences of the years of neglect suffered by the British army since 1815. It is richly ironic that one of the most celebrated actions of the war, the Charge of the Light Brigade at the Battle of Balaclava, resulted from a woefully misinterpreted order.

> Theirs not to reason why,
> Theirs but to do and die
> Into the valley of death
> Rode the six hundred

– gushed Alfred Lord Tennyson in 'The Charge of the Light Brigade', a poem which captured the imagination of the nation. But it was the wrong valley – and a total waste of time and life.

Palmerston and his critics

Palmerston's foreign policy only *appears* to match the bulldog spirit of John Bull. It is true that he was prepared to browbeat weaker opponents. He ordered the blockade of Piraeus, the port of Athens in 1850, demanding compensation from Greece for loss and damage done to the property of the dubious Portuguese Jewish adventurer and speculator, Don Pacifico, who had claimed British citizenship since he had been born on the British territory of Gibraltar. He was also prepared to read lessons in the virtues of representative government to the central European powers, notably the Austro-Hungarian Empire. He was certainly not above using the press (as one of his early mentors, George Canning, had done) to build up a reputation for bluff patriotism and to give out messages that Britain would not be pushed around. He manipulated long-standing British anti-Catholic prejudice at various times as an aid to his frequently anti-French foreign policy.

The courts of the central European powers – Austria and Prussia – hated Palmerston, regarding him as boorish, dangerous and unreliable. Well-publicised support for liberal and nationalist principles went down particularly badly there during the revolutions of 1848–9. Most of Melbourne's Whig colleagues were severely critical of Palmerston's diplomatic isolation of France during attempts to settle the question of Mehemet Ali and his threat to the Ottoman Empire in 1839–41. They thought that he risked a war for which the country was not prepared. In the late 1840s Queen Victoria and Prince Albert were severely critical of Palmerston's policy and demeanour. They also feared that some of his 'liberal' statements might encourage revolutionaries and weaken established authority throughout the continent. Albert believed that Britain's low reputation in continental Europe in the late 1840s resulted from the lack of trust in Palmerston.

Change or continuity?

In reality, Palmerston's policies were usually much more cautious than they sounded, especially when magnified in newspapers or embellished during the public speeches he made during tours of the country as prime minister in the late 1850s and early 1860s. Palmerston adapted long-standing foreign policy objectives to changing conditions:

1 He believed in a balance of power in Europe. This involved keeping France in check in the west and, of ever-growing importance, curbing Russia's ambitions in the Mediterranean.

KEY TERM:

Populist

Populism, as a specific term, was first coined to describe different popular political movements in the United States and Russia at the end of the nineteenth century. It has acquired a more useful general meaning, however, which is the relevant one here. Populism involves taking up policies with wide appeal – often policies which seem too simple, or otherwise do not appeal – to the political elite or to a sophisticated audience. Thus, the patriotic element in Palmerston's policies undoubtedly struck a chord with many working people and also among the non-political middle classes. It was precisely Palmerston's appeal beyond the political elite which many of his fellow aristocrats found so distasteful.

2 He did not want direct involvement on the European continent, but he supported moves towards more 'constitutional' (*i.e.* non-absolutist) regimes. He did this partly because public opinion was much more liberal than absolutist and partly because he knew that representative governments would have substantial middle-class involvement. A large proportion of the middle classes were traders, bankers and manufacturers. Industrial Britain could do business with them.

3 His objectives lay in the advancement of Britain as an industrial and trading nation. This involved giving priority to the navy over the army and had important consequences:

a The geographical over-extension referred to above. As shrewd diplomats in Europe realised, because so many interests central to Britain's commercial well-being lay outside Europe, it was highly unlikely that Britain would challenge the larger powers on the continent. Bismarck exploited this perception brilliantly, knowing that Palmerston's bark was usually much worse than his bite.

b The army was underfunded. Palmerston's political career benefited from public criticism of the Aberdeen government's Crimean War policy but Palmerston as Foreign Secretary had done nothing to reverse two generations of military neglect.

Palmerston's approach to foreign policy can be criticised as being too **populist**. It might be objected that he underestimated two growing threats: that to European stability presented by the aggressive policies of Bismarck's Prussia and that to British commercial supremacy by the United States. However, it is difficult to see what Britain could have done about either. Nor is it plausible to suggest that other ministers in charge of foreign affairs had a radically different agenda. Differences lay much more in tone and personality than in ultimate objective.

The **Earl of Aberdeen** might perhaps be presented as offering a distinctively different contribution in foreign affairs. When he became Foreign Secretary in 1841, for the third time, and for what turned out to be his longest and most influential stint, he began by continuing Palmerston's policy towards the United States, but his emollient personality may have helped to resolve outstanding disputes between Canada and the US more effectively. In European affairs, also, Aberdeen was much keener on forming harmonious personal relations with ministers such as Metternich and Guizot than ever Palmerston was. There is no doubt which foreign secretary was the more appreciated in European courts. For Palmerston, that was precisely the point. He believed that a degree both of bluff and sabre-rattling was necessary in order to carry on diplomacy from a position of strength. There is, however, little evidence that Aberdeen, or indeed Russell or Clarendon, who both succeeded him in the early 1850s, jeopardised any significant British interests. Palmerston is the foreign secretary who is remembered from this era. Fame is, however, not invariably the same thing as effectiveness. Britain's diplomatic hand was never as strong as the nation's economic strength might lead unwary observers to think. This was especially so in respect of affairs in central Europe. Despite Palmerstonian bluster and his frequent detailed, and withering, criticisms of the efforts of those he considered lesser men, all administrations in mid-nineteenth-century Britain recognised the fact.

PROFILE: *Earl of Aberdeen*

George Hamilton Gordon, fourth **Earl of Aberdeen** was born in 1784, the same year as Palmerston, into a Scottish family which had been supporters of the Stuarts until well into the eighteenth century. Like Palmerston, he was educated at Harrow and a rivalry developed between them. Aberdeen entered the House of Lords as a Scottish representative peer in 1806, and was keen to uphold the traditions of Pitt the Younger, who had died just before he entered Parliament. He first held high office as Foreign Secretary in 1828 after Wellington had stimulated the resignation of Huskisson, Palmerston and other so-called 'liberal Tories'. He was briefly Secretary at War in the first Peel administration but is much better known for his service as Foreign Secretary in the second administration of 1841–6. Here he gained the reputation for careful statesmanship and a determination to avoid war. He helped to settle various border disputes with the United States. He left office with Peel and remained a prominent member of the 'Peelite' group in Parliament. He became Prime Minister in 1852, heading a coalition of Peelites and Whigs. He was never able to establish authority over Palmerston, his Home Secretary who despised him, or Lord John Russell, who found it difficult to cede seniority to him. The crises in the Crimea brought his government down in 1855 and he did not hold office again. Compared with Palmerston, he had a calm and reflective temperament, and also pursued scholarly researches into the ancient world. He died in 1860.

Tasks

1 Study Figures 18.1, 7.1, 7.2 (page 55) and 10.1 (page 89). Use the information in these maps to get a sense of the *extent* of British influence and involvement in the mid-nineteenth century. Now link the evidence of the maps with the information given in the time chart at the beginning of the chapter (pages 165–7).

2 Split into two groups:
  - **a** One group should look at the treatment of Palmerston's foreign policy given in this chapter. Do you think it is a favourable one or not? Report back to the class as a whole, giving the reasons for your judgement.
  - **b** Some historians have said that Palmerston represents a different tradition in foreign policy from Aberdeen. How strong is the evidence for this view? Report back to the class, giving reasons to support your opinion.

3 Look back to chapter 10. Which aspects of Palmerston's foreign policy attitudes and methods are closer to those of Castlereagh and which to those of Canning? Make a list of the points in separate columns, headed 'Castlereagh', 'Canning' and 'Either/both'.

Further reading

The books by Chamberlain and Cain and Hopkins, referred to at the end of chapter 10, remain useful. See also:

M. Chamberlain, *Lord Palmerston* (GBC Books, Cardiff, 1987) – a brief, but authoritative biography.

D. Southgate, *'The Most English Minister': The Policies and Politics of Palmerston* (Macmillan, 1966).

J. Ridley, *Lord Palmerston* (Constable, 1970) – both of these are weighty and detailed biographies.

M. Chamberlain, *Lord Aberdeen: A Political Biography* (Addison Wesley Longman, 1983) – the best modern biography of a neglected prime minister whose foreign policy also receives less praise than it deserves.

THEMATIC

19 The age of the railway: social change and industrial maturity in mid-Victorian Britain

Time chart

1825: Stockton to Darlington railway opened in north-east England: the world's first passenger railway but used mostly for taking coal from County Durham to the Tees, and then by ship to London. It used stationary engines and horses as well as steam

1830: Liverpool to Manchester railway opened; William Huskisson accidently killed at the celebrations to mark its opening

1836: Railway opened from London to Birmingham, and a spur to Manchester opened in the following year

1837–40: First major burst of railway investment – 'railway mania'

1840s: Decade of great railway expansion and mergers between companies produces one or two 'giants' such as the Midland, Great Northern and the London-North Western. By 1850 only 22 railway companies are in business, compared with about 200 in 1843

1840: 1,500 miles of track open

1841: First railway in Wales opened (from Cardiff to Merthyr); Thomas Cook organises the world's first passenger excursion (from Loughborough to Leicester)

1842: Line opened from Edinburgh to Glasgow

1844: Railway Act creates a separate Railways Board with powers of inspection and accident investigation. Railway companies obliged to run at least one service a day for passengers who would pay no more than 1d a mile ('Parliamentary Trains')

1846–7: Second 'railway mania' – heavy investment in railways

1850: 6,000 miles of track open; line opened from London to Edinburgh

1851: Great Exhibition in London's Crystal Palace: an international showcase for industrial and technological exhibits. It is designed, in part, to demonstrate Britain's industrial lead. Thomas Cook's excursions enabled thousands of relatively humble folk to travel to London to visit the Exhibition

1856: Development of Bessemer process for manufacture of steel helps to boost metals industries

1860: 9,000 miles of track open

1862–5: Third main instalment of 'railway mania'

1864: Opening of Metropolitan Railway in London helps to speed the process of suburban housing development

1870: 13,000 miles of track open

Railways are the most evocative and powerful symbol of Victorian progress. Though the first purpose-built railway, from Stockton to Darlington, opened 12 years before the Queen ascended the throne, the early years of her reign witnessed the most extraordinary explosion of activity. Thousands of miles of track were rapidly laid, by companies funded by investors, small and large, who appeared to believe – at least during the three 'railway manias' (see time chart) – that no railway could ever fail. Investment in railway companies was particularly popular in the north-west of England. Though railway shares were not always a licence to print money, and many companies were short of capital during construction of track, returns were frequently very impressive. In the mid-1840s the Stockton–Darlington railway was paying investors a massive 15 per cent dividend.

In the peak year 1847, more than a quarter of a million railway workers – 'navvies', carrying on the name from the original canal 'navigators' – were employed. We may think that we know who built the railways. The stereotype 'navvy' is the unskilled Irishman, desperate for employment and prepared to work on the most laborious and dangerous projects. This is largely myth. Recent immigrants from Ireland did find much employment on railway construction at the time of the Irish potato famine (1845–7) and afterwards, many moving around the country following the work. Most railway labourers were recruited from within local populations and did not travel long distances once the railway moved on.

Railways also helped the development of several professions. Railway engineering was a specialised and highly skilled task. Construction helped to separate the distinct elements of mechanical and civil engineering. Some of the most impressive evidence of the skill of nineteenth-century civil engineers remains with us in the form of railway viaducts, such as the Sankey Viaduct on the Liverpool–Manchester railway, which linked with the boats of the Sankey Navigation, or the Lockwood Viaduct, with its 32 arches, completed just west of Huddersfield in 1848. Tunnels are less obvious, but require no less skill to design and build. The Woodhead tunnel, through Pennine moorlands on the line between Sheffield and Manchester, was more than three miles long, took from 1839 to 1845 to build and was worked on by 1,500 navvies at a time.

The legal profession gained profitable employment in sorting out the often contentious area of landownership, sale and conveyancing. Several lawyers made themselves almost as rich as shrewd landowners from negotiations over the sale of highly prized land. Railways needed sharp lawyers to protect their interests in contests with the agents of such prominent landowners as the Earls of Derby and Sefton, for example, who owned substantial property in Liverpool and made large sums out of their sale for railway development. The actuarial side of railway business also helped the emergence of accountancy as a separate profession. Accountants were also needed to sort out the mess when companies failed and when compensation claims were under consideration.

The main benefits of steam technology in transport were heavily reduced journey times. Journeys from London to York in the 1820s, for example, took almost 36 hours by even the speediest stage coaches. Even this was a huge improvement on the 3–4-day journeys common for the rich in the 1750s. The railway made the same journey in the early 1840s in about eight hours. Some have argued that the advent of the railway made Britain an integrated nation – rather than a series of overlapping but distinct regions and countries – for the first time.

As in so much else concerning the industrial revolution, Britain was first in the field. Other nations initially followed at what was both a respectful and an envious distance. It is not surprising that British expertise was in heavy demand from abroad from the 1840s onwards. The British passion for railways also extended to investment. In the second half of the nineteenth century many investors happily supported new schemes, especially in the Americas, to link places they had never heard of in countries which they could not certainly identify on a map. It was a common, and perhaps a justified, complaint of late nineteenth-century businessmen that too much capital was invested abroad. Much of this investment was in speculative railway schemes. At mid-century, Britain's railway lead was substantial. In 1850 it had opened almost twice as much railway track as Germany and more than three times as much as France.

Railways also helped existing industries. Their impact on iron, for example, was massive. In the second half of the 1840s, almost 20 per cent of pig-iron output was used in constructing the track ('permanent way'). Economic linkage between railways and iron, however, went well beyond this. Pig-iron output was almost four times higher in 1850 than in 1830. The application of steam technology to shipping in the 1850s and 1860s advanced it still further. Exports of iron and steel products were three times more valuable in the 1850s than the 1840s.

Coal was the mineral which provided the power for railway engines and for most other forms of power. Figure 19.1 shows how rapidly coal production expanded in the first half of the nineteenth century.

Mining was a labour-intensive industry and both the numbers and output of the pits in the North-East, central Scotland, South Wales and Yorkshire expanded massively. Some economic historians speak of a 'second', and more far-reaching, industrial revolution. Recent work, making use of **counterfactual analysis** and terms like **social savings**, has weakened the case for revolutionary change. However, the most sophisticated estimates suggest that, by the middle of the 1860s, the British economy would have been more than 10 per cent smaller if railways had not been constructed. Some important new developments, such as the new Post Office service after 1840, could not have happened without railways. The main effects of railways on larger industries seem to have been expansionist rather than innovatory. The *technology* of iron production, engineering, mining and the like was not fundamentally changed by the railways, but *output* was substantially increased.

It was to the railways, also, that politicians and other influential folk most naturally turned as they sought ways of celebrating progress. Queen Victoria's husband, Prince Albert, was heavily involved in designing the Great Exhibition of 1851. It was to be both an international festival and an elaborate hymn to the human ingenuity involved in harnessing the bounties of nature for the general benefit. But it was held in London and it proved an unrepeatable opportunity to demonstrate Britain's superiority in many economic and technological fields. Those who inspected the many foreign exhibits with a discriminating eye could detect that there were already specialised areas in which British was not 'best'. Only a tiny handful, however, doubted Britain's continued ability to set the pace. They were even outnumbered by aesthetes who condemned the vulgarity of an exhibition housed in a vast glass dome more than one-third of a mile long which had patently captured the imagination of all classes. Secretly, they resented its immense popular success. The message of the Great Exhibition was insistently upbeat: free trade, peace and prosperity were the triple stars moving in profitable conjunction to augur Britain's continued role (even its manifest destiny) as the most prosperous nation on earth.

KEY TERMS:

Counterfactual analysis

Counterfactual analysis is concerned with attempting to work out what would have happened had some key variable been absent. It is 'what if?' history. In the case of railways, economic historians have tried to calculate the value of railways by taking them out of the equation. Thus, counterfactual analysis on the savings made in transporting goods and people uses actual costs of transport by the best alternative means available in a given location – ships, barges, stage-coaches, etc. These are measured against known costs of rail transport.

Social savings

The term **social savings** has been devised by economic historians attempting to estimate the benefits derived from railways. It is closely linked with counterfactual analysis. One measure is obtained by subtracting the total cost of transporting passengers and goods by rail from that involved in transporting them by water or road. The difference in the mid-nineteenth century was almost always in favour of rail and is termed the social saving. The sum is simple, but the assumptions are complex. For example, in order to agree that a genuine social saving has been achieved, we need to assume that the amount of money earned by investors who put their money into railways was much the same as from other forms of investment over a period of time. This, and other assumptions, are impossible to test precisely.

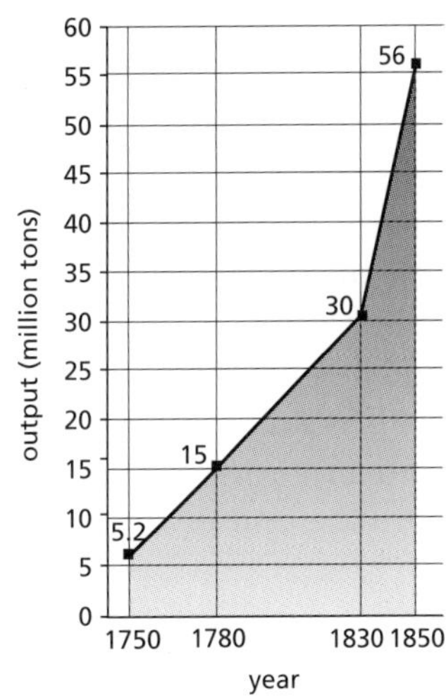

Figure 19.1 *Coal output 1750–1850*

> *'Never have I seen clearer evidence of general well-being. Our country is, no doubt, in a most happy and prosperous state. Free trade, peace, and freedom.'*
>
> The view of Absolom Watkin, an old campaigner for the repeal of the corn laws, in 1853. [The next year the Crimean War began.]

Change

What features of nineteenth-century life were most changed by the advent of the railways? The obvious ones seem to be:

- *speedier and more efficient transport* – of freight, especially bulky goods
- *stimulus of other industries* – particularly coal and iron
- *new opportunities for investment* – especially during 'railway manias', when many small investors unwisely committed more than they could afford
- *expanded opportunities for migration* – railways assisted movement both short- and long-term. They also improved flows of information about job opportunities. The damaging over-supply of rural labourers in the south of England became less acute once railways began to serve agricultural communities extensively after mid-century.
- *extended opportunities for many,* especially the more prosperous, *to work at a distance from home.* Commuting became increasingly common. Manchester's middle classes, for example, moved out of the centre of the city, following railway lines which transformed first Didsbury and Victoria Park three or four miles to the south and, by 1860, Sale, Altrincham, Cheadle Hulme, Bramhall and Wilmslow. Places in a radius between 5 and 12 miles south and east of Manchester became, and have remained, highly eligible and fashionable suburbs.
- *substantial alterations in the physical appearance of cities* – railway construction often displaced ordinary people and many dwellings were knocked down to make room. Much time and effort was spent on the construction of railway stations. Classical designs, such as the arch at Euston (now demolished), were common and many large stations were so opulently designed that they can be seen almost as secular cathedrals. Cubitt's glass and stone structure at London's King's Cross in 1850 has been widely praised. So was J. P. Pratchett's classical design for Huddersfield (1847–8) and, in 1877, Thomas Prosser's completely redesigned York station built in iron and glass and on a curve.
- *the creation of new towns* – some places, like Crewe, Swindon and Wolverton, were new 'one-industry' towns created by the railway.

Other new towns, like Barrow-in-Furness at the extreme north-west of Lancashire in the 1850s and Middlesborough, at the north-eastern edge of the old county of Yorkshire, were based on the iron industry but dependent on an efficient railway system. For many years, the railway was the only direct means of approaching Barrow by land from the south or east since engineers had built bridges across the rivers Kent and Leven. Travel by poor-quality road involved long detours. The advent of the railways also fundamentally altered the economic structure of several ancient towns. It would not be a wild exaggeration to describe Darlington (Co. Durham), York, Derby and Ashford (Kent) as 'railway towns' well before the end of the nineteenth century.

- *greater emphasis upon time* – all previous forms of transport depended to a greater or lesser extent on time. Operators had to let passenger and freight users know when they intended to depart and arrive at agreed destinations. However, the much greater speeds of which steam locomotives were capable placed a greater emphasis on punctuality. In many jobs, even as late as 1850, precise times did not matter very much. As railways became more extensively used, the importance of accurate timekeeping increased and more people in Britain became aware of the need to keep to time.
- *expanded leisure opportunities* (this aspect is developed in chapter 28).

Continuity

No one can deny the enormous importance of railways but they must be seen in context. The following points should help you to understand that railways consolidated and encouraged existing trends as well as developing new ones:

1 Canals were not eclipsed overnight by the railways. Many waterways continued to be profitable. Hauliers preferred them in many areas until well into the second half of the nineteenth century when railway freight rates finally began to fall significantly.

2 Early railways stimulated the coastal shipping trade rather than challenging it. Coal from the North-East continued to go to London by ship. It was now brought more efficiently to the ports.

3 The economic models referred to above suggest only that railways were extremely important to the economy, not that they revolutionised it. It is certainly not true to suggest that railway development stimulated revolutionary change in all other aspects of the economy.

4 Though the coming of the railways affected the physical appearance of cities, they tended to reinforce existing trends rather than create new ones. From the end of the eighteenth century a trend towards 'residential zoning' was already apparent. Generally, the poorest workers, who could not afford transport, would live nearest their places of work – usually in town centres. The movement out of city centres to the leafy 'commuter suburbs' was already well under way before the railways came. Here, as elsewhere, railways accelerated an established trend.

Consolidation and maturity

The 1850s and 1860s were decades of growth and consolidation. Our railway chronology tends to be front-loaded. We now remember when the largest cities were linked, the major trunk routes opened and who the railway pioneers were (e.g. **George Hudson** and **Isambard Kingdom Brunel**).

Many students in consequence retain the erroneous notion that, a few bits of 'infilling' apart, the essential railway network was complete by 1850. In fact the next 20 years were even more significant, for two main reasons. Firstly, as so often happens when new developments have 'bedded in', costs came down. It has been estimated that the cost of

PROFILE: *George Hudson*

George Hudson was certainly the most famous, and probably the most unscrupulous, railway entrepreneur of the nineteenth century. He certainly earned his nickname 'The Railway King', though by dubious means. He was born in 1800 and first took up trade as a linen draper. He inherited a substantial fortune in the late 1820s and used it to invest heavily in railway development. His speculations were so successful that, by the middle of the 1840s, he controlled about half the track in Britain, with virtual monopoly control over much of the Midlands and the North-East. He was one of the earliest exponents of aggressive 'take-over bids' as he schemed and gambled his way through the company amalgamations of that period. He entered Parliament at a by-election for Sunderland in 1845. In a high-profile contest he appeared as a defender of the landed interest (on whose cooperation much of his railway ventures depended) and supported the existing corn laws against a prominent Anti-Corn Law League candidate. He was accused of fraud and lost much of his fortune in 1849. He continued as an MP until the election of 1859, however, as one of about 100 MPs in the 1850s with substantial railway interests.

PROFILE: *Isambard Kingdom Brunel*

Isambard Kingdom Brunel was perhaps the most gifted British engineer of the nineteenth century. He was born in Portsmouth in 1806 and worked with his father, Marc, on the first tunnel under the Thames. This eventually formed part of the London Underground system. His most famous monuments are probably the Clifton Suspension Bridge (Bristol), which he planned between 1829 and 1831 and which opened after his death, and the steamships *Great Western* (1845) and *Great Eastern* (1853–8), the latter being the largest steamship then built. He was for many years Chief Engineer to the Great Western Railway, much of which he designed including its distinctive broad-gauge track. He also designed London Paddington and Bristol railway stations. He died in 1859.

transporting freight fell by about 30 per cent between the mid-1840s and 1870, while passenger fares dropped by about 40 per cent. With reduced costs came new markets and expanded opportunity.

Secondly, it was from the development of linking branch lines, mostly traversing rural and highland Britain, after 1850 that ordinary people enjoyed greatest benefits. The earliest railways were built primarily for freight but were widely used also by richer travellers. The number of passenger journeys made in 1870 was almost five times as great as in 1850. Far more 'third-class' passengers – as those paying the lowest fares to sit on wooden benches in the open air were called – travelled. Darlington, the world's oldest railway town, was linked across the north Pennines to Penrith by 1862 via a track which crossed some of the bleakest and most inhospitable upland in England. The rural lines opened up possibilities for travel to many thousands. Faster and cheaper transport costs also made a wider range of perishable agricultural produce affordable for townsfolk. Lines now remembered only by enthusiasts and romantics, therefore, mattered. Thus, in Lincolnshire, Holbeach was linked to Spalding in 1858 and 56 miles of track in previously inaccessible mid-Wales linked Talyllyn to Llanidloes in 1864.

Some large and challenging enterprises remained to be completed after 1870. Most of these were in Scotland and the more remote parts of northern England. The Midland Railway Company's famous alternative direct route from Glasgow to London across the Pennines was not opened until 1876. Many navvies died building the 71 miles of scenic, but brutally gruelling, track north-west from Settle to Carlisle. During the construction of the Ribblehead Viadict on that line, an area of bleak moorland around Ribblehead was transformed for a decade into a roistering, hard-drinking and licentious shanty town before giving way once again to sheep – the place's natural, and far more placid, inhabitants. In Scotland the West Highland line from Glasgow to Fort William and Mallaig – the southern point of departure by ferry to the Isle of Skye, was not opened until 1889. The east–west line from Inverness to Kyle of Lochalsh, and the shortest crossing to Skye, was completed only in 1897, more than 30 years after an Act authorising the route was passed in Parliament.

Railways were the most important development which contributed to the growing economic maturity in mid-Victorian Britain. They provided large-scale opportunities for investment and helped to consolidate the money market. They contributed towards stabilising growth in the economy. Before about 1850, large booms were followed by substantial slumps. The so-called mid-Victorian boom of about 1850 to 1870 was more important for its length than its strength. Stable growth helped to reduce social tensions and drew the sting from radical politics (see chapters 5, 6, 11 and 16). To this stability railways contributed substantially. Railways also promoted substantial changes in society, not all of them for the better, but long-lasting and significant nevertheless. To name only the most obvious, they created a more mobile population, helped people to become better fed and they accelerated the trend towards the development of Britain as an urban nation. In 1801 the great majority of British people lived in the countryside. By 1851 the proportion of rural and urban dwellers was about even. By the early 1880s more than two-thirds of the population lived in towns. Railways probably contributed more than any other single factor towards the making of modern Britain. The following summary by an eminent transport historian puts matters clearly and fairly:

> *'Railways may not have been essential to Britain's economic growth in the nineteenth century, nor did they... produce a "take off", which was already under way by 1830. But they were of enormous significance in the 1840s and 1860s, and throughout the period had a considerable impact upon the capital market, supplying industries, and transport services generally. There is no doubt that railways had a greater influence than any other single innovation before the age of oil and electricity.'*
>
> T. R. Gourvish, 'Railways 1830–70', in M. J. Freeman and D. H. Aldcroft (eds), *Transport in Victorian Britain* (1988).

Task: working with visual sources

Examine the following sources. You can use them alongside the material in this chapter to develop your understanding of the impact of railways in Victorian society:

Source 1 *'Rain, Steam and Speed' by J. M. W. Turner, 1844*

Source 2 *The Sankey Viaduct*

Source 3 *Navvies digging a cutting for the London–Birmingham line, from a painting by J. C. Bourne in 1837*

Source 4 *York Railway Station in the late nineteenth century*

MANCHESTER, BUXTON, MATLOCK, & MIDLANDS JUNCTION RAILWAY

June 1st, 1852, and until further Notice.

LEAVE (IN CONNECTION WITH TRAINS)	From DERBY	From LEEDS, and the North From DERBY, NOTTINGHAM, BIRMINGHAM, &c	From LEEDS, and the North, From DERBY, NOTTINGHAM, LINCOLN BIRMINGHAM, &c	From LEEDS, and the North, From DERBY, NOTTINGHAM, LINCOLN BIRMINGHAM, &c	From LONDON DERBY, NOTTINGHAM, BIRMINGHAM, &c	From LEEDS, and the North, From DERBY, NOTTINGHAM, BIRMINGHAM, &c	SUNDAY TRAINS
	A.M.	A.M.	P.M.	P.M.	P.M.	P.M.	A.M.
DERBY	7.45	9.30	12.55	3.50	6.0	9.00	9.00
AMBERGATE	8.20	10.08	1.25	4.20	6.55	9.25	9.35
CROMFORD	8.34	10.22	1.39	4.34	7.09	9.39	9.49
MATLOCK BATH	8.37	10.25	1.42	4.37	7.12	9.42	9.52
MATLOCK BRIDGE	8.40	10.28	1.45	4.40	7.15	9.45	9.55
DARLEY	8.45	10.33	1.50	4.45	7.20	9.50	10.00
ROWSLEY Arrive	8.50	10.38	1.55	4.50	7.25	9.55	10.05

LEAVE (IN CONNECTION WITH TRAINS)	To LEEDS, and the North, To DERBY, NOTTINGHAM, LINCOLN BIRMINGHAM, &c	To DERBY, LONDON, &c	To LEEDS, and the North, To DERBY, NOTTINGHAM, LINCOLN BIRMINGHAM, &c	To LEEDS, and the North, To DERBY, BIRMINGHAM, and Express to LONDON	To LEEDS and the North, To DERBY, BIRMINGHAM &c	To LEEDS, and the North, To DERBY, LONDON, BIRMINGHAM, &c	SUNDAY TRAINS
	A.M.	A.M.	P.M.	P.M.	P.M.	P.M.	P.M.
ROWSLEY	9.15	11.15	9.50	5.0	6.15	8.40	7.00
DARLEY	9.20	11.20	2.55	5.5	6.20	8.45	7.05
MATLOCK BRIDGE	9.25	11.25	3.0	5.10	6.25	8.50	7.10
MATLOCK BATH	8.37	10.25	1.42	4.37	7.12	9.42	9.52
CROMFORD	9.30	11.30	3.5	5.15	6.30	8.55	7.15
AMBERGATE	9.45	11.45	3.20	5.27	6.45	9.10	7.27
DERBY Arrive	10.45	12.15	3.55	6.05	8.00	10.47	8.05

N.B. At the Rowsley Station, Omnibuses to and from Chatsworth, Bakewell, and Haddon, meet the Trains:–Fare, 6d. each.
Post-Horses and Conveyances always in readiness.

Source 5 *Extract from railway timetable, 1852*

1 Source 1 presents a striking image of a train. It was painted near the beginning of the railway age.
  a What message do you think Turner is trying to convey about this new method of transport?
  b Is its message altered, or confirmed, when you look at the title in addition to the picture itself?

2 Sources 1, 2 and 3 are all paintings from the 1830s and 1840s.
  a Do you think any of them gives a more realistic picture than the others? Give reasons for your answer based on information in this chapter.
  b Would it have been more useful to have had a photograph to replace any of these pictures? Explain your answer.

3 Look at sources 4 and 5. What aspects of railway development are emphasised in these two sources?

4 Use these sources, and the information in the chapter, to decide how much change railways had brought to Britain by 1870.

Further reading

C. More, *The Industrial Age: Economy and Society, 1750–1985* (Addison Wesley Longman, 1989) – this recent textbook has a very good section on the impact of railways.

M. J. Freeman and D. H. Aldcroft (eds), *Transport in Victorian Britain* (Manchester University Press, 1988) – a collection of lively essays.

T. R. Gourvish, *Railways and the British Economy, 1830–1914* (Macmillan, 1980) – written by an expert economic historian, and it shows.

H. J. Dyos and D. H. Aldcroft, *British Transport* (Leicester University Press, 1969).

H. J. Perkin, *The Age of the Railway* (Panther, 1970) – a social history treatment, especially good for showing how railways increased opportunities for humble folk and how it gave a boost to the holiday industry.

M. C. Reed, *Investment in Railways in Britain, 1820–44* (Oxford University Press, 1975) – a very detailed and careful research study which throws light on the people who actually risked their money and, sometimes, made fortunes.

J. R. Kellett, *The Impact of Railways on Victorian Cities* (Routledge, 1979) – concentrates on the balance between railways as a destructive and a constructive force.

CHANGE AND CONTINUITY

20 Parties and policies, 1846–65

Time chart

1846: Conservative Party splits over the repeal of the corn laws. Peel's government is replaced by a Liberal one headed by Lord John Russell, which wins a general election in 1847 and retains power

1850: Russell's government weakened by disputes over Palmerston's foreign policy

1851: Ecclesiastical Titles Act prohibits Roman Catholic bishops from using their titles in Britain. The measure passed through Parliament with a huge majority, but alienated the Liberals' Catholic supporters, weakening the government still further

1852: Russell's government resigns and is replaced by a minority Tory government led by the Earl of Derby. General election reduces the number of Peelites and increases Conservative support by about 70 seats, but Derby fails to get a majority. Disraeli proves a disaster as Chancellor of the Exchequer and the weak government resigns in December, being replaced by a Liberal-Peelite coalition headed by the Earl of Aberdeen

1853: Gladstone's first budget continues trend towards complete free trade

1855: After criticism of Crimean War policy, Aberdeen's coalition is replaced by a Liberal government headed by Palmerston

1857: Palmerston exploits nationalist sentiment to increase Liberal majority to about 80 seats, though some 'pacifist' Liberals and radicals defeated in the election

1858: Palmerston's government brought down by discontented Liberals allying with Conservatives. Replaced by a second Derby minority government. All political restrictions on Jews removed. Property qualifications for MPs removed, thus achieving one of the Chartists' 'six points'

1859: General election in May increases Tory support by about 45 seats but leaves Derby still short of a majority. His government defeated the following month by a combination of Liberals and radicals after a meeting at a club (Willis's rooms) in London. This is seen by many as the origin of the modern Liberal Party. Palmerston becomes Prime Minister again

1860: Cobden–Chevalier trade treaty and Gladstone budget sustain free-trade policies

1861: Gladstone repeals paper duties, making newspapers cheaper and helping his reputation as the supporter of working men: 'the People's William'. Gladstone also sets up Post Office Savings Banks to attract habits of saving and thrift. They rapidly establish themselves as secure havens for small savings

1865: The Liberals win a large victory over the Conservatives and increase their majority to about 80. Three months later, in October, Palmerston dies and is succeeded as Prime Minister by Russell

The hole in the middle of the nineteenth century?

This is the period of British domestic political history which students of the nineteenth century study least. Superficially, it is easy to see why. It is a period, broadly speaking, of prosperity. After the last Chartist outbreak of 1848 (see chapter 16) there is widespread tranquillity, punctuated from time to time by strikes. Some of these, like that of the Lancashire textile workers in 1853–4, were bitter and violent, but popular movements did not threaten the authority of government. This period is not one of heroic struggle.

Party politics appear to be confused after the Conservative Party split over the corn laws (see chapters 13 and 17). Until the late 1850s, the 'Peelites' refused to support either of the main political parties. Of the five governments which held office between 1846 and 1859, three were either minorities or coalitions. Big issues and clear patterns seem elusive.

This is not a period bereft of big political names and 'personalities'. However, most of the action appears to be in foreign affairs and the dominant politician of the age, Viscount Palmerston, was undeniably more interested in foreign affairs than in domestic politics (see chapter 18). **Lord John Russell** and the **Earl of Derby**, who led the Liberal and Tory Parties respectively for much of the period, are generally considered to have been second rate, while William Gladstone and **Benjamin Disraeli,** who certainly were not, are in less senior positions than they will hold in the late 1860s and 1870s – so why not wait a little to study them in detail?

PROFILE: *Lord John Russell*

Lord John Russell was born in 1792 into one of the wealthiest families in Britain as a son of the Duke of Bedford. He became an MP in 1813 and remained in Parliament until his death in 1878. From 1861, however, he sat in the House of Lords, as Earl Russell. He earned the reputation of a reformer early in his career, being responsible for getting the Test and Corporation Acts repealed in 1828 and playing an active role in promoting the First Reform Act in 1831–2. His first cabinet post was as Paymaster General of the Forces (1831–4) under Grey. He served first as Home Secretary (1835–9) and then as Colonial Secretary (1839–41) under Melbourne. He had two stints as Prime Minister, the first long (1846–52) and the second short (1865–6). He also served as Foreign Secretary under Aberdeen (1852–3) and Palmerston (1859–65). His length of political service bears comparison with almost anyone in the nineteenth century. However, he was neither a strong speaker nor a convincing leader.

PROFILE: *Earl of Derby*

The **Earl of Derby** was born **Edward Stanley**, son of the thirteenth earl, in 1799 and inherited the title himself in 1851. He was first elected to the Commons in 1820 as a Whig and was given minor office as a Whig in Canning's brief coalition government of 1827. He remained in the Whig camp during the Reform crisis and served as Chief Secretary for Ireland, 1830–33, entering the cabinet in 1831. As Colonial Secretary (1833–4), he carried out the legislation which abolished slavery in the British colonies. He left the Whigs because of disagreements about the use of Church of England funds to support measures which would benefit Catholics in Ireland. He served as Colonial Secretary (1841–5) in Peel's famous government and inherited leadership of the Conservative Party after the split in 1846. He continued as its leader, being prised from the post – with some reluctance – by Disraeli in 1868. He was three times Prime Minister in minority Conservative governments (1852, 1858–9 and 1866–8). An intelligent man, with scholarly interests outside politics, he was probably the senior politician most disadvantaged by the split over the corn laws, since most of his political maturity was spent in opposition. Despite his intellectual interests, his political determination and drive should not be underestimated.

PROFILE: *Benjamin Disraeli*

To many students of the nineteenth century, **Benjamin Disraeli** is its most attractive political figure. He is admired for his wit, charm and fluency and, perhaps above all, for seeming never to take the 'great game' of politics entirely seriously. Others, an increasing minority, see him as a philandering and crooked charlatan who loved fame and power for its own sake and who – despite the calculated decision to marry a rich widow – never quite shook off the self-pity of a relatively humble background which, he believed, saddled him with enormous disadvantages compared with his rival Gladstone. His family was wealthy enough – his father Isaac was a Jewish author and intellectual – but his racial origins made it difficult to break into the social circle where high politicians moved. Like his father, he had some success as an author. His novels *Coningsby* and *Sybil, or the Two Nations* have not stood the test of time, but they were successful in their day and revealed at least some interest in social questions. After several attempts, he was finally elected as MP for Maidstone in 1837. He believed that Peel should have given him a job in his government and his attack on Peel over the corn laws was motivated in part by spite. His attacks on Peel brought him instant fame and he became leader of the Conservatives in the Commons in 1848. During a long, and sometimes uneasy, relationship with Derby he served as Chancellor of the Exchequer in all three of his leader's minority governments, before supplanting him as prime minister for a few months soon after brilliantly managing the passage of the Second Reform Act. During his time in opposition (1868–74) he helped to improve the organisation of the Conservative Party and established policies designed to make it attractive to the new voters. He was rewarded with victory in 1874 and served as prime minister until 1880. During this time he was much more concerned with foreign than with domestic affairs and was also periodically wracked by ill health. He was created Earl of Beaconsfield in 1876 by Queen Victoria, one of many women who found his charm captivating. He died in 1881.

For most students, strife is more racy than stability and depression more interesting than prosperity. Yet this period is important and worth studying at least in outline. Unless you know what is going on in politics in the years 1846–65, you will not get a proper understanding of the ways in which the modern Liberal and Conservative Parties developed and you will certainly not understand why it was that Gladstone and Disraeli came to be bitter personal enemies as well as political rivals.

Figure 20.2 'The burning of the Houses of Lords and Commons' by J. M. W. Turner, 1834

The consequences of the Conservative split: how much instability?

After 1846 a distinct group of Conservative free-traders operated separately from the Conservative and Liberal Parties. About 90 MPs in the Commons followed the line of their leader Sir Robert Peel, who told a close friend in 1846: 'I intend to keep aloof from party combinations'. The Liberals were the obvious beneficiaries of the split. Russell's government was a mediocre one, but it held office with little challenge for six years, often buoyed up on crucial votes by the Peelites.

Yet, though the Peelites refused to support either main political party on a regular basis, they did not necessarily agree among themselves, especially after Peel's death in 1850, and they showed no inclination to become a separate party. In fact, the extent to which the Peelites disrupted party politics in the late 1840s and 1850s is easily exaggerated. Peel himself had been a great supporter of the strength of executive government. He cared much more for efficient and appropriate measures than he did for party labels. Not surprisingly, prominent Peelites like Aberdeen and Gladstone took the same view. Thus, when a weak Liberal government was proposing economic measures they agreed with, they readily supported it – just as Peel had supported the Whigs over controversial issues like the Poor Law Amendment Act in the 1830s. The Peelites wanted to see political stability. This attitude both underpinned their frequent support for Russell from 1846 to 1852 and sustained their alliance with the Whig-Liberals during the Aberdeen coalition of 1852–5. The fact of the Peelite split did not make for unstable government by itself.

The Peelites could claim one negative achievement: they kept the Conservatives out of power for most of this period. The Tory leader, the Earl of Derby, was desperate to bring them back and these years are littered with overtures, negotiations and entreaties to their old colleagues. They had some success, especially with some of the lesser known free-traders of 1846. Among Peel's old lieutenants in government, however, they were less successful. There are three main reasons for this:

1 Peelites were absolutely committed to free trade, and they feared that Derby's Conservatives, though never so unblinkingly Protectionist as the bitter debates of 1845–6 suggested, were still not convinced of its benefits. In office as Chancellor of the Exchequer in 1852, Disraeli was perfectly happy to announce his conversion to free-trade policies. All but about 40 Conservatives went along with the change of policy. However, Peelites remained unconvinced of Conservative good faith on this most important of issues. Disraeli's conversion is, however, very significant. It meant that there was no significant disagreement in Westminster over the broad direction of economic policy. Whether Liberal, Conservative or coalition governments were in office, Britain moved steadily towards free trade. Free-trade policies were absolutely central to what many have called the period of 'Victorian liberalism'. It is important to understand that the policy was not unique to the Liberal Party.

2 Most leading Peelites were also in favour of religious toleration and had followed their leader in his policies to give greater freedom and educational opportunity to Roman Catholics in Ireland (see time chart, chapter 13). By the 1850s, even Gladstone, the most prominent opponent of the Maynooth grant in 1845, had softened his views. The most steady religious intolerance in British politics was to be found among the rank and file of the Conservative Party. Documents I and III from the 'examination question' on pages 195–6 indicate other aspects of backbench Conservatism which well-educated and experienced Peelites would not willingly embrace. For some Peelites in the early 1850s, then, the Whigs were becoming more congenial colleagues than the Conservatives. The experience of the Aberdeen coalition, despite its many difficulties over foreign affairs, strengthened the links.

3 Very few Peelites had any time whatever for Benjamin Disraeli. They disliked his flashy, dandified ways – especially the tone of levity

which many thought he brought to politics. They resented the fact that his rapid climb through the ranks of the Conservative Party had been so dependent on free trade, the issue on which they felt most strongly, and on which he had brought their chief down. Most of all, they distrusted him. Gladstone confessed to feeling a 'sentiment of revulsion' against Disraeli. Derby's negotiations to bring leading Peelites back into the Conservative fold were often wrecked by the presence at his side of 'the Jewish adventurer'.

We should never underestimate the importance both of personality and personal ambition in determining political fortunes. They played a specially important role in the politics of the 1850s and early 1860s, and helped to keep the Earl of Derby out of power for much longer than his talents merited. They also kept Disraeli from any lengthy spell in office when he was relatively young and fit. Outside Westminster, indeed, the old Conservative/Whig-Liberal divisions remained clear. Local politics were not much influenced by Peelite opinions. Between 1846 and 1859 steady progress was made in grass-roots party organisation, and in places like Liverpool, Birmingham and Leeds, the distinction between Conservatives and Liberals became ever sharper. Overall, this is *not* a period of confused party allegiance.

It was disputes among political leaders at Westminster which created an atmosphere of instability in the 1850s and the consequent minority governments and 'coalitions' which Disraeli so much deplored (see document III, on page 196). Even here, however, we should not attribute discord specifically to the Peelites. In their very different ways, both Lord John Russell and Palmerston were *prima donnas*, with a strong sense of their own importance and a disinclination to concede seniority to the other. Their disputes fatally weakened the Liberal government after 1850 and led to Russell's fall in 1852. Palmerston cleverly exploited his popularity with the public and eventually won his power struggle with Russell. In doing so, however, he weakened the anti-Conservatives by demonstrating how far apart he and leading 'pacifist radicals' like Cobden and Bright were in the mid and late 1850s.

The liberalisation of Mr Gladstone

Personal ambition was probably the factor which determined Gladstone's course of action in the late 1850s. By the time the Aberdeen coalition fell in 1855, it was clear that the Peelites would not remain a separate group for much longer. Their numbers were declining both by natural wastage as members died and because many had already given their support to one party or the other. Paradoxically, the inevitability of these decisions testifies to the *strength* of party politics even at a time of apparent confusion. Politicians knew that they must be party men if they were to have successful careers and discharge the government business for which Peel's training had fitted them. The dilemma was particularly acute for Gladstone. Temperamentally, he was more of a Conservative than a Liberal. He was a strong supporter of the Church of England. He believed in order and stability. In the first half of his career, he was less 'reformist' (except on matters of administration) than any other Peelite. However, two considerations weighed with him above all others:

- He was ambitious and recognised that he needed a firm party base in order to hold office for long periods.
- He hated Disraeli with quite extraordinary virulence.

John Bright, the leading Quaker radical, played on these factors with skill in the late 1850s. He pointed out that Disraeli's position in the Conservative Party was now so entrenched that it would be all but impossible to stop him succeeding Derby when the time came. Furthermore, in 1859 Disraeli was 54 years old. Palmerston and Russell, Queen Victoria's 'two terrible old men', were 75 and 67 respectively. It was obvious where the longer wait for the leadership would be. Gladstone's tenure as Chancellor of the Exchequer had won him much esteem as a highly competent free-trade minister. He was recognised on all sides as 'the coming man'. Other Peelites were near the end of their careers. Two of the most prominent, Aberdeen and Herbert, were to die in 1860 and 1861 respectively. Gladstone was the remaining big Peelite catch. A combination of self-interest and hatred determined his decision. He threw in his lot with the Liberals in 1859, remaining as Chancellor of the Exchequer – the post he coveted – under first Palmerston and then Russell until the Liberals fell from office in 1866. His disapproval of Palmerston's reputation with women and of his sometimes sharp political practice was certainly noted, but Palmerston, whose origins at least were Anglican, was much less of a personal stumbling block to a fastidious churchman than was Disraeli. Within a year or two William Gladstone, once 'the rising hope of those stern unbending Tories' in T. B. Macaulay's famous phrase, had become 'the People's William'. He would continue to dominate British politics for another 35 years.

In June 1859 Liberals and radicals met together at Willis's rooms in London (see document IV on page 196) to agree upon a programme to defeat Derby's minority Conservative government. This defeat was accomplished within a week of the meeting. Some have seen it as the real beginning of the modern Liberal Party. This is a contentious claim. After all, a similar meeting, involving Whigs, radicals and Irish nationalists, had produced the so-called Lichfield House Compact which had ended Peel's minority government in 1835. The anti-Tory group in Parliament had rarely been cohesive or united and it contained a very wide range of opinion. More MPs in the 1840s and 1850s began calling themselves 'Liberals'. They did so, whether their own origins were urban or rural, to indicate that their appeal was to a broader base of opinion than was represented by the 'Whig' leadership.

The party was invariably led by great landowners, many of whom asserted that their credentials as 'reformers' dated back to the actions of their ancestors who turfed James II off his throne in 1688 and thus ended royal absolutism in England. This was uncertain history but powerful symbolism. It also served to validate the continued leadership of a political party with increasing strength among the urban middle classes in the hands of men like Viscount Palmerston, Lord John Russell and the Duke of Argyll. The Liberal Party which resumed office after 1859 contained considerable breadth of opinion and much internal disagreement. It was at least a workable machine for government and this was the aspect which Gladstone most appreciated as he set to work as Chancellor to consolidate Britain's reputation as the world's leading free-trade nation.

Examination question: Party politics in the 1850s

Before you tackle this question re-read the hints given at the end of chapter 11. They should help you direct your answers as required.

Document I

'In politics, Mr Thorne was an unflinching Conservative. He looked on those 53 Trojans who ... censured Free Trade in November 1852 as the only patriots left among the public men of England. When that terrible crisis of Free Trade had arrived, when the Repeal of the Corn Laws was carried by those very men whom Mr Thorne had hitherto regarded as the saviours of his country he was for a time paralysed. Now all trust in human faith must be for ever at an end.'

(An extract from Anthony Trollope's novel, *Barchester Towers* (1857). This novel is about the Church of England and politics. Trollope, besides being a novelist, was a civil servant and a keen observer of political affairs. In 1868 he was elected as a Liberal MP.)

Document II

'Dislike (personal I mean) of Disraeli in the first place and of Derby in the second is a ruling passion with the Peelites; and it has always struck me that the personal difficulty as to Disraeli would stand in the way of any junction between even the Gladstonian section and the present government.'

(Sir Charles Wood, who had been Chancellor of the Exchequer in Russell's Liberal government of 1846–52, assessing the chances of the Peelites returning to the Conservative Party during the Derby government of 1852, quoted in J. B. Conacher, *The Peelites and the Party System, 1846–52* (1972).)

Document III

'[During the parliamentary session of 1852–3 Disraeli] complained loudly of the apathy of the party: they could not be got to attend to business [in Parliament] while the hunting season lasted: a sharp frost would make the difference of twenty men. They had a good natural ability, he said, taking them as a body but wanted culture: they never read: their leisure was passed in field sports [hunting, shooting, fishing, etc.]. The wretched school and university system was at fault: they learned nothing useful, and did not understand the ideas of their own time.'

(An extract from the diary of the Conservative Edward Stanley, son of Lord Derby, in J. R. Vincent (ed.), *Derby, Disraeli and the Conservative Party: the Political Journals of Lord Stanley, 1849–69* (1978).)

Document IV

'The Liberal party met at Willis's rooms. I attended. Palmerston was speaking on the platform – a few others equally conspicuous – Lord John [Russell] among them.

The general tone and feeling of the meeting were very good. Bright was remarkably discreet and moderate. Lord John and Palmerston rivalled each other in expressing disinterestedness and readiness to cooperate. The entente cordiale *[hearty agreement] seemed perfect till Roebuck threw his shell ... of disunion. The gist of his speech was this: he disbelieved in the possibility of a cordial combination of the various sections of the Liberal Party, he doubted whether the two rival Lords [Palmerston and Russell] would long cooperate in the same Cabinet. He also thought that it was not a good policy to turn out the existing government without some approach to certainty of securing better men.*

Bright was hardly satisfied with Palmerston's assurances of a more pacific [peaceful] [foreign] policy – till Lord P. had spoken again, when he gave more satisfaction.

It was a curious meeting ... I noted that, when Roebuck was making his onslaught, Lords Palmerston and John Russell were very skilled in their mode of dissembling [covering up] their annoyance ... Palmerston ... used his hand as if deaf – so as to leave it uncertain whether the worst hits reached him. Lord John bore his share with good temper. I observed that at one passage [in Roebuck's speech] he drew a deep sigh. Roebuck had several interruptions – but no cheers of approval.'

(Diary of Sir John Salusbury-Trelawny, Liberal MP for Tavistock (Devon), 6 June 1859, in T. A. Jenkins (ed.), *The Parliamentary Diaries of Sir John Trelawny*, Camden Series, vol. 40 (1990).)

Document V

'Aberdeen, only a month away from his sixty-ninth birthday ... returned [from an audience with the Queen in December 1852] with a commission to form a government. Since neither Palmerston nor the Peelites would serve under either Russell or Derby, it was in fact the only solution. The party alignments which had dominated politics since 1828 were no longer capable of fulfilling their primary function of providing an administration. The central government of liberal-conservatives and conservative-liberals, for which many hoped after 1846 had materialised at last, though without the commanding figure of Peel and under the man who was temperamentally one of the least forceful of Peel's senior colleagues.

"England does not love coalitions," said Disraeli dismissively when about to be defeated by one in the Commons in December 1852. It would have been truer perhaps to say that politicians do not love coalitions, as Disraeli himself had discovered when hunting desperately for alliances with Peelites, radicals and Whigs in the preceding half-dozen years. There are too few posts for all the claimants; too many compromises on policy; too many old animosities to be smoothed over.'

(N. Gash, *Aristocracy and People: Britain, 1815–65* (1979).)

Questions

a What, according to document III, were Disraeli's main criticisms of the Conservative Party in 1852–3? *3 marks*

b Study documents I, II and III. What can you infer from these documents about the reasons why the Conservatives were so rarely in government during the 1850s? *5 marks*

c Study document IV and use your own knowledge. How does Sir John Salusbury-Trelawny's account explain what Russell and Palmerston wanted to achieve from the meeting of Liberals and radicals held at Willis's rooms in June 1859? *4 marks*

d Study the origins and content of documents I and IV. Do you think either of these documents gives a more useful account of the features of party politics which it describes than the other? Explain your answer by reference to the origins and content of both documents. *6 marks*

e 'The party alignments which had dominated politics since 1828 were no longer capable of fulfilling their primary function of providing an administration' (Gash). Use all of the documents, and your own knowledge, to explain why this was so for much of the 1850s. *7 marks*

Further reading

E. J. Evans, *Political Parties in Britain, 1783–1867*, Lancaster Pamphlet (Routledge, 1985) – offers useful guidance on what is often seen as a confusing period.

M. Winstanley, *Gladstone and the Liberal Party*, Lancaster Pamphlet (Routledge, 1990) – the best brief account of the Liberal *Party* which puts Gladstone's contribution in context.

R. Stewart, *The Foundation of the Conservative Party, 1830–67* (Addison Wesley Longman, 1979) – a detailed study which is particularly good on the Conservative split and its consequences.

J. R. Vincent, *The Formation of the Liberal Party, 1857–68* (Constable, 1966).

J. B. Conacher, *The Aberdeen Coalition, 1852–5* (Cambridge University Press, 1968) – still the best detailed study of this government.

J. B. Prest, *Lord John Russell* (Macmillan, 1972) – a detailed biography.

A. Hawkins, *Parliament, Party and the Art of Politics, 1855–9* (Stanford University Press, 1987) – a long and detailed study which is full of insight about mid-Victorian politics. Best used by those who are fascinated by the political process.

CAUSE AND CONSEQUENCE

21 The revival of parliamentary reform

Time chart

1852: Bill by Lord John Russell to extend the vote for those occupying property in the towns worth £5 a year, and in the counties £10. The bill fell with the Russell government

1854: Russell proposal to extend vote to £10 county and £6 borough householders presented, but withdrawn on outbreak of Crimean War

1859: Derby's minority government introduces a proposal to extend the vote to £10 householders in counties and boroughs, together with various disfranchisements of seats and transfer to larger boroughs and counties. Defeated by 39 votes in Commons

1860: Russell presents another bill with similar clauses to that of 1854, and again withdraws it

1865: Death of Palmerston removes a leading obstacle in the way of further parliamentary reform

1866: Russell's Liberal government introduces developed proposals for reform:

- vote to be given to £14 county and £7 borough householders
- lodgers paying rent of £10 a year to receive the vote
- vote to be given to those with at least £50 in savings banks
- 49 small boroughs to be disfranchised: 26 seats to go to counties, 22 to larger boroughs and one to London University

Conservatives, with some Liberal help, defeat the bill on amendment and Russell's government falls

1867: Disraeli pilots a much-amended Conservative bill through Parliament. Introduces parliamentary reform in England and Wales

1868: Separate parliamentary Reform Bill for Scotland passed

1872: Secret ballot introduced by Gladstone's Liberal government

Why was a Second Reform Act passed?

The Whigs who passed the Great Reform Act of 1832 (see chapter 12) argued to the opponents of that highly controversial measure that it

Figure 21.1 *The Palace of Westminster, 1856*

would settle a festering sore for good and all. It rapidly became clear that it did nothing of the kind. Virtually all in Parliament could unite to oppose the wild extravagances of universal manhood suffrage, as advocated by the Chartists (see chapter 16), but many MPs could see nothing wrong with increasing the electorate to embrace those solid, educated working men who did not occupy property worth £10 a year or more, but who could certainly be trusted to vote wisely if given the chance. The reduction of social tension and the long period of boom also helped create a climate of optimism rather than fear. The impact of gentle inflation and substantially improved electoral organisation had already combined to increase the number of voters under the old rules. There were about 400,000 more voters on the electoral registers in the year before the Second Reform Act was passed than there had been in the year after the Great Reform Act became law. This large increase went largely unnoticed.

By the 1850s Lord John Russell was only one of a considerable number of Liberal MPs urging further reform. As you can see from the time chart, no fewer than four serious attempts were made at reform in the years 1852–60. Additionally, seven motions to introduce a secret ballot were debated in Parliament between 1851 and 1864. Reform was a live, if never a burning, issue. For the Liberals, the matter was one of principle:

many radical MPs, like Bright, were convinced parliamentary reformers. William Gladstone was in the early 1860s greatly impressed by the sacrifices made by Lancashire cotton workers during the 'Cotton Famine'. In a famous speech of 1864 he stated – with wonderful pomposity – that 'every man who is not presumably incapacitated by some consideration of personal unfitness or of political danger is morally entitled to come within the pale of the constitution'.

In 1863 and 1864 a Reform Union begun by businessmen in the north of England and a Reform League, dominated by trade unionists like Robert Applegarth and George Odger, were both established. However, the Liberal Party was divided over reform. A vocal minority, led by **Robert Lowe**, and supported by leading peers like Lansdowne and Grey, opposed it strenuously. The Prime Minister, Palmerston, saw no reason to open up an issue which might again divide a Liberal Party so recently united (see chapter 20). The Conservatives, out of office for most of the 1850s and 1860s and looking for any opportunity to exploit weaknesses in their opponents, took up parliamentary reform on tactical grounds. Anything which split the Liberals would be good for them.

What debates on reform in the 1850s and 1860s did *not* have, in great contrast to those in the late 1820s and early 1830s, was fervent extra-parliamentary agitation. The 1867 Reform Act was the product of debate and party-political manoeuvring within Westminster rather than pressure from outside. The famous Hyde Park demonstrations, during which some railings were knocked down by protesting crowds, took place long after the Liberal Reform Bill had been introduced. Lord Derby's son, Edward Stanley, was nearer the mark when he wrote in his diary on 26 July 1866: 'The political excitement among the upper classes is greater than it has been for the last seven or eight years. I do not believe it is shared to any considerable extent by the people.'

Certainly, the death of Palmerston in 1865 precipitated matters, if only because his successor as Prime Minister, Lord Russell, was a leading advocate of reform. His own proposals (see time chart) were relatively modest. They would probably have added about 400,000 men to the electoral register. However, Lowe and 47 other anti-reform Liberals worked with the Conservative opposition to defeat the bill. Russell resigned almost immediately, leaving Derby to form his third minority government in 14 years. What Lowe and his colleagues had left out of their calculations was that the Conservatives, and particularly Benjamin Disraeli, were desperate for a high-profile political success. Derby himself said that he was not prepared yet again to be 'a stop-gap' prime minister, serving only until the Liberals reunited again. Disraeli saw reform as the ideal opportunity of delivering what his boss wanted: attention-grabbing victory. Succeeding

PROFILE: *Robert Lowe*

Robert Lowe was born in 1811 the son of a well-to-do clergyman. His education was a conventional one for a rich young man – Winchester and Oxford. Thereafter, it took an unconventional turn because he emigrated to Australia in 1842, serving on the New South Wales legislative council. Here he formed distinctly unflattering opinions about governments elected on a wide franchise. He returned to Britain in 1850. He was elected Liberal MP for Kidderminster in 1852, where he expressed distaste for many of the opinions of uneducated voters. He was happier representing the smaller borough of Calne from 1859 to 1867. He served in minor office in the Aberdeen coalition and the first Palmerston government, before becoming Vice-President of the Committee of Council on Education from 1859 to 1864 (see chapter 15). An extremely able man with a very clear mind and acute debating skills, he led the successful Liberal opposition to Russell's Reform Bill of 1866, but this did not impede his subsequent progress. He was Home Secretary from 1868 to 1873, in Gladstone's government of 1868–74 and then moved to the post of Chancellor of the Exchequer. He died, ennobled as first Viscount Sherbrook, in 1882.

on parliamentary reform when the Liberals – historically, the party of reform – had failed would be an immense coup. As always with Disraeli, tactics and ends were far more important than principle and means.

Disraeli's success in piloting reform through Parliament was a triumph of political dexterity and quick-wittedness. It was achieved by outflanking the Liberal middle ground, occupied by Russell and Gladstone. They wanted considered, measured reform. Disraeli wanted reform, almost at all costs. During the debates, rather than risk defeat, he accepted amendment after amendment from Liberal radicals, gaining their trust in the process. He relied on his own troops and on the radicals to vote down a 'sensible' amendment proposed by Gladstone, which would have extended the vote to householders in the boroughs. The specific proposal did not matter to Disraeli; defeating the Liberal leadership did, and here he was triumphant. He accepted a decisive amendment by another Liberal radical, Grosvenor Hodgkinson, which extended the vote to those occupying any house in the boroughs, whether they paid rates directly to that borough or 'compounded' them in with the rent they paid to landlords. For Gladstone and the Liberals 'compounding' was the touchstone: those who paid rates separately tended to be respectable, and long-term, tenants; those who did not were often poorer, less well-established and likely to 'flit' without paying rent or rates when times got hard.

As it turned out, the Hodgkinson amendment was unworkable in practice, but details never bothered Disraeli. Accepting this proposal, and voting down Gladstone's, got him his Reform Bill. He hoped to use this triumph as the basis of a direct appeal to the new voters. He had visions of 'marketing' the Conservatives as the party of the working man. The appeal failed at the general election of 1868, as we shall see (chapter 22), but the notion of 'Tory democracy', as yet a gleam in Disraeli's eye, would bring immense political advantage during the next generation.

The changes made in 1867

As in 1832 (see chapter 12), qualifications for the vote continued to differ as between counties and boroughs. The main distinction was that, because this was a Conservative Act and the Conservatives were in general much stronger in the counties than in the boroughs, a systematic attempt was made to reduce the number of urban voters in the counties, keeping the landed interest as strong as possible there while allowing the anyway Liberal majority in many boroughs to be consolidated.

In county seats the following could vote:

- men owning, or having leases of more than 60 years for, land worth at least £5 a year
- men occupying land with a rateable value of at least £12 a year, provided they had paid the relevant poor rates
- otherwise, voting rights were as established in 1832.

In borough seats the following could vote:

- men owning, or occupying, dwelling houses, if resident for at least 12 months
- lodgers of property worth at least £10 a year for at least 12 months.

'The Minority Clause':

Where a borough, or a county, seat had three members, no voter could vote for more than two candidates. The intention here was to allow strong minority interests representation. In many boroughs between 1832 and 1867, the two Conservative candidates in two-member seats often polled well, obtaining, say, 40 per cent of the support. However, they were regularly beaten by Liberals with more support. The Conservatives were attempting to ensure that at least one Conservative MP would be elected in the largest boroughs: Birmingham, Leeds, Liverpool and Manchester.

'The first stage, I have no doubt, will be an increase of corruption, intimidation, and disorder, of all the evils that happen usually in elections. But what will be the second? The second will be that the working men of England, finding themselves in a full majority of the whole constituency, will awake to a full sense of their power. They will say: "We can do better for ourselves ... Let us set up shop for ourselves. We have objects to serve as well as our neighbours, and let us unite to carry those objects. We have machinery; we have trade unions; we have our leaders all ready."

The result [of the proposed changes] will be that the working classes will have a majority in ninety-five boroughs, almost a majority in ninety-three, and more than one-third of the representation in eighty-five ... It is an old observation that every democracy is in some respects similar to a despotism ... As courtiers and flatterers are worse than despots themselves, so those who flatter and fawn upon the people are generally very inferior to the people – the objects of their flattery and adulation. We see in America, where the people have undisputed power, that they do not send honest, hard-working men to represent them in Congress, but traffickers in office, bankrupts, men who have lost their character and been driven from every respectable way of life and who take up politics as a last resource ... Now, Sir, democracy has yet another tendency which it is worthwhile to study at the present moment. It is singularly prone to the concentration of power. Under it, individual men are small, and the Government is great. That must be the character of a Government which represents the majority, and which absolutely tramples down and equalises everything except itself.'

Robert Lowe, speaking in the House of Commons against Russell's Liberal Reform Bill in 1866. [Look at the profile on him in this chapter for further information. Lowe had been trained as an academic, had served as a barrister and had spent some time in Australia, where he had seen colonial governments elected on a wide franchise.]

'It has been thought strange, but there are nations in which the numerous unwiser part wishes to be ruled by the less numerous wiser part. The numerical majority ... is ready, is eager to delegate its power of choosing its ruler to a certain select minority. It abdicates in favour of its elite, and it consents to obey whoever that elite may confide in ... it has a kind of loyalty to some superior persons who are fit to choose a good government, and whom no other class opposes. A nation in such a happy state as this has obvious advantages for constructing a cabinet government. It has the best people to elect a legislature, and therefore it may be fairly expected to choose a good legislature – a legislature

competent to select a good administration ... A life of labour, an incomplete education, a monotonous occupation, a career in which the hands are used much and the judgement is used little, cannot create as much flexible thought, as much applicable intelligence, as a life of leisure, a long culture, a varied experience, and existence by which the judgement is incessantly exercised.'

Walter Bagehot, *The English Constitution* (1867). [This became the leading book on the subject and was widely used by the educated elite in late Victorian Britain.]

The main consequences

1 The 1867 and 1868 Reform Acts in Britain increased the number of voters substantially. The electorate comprised just short of 2 million adult men in 1869, compared with just over 1 million immediately before the Second Reform Act was passed. The total increase was about 89 per cent, though much greater in the borough seats (134 per cent) than in the counties (46 per cent).

2 In several of the industrial boroughs the majority of the electorate was now working class. The electorates of Oldham (Lancashire) and South Shields (Co. Durham) were six times as large in 1868 as they had been in 1866. The enfranchisement of iron workers in Merthyr Tydfil increased that borough's voters tenfold. The Scottish Reform Act of 1868 produced a radical change in Glasgow's electorate. In 1867 about 57 per cent of the electorate there had been middle class, 23 per cent skilled working class and about 13 per cent semi-skilled or unskilled. By 1869 the proportions were 34 per cent, 35 per cent and 40 per cent respectively. Thus, Glasgow's electorate was overwhelmingly working class, much of it what Gladstone would have called 'the lower sort', *i.e.* the non-respectable and ill-informed whom he would not have trusted to vote sensibly.

3 The redistribution of parliamentary seats was also substantial. You can easily detect the different emphases of a Conservative from a Liberal government. The boroughs (where the Liberals tended to be stronger) suffered a net loss of 30 seats (52 disfranchisements and 22 extra seats for larger boroughs); the counties (where the opposite bias obtained) gained 27 of these and the universities (two of them from Scotland's Glasgow and Edinburgh) gained three. Unlike in 1832, however, a general rule of thumb about size of population governed decisions about the parliamentary boroughs. All populations of fewer than 10,000 were at risk. After the usual horse-trading, seven from England disappeared altogether and 22 kept only one of their two members.

KEY TERM:

First-past-the-post

This term, borrowed from horse-racing, describes a situation in which an election is won by the candidate who wins the largest number of votes, irrespective of the numbers of electors voting against him or – since British elections still retain the system – her. Thus, someone in an election with three candidates who had 10,000 votes would automatically be declared elected, even though both of his rivals had won 9,999 votes each. A candidate can, in theory, be successful even if two-thirds of those voting actually voted against him. When those who could have voted, but did not bother to do so, are taken into account the proportion of positive support can be very small, sometimes as little as a quarter. A **first-past-the-post electoral system** makes it virtually impossible for minority parties to get the number of seats their share of the popular vote across the country suggests that they should get. It is not surprising, therefore, that small parties strongly support some form of 'proportional representation', whereby minority votes are given greater weight, rather than 'first past the post'.

4 Decisions about boundaries of boroughs and counties were also made by a parliamentary commission on which the governing Conservative Party had a majority. The general effect was to extend the boundaries of boroughs much more extensively than before 1832, such that suburban areas, where men had previously voted in county seats, were usually considered part of the relevant borough seat. The intention was clearly to reduce as far as possible the number of urban, and predominantly Liberal, voters in the county seats. In a **first-past-the-post** electoral system, as Disraeli well knew, political parties gain no extra advantage in winning a particular seat by a large, rather than a very small, majority. He was keen on having Liberal candidates piling up large majorities in seats unwinnable by the Conservatives, especially if the effect was to ensure that the Conservatives might narrowly win a few seats they might otherwise have lost.

5 We need to be careful about simple generalisations which suggest that the 1867–8 changes 'gave the vote to the industrial working classes'. In many places, of course, it did. However, most miners were *not* enfranchised by the Second Reform Act. Many lived not in parliamentary boroughs but in smaller communities which were part of a county constituency. They did not receive the vote until 1884. Also, even in the boroughs, the vote was far from universal for working men. A one-year residence qualification cut many out. The very poor tended to move accommodation more frequently, and were anyway suspicious about 'registering' to vote. Many had good reason not to be on official lists. Ordinary lodgers did not get the vote and nor did most adult males who still lived with their parents.

6 As we have seen, most amendments which were put forward to increase the number of voters during the progress of Disraeli's bill through the Commons were accepted. One significant amendment, however, did not get through. The philosopher and Liberal MP John Stuart Mill argued that, in logic, there was no reason for withholding the vote from women on the same terms as men. This was the first occasion on which the idea of giving women the vote was seriously debated by an all-male Parliament. It received very little support, the great majority of MPs much preferring their own 'instincts' to Mill's logic. Neither for the first, nor the last time, logic was discovered to be an extremely feeble weapon in parliamentary debate.

Whatever reservations can be made about the extent of the changes in 1867–8, however, no one can deny that Disraeli's Reform Act changed the political map irrevocably. The trouble was that no one, least of all Disraeli himself, knew how it would actually *work*. In the next two chapters, we will see how the two major political parties responded to the challenges.

Task: class debate

One of the most important skills which historians develop is the ability sympathetically to evaluate arguments they do not themselves accept.

Almost no one nowadays would accept the arguments provided by Robert Lowe and Walter Bagehot against a large extension of the franchise or, if they did, would find it almost impossible to express them publicly and be taken seriously. As historians, your task should be to understand *why* such attitudes and beliefs were widespread among the political elite whom Bagehot was referring to in *The English Constitution*.

Many historical exercises with sources require you to reach judgements about the strength and weaknesses of different viewpoints. This debate gives you an opportunity to do something different. You should divide into two groups:

- *Group A* will study the arguments of Lowe and Bagehot and pick out the points made in the sources which seem to you to derive from self-interest.
- *Group B* will look at the same sources, but pick out the points made which seem to you to suggest disinterested (*i.e.* neutral) concern for the best kind of government.

The two groups should then present those arguments and decide which of the two reasons for holding non-democratic views were the more important. Both groups should use information from this chapter, and elsewhere if you have it, about the Second Reform Act to help you come to a decision.

You might also like to decide from your own experience how many of the fears of Lowe and Bagehot about democratic government have proved justified.

Further reading

J. K. Walton, *The Second Reform Act* (Routledge,1987) – now the best brief study of the Act's importance.

D. G. Wright, *Democracy and Reform, 1815–85*, Longman Seminar Studies (Addison Wesley Longman, 1970) – just a little dated but still useful to get the Act in its context.

H. J. Hanham, *Elections and Party Management* (Addison Wesley Longman, 1969) – a splendid detailed study of how agents tried to increase their party's chances in elections.

M. Cowling, *1867: Disraeli, Gladstone and Revolution* (Cambridge University Press, 1967) – a detailed research study by a leading right-wing historian whose 'revolution' is safely contained within the Palace of Westminster.

F. B. Smith, *The Making of the Second Reform Bill* (Cambridge University Press, 1966) – unravels the complexities of this process splendidly, if at length.

Part Three Democracy, empire and welfare, 1867–1914

ROLE OF THE INDIVIDUAL

22 What was Gladstonian Liberalism? The Liberal Party, 1866–85

Time chart

1866: Liberals resign from office after defeats over their Reform Bill

1868: Lord John Russell resigns the party leadership; Gladstone becomes first party leader and then, after general election victory, Prime Minister. Compulsory payment of church rates abolished

1870: Forster's Elementary Education Act provides for rate-supported board schools to 'fill in the gaps' of voluntary (church school) provision. Edward Cardwell's army reforms prohibit purchase of commissions. Introduction of competitive examinations for entrance to the civil service

1871: University Tests Act permits non-Anglicans to be admitted to the Universities of Oxford and Cambridge. Establishment of a new Local Government Board. Trade Union Act and Criminal Law Amendment Act help secure legal status of unions but does not recognise right to peaceful picketing

1872: Establishment of secret ballot helps to reduce opportunities to influence voters at elections. Licensing Act imposes new restrictions on the sale of drink

1873: Government resigns after defeat on a bill to reform higher education in Ireland, but Disraeli refuses to become leader of another minority Tory government. Liberals resume office

1874: Liberals defeated in the general election. Conservatives have an overall majority of about 50 seats

1875: Gladstone resigns leadership of Liberals in the Commons and is replaced by Hartington. He becomes an irregular attender of Parliament for a time

1876: Gladstone's pamphlet on 'The Bulgarian Horrors' brings him back into public life

1877: Formation of the National Liberal Federation – controlled by radicals. Joseph Chamberlain exercises considerable influence from Birmingham

1879: Gladstone pioneers new forms of direct electioneering to mass audiences in the Midlothian Campaign

1880: Liberals win an overall majority of almost 60 seats; Gladstone becomes party leader and Prime Minister again

1881–2: Irish nationalist MPs disrupt parliamentary business. Much disunity within the Liberal Party

1883: Corrupt and Illegal Practices Prevention Act regulates amounts that can be spent on election expenses

1884: Third Reform Act establishes a uniform franchise qualification in both boroughs and counties. About two-thirds of adult males in England and about one half in Ireland have the vote after this Act

1885: Major redistribution of parliamentary seats sees 159 old seats removed and 175 new ones created. At the general election, Liberals retain substantial majority over the Conservatives but have no overall majority because of the presence of 86 Irish nationalists

Gladstone: man and beliefs

William Ewart Gladstone is one of the most compelling characters in nineteenth-century politics. As the biography on page 113 indicates, his political career spanned more than 60 years and for much of that time he was absolutely at the centre of affairs. His energies and abilities alike were legendary. In addition to being a full-time politician and administrator, he found time to write closely argued pamphlets on the great issues of the day, notably the Church and foreign affairs. He was a loyal and passionate Churchman, and he proved passionate in much else. He was highly sexed; his wife, from whom political activity often required lengthy periods of separation, became pregnant nine times in 14 years. His odd, almost driven, habit of visiting prostitutes on 'rescue' missions – often after delivering a lengthy Commons speech – risked ridicule and politically damaging exposure. His aim of converting them to respectable employment achieved predictably limited success. The entries in Gladstone's meticulously maintained diaries reveal that, from the 1840s, he took to scourging himself with a whip after many of these nocturnal visits. The same diaries also reveal a man of huge learning and intense intellectual curiosity.

Partly because he was in the political spotlight for so long and partly because so much was written both by and about him, we know more about William Gladstone than about any other British politician of the nineteenth century. Given his successes as Chancellor of the Exchequer and Prime Minister, furthermore, it is easy to assume that Gladstone led the Liberal Party much as he wanted and that the party gladly followed such an able and successful leader. This chapter title includes the phrase 'Gladstonian Liberalism', which only seems to reinforce the image of Gladstone as the essence of Liberalism. The paradox is that he was not. As we know, Gladstone came to the Liberal Party quite late in his career. His background, instincts and early political guidance all came from Tory, or Conservative, sources. The Conservative Prime Minister Sir Robert Peel gave Gladstone his first government job; he remained his political tutor until he died in 1850.

From Peel, Gladstone learned to prize free trade as the economic objective to follow above all others. Gladstonian Liberalism was committed to free trade, low taxation and limited government interference. In 1874, as proof that he was committed to cheap government, he promised that he would abolish the income tax if his party won the election. Peel had only reintroduced income tax in 1842 in order to get the nation's finances back in order after the mismanagement of Melbourne's Whigs. After a generation of peace and prosperity, Gladstone argued, the nation could afford to get rid of it again.

Gladstone's economic policy, therefore, was Peelite rather than Liberal. Other, more thoroughgoing, Liberals like Richard Cobden and John Bright were also convinced free-traders, but it was Gladstone's senior position in the party during its long periods in office in the 1860s and early 1870s that helped to confirm the Liberals as 'the party of free trade'. Perhaps from Peel, also, Gladstone learned what he always temperamentally wanted to hear anyway: that political parties were subordinate to great moral and ethical questions. Peel did not flinch from breaking up his party in 1846 to secure the great prize of free trade in corn. As we shall see, Gladstone was prepared to risk exactly the same outcome for the Liberals over his conversion to the highly controversial cause of Irish Home Rule. Gladstone, like Peel, was not fundamentally a party man. Though his immense abilities and his increasing liking for taking politics direct to the people proved enormous political assets for the Liberals, many in his adopted party had substantial reservations about him.

For the Whig aristocrats, who still provided the party with much of its money and were used to leading it, both Gladstone's commercial background – he was no tenth-generation aristocrat – and his disloyalty to his old party (if he could desert the Conservatives over one issue, why not the Liberals over another?) – told against him. He was not readily assimilated into the old traditions and myths of Whiggery as the guardian of the nation's liberties. For the new generation of professional politicians – men like **Joseph Chamberlain** who were coming to maturity in the age

PROFILE: *Joseph Chamberlain*

Joseph Chamberlain is perhaps best remembered nowadays as the man who brought both major political parties close to collapse. He was born in London in 1836 the son of a tradesman, but made his fortune in Birmingham as a screw manufacturer. Birmingham was his early political power base and he introduced many reforms while its Mayor from 1873 to 1875. He was elected MP for Birmingham in 1876, and he helped to make the new National Liberal Federation into a very efficient political organisation, claiming much credit for the Liberal victory in 1880. He served Gladstone as President of the Board of Trade in the government of 1880–85 but broke with Gladstone over Ireland, becoming first a Liberal 'Unionist' and then crossing over into the 'Conservative and Unionist Party'. He was Colonial Secretary in Salisbury's government of 1895–1902, when he supported both imperial policies and policies of social reform. He resigned from Balfour's government in 1903 to campaign for 'imperial preference' rather than free trade. It is widely believed that the divisions to which this led brought about the Liberal landslide victory in 1906. In the same year, Chamberlain suffered a severe stroke and, though he lived on until 1914, this finished his political career.

of mass politics – Gladstone's preference for giving what he called 'great moral questions' such a high priority and the details of electoral management and 'fixing' such a low one was both perplexing and unsettling. Chamberlain was an able man with a genius for political organisation. His views about how to exploit what *Macmillan's Magazine* called the 'new conditions' created by the Reform Act differed sharply from those of Gladstone.

'After the passing of the Reform Bill [in 1867] the leaders of the Liberal Party in Birmingham recognised the new conditions under which alone success would be possible. They saw the absolute necessity of taking their party as a whole into their . . . confidence. It was evident to them that the day had gone by for attempting to control a large constituency by cliques composed of a few wealthy men. A whole suburb could be outvoted by a couple of streets . . .

It was soon perceived that the development of the life of a great town needs some agency far more powerful and more worthy than a mere election committee . . . Time, trouble and thought were . . . lavished in Birmingham

> *. . . to persuade the people at large that political interests are the interests of civilisation in its broadest sense. The improvement of the dwellings of the poor; the promotion of temperance; the multiplication of libraries and art galleries; the management of grammar schools, as well as public elementary schools, were all discussed as questions of Liberal politics . . . The problem presented [to the people] was how to obtain [support for] a programme of public improvement as well as a vote for a parliamentary candidate. It was decided that the Liberal Party, as a party of avowed Liberals, should, if possible, secure a working majority in every representative body connected with the borough . . . In the council of a town, which is almost a state in size and importance, men . . . are wanted who will stand on the same side of Liberal progress in municipal affairs that Liberal members of the House of Commons take on in national affairs, and who will make the town as great in its educational and scientific institutions as it is in commercial activity, and address themselves to the removal of preventible causes of ignorance, disease, and crime.'*
>
> *Macmillan's Magazine*, vol. 35, 1876–7.

For the new men, Gladstone was of the old school; they felt that they could never quite trust either his political loyalty to them or his assertive and embarrassingly public conscience. Gladstone presented himself as a man of action prepared to take up a series of high-profile causes, and he used the party as his vehicle. As he put it in a letter to Granville in 1877: 'My opinion is and has long been that the vital principle of the Liberal Party. . . is action, and that nothing but action will ever make it worthy of the name of a party'. Since Gladstone frequently seemed to have more moral and physical energy than the rest of the party put together, you can see why many Liberals yearned for a bit of peace and quiet.

The Liberals

Increasingly, influential Liberals were reluctant to follow where Gladstone wanted to lead. Students generally know much more about Gladstone than they do about the party in which he spent the last 35 years of his active political life. Yet, if we are to understand the importance of the individual in politics, it is important to appreciate that even the most dominant of them needs to be seen in an appropriate context.

a Whigs and aristocrats

By the late 1860s, the Liberals had grown accustomed to holding office. Most of the party's leaders, men like Lord John Russell and the **Marquis**

PROFILE: *The Marquis of Hartington*

Spencer Cavendish, **Marquis of Hartington** was born in Lancashire in 1833 and succeeded to the title of marquis, as the heir to the earldom of Devonshire, in 1858. He entered Parliament as a Liberal in 1857 and served in Gladstone's first cabinet both as War Secretary and as Chief Secretary for Ireland. He took over, with Granville, as leader of the Liberals on Gladstone's resignation in 1875 and served him again as Secretary for India (1880–82) and War Secretary (1882–5). He opposed Gladstone's Irish Home Rule policy in 1886 and became leader of the Liberal Unionists. He became eighth Duke of Devonshire in 1891 and served in the Conservative and Unionist government as Lord President of the Council (1895–1903). Hartington's break with Gladstone was of first importance. He was the leading Whig in the party and, as such, took many Liberal Unionists with him. This ensured that Gladstone's last eight years as leader would be of a party which had lost most of its support among the great landowners. He died in 1908.

of Hartington (eldest son of the Duke of Devonshire), came from families which felt that they had been born to rule. Throughout the 1850s and 1860s the party had been led by people from the same immensely privileged backgrounds as had dominated British political life since the early eighteenth century. There are very strong elements of continuity in the Gladstonian Liberal Party. Anthony Trollope, one of the nineteenth century's most celebrated novelists, knew a lot about politics and politicians, working for many years as a senior civil servant. In a series of political novels, he recreated the mid-Victorian political scene. Though he recognised the newcomers from business, trade and the northern industrial towns, his novels told a story of political power being controlled from the centre by great landlords. He called his leading power-broker 'The Duke of Omnium'. *Omnium* is Latin for 'everything' and Trollope was making the point that inherited landed wealth continued to bestow immense political influence. Until 1880, landowners remained the largest group in the House of Commons and many of the 320 or so landowners and ex-officers from the armed services who were elected to the 1874 Parliament were related to the aristocracy. Gladstone himself respected high breeding and much preferred the company of wealthy landowners to that of northern businessmen or bankers. His cabinets reflected strong aristocratic prejudice; they were far from being dominated by 'new men' like John Bright. When Gladstone gave up the leadership of the party in 1875, it passed to two leading Whigs, Hartington and Granville. When Gladstone seized the leadership of the party back after the famous election victory of

1880, these two were given senior posts in the second Gladstone cabinet – Granville as Foreign Secretary, Hartington as Secretary for India, Britain's greatest imperial asset.

Though the agricultural depression of the later 1870s and the rapidly changing electoral system finally reduced the social and political dominance of the Whigs in the 1880s, they remained an important element in Gladstone's Liberal Party; the party was hardly ever the force it had been once their influence began to decline. Paradoxically, the political party which is generally associated with 'progress' and 'reform' still owed much to the influence and involvement of aristocratic Whig politicians.

b Commoners and radicals

For many years, students have been encouraged to think in terms of a Liberal Party under Gladstone which was divided into three parts – the Whigs, the radicals and a large, loyally Gladstonian 'middle group'. This is not a particularly helpful division. Although the Whigs can be clearly identified as a separate group, there is much overlap between the others. The so-called 'radicals' did not stand on a common platform; they supported a wide variety of issues, some of them in opposition to each other. While some radicals were anxious to extend the principle of democracy, some embracing the cause of women's suffrage from the late 1860s, others had different priorities. Temperance reformers wanted to improve the working man and, by depriving him of access to drink, ensure that a larger proportion of his wages would get back home to benefit his wife and children. Teetotallers tended to be intolerant and to believe that people should earn their privileges by sober commitment to respectable behaviour and to improvement. Led by Sir Wilfred Lawson, the grandly titled 'UK Alliance for the Suppression of Liquor' was a one-issue pressure group which sheltered under the broad umbrella of the Liberal Party. There were many others, on issues such as the disestablishment of the Church of England, compulsory education, improved legal status for trade unions, home rule for Ireland and support for the Welsh language. The more enthusiasts for one particular cause banged their own drums, the louder and more discordant the noise they made.

As in Palmerston's day, so-called radicals divided sharply in their attitudes to foreign policy. Some, led by John Bright, were pacifists, believing that active foreign policy risked war. For them, war was morally wrong. It was also bad for trade and thus for prosperity. Others took precisely the opposite view. While wishing to see increased state involvement to improve the conditions of working people, they believed that it was Britain's destiny, as the most powerful nation in the world, to give a moral lead to the rest. Britain could use its naval strength to impose its will on others. They were prepared to go to war in defence of British interests abroad. By the 1880s, a distinct group of 'Liberal Imperialists' was emerging. The division between imperialists and anti-imperialists threatened party unity for much of the remainder of the century.

Similarly, the so-called middle group, though it usually supported the leadership, contained many members who felt passionately about one issue or another. Some Gladstone loyalists, for example, were strongly committed to the cause of secular education and were disappointed that Forster's Education Act of 1870 continued to give grants to Church of England schools. The Church remained the dominant force in popular education in the English countryside.

The more the subject is studied, the less clear-cut are distinctions between 'radicals' and the remainder of the Liberal Party. It is much more helpful to identify where Liberal support was strong. From the following points, you can build up a picture of the kind of interests which comprised the party which Gladstone led in the 1870s and 1880s.

- *Nonconformists* supported the Liberal Party in large numbers. Areas in which Nonconformity was strong tended to be areas where the Liberals did well in almost every election. More than 60 Liberal MPs were Nonconformists in the Parliament of 1868–74; almost no Conservatives were. More importantly, those Anglicans who represented the large majority of the parliamentary Liberal Party were sensitive to those issues which mattered to Nonconformists, like compulsory payment of church rates and education.
- Most *skilled workers* looked upon the Liberals as the party of the working man. The first working men, Alexander MacDonald and Thomas Burt, elected to Parliament took their seats in 1874; they were among the strongest supporters of Gladstone.
- Liberals tended to do well in the *northern manufacturing areas* of England, and particularly the woollen textile areas. Even in 1874, when a general election was lost, the Liberals still managed to defeat the Conservatives by 60 seats to 27 in northern boroughs which had more than 5,000 voters.
- Liberalism was particularly strong in *Scotland, Wales* and parts of the *south-west of England*. In all of these areas, national and regional identity was of importance and in most the Anglican Church was an object of opposition, distrust or even hatred.
- The Liberal Party tended to have disproportionate attraction for *writers* and *intellectuals*. Though a tiny group numerically, their importance lay in the ideas they generated. They contributed to sustaining liberalism's image as the party of progress and reforming zeal.

The price of reform

The government of 1868–74 is rightly recognised as one of the great reforming ministries of the nineteenth century. The time chart gives some indication of the range of its reforms. To them should be added important changes in Ireland which are dealt with separately (see chapter 24).

Three points should be made about this torrent of reform:

1 Reforms are frequently better appreciated in hindsight than at the time. Gladstone's commitment to administrative reorganisation and efficiency helped both local and central government to work better. The quality of entrants to the civil service, for example, became impressively high. Efficiency in administration, however, does not win many votes.

2 These reforms often showed up Liberal divisions, rather than emphasising their strength. Forster's Education Act was a compromise between Anglicans and Nonconformists which satisfied neither side – though it happened to be a major turning-point in opportunity for working-class children. Gladstone himself worried that it would weaken the Church of England, to which he still remained devoted. Similarly, the trade union reforms of 1871 stopped frustratingly short of giving the skilled workers the assurances they wanted. Even the famous Secret Ballot of 1872 was conceded grudgingly by Gladstone (who saw little point in it) in order to get John Bright back into the cabinet and to put on a show of Liberal unity when it was becoming frayed.

3 Some of this legislation was easily exploited by the party's opponents. The Licensing Act of 1872 failed to satisfy temperance reformers, while also playing into the hands of the Conservatives who could portray the Liberals as killjoys bent on depriving the working man of drinking time.

By 1873, it was obvious to all that the Liberals were deeply divided, their reforming impulse apparently played out. Disraeli exploited the situation brilliantly (see chapter 23). The eventual Liberal recovery of the later 1870s owed something to Gladstone's discovery of a great moral cause in foreign policy, championing Bulgarian Christians against 'Infidel' Turks in eastern Europe and rubbishing 'Beaconsfieldism' in the process (see chapter 23). Gladstone also developed his love affair with the electorate by direct appeals in national campaigns. Liberal revival probably owed most, however, to the fact that the Conservatives had to face the electorate in 1880 in the depths of an economic depression.

Figure 22.1 *A post-1870 Board School*

ROASTING THE MINISTERS.

Figure 22.2 *Cartoon from* Judy, or the London Serio-comic Journal, *1873*

The second Gladstone government of 1880–85 was dominated by foreign affairs and, especially, by Ireland (see chapters 24 and 26). It had little of the reforming zeal of its predecessor. Perhaps, however, it emphasised even more the double-edged quality of Gladstone's outsize personality. Gladstone had seized back the leadership in 1880 from Hartington and Granville on the back of his evident appeal to the electorate. Queen Victoria viewed this development with horror:

'Windsor Castle, 22 April 1880

Wrote last night to Lord Hartington, asking him to come today, as I wished to charge him with forming a Government. I saw him at that hour, and he spoke quite frankly. I was equally frank with him. But the result was unsatisfactory. When I stated that I looked on him to form a Government, he said that though they had not consulted Mr Gladstone, both he and Lord Granville feared that they would have no chance of success if Mr Gladstone was not in the Government, and that they feared he would not take a subordinate position. If he were to remain a sort of irresponsible adviser outside the Government, that would be unconstitutional . . . and that if he were quite *independent, he might make it impossible for any Liberal Government to go on. They therefore thought it would be best and wisest if I at once sent for Mr Gladstone.*

I said there was one great difficulty, which was that I could not give Mr Gladstone my confidence. His violence and bitterness had been such, the way in which he had, in times of great anxiety, rendered my task and that of the Government so difficult, and the alarm abroad at his name being so great, it would be impossible for me to have the full confidence in him I should wish, were he to form a Government.'

Extract from Queen Victoria's journal, *Letters of Queen Victoria*.

The very personality which the Queen found so distasteful, however, helped to give an increasingly divided party a semblance of unity. Even so, Gladstone's high-handed ways and his moral certainties continued to upset both aristocrats like Hartington and young politicians on the make, like Joseph Chamberlain who suspected (not without reason) that Gladstone was finding reasons to avoid promoting him as high as his political talents warranted. It is well known that the Liberal Party split in 1886 over Irish Home Rule (see chapter 24). We need to remember, also, that a number of Whig landowners were already deserting the party before this crisis. The Marquis of Lansdowne was the best known, but the Dukes of Argyll and Bedford represented significant defections as well. Many Whigs disliked Gladstone's leadership and resented the way that (as they saw it) he had snatched back the leadership in 1880. More were deeply concerned about the growing importance, especially at grassroots level, of ideas which aimed at increasing the role of the state and using it to reduce economic and social inequalities. Many feared that their party was being used by men like Chamberlain and even Bright to advance the cause of 'socialism'.

Among the majority who stayed loyal to Gladstone in the early 1880s, the feeling was growing that, while Liberals could not do without Gladstone's leadership, he was nevertheless driving the party ever closer to the rocks. When deprived of big issues in the middle 1870s, Gladstone talked incessantly of retirement. First foreign affairs and then Ireland, however, gave him his big 'issues'. During the 1880s and into the 1890s the 'Grand Old Man' hung limpet-like to the leadership, blighting the ambitions of the next generation, while impaling the party on policies which could hardly fail to divide the party irrevocably.

Group task

You should now be able to reach some conclusions about the role of a key individual. Use the evidence in this chapter – and any other information you may have – to draw up a list of the 'plus' and 'minus' points of Gladstone's leadership of the Liberals in this period. Different groups could look at particular aspects. Concentrate on:

- his beliefs
- his relations with political colleagues
- his style of leadership
- his appeal to the electorate.

You should then be in a position to reach a conclusion on the following question: 'Was Gladstone more of a help or a hindrance to the fortunes of the Liberal Party in these years?'

Further reading

M. Winstanley, *Gladstone and the Liberal Party,* Lancaster Pamphlet (Routledge, 1990) – a good, brief introduction to both man and party.

T. A. Jenkins, *The Liberal Ascendancy, 1830–86* (Macmillan, 1994) – a very useful survey which incorporates much recent research.

R. Jenkins, *Gladstone* (Macmillan, 1995) – a major new study whose insights are informed by the fact that the author was a senior politician himself.

H. G. C. Matthew, *Gladstone* (Oxford University Press, 1988).

J. P. Parry, 'Religion and the collapse of Gladstone's first government, 1870–74', *Historical Journal,* vol. xxv (1982).

J. P. Parry, *The Rise and Fall of Liberal Government in Victorian Britain* (Yale University Press, 1993) – an excellent and up-to-date survey which puts Gladstone in a wider focus.

CHANGE AND CONTINUITY

23 What was Disraelian Conservatism? The Conservative Party, 1867–80

Time chart

1867: Disraeli pilots a second Reform Act through Parliament. In addition to greatly increasing the number of voters in the boroughs, the measure removes many non-Conservative voters from county seats. Conservative National Union founded – the beginnings of modern party organisation

1868: Derby resigns; Disraeli becomes leader of the Conservative Party and, briefly, Prime Minister. General election brings Conservative defeat but considerable increase in support in Lancashire and some other counties

1870: Establishment of Conservative Central Office under John Eldon Gorst

1872: Disraeli's famous speeches attacking the Liberal government as 'a range of exhausted volcanoes' and asserting that 'the health of the people was the most important question for a statesman'

1873: Gladstone resigns after suffering a defeat on an Irish measure. Disraeli refuses to assume office at the head of a minority government

1874: Conservatives win an overall majority of about 50 seats and Disraeli becomes Prime Minister again. Disraeli moves quickly to amend the Liberal Licensing Act and increases hours of drinking – pleasing working men and the mostly Conservative brewers. Factory Act reduces maximum working hours of women and children and prohibited full-time work before age of 14

1875: Passage of Trade Union Acts. Artisans' Dwelling Act enables local authorities to buy land on which new houses might be built. Public Health Act brings together principles found in much legislation passed previously. Sale of Food and Drugs Act aimed to reduce adulteration of food, but local authorities not compelled to appoint food analysts

1876: Rivers Pollution Act aimed to reduce discharge of poisonous waste into rivers, but this was only a milder version of sterner legislation which the government had withdrawn. The Merchant Shipping Act introduced load lines to prevent dangerous overloading of vessels but it had limited effect. Queen Victoria accepts the title 'Empress of India'. Disraeli accepts a peerage as Earl of Beaconsfield. Gladstone returns to public life with his pamphlet 'The Bulgarian Horrors and the Question of the East'

1877: War breaks out between Russia and Turkey. British interests in the Mediterranean affected

1878: Derby, the British Foreign Secretary, resigns over Middle-East policy, fearing that Disraeli would declare war on Russia. Salisbury succeeds him. Congress of Berlin settles the Russo-Turkish question and preserves the Turkish empire. Britain occupies Cyprus

1879: Zulu war; British troops defeated at Battle of Isandhlwana

Conservative revival in opposition

Disraeli talked of climbing to 'the top of the greasy pole' when he replaced Derby as Prime Minister in February 1868. He did not stay there long at first. The electorate proved less grateful than he had hoped for increasing its size so extensively. The Conservatives returned to their accustomed opposition role after the general election and Disraeli broke with tradition by choosing to resign before the new Parliament assembled. Always the supreme political tactician, he recognised that the will of the people was now expressed through support for one party or another. There was little point in trying to stitch together parliamentary alliances when the electorate's preference for Gladstone had been so clearly expressed.

The years of opposition which stretched ahead, however, proved less futile than those in the 1850s and early 1860s for two main reasons: improved organisation and recast policies.

After 1868 the Conservatives took the opportunity to improve their organisation. The new Central Office became involved in selecting candidates. J. E. Gorst helped to ensure that Conservative policies were properly explained in the constituencies by publishing pamphlets designed to be read by working people. Disraeli was also anxious to ensure that working men had good reasons to support the Conservatives. Local parties developed extensive programmes of social, as well as political, events. It was not unusual to find local parties boarding excursion trains for a day of fun, frivolity – and to hear the occasional political speech. In 1875, for example, Stockport Conservatives hired two trains to take their supporters to Southport and the beach.

Improved political organisation was a feature of both political parties as they responded to new challenges after 1867. There is no doubt, however, that by the next election in 1874, the Conservatives were the better organised and had the higher morale. In particular, they were now a significant presence in constituencies which had previously been almost unchallengeably Liberal. At the election of 1874, the Conservatives won seats from the Liberals in 74 constituencies of England and Wales; 65 of these had local Conservative organisations, most of them founded in the early 1870s.

Disraeli took the opportunity to reappraise traditional Conservative policies and attitudes. The challenge he faced was to rescue the party from apparently permanent minority status. His solution was to present it as the 'national' party and also as one which had the interest of all the nation's citizens at heart. These two themes were at the heart of two speeches made in 1872 at Manchester's free trade hall and London's Crystal Palace. Both were long on general impression – support for 'the Empire' which the Liberals were letting go to waste; declarations of concern for the health of the nation – but significantly short on precise detail.

Nevertheless, Disraeli was perhaps the first major politician to realise that most people are not much interested in the detail of politics. For him, image mattered more than content; detail he always left to others. He presented the Tories both as the patriotic and the practical party. Queen Victoria was personally enchanted to be titled 'Empress of India'. The title also conveyed the indelible impression that Britain was a major imperial power. British citizens were intended to take pride in the fact. Conservatives were also suspicious of ideology; they preferred common sense to theory. Thus Conservatives cut across crude class divisions to appeal to the best in everyone. Submitting these airy assertions to rigorous specific criticism nearly always leaves the balance of intellectual advantage with the opponents of the Conservatives. But most people are neither intellectual nor red-hot politicians. Disraeli's clever mixture of mildly stirring patriotic rhetoric and cosy banality has proved to be a bankable asset for his party ever since. Disraeli did more than any other single politician to make the Conservatives not only electable but the normal preference at least of English, if not British, voters ever since.

'The elections of 1868 had brought home to the statesmanship of Disraeli the necessity of creating some kind of organisation to meet the new conditions created by the Reform Act which he had passed for the purpose of dishing the Whigs [defeating the Liberals] . . .

With few exceptions, the counties voted solidly for the Tory Party [in the General Election of 1868], and occasioned no trouble. The boroughs, on the other hand, were nearly all Radical; and . . . the whole of London returned only one Conservative. The municipal corporations were almost invariably Radical and the political influence exercised by them was of course enormous . . .

While . . . several influential members of the Tory Party thought that the Conservative cause was absolutely ruined, Disraeli's brains perceived that the remedy for this state of affairs lay in the invention of an entirely new system of conducting elections. Disraeli believed that personal zeal or ambition would prove more successful than paid services; accordingly, after the Liberal triumph of 1868 he began to look about for a young and ambitious member of the party, who would be willing to give his services to the Conservative cause, and who would devote his best years to working out a complete scheme of party organisation. His choice fell on Mr [John Eldon] Gorst, who had entered the House of Commons in 1866 . . . but had lost his seat in the election of 1868. What was most wanted, said Disraeli to his new party manager, was that every constituency should have a candidate ready beforehand. That ought to be the first consideration in organising a permanent system of electoral machinery. Offices and an adequate staff were provided in Parliament Street; and at these headquarters the party manager and his able assistants duly installed themselves as "The Conservative Central Office" . . .

The satisfactory results achieved by this new system of organisation were manifested at the by-elections which occurred from time to time. Disraeli took a great interest in the working of the new machinery.

When parliament was suddenly and unexpectedly dissolved in 1874 there was no confusion or embarrassment among the ranks of the Conservative Party. Telegrams were sent immediately to all the constituencies, telling them to get ready for the election, and asking them who was going to contest the seat in the Conservative interest . . . The plan of campaign was to throw the whole energies and resources of the central organisation into those contests which received inefficient local help, but which gave a reasonable expectation of a successful issue. And in this way the election of 1874, which might otherwise have proved disastrous to the Conservative Party, was turned into a brilliant victory.'

From a biography of Disraeli entitled *Earl of Beaconsfield* written by H. E. Gorst (1900).

The 1874 general election: continuity or change?

Disraeli's triumph at the polls in 1874 is of first importance. It was the first majority the party had won since Peel's in 1841 and it was to be the turning-point of Tory fortunes. Thirty-one general elections were held in the years 1874–1992 inclusive. The Conservatives, either alone or as the dominant element in coalitions, had a majority over their main opponents in 19 of them. In 1874 the Conservatives consolidated earlier gains in Lancashire and Cheshire, winning 34 of the possible 46 seats. They greatly improved their position in the largest borough seats. The Liberals had been used to winning at least three-quarters of the seats with the largest electorates. Yet in 1874 the Tories won 44 of the 114 seats with the largest number of voters. For the first time, they approached parity in London, winning 10 out of the capital's 22 seats.

This proved to be the start of something really big: Conservative domination of the votes of the lower middle classes in the growing suburbs. The victory seemed a wonderful reward for Disraeli's policies since 1868. He had supervised a thorough overhaul of the Conservatives' electoral machine. Disraeli's biting attacks on the disunited, exhausted Liberals also struck a chord. In 1874 Gladstone promised to reduce taxes, yet still lost convincingly.

The Conservative victory seemed to signal a radical shift in the electorate's allegiance, and in some sense it was. Yet, on closer inspection, we may seem in some respects still to be in the old political world rather than the new.

1 A substantial majority of the Conservative MPs returned in 1874 represented rural seats. About 250 of the 350 or so Tory MPs were landowners. Like Peel in 1841, Disraeli dominated the English counties, where he won 153 of the 180 seats. In Parliament, the Conservatives were dominated by English squires and country gentlemen.

2 Even in Lancashire and Cheshire, where Conservative advance was most striking, it is very difficult to argue that the reason was the increased popularity of Conservative policies among working men. Conservatives in the North-West did especially well in places where there was a large Catholic minority. Many working men were voting more out of fear of, or hostility to, Irish immigrants. The Conservatives traditionally strongly supported England's established religion, the Church of England.

3 Scotland and Wales were nothing like as enthusiastic for the Conservatives as England was. The Liberals won 40 seats to the Conservatives 20 in Scotland and 19 to the Conservatives 11 in Wales. In Ireland, the first general election fought on a secret ballot brought no fewer than 58 nationalists to Westminster; the Conservatives won 33 seats in Ireland. The 1874 election confirmed that the Conservatives were the party of England and not Britain and rural, rather than urban, England.

4 Though the number of seats which were not contested at general elections declined sharply after 1867, they still represented a significant minority of the total – and Conservatives were disproportionately returned for them. This helps to explain the paradox that the Conservatives (who outnumbered the Liberals in England by 288 seats in 171 at this election) nevertheless did not win any larger share of the popular vote than the Liberals did.

Disraeli undoubtedly had a vision of a modernised Conservative Party which would sweep the Liberals aside. Beneath the surface of the election result, and despite some very hopeful signs in suburban areas, the basis of support for the Tories remained much as it had been in Peel's day.

Disraeli's government of 1874–80

In his famous Crystal Palace speech of June 1872, Disraeli had said that a great objective of the Conservative Party was 'the elevation of the condition of the people'. It is perhaps natural, therefore, to look at the record of the Conservative government and to judge it by how far it met this objective. Superficially, it might seem that social issues were at the forefront of the Conservative strategy. The time chart gives details of what we might call the 'social legislation' passed in the years 1874–6.

In recognition of Tory successes in Lancashire, Disraeli made the previously obscure, but wealthy, banker from that county, **Richard Cross**, his Home Secretary. Cross laboured hard on measures such as the Artisans' Dwelling Act, the Public Health Act and the Sale of Food and Drugs Act. The Employers' and Workmen's Act and the Conspiracy and Protection of Property Act, both passed in 1875, produced perhaps the most radical departure from existing practice. The first Act put employers and employees on an equal footing before the law. The second freed trade unions from the threat of being prosecuted for taking strike action collectively.

> *'An agreement or combination by two or more persons to do or procure to be done any act in contemplation or furtherance of a trade dispute between employers and workmen shall not be indictable as a conspiracy if such act committed by one person would not be punishable as a crime.'*
>
> Conspiracy and Protection of Property Act, 1875

Disraeli's motives in promoting trade union legislation were political. Recognising that earlier Liberal legislation had fallen short of union expectations, and knowing that the unions were strongly Liberal in their support, he made a bold play for the working man's vote. Just as the Liberals had proved too cautious over parliamentary reform in 1866, so Disraeli would now exploit the fierce opposition to trade union reform from many Liberal businessmen.

In August 1875 Disraeli announced himself satisfied with the extent of legislative achievement on the social question:

> *'We have been successful ... The [ordinary people] did not coerce us but assisted and aided us ... During the five years that we spent in Opposition we endeavoured to impress upon the country our sincere convictions that the time had arrived when political change was no longer required, when the distribution of political power was no longer the problem to solve in this country, but that its intelligence and energy should be directed to the improvement and elevation of the condition of the people ... When ... we had acceded to power it became our first duty, and I can say our most ardent desire, to bring practice into policy.'*
>
> Speech at the Mansion House, 4 August 1875, quoted in *The Times*, 5 August 1875.

It is easy to exaggerate the importance of 'social legislation' in Disraeli's thinking. Tory legislation did little to increase the role of the state or to challenge the near-universal belief among established politicians in the superiority of free trade and *laissez-faire* in economic policy. Much legislation only extended principles already established by the Liberals in 1868–74, usually with a political spin on the ball designed to woo Conservative voters. Thus, the Sandon Education Act of 1876 modified its more famous predecessor, passed by the Liberals in 1870, by introducing local School Attendance Committees with powers to compel attendance. Sandon wanted to improve the attendance at Anglican rural schools. Absentee pupils did less well in the tests which helped to

PROFILE: *Richard Cross*

Richard Assheton Cross, who was born in 1823, had a long political career, but is best remembered as Disraeli's Home Secretary in the government of 1874–80. He also served Salisbury briefly in that capacity (1885–6), before moving on to be Secretary for India (1886–92) and Lord Privy Seal (1895–1900). Cross was responsible for working out the details both of the reform of the Liberal Licensing Act in 1874 and the Artisans' Dwelling Act in 1875. Though the powers which local authorities could take to improve housing under the latter measure were extensive, Cross's Act was not especially successful. Only 10 of the 87 local authorities which could have made use of it had chosen to do so by 1881. Cross was more committed to social reform than his leader and famously expressed surprise that Disraeli, who had spoken of improving the health of the nation before taking office, had no specific proposals for doing so. Cross and Disraeli were never close. Cross found Disraeli's preference for image over substance perplexing, while Disraeli disliked Cross's bourgeois manners. Cross died in 1914.

determine the level of government grant. Evidence was mounting that performance was better in urban schools, run by the new school boards. The older Anglican or 'national' schools were being left behind and the Church's educational supremacy threatened. The Conservatives therefore sought to redress the balance in the interests of their Anglican rural supporters.

Cross himself was one of the few Conservatives to complain at the lack of vigour with which social reform was being pursued. He was swiftly brought into line by Disraeli who reminded him that he had promised in his election addresses to give the British people a rest from what he called 'incessant and harassing legislation'. Such legislation, Disraeli was convinced, had contributed to Gladstone's downfall and he had no intention of repeating his rival's mistake. The Conservative Party, after all, was the party of solidity and consolidation, not of rash and hectic reform. So, after the legislative flurry of 1874–5, Conservative pledges on social reform were considered redeemed. Attention now needed to be diverted to foreign affairs. Significantly, the Conservative social reforms were hardly mentioned by Conservative leaders when they next faced a general election in 1880.

Foreign policy during Disraeli's ministry was dominated by the implications of the steady decline of the Ottoman Empire (Turkey). British interests were bound up with preserving stability in the Mediterranean and,

KEY TERM:

Jingoism

Jingoism now means reckless patriotism. A 'jingoist' will risk war to preserve his or her country's honour. The term originates in a music hall song written at the time of the Bulgarian crisis. When Disraeli sent a British fleet to the Mediterranean, the song asserted that 'We don't want to fight but, by jingo, if we do, we've got the men, we've got the ships, we've got the money too'. It should not be thought that everyone supported jingoistic policies at this time. A much less well-known parody of the song also did the rounds of the music hall. It said, 'I don't want to fight; I ain't no Briton true, and I'd let the Russians have Constantinople.'

most particularly, in preserving the route to India and the profitable trade in the East. In purely economic terms, therefore, Britain wished to ensure that Turkey did not weaken too fast because Russia was waiting to step into the breach and had ambitions of its own to dominate the Mediterranean (see chapter 18). In the 1870s, however, moral and nationalist factors complicated the issue. The weakening of the Ottoman Empire encouraged nationalist movements in the Balkans, especially Bosnia, Serbia and Bulgaria. These enjoyed initial success but the Turks recovered ground in 1876 and, in doing so, committed numerous atrocities, including the massacre of numerous Bulgarian citizens.

Gladstone's famous pamphlet (see time chart) was partly a rallying cry for Christian Britain to support nations struggling to be free against the oppressive and barbaric rule by a corrupt Muslim empire. It was also calculatedly political. Gladstone was anxious to stress that Disraeli's policy was immoral. The Conservatives were soon accused of using **jingoism** to shore up an intolerable regime.

The Bulgarian crisis stirred passions over foreign policy issue as no other in the nineteenth century did. In the hands of a political master like Gladstone, the issue could be presented as one between good and evil, reaction and progress. Disraeli, too, had high cards to play. The Turks might be corrupt and played out but would British interests be served by helping the Ottoman regime to collapse, when the certain consequence would be an increase of Russian influence in the Mediterranean? He also knew that Gladstone was not the Liberal Party. He could, and did, rouse Nonconformist consciences and raised the morale of party activists on an undeniably 'big issue', but the party leaders were much more cautious. They were not willing to risk war in the Mediterranean, especially against the Turks. Hartington and Granville feared that the Liberals might split if Gladstone continued his crusade.

Disraeli eventually emerged with a substantial diplomatic triumph. The war between Russia and Turkey produced a Russian victory and the imposition on Turkey of a new, independent territory labelled 'big Bulgaria' – Christian but also effectively a Russian satellite. The other European powers were not prepared to see such a dramatic increase in Russian influence in south-east Europe. Britain and Austria took the lead in bringing Russia to the conference table. The Congress of Berlin substantially reduced the amount of Bulgarian territory under Russian influence. Turkey remained a power in the area, but Britain occupied Cyprus. This action eloquently indicated that Britain no longer believed that Turkey could ensure stability on its own. The Congress did not 'solve' the Eastern Question but it did avoid sucking Britain into war. Disraeli, naturally and not unreasonably, claimed the credit. From a

Figure 23.1 *Cartoon showing Disraeli at the Congress of Berlin*

window in No. 10 Downing Street, he said that he had brought back from the conference 'peace, I hope, with honour'. Characteristically, though, most of the detailed preparatory work on Britain's brief at the Congress was undertaken by Salisbury. Disraeli was not a details man.

Though Disraeli lost the general election of 1880, the policies, and more particularly the images of Conservatism, which he advanced proved very soundly based. Disraeli died a year after leaving office. He left the Conservative Party ideally placed to profit from the social and political changes of the last two decades of the nineteenth century. Disraeli had helped to make the Conservatives the natural party of government.

Preparing an examination answer bringing together material from different sources

This activity is mostly based on the material in this chapter and the previous one. You will also find useful the list of changes brought about by the 1867 Reform Act on page 202.

This exercise is designed to help you to develop this skill by bringing together material from different chapters of the book. Success in this can bring great benefits.

- You will gain confidence in the collection of material.
- Having collected this material, you will be able to develop skills of selection for a particular purpose.
- You will also develop flexibility. Examiners don't always test your understanding of one topic only; they sometimes ask you to compare and contrast different issues, individuals or factors. You might be required to compare the causes of the 1832 and 1867 Reform Acts, for example, or, as here, to compare the fortunes of the two political parties after 1867.
- Most students do not prepare themselves properly to cope with these types of question. Yet the skill is easily acquired – with practice. High marks are always earned by students who can confidently compare and contrast.

Examiners are fond of asking which of the two major political parties adapted better to the changed conditions which the Second Reform Act brought about. Sometimes, they deliberately put one opinion in the foreground and ask you to say what you think about it. This is often called 'debating the issue'. Here is a typical question of this type:

> 'Disraeli and the Conservatives adapted much better than Gladstone and the Liberals to the new political world created by the 1867 Reform Act.' How far do you agree with this judgement, as applied to the period 1867–80?

Your task is to draft an answer to this question, based on material from chapters 21–23. The following 'pegs' might help you to frame the right questions, and also to organise your material. You should first draw up an essay plan and these 'pegs' will help you. Some relevant material attached to each 'peg' will help you to select and also to organise a logical response. Make sure that your answer makes use not only of the text but of the written and visual sources:

a Introduction: in what ways *did* 1867 create 'a new political world'? *Hint:* introductions can be tricky to write. The following points may help:

- **i** They should be quite short: one paragraph is often enough; there should not normally be more than two.
- **ii** They should not go into any details – leave these to the main body of the answer.
- **iii** They should show that you have understood what the question is getting at. Thus, some direct reference here to the 'new political world' will help you. Presumably this phrase relates to the greatly widened electorate, to working-class majorities in many urban seats. Perhaps also it might give you an opportunity to say that you will develop ideas later on about both party organisation and party policies.
- **iv** There are some key phrases to avoid, such as the following: 'Before we answer this question, it is first necessary to . . .'. Whatever the candidate feels it is first necessary to do it is rarely a good idea to spell this out. Remember that you won't have more than one hour at the most to answer the question, so you will want to keep everything tight and relevant. Also, most answers which begin this way then usually ramble into irrelevance or into excessive descriptive material which could be drawn upon to answer the question but which won't answer it just by being written down.

b Liberal approach: flurry of 'domestic' legislation; administrative achievement; search for 'big' issues. Is foreign policy a 'negative' issue?

c The specific contribution of Gladstone.

d Conservative approach: early concentration on organisation; identification of key issues; attempts to 'win the working man'; nationalism and patriotism. Is foreign policy a 'plus' issue?

e The specific contribution of Disraeli.

f Compare the electoral successes of the two parties. The Liberals win two elections in this period and the Conservatives one. Does this make the Liberals more successful?

g This final 'peg' relates to the conclusion, which should be *your own*. You should be working towards a final statement which summarises material developed at greater length early on and which then does offer your own view. That view should:

- **i** be supported by relevant evidence from the chapters
- **ii** be directly related to the quotation – do you think it is broadly right, or not?
- **iii** recognise that there is plenty to be said on both sides of the question. If the quotation was, without doubt, true it would not have been selected for an examination question.

These are only suggestions, of course. There are many ways to compile an essay answer. You might want to make the whole of your answer comparative. This would be a good strategy, but it is best attempted when you are confident that you can develop ideas which are a bit less ambitious and which lead on to sustained comparison in the second half of the essay.

Further reading

J. K. Walton, *Disraeli,* Lancaster Pamphlets (Routledge, 1990) – a useful introduction which highlights all the main issues.

R. Blake, *Disraeli* (Methuen, 1966) – a truly great biography; detailed, scholarly, and critically sympathetic towards his subject.

R. Blake, *The Conservative Party from Peel to Thatcher* (Fontana, 1991).

P. Ghosh, 'Style and Substance in Disraelian Social Reform' in P. Waller (ed.), *Politics and Social Change in Modern Britain* (Wheatsheaf, 1987).

P. Smith, 'Disraeli's politics', *Transactions of the Royal Historical Society*, 1977.

CHANGE AND CONTINUITY

24 Pacifying Ireland and its cost: the importance of the Home Rule Crisis

Time chart

1845–7: Irish potato famine. Over the next few years, Irish population drops from about 8.3 million to 6.5 million. About 2 million Irish people starved. Emigration rates greatly increase. Population continues to drop. By 1901 the population of Ireland is 4.5 million

1852–1910: About 4.5 million Irish people emigrated. About a quarter of these went to Britain. The majority of the remainder went to the United States

1850s: Irish Republican Brotherhood, an organisation committed to achieving Irish Home Rule, established and wins many converts. The Fenian Brotherhood founded in 1858

1867: Fenian (nationalist) uprising in Ireland. Escape of Fenian prisoners from Manchester gaol. Explosion at Clerkenwell (London) during attempted breakout of Irish prisoners kills many

1869: Gladstone's government disestablishes the (Anglican) Church of Ireland – the first instalment of Gladstone's attempt to 'pacify Ireland'. The money it had received was placed in a fund to be used for educational and other social purposes in Ireland

1870: Irish Land Act attempts to give tenants protection against eviction and against sudden rises of rent. Tenants given limited rights to purchase land but the Act proves ineffective

1873: Gladstone's Irish Universities Bill attempts to promote 'mixed education' of Protestant and Catholic in a new University of Dublin. Opposed by Catholic bishops and secularists, it fails and marks a turning point in the fortunes of the government

1874: The first use of the secret ballot (1872) enables 59 Irish Nationalist MPs to be elected

1875: Charles Stewart Parnell first elected to Parliament. He becomes leader of the Home Rule Party in 1877

1879: During a severe agricultural depression the Irish Land League formed by Michael Davitt to secure greater rights for Irish tenants and land 'for the people of Ireland'

1879–82: 'Land War' in Ireland, with many instances of cattle-maiming, arson and other forms of rural terrorism. Massive protest against eviction of Irish tenants. Government retaliated with 'Coercion' Acts. That of 1881 allows for arrest without trial

1881: In an attempt to end the rural violence, Gladstone passes another Land Act which secures the '3Fs': fair rents for tenants; freedom of sale; fixity (or security) of tenure for Irish tenants. Parnell arrested and taken to Kilmainham gaol

1882: Parnell negotiates the 'Kilmainham Treaty' with Gladstone, whereby he agrees to cooperate with the Liberals' policies for improvement of tenants' position in Ireland provided tenants' arrears were wiped out. Murder of the new Chief Secretary, Lord Frederick Cavendish, and his deputy by the 'Invincibles' in Phoenix Park

1884: Third Reform Act increases the Irish electorate fourfold

1885: The return of 85 Irish nationalist MPs makes it difficult for either British party to govern without coming to an agreement with them. Gladstone announces his conversion to Irish Home Rule

1886: Gladstone's first Home Rule Bill introduced but fails by 30 votes to pass through the Commons. More than 90 Liberals vote against Gladstone; many Liberals leave the party permanently

1890: Parnell's political career ended by the O'Shea divorce case. Nationalist MPs split between allegiance to Justin McCarthy and Parnell's successor, John Redmond

1893: Gladstone's second Home Rule Bill presented. It was very little different from the first, though having provision for 81 Irish MPs at Westminster. It passes through the Commons with a majority of 43, but is defeated by 419 votes to 41 in the Lords

1903: Conservative government passes a successful measure of land reform (Wyndham's Act) which extended the right of Irish tenants to buy their own land. Government aid provided to help tenants to buy their land. By 1914 more than 300,000 of 500,000 Irish tenants at the time of this Act had bought themselves into landownership

1910: After the two general elections of this year, Irish nationalist MPs, led by John Redmond, hold the balance of power and can keep Liberals in power

1912: Third Home Rule Bill introduced. Ulster mobilised against Home Rule and in defence of the Union by Edward Carson

1913: Home Rule passed by Commons but rejected by Unionist majority in the Lords. Ulster and Nationalist volunteers arming to defend their respective positions

1914: An inter-party conference summoned to try to stop civil war in Ireland. Immediate issue of Home Rule shelved by outbreak of First World War

Changing the question?

In 1937 a spoof history book was published called *1066 and All That*. It is wonderfully funny and becomes funnier the more history you actually know. It presents a series of comic judgements about important historical issues. Not surprisingly, the book has something to say about Gladstone and Ireland. Much of the latter part of the great prime minister's career was dominated by characteristically single-minded and energetic, but unavailing, attempts to solve what was called 'the Irish question'. *1066 and All That* summed it all up by saying that whenever Gladstone looked likely to solve the Irish question, the Irish changed the question. You get the flavour. Like so much humour based on irony, the judgement contained just enough truth to be funny but not enough to be authoritative. In this chapter, you will be able to judge for yourself both why Irish issues were so important to Britain in this period and why 'the Irish question' remained unsolved when the First World War broke out in 1914.

Gladstone announced on taking up office as Prime Minister in 1868 that his 'mission' was 'to pacify Ireland'. As we have seen, Gladstone was a big believer in missions and Ireland was perfect for his purposes. Since the devastating Irish potato famine, nationalist pressure for a complete separation of Ireland from Britain had grown (see time chart). The mass exodus of Irish from their homeland only added to the pressure since emigrants to the United States lost no time in asserting their case that they were exiles from their native land, forced out by the uncaring and brutal policies of an occupying power. From the 1850s to the present day, the east coast of the United States has been an unfailing, if sometimes ill-informed and uncritical, source of financial and moral support for Irish nationalist causes. A significant minority of nationalists in Ireland were already looking to violence to achieve their ends. Look at the argument for 'force' advanced below by the so-called 'Irish People of the World' in 1867. It sums up much of the nationalist case for separation from Britain and, as Gladstone was to learn to his cost, the arguments would not go away.

During 1867, also, the Irish case was brought directly to Britain via terrorist activity (see time chart). As so often, Irish nationalist agitators saw that the only way to get Britain to take Ireland seriously was to bring it directly to the attention of British citizens.

> *'We have suffered centuries of outrage, enforced poverty, and bitter misery. Our rights and liberties have been trampled on by an alien aristocracy, who, treating us as foes, usurped our lands and drew away from our unfortunate country all material riches. The real owners of the soil were removed to make room for cattle, and driven across the ocean to seek the means of living, and the political rights denied to them at home, while our men of thought and action were condemned to loss of life and liberty . . .*
>
> *Today, having no honourable alternative left, we again appeal to force as our last resource . . . manfully deeming it better to die in the struggle for freedom than to continue an existence of utter serfdom . . .*
>
> *We aim at founding a Republic based on universal suffrage, which shall secure to all the intrinsic value of their labour. The soil of Ireland, at present in the possession of an oligarchy, belongs to us, the Irish people, and to us it must be restored.'*
>
> Proclamation by 'The Irish People of the World' of an Irish Republic, 1867.

Having read this source, you can perhaps see why *1066 and All That* was wrong. It was not the 'question' which changed so much as Britain's response to it. Gladstone's attempted 'solution' concerned three factors of the problem: the Church, land and, ultimately, national identity. His initial strategy was to improve the material conditions of Irish Catholics and thus remove (or greatly reduce) the economic arguments in favour of the repeal of the Act of Union. What this strategy could not tackle, of course, was the growing support within Ireland for separate nationhood. Nationalism in Ireland proved to be an intoxicating mixture of three ingredients:

- *Economic hard-headedess* – only when Ireland was in control of its own destiny could conditions be put in place for a genuine recovery. The Irish knew their own country best.

- *Anger* – at an occupying power which had let 2 million Irish people starve in the late 1840s and which still showed little sign of wanting to take the country seriously unless acts of violence disturbed the complacency of the ruling Victorian elite.
- *Romanticism* – nationalism as an ideal to liberate the spirits of a passionate and ingenious people. Irish literature, and especially poetry, was to prove a strong complement to political agitation. Men like J. M. Synge and W. B. Yeats would, in the early twentieth century, give the Irish a distinctive and formidable voice.

Against such obstacles, it is hardly surprising that even such a formidable and determined character as Gladstone could make little headway.

The Irish Church Disestablishment Act did at least rid the Irish of one grievance. No longer would the tenantry be forced to pay for the support of the Church of Ireland, an Anglican establishment which substantially fewer than 10 per cent of the population belonged to. Gladstone's strategy was very similar to Peel's over Maynooth in 1845 (see chapter 13). He was trying to give Catholics, and especially the educated Catholic middle classes, reasons for supporting the Union. The irony was, of course, that Gladstone – then a self-righteous and intolerant high Anglican – had resigned from Peel's government over a proposal less radical than the one he now offered to Liberal supporters as a means of quieting Irish agitation.

The rocky road to Home Rule

Church disestablishment was never likely to have much more than symbolic significance, though it did increase the social status of the more senior Catholic priests. The Land Act of 1870 promised more direct benefits. It introduced the principle of compensating tenants who faced eviction by their landowners. For the first time in relations between landlord and tenant in Ireland, the government had defined specific rights which tenants could, in theory, exercise. The Act was, however, ineffective. It did not alter the power relationship between landowner and tenant and it did not meet the main nationalist objection that too much land remained in 'alien' hands. By the 1870s, in fact, it is easy to show that a substantial number of landlords in Ireland were both Irish and Catholic. Landowners were by no means exclusively English and Scottish 'occupiers' who cared nothing for Ireland except to exploit its natural resources. The image presented to the Irish of an alien occupying power, carefully burnished by the nationalists, however, easily overcame the increasingly complex reality.

'This conference cannot separate without calling on the Irish constituencies at the next general election to return men earnestly and truly devoted to the great cause which this conference has been called to promote, and who, in any emergency that may arise, will be ready to take counsel with a great national conference to be called in such manner as to represent the opinions and feelings of the Irish nation.'

Resolutions of the Home Rule Conference held at the Rotunda Café, Dublin, 21 November 1873.

'In the opinion of this Conference the time has arrived when Irish members who have been elected to represent the national demand for Home Rule ought to form a separate and distinct party in the House of Commons, united in the principle of obtaining self-government for Ireland ... It is essential to the due discharge of our duties to our constituents and the country that we should, collectively and individually, hold ourselves aloof from, and independent of all party combinations, whether of ministerialists or of the opposition.'

Resolutions approved at a Home Rule Conference held at City Hall, Dublin, 3 March 1874.

The main weaknesses of the nationalists in Ireland until the late 1870s were lack of unity and disagreement over tactics. In particular, land reformers and nationalists had divided into revolutionary (Fenian) and parliamentary (constitutional) camps. From 1879 on, however, the British had to encounter greater unity of purpose. The agricultural depression, which hit Britain as hard as Ireland (see chapter 25), meant that many Irish tenants could not afford to keep up their rents and so, despite the Act of 1870, faced eviction. Secondly, the various Irish groups now agreed to unite under **Charles Stewart Parnell** and Michael Davitt to press for a programme of land nationalisation.

The early 1880s, which saw Gladstone's return to power, witnessed unprecedented agitation and considerable disruption in Ireland, including **boycotting** and high-profile assassinations (see time chart). His policy was a mixture of conciliation and coercion. The Land Act of 1881 held out the prospect of Irish tenants becoming landowners and more than £30 million worth of rent arrears were cancelled in 1882 under the terms of the Kilmainham Treaty. This treaty was too much for W. E. Forster who, as Chief Secretary for Ireland, had piloted a Coercion Act through Parliament the previous year. Coercion, however, remained firmly on the agenda, especially after the Phoenix Park assassinations of 1882.

KEY TERM:

Boycotting

Boycotting is now used as a general term to describe people who are shunned, or organisations which are ignored. Its origins lie in the nationalist agitation in Ireland orchestrated in the late 1870s and early 1880s by Parnell. Tenants during the depression of the late 1870s were frequently evicted and their land taken over by others. Frequently, those who took over the land from evicted tenants were treated with extreme hostility and given no help to farm their land. This fate befell Captain Charles Boycott (1832–97), the agent of Lord Erne in County Mayo. The government had to come to his aid, spending far more in protecting him and getting his crops harvested than the crops were worth.

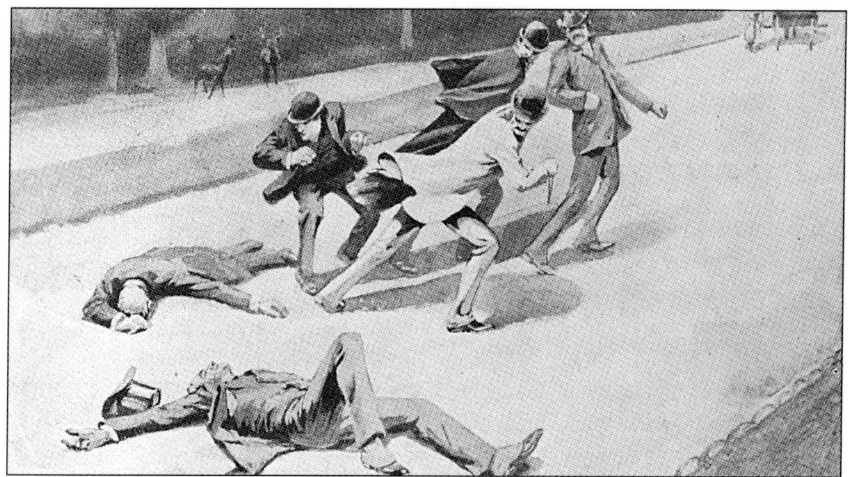

Figure 24.1 *The Phoenix Park, Dublin, murders, 1882*

The initiative, however, remained with Parnell and the nationalist cause was considerably strengthened by the increased number of voters created by the Third Reform Act and then by the general election of 1885. During 1884–5 Gladstone spent much time reflecting upon the inadequacy of the government's legislative response. His fateful decision to promote a bill for Home Rule was announced in December 1885 and immediately had profound consequences, especially in Britain. Gladstone knew, of course, that his decision would provoke fierce controversy within the Liberal Party but hoped that a measure which after all stopped a long way short of independence since the UK Parliament retained important powers could be 'sold' to the great bulk of his supporters.

PROFILE: *Charles Stewart Parnell*

Charles Stewart Parnell was born in 1846 into a prosperous Protestant Anglo-Irish family. His enthusiasm for the nationalist cause was probably fired by his American mother. He entered Parliament in 1875 and rapidly developed obstructive tactics there designed to focus attention on Irish matters by impeding debate on all others. He also organised boycotting campaigns to impede the eviction of poor Irish tenants. As leader of the Irish nationalists he exerted great influence both in Ireland and Westminster during the 1880s. One of his main skills lay in his ability to unite both revolutionary and constitutionalist factions in the Irish cause. Gladstone was impressed with his abilities. The end of his career was sudden and ignominious. He was deserted by most of his Catholic followers following his citation in a divorce petition in 1890. Some stayed with him, thus provoking just the kind of split he had striven so hard to avoid. He died in 1891.

The Irish Home Rule Bill, 1886

1 Proposed to establish an Irish Parliament of two houses. The Upper House could veto legislation in the Lower for a maximum of three years.

2 The Lower House to contain 204 MPs.

3 Irish Parliament would have control over most domestic issues, but UK Parliament retained overall control over making peace and war, raising troops, trade and many other economic issues.

4 Irishmen not to be permitted to sit in the British Parliament.

The following source shows how Gladstone proposed Home Rule both as a solution to short-term agitation and as a recognition of genuine nationalist sentiment.

'Agrarian crime has become, sometimes upon a larger, and sometimes upon a smaller scale, as habitual in Ireland as the legislation which has been intended to repress it . . . although at the present time it is almost at the low water mark, yet [it] has the fatal capacity of expansion . . . to dimensions and to an exasperation which becomes threatening to general social order, and to the peace of private and domestic life . . .

The agrarian crime in Ireland is not so much a cause as it is a symptom . . . It is impossible to depend in Ireland upon the finding of a jury in a case of agrarian crime according to the facts as they are viewed by the government, by the judges, and by the public . . . at large. That is a most serious mischief, passing down deep into the very groundwork of civil society . . . The consequence is to weaken generally the respect for law . . . among a people who, I believe, are as capable of attaining to the very highest moral and social standard as any people on the face of the earth . . .

Nothing has been more painful to me than to observe that, in this matter, we are not improving, but, on the contrary, we are losing ground . . . In [the] years 1833 to 1885 there were but two years which were entirely free from the action of the special [coercive] legislation for Ireland. Is not that of itself almost enough to prove that we have arrived at the point where it is necessary that we should take careful and searching survey of our position? . . . Rightly or wrongly . . . law is discredited in Ireland, and discredited in Ireland upon this point specially – that it comes to the people of that country with a foreign aspect and a foreign garb . . .'

William Gladstone, introducing the Home Rule Bill to the Commons, 8 April 1886.

Gladstone's arguments had only limited success. More than anything else, the proposals showed how alienated the overwhelming majority of Irish Protestants were. Almost all of these, of course, lived in the ancient northern kingdom of Ulster which, during the second half of the nineteenth century, had experienced the bulk of what industrial expansion and economic growth Ireland had seen. John Bright, an old-style principled Liberal, said that he could not 'consent to a measure which is so offensive to the whole protestant population of Ireland and to the sentiment of the province of Ulster so far as its loyal and protestant people are concerned'. The Conservative Lord Randolph Churchill mobilised the Protestants with the chilling slogan 'Ulster will fight and Ulster will be right'. MPs were left in no doubt that the likely consequence of a Home Rule Act would be civil war in Ireland. The following Unionist contribution to the debate was relatively moderate:

> *'The Party to which he belonged had been returned to that House with one distinct order from their constituents, which was to oppose as much as they could, and resist to the utmost of their power, anything like an approach to a violation of the Act of Union ending in a separation of England and Ireland. For a number of years past what had been called remedial legislation had been passed by that House, and hon. Members had flattered themselves, from time to time, that they had passed measures which would be final, and of a character to gain the affections of the Irish people. But not a single measure that had been passed had gone one step towards attaining that object. The fact was that there existed among the great mass of Irish people an innate hatred of England . . . [the passing of the present bill] would be regarded by certain classes in Ireland as nothing more than an instalment towards an end, which meant the Repeal of the Union . . . the result would be the establishment of an Irish Republic, which would be the focus of foreign intrigue in time of peace and would be a source of imminent danger in England in time of war.'*
>
> R. T. O'Neill, MP for Mid-Antrim, replying to Gladstone's speech, House of Commons, April 1886.

Though divisions within the Liberal Party were about more than Home Rule (see chapters 22 and 29), it can be argued that the Liberals never recovered from the trauma of 1885–6. Gladstone did not get Home Rule through and, in the attempt, split his party. More than 90 Liberals joined the Conservatives to vote Home Rule down in 1886. Hartington and most of the Whigs left permanently. So did that arch-fixer and organiser Joseph Chamberlain, although many of Chamberlain's radical allies drifted back to the Liberals in the later 1880s and early 1890s. The Liberal split was not pre-ordained. Almost certainly, had Gladstone decided to retire gracefully in, or soon after, 1886 the party would have reunited. The consequences for later British political history were incalculable. The Grand Old Man, who had talked of little other than resignation in the mid-1870s, would have none of it in the mid-1880s. He was unswerving in his determination to give the Irish what he believed they needed. In the absence of Hartington and Chamberlain, he was an even more dominant figure than before, though his single-issue obsessions did the Liberals little good in the last decade of his leadership. While his successors, Rosebery, Campbell-Bannerman and Asquith were far less enthusiastic Home Rulers, the damage had already been done. Between them, Gladstone and Ireland had dealt near-fatal blows to the Liberal Party.

Gladstone did at least get his second Home Rule Bill through the Commons in 1893, though there was never the remotest prospect of its succeeding in the Lords. Meanwhile, both Liberals and Conservatives pressed ahead with proposals which encouraged absentee British landlords to sell up and leave the land for the Irish to buy. The Wyndham Act of 1903 was only the most famous of several initiatives which largely returned the land to Irish ownership. It was, however, too late for even such a radical change to halt the impetus behind independence. In the 1890s and 1900s, cultural developments in Ireland gave more emphasis to 'separateness', not least in the promotion of the Gaelic language. When the general elections of 1910 gave the nationalists the balance of power, they used it to force Liberal politicians to take up the cause once again.

The passing of the 1911 Parliament Act (see chapter 31) introduced a new, and for Unionists, alarming dimension. After 1911, the Lords could only delay Home Rule for a maximum of two years; its inbuilt Unionist majority was now of limited value. However, it did duly reject Asquith's first two Home Rule Bills. It is hardly surprising that the years 1912–14 saw the polarisation of Irish society as never before. For the first time, Unionists were now as fearful of absorption into a hated priest-ridden independent Ireland as they were defiant of majority opinion in that country. **Edward Carson**'s leadership of the Unionists emphasised the likelihood of violence if the Liberals persisted with their Home Rule proposals.

'Being convinced in our consciences that Home Rule would be disastrous to the material well-being of Ulster as well as to the whole of Ireland, subversive of our civil and religious freedom, destructive of our citizenship, and perilous to the unity of the Empire, we, whose names are underwritten, men of Ulster, loyal subjects of his gracious majesty King George V . . . do hereby pledge ourselves in solemn covenant throughout this our time of threatened calamity to stand by one another in defending for ourselves and for our children our cherished position of equal citizenship in the United

PROFILE: *Edward Carson*

Edward Carson, the spokesman of Protestant Ulster was actually born in Dublin, in 1854. He trained as a lawyer and played a major part in the humiliation of the playwright Oscar Wilde when he defended the Marquis of Queensbury in the libel action which Wilde brought in his vain attempt to clear himself of charges of homosexuality. His powerful leadership of the Unionists involved getting more than a quarter of a million Protestants to sign a solemn covenant declaring undying opposition to Home Rule. The Ulster Volunteer Force, an unofficial armed force also organised by Carson, was set up in 1913 and helped to bring Ireland to the brink of civil war by 1914. During the First World War, Carson served as Attorney General and, later, as a member of Lloyd George's war cabinet. He died in 1935.

Kingdom and in using all means which may be found necessary to defeat the present conspiracy to set up a Home Rule parliament in Ireland. And in the event of a parliament being forced on us we further solemnly mutually pledge ourselves to refuse to recognise its authority.'

Sir Edward Carson introducing the so-called 'Ulster Covenant', signed by almost half a million men and women in Ulster. Reported in *The Times*, 20 September 1912.

The British Prime Minister, Herbert Asquith, tried to avert conflict in early 1914 by promising that a simple majority vote by any Irish county would exclude that country from Home Rule for a period of six years. This olive branch to the Unionist minority was rejected with contempt. The war put the Irish question on to the back-burner, though only for a year or two. The nationalist leader, John Redmond, pledged Ireland's support for Britain against Germany but he knew that many of his followers wanted nothing to do with either Britain or Britain's war.

Further reading

M. J. Winstanley, *Ireland and the Land Question, 1800–1992*, Lancaster Pamphlet (Routledge, 1984) – gives a brief, informative survey of one of the main sources of dispute.

K. T. Hoppen, *Ireland since 1800: Conflict and Conformity* (Addison Wesley Longman, 1989) – useful particularly for treatment of land ownership and population.

R. F. Foster, *Modern Ireland 1600–1972* (Penguin, 1988).

J. C. Beckett, *A History of Modern Ireland* (Hutchinson, second edition, 1981).

F. S. L. Lyons, *Ireland since the Famine* (Weidenfeld, 1972).

T. R. Gourvish and A. O'Day (eds), *Later Victorian Britain 1867–1900*, (Macmillan, 1988), chapter by A. O'Day on Ireland surveys why the Irish issue became ever more critical.

H. Matthew, *Gladstone, 1875–98* (Oxford University Press, 1995).

HISTORICAL CONTROVERSY

25 Was there a 'Great Depression' in business and agriculture?

The performance of the economy in the last quarter of the nineteenth century has been the subject of enormous controversy. Contemporaries became uncomfortably aware of the consequences of other nations' catching up after about 50 years during which Britain had been incontestably the world's leading industrial power. In 1896 an author called E. E. Williams produced a book entitled *Made in Germany*. It enjoyed enormous sales and alarmed many people. Its central argument was that Germany was, in many respects, outpacing Great Britain. German technology was more sophisticated and German education better targeted on improving the country's industrial and commercial output.

The United States was also making impressive strides. Important technological innovations like the sewing machine and the typewriter were being made in the USA rather than Britain. By far the most important technological innovation of the period – the harnessing of electricity for power – was being exploited more cheaply and effectively in the USA and in Germany than in Britain. It was US know-how which was playing a leading part in the expansion of London's underground system in the 1880s and 1890s. The economies of the newer industrial countries seem to have grown a lot faster. By one estimate, the average growth rate of the British economy in the years 1873–1913 was 1.3 per cent whereas that of the United States was 4.8 per cent and Germany 3.9 per cent.

Two important symbols seemed to confirm the gloomy picture. Between 1880 and 1900, the value of exports by Britain's cotton industry, traditionally in the vanguard of industrial progress, actually went down from about £105 million a year to about £97 million. Baring's famous merchant bank (which did collapse in 1995 because of the under-supervised gambling of one arrogant and foolish young man) was almost brought down in 1890. The supremacy of the City of London as the world's money market was called into question.

Nowhere was the impact of US competition more devastating than in agriculture, and especially the production of corn. The combination of the opening up by railways of the United States's prairies and the firm maintenance of a policy of free trade had devastating consequences. Look at Figure 25.4 (page 248) and notice how rapidly the acreage sown with corn in Britain declined in the years 1871 to 1911. Then look at view 5 (page 252) which points to some of the broader social consequences.

How 'depressed' the British economy actually *was* has been a subject of furious debate, especially during the last 25 years. A linked question has generated equally heated disagreement. Insofar as the British economy was depressed, who, if anyone, was to blame? This chapter provides you with a selection of the relevant evidence. The questions at the end of the chapter will lead you through this detailed material:

1 Whatever *historians* now think, contemporaries were *sure* that Britain was in depression. Contemporaries cannot, by definition, see things in perspective. What they *did* see, however, was other nations catching up. Look at the evidence on page 249 from *The Economist* in the early 1880s. *The Economist* was one of Britain's most informed and respected journals and not normally alarmist at all. What people think at the time is at least as important as what historians decide much later. In one sense, it hardly matters whether historians believe contemporaries to have been right or wrong. What contemporaries felt affected behaviour and policy. Perceptions have consequences.

2 Perceptions of decline caused influential people to have radical thoughts:

a If other nations were catching up and passing Britain by, might it possibly be that the doctrine of *laissez-faire* (free trade) was fallible? The middle classes had believed, almost as they believed in the Bible's New Testament, that *laissez-faire* was the only true economic faith. Had they been following a false economic god? The delicious irony suggested itself to some heretics: might Britain profit from free trade only while it held what amounted to a monopoly of industrial production know-how? Of course, most of the middle classes continued in their blind allegiance to *laissez-faire*, but it was enough that, by 1914, the question was being increasingly asked.

b If both landowners and middle classes were feeling the pinch in the last quarter of the nineteenth century, they might be inclined towards another radical thought. Perhaps poverty was not always, and necessarily, the fault of the individual.

3 To get a sense of this topic, it is as well to be aware of the crucial distinction between *relative* and *absolute* decline. Almost all of the indicators suggest that the British economy continued to grow. There was no absolute decline. Some sectors did well, especially those concerned with providing food, services and transport. The great armaments manufacturer **William Armstrong** enjoyed a hugely successful career which

PROFILE: *William Armstrong*

William Armstrong was born in Newcastle in 1847 and trained for the law before going into business as an engineer. He invented new techniques for loading artillery and sold these to both army and navy. After initial setbacks, he made a huge fortune and became one of the world's most successful gun-makers. He was also heavily, and profitably, involved in shipbuilding and established a large shipyard on the River Tyne. He died in 1900.

was not impeded by any 'Great Depression'. He built a massive Gothic castle in Northumberland (Figure 25.1) out of his profits. However, most industrial sectors' growth in the late nineteenth century was slower. Other nations were now growing much quicker; hence the perception that Britain was being 'passed by'. Most economic historians agree that British growth rates were closer to the more modest levels being achieved by newly independent Italy and the old Austro-Hungarian Empire than by Germany and the USA.

4 Economists tend to think in terms of depression when prices are falling and share values on the decline. Neither of these factors need

Figure 25.1 *Cragside, Northumberland, built by Armstrong*

Figure 25.2 *St Helens Library and Institute*

make ordinary workers worse off – rather the contrary. Living standards for many workers rose substantially in this so-called period of depression. If they stayed in work, they benefited from sharply falling food prices. Workers also benefited from the general reduction in hours of work from the 1870s onwards. Differences in income between the highest and lowest in society did not change all that much in the period 1870–1914, although there were some shifts in the direction of greater equality. What is much more important is that the working classes were now able to afford items which would previously have been beyond all but the wealthy: access to better quality food, the ability to travel sometimes quite long distances, more choice in terms of leisure and sport (see chapter 28). It is no accident that both mass grocery chains and professional football became commercially viable at this time. Both depended on higher disposable income by the majority of the population.

5 The political consequences of the great changes in arable agriculture were probably highly significant too. It is true that Britain's prime minister at the end of the nineteenth century was a peer of the realm – the third Marquis of Salisbury. However, the effortless control of the landed interest over the main levers of central power were now being rapidly loosened. Fewer landowners could afford to make politics an alternative career. More and more the House of Commons was being dominated by the middle classes – bankers, lawyers and lecturers in

Figure 25.3 *Cartoon titled 'Depressed Dukes'. The Duke of Devonshire is saying: 'If this Budget passes, I don't know* how *I'm going to keep up Chatsworth.' The Duke of Westminster replies: 'If you come to that, we may consider ourselves lucky if we can keep a tomb over our heads!'*

particular. A few working men were beginning to find their way into Westminster (see chapter 29). The old political order was finally being dismantled, without revolution but in response to substantial economic changes.

Figure 25.4 *Agriculture statistics, 1871–1911 (in millions)*

	1871	*1881*	*1891*	*1901*	*1911*
Acreage sown:					
Corn	3.57	2.81	2.31	1.70	1.91
Vegetables	3.74	3.51	3.30	3.13	3.04
Grasses	4.37	4.34	4.72	4.86	4.12
Sheep kept	27.12	24.58	28.73	26.38	26.49

Figure 25.5 *Coal and pig-iron production, 1875–1914 (in millions of tons)*

	1875	*1885*	*1895*	*1905*	*1914*
Coal	131.87	159.35	189.66	236.13	265.66
Pig iron	6.36	7.42	7.70	9.60	8.92

Figure 25.6 *Registration of shipping, 1875–1914*

	1875	*1885*	*1895*	*1905*	*1914*
Numbers of ships	25,461	23,662	21,003	20,581	21,065
Ships' weight (in millions of tons)	6.15	7.43	8.99	10.74	12.42

Views on the state of the economy from The Economist, *1880–81*

a On iron, 13 March 1880

'Up to the commencement of the last quarter of the present year the thick darkness was appalling, for out of the once busy 2,158 puddling furnaces of the North of England and Cleveland, only 838 were at work ... The Cleveland blast furnace men have recently added on 10 per cent to their [wage] rates ... In manufactured iron and steel the increase of tonnage is very distinctly owing to the large make and delivery of steel rails from Eston, the exports owing to the large make and delivery of steel rails from that part of Middlesborough alone having exceeded 200,000 tons ...

It may be interesting to know that the production of steel is being developed in America at a much more rapid rate than in England ... In the United States the production of Bessemer ingots was eighteen times as great as it was in 1870, having risen from 40,000 tons in that year to 730,000 tons in 1878, whilst in Britain the production had not become four times as great as it was nine years ago, the total output in 1870 having been 215,000 tons and in 1878 ... 807,000 tons.'

b On agriculture, 13 March 1880

'We publish today our annual crop returns for 1879, as contributed by 453 correspondents, representing every county in England and ten counties in Wales. They fully confirm the worst accounts that have appeared from time to time as to the serious failure of the crops, being the most discouraging that we have ever published.'

c On agriculture, 12 March 1881

'In the cereal year ending August 1879, wheat production in America first astonished Europe; in 1880 increased exports were partly attributed to extraordinary efforts made to substitute the great European crop deficiencies of England, France and other continental countries from the bad harvest in 1879; but the present season, commencing from 1 September 1880, shows the clear truth that now the wheat acreage of the United States will yearly produce, with only middling yield, a bulk of grain that must entirely change the general situation of the wheat trade – and of land value – in England and France ... 1880 has read merchants a lesson that demands careful consideration in the present and in the future.'

View 1: As well as can be expected?

'Few beliefs are so well established in the credo of British economic history as the belief that the late Victorian economy failed. Statistical economists and literary historians, Englishmen and foreigners, late Victorians and moderns have accepted some version of it. The three senses in which Britain is said to have failed are that output grew too slowly because of sluggish demand, that too much was invested abroad because of imperfect capital markets, and that productivity stagnated because of inept entrepreneurship . . . The argument of this essay is that these beliefs are ill-founded.

[McCloskey then studies economic data relating to exports and also the scope which the British economy had for growth. He concludes:]

It is likely that there were binding **resource limitations** *on the growth of the British economy in the late nineteenth century . . . the resources available to the economy were not* **elastic** *in supply and reallocation of them . . . would have brought little or no additional growth. The growth of output depended on how productively the available resources were used . . . There is little left of the dismal picture of British failure painted by historians. The alternative is of an economy not stagnating but growing as rapidly as permitted by the growth of its resources and the effective exploitation of the available technology.'*

Donald M. McCloskey, 'Did Victorian Britain Fail?', *Economic History Review* (1970).

View 2: An interpretation of the reason for Britain's long-term decline

'Nineteenth-century Britain was a pioneer of modernisation. Yet . . . the extent of the transformation was more limited than it first appeared to be. New economic forces did not tear the social fabric. Old values and patterns of behaviour lived on within the new . . . The end result of the nineteenth-century transformation of Britain was indeed a peaceful accommodation [between the interests of land and industry] but one that entrenched pre-modern elements within the new society and [allowed the existence of] anti-modern elements . . .

Was . . . the death knell tolling for the English aristocracy as a ruling class [as a result of the industrial revolution]? In the long view, no doubt. Yet not before the aristocracy had succeeded in both prolonging its reign and educating its successors in its [own] world view. Power was peacefully yielded in return for time and the acceptance of many aristocratic values by the new members of the elite . . .

The children of businessmen were admitted to full membership in the upper class [through an education in public schools] at the price of discarding the distinctive, production-oriented culture shaped during the century of relative isolation [the 18th century] . . . The adoption of a culture of enjoyment by new landowners [men of business who had invested their profits in land] . . . meant the dissipation of a set of values that had projected their fathers as a class to the economic heights, and the nation to world prominence . . . Indeed, Bertrand Russell [the famous philosopher] – himself a hereditary peer – was to suggest that "the concept of the gentleman was invented by the aristocracy to keep the middle classes in order".'

Martin J. Wiener, *English Culture and the Decline of the Industrial Spirit, 1850–1950* (1985).

View 3: Digging beneath the surface

'There was an impressive range of new enterprises in late Victorian Britain which is difficult to square with the pessimistic view of British businessmen. Several of the sources of entrepreneurship are easily overlooked. For example, many men moved into the south and east of the country, taking advantage of falling land prices, to set up as dairy farmers and market gardeners supplying the huge London market with fresh produce. Another neglected area is that of women. Among the middle classes this typically took the form of careers as novelists; but innumerable working-class women who took lodgers to help make ends meet moved on to become proprietors of guest houses and small shopkeepers. Perhaps the most notable evidence of the latter was the rapid spread of the fish-and-chip shop during the late Victorian period ... The 1890s particularly saw a major expansion of bicycle production by firms like Raleigh, using the traditional metalwork skills of the towns of the Midlands. William Lever advanced in the classical manner from the small beginnings of his father's shop to become the leading manufacturer of soap and the architect of Port Sunlight. In addition, a number of men made their fortunes through the development of chains of grocery stores, such as ... Thomas Lipton who bought his own tea plantations so as to cut out the middle men and reduce the price of tea to the consumer.'

Martin Pugh, *State and Society: British Political and Social History, 1870–1992* (1994).

View 4: British performance in context

'Even in an international context, there were some strong elements in British economic performance during the period. Dominance in the field of international financial services continued, although the USA provided a growing challenge. The shipping industry was very successful. The manufacturing sector, however, failed to move quickly enough into the production of more sophisticated goods, while some existing industries' performance may have been less than optimum. The failure to invest enough, and to exploit new technologies, can be linked in particular to the existing organisation of industry and the unwillingness to change it, and to the lack of adequate technical and managerial training.'

Charles More, *The Industrial Age: Economy and Society in Britain, 1750–1985* (1989).

KEY TERMS:

Resource limitations

All of the social sciences treasure their jargon. This example is easily explained. **Resource limitations** refer to the limits imposed on Britain's ability to sustain growth in the economy by natural resources, such as the size of the country, the extent of its productive land, its coal mines and the rest. Ultimately, Britain is a small country in the far north-west of Europe. Other nations are more centrally placed, are bigger and have larger natural resources of these kinds.

Elastic

When economists describe something, like demand or resources, as **elastic** they mean that it is capable of easy change, for example, by expansion or contraction. 'Inelastic' means the opposite. So if resources are inelastic, there is little or no capacity for change. In this context, Britain, as a small country, was bumping up against a natural ceiling of resources.

View 5: The consequences of US competition for British agriculture

'From 1846 onwards, the prosperity of British agriculture had been dependent on high prices and low imports. But a generation on, those opponents of repeal who had argued that free trade in corn would destroy British agriculture by letting in cheap foreign produce seem to have been vindicated [justified] – and in the most unhappy way possible.

It is clear that this worldwide fall in agricultural prices led to an unprecedentedly gloomy period for British landowners. Undeniably, some contemporaries over-reacted to the late-nineteenth-century depression, there were considerable local variations, and pastoral farming was less hard-hit than arable. But even so, it was impossible to see signs of recovery, there was a continuous contraction of cultivation, and rents collapsed almost everywhere. In England, between the mid-1870s and the mid-1890s, they fell on average by 26 per cent: only 12 per cent in the pastoral north-west but 41 per cent in the arable south-east . . . In addition, many landowners now found themselves squeezed between what seemed to be inexorably [unstoppably] declining income, and outgoings that could not be correspondingly reduced . . . as the income that land generated declined, its capital value fell by at least 30 per cent.'

David Cannadine, *The Decline and Fall of the British Aristocracy* (1990).

View 6: Asking the wrong question?

'The most fundamental assumption made by advocates of the "cultural critique" [such as Martin Wiener – see view 2] is wrong, namely that Britain's was centrally an industrial *economy whose industrial and manufacturing lead vanished through qualitative decline after 1870 . . . Britain's was* never *fundamentally an industrial and manufacturing economy; rather, it was* always*, even at the height of the industrial revolution, essentially a commercial, financial, and service-based economy whose comparative advantage [against other nations] always lay with commerce and finance. Britain's apparent industrial decline was simply a working out of this process, a working out which became increasingly evident from about 1890, and which was, manifestly, coincidental with a continuing rise in the average standard of living in Britain rather than a decline. What is so often seen as Britain's industrial decline or collapse can be seen, with greater accuracy, as a transfer of resources and entrepreneurial energies into other forms of business life . . . in moving from industry to commerce, Britain's entrepreneurs were responding intelligently to perceived opportunities.'*

W. D. Rubinstein, *Capitalism, Culture and Decline in Britain, 1750–1990* (1993).

Tasks: making sense of a historical controversy

1 Does Donald McCloskey himself think that Victorian Britain failed (view 1)? Show your understanding of his interpretation in explaining your answer.

2 What does Martin Wiener (view 2) think was the reason for Britain's economic decline in this period?

3 **a** Which evidence from the rest of the chapter could Charles More (view 4) draw upon to support his opinions about British economic performance?

b Does any part of More's argument support that of Wiener (view 2)? Explain your answer.

4 Which of Martin Pugh (view 3) or W. D. Rubinstein (view 6) do you think mounts the more effective attack on Wiener's interpretation of Britain's decline? Explain the basis of your choice by reference to the arguments advanced in all three views.

5 Does David Cannadine (view 5) believe that the British economy was in rapid decline in this period? Explain your answer.

6 Do views 1–6, taken together, suggest that contemporaries were wrong about the 'Great Depression'? Explain your answer.

7 'Historians produce different interpretations of past events not because they directly contradict each other but because they study different aspects of the same problem.' How far does your study of the different views of the so-called 'Great Depression' lead you to support this conclusion?

Further reading

S. B. Saul, *The Myth of the Great Depression* (Macmillan, Studies in Economic and Society History, 1969) – a useful summary of the issues.

C. More, *The Industrial Age* (Addison Wesley Longman, 1989).

P. Mathias, *The First Industrial Nation* (Routledge, second edition, 1983).

T. May, *An Economic and Social History of Britain 1760–1990* (Addison Wesley Longman, second edition, 1990) – a useful student text.

D. McCloskey and R. Floud (eds), *The Economic History of Britain Since 1700* vol. 2 (Cambridge University Press, second edition, 1994) – an up-to-date study which quantifies the problem of 'depression'.

Keith Burgess, 'Did the Late Victorian Economy Fail?' in A. O'Day and T. R. Gourvish (eds), *Later Victorian Britain, 1867–1900* (Macmillan, 1988).

EXPLANATION AND HISTORICAL CONTROVERSY

26 What was the Empire for? Imperialism in the late nineteenth century

Time chart

1874–7: The explorer Henry Morton Stanley crosses Africa from east to west and attracts much interest in Britain to the 'Dark Continent'

1876: Disraeli engineers the title of Empress of India for Queen Victoria

1879: War between British and Zulus in southern Africa. Zulu victory at Isandhlwana before British victory at Nkambule led to overall success in the war and eventual extension of British control over southern Africa

1880–81: In first Anglo-Boer War, Boers in the Transvaal defeat a British force at Majuba Hill. Gladstone agrees to withdraw British troops and the Convention of Pretoria confirms Transvaal's internal independence

1882: Britain begins its occupation of Egypt

1884: Conference held at Berlin. It recognised Belgium's ownership of the Congo and decided many issues of colonial policy which enabled the European powers to expand their territories without coming into conflict with each other. Britain confirms the semi-independent status of Transvaal

1885: Gladstone attracts much criticism for failing to send sufficient resources to save General Gordon in his attempts to defend Khartoum, the capital of the Sudan, against attacks by the Mahdi

1886: Discovery of gold in the Transvaal rapidly transforms the political situation in the area

1890: Imperial congress held in Brussels and decides many boundaries between the European powers. Britain agreed boundaries of territories with the Portuguese in west Africa and with the Germans and French in east Africa. The balance of advantage in terms of territory went to Britain, which agreed to give the north European island of Heligoland to Germany in return for concessions in Africa, notably Zanzibar

1896: The Jameson Raid fails in its attempt to overthrow the Boer government of the Transvaal. It leads to Rhodes's overthrow

1898: General Kitchener, at the head of Anglo-Egyptian forces, recaptures the Sudan after the Battle of Omdurman

1898–9: Crisis between British and French at Fashoda on the River White Nile almost leads to war

1899: Second Boer War breaks out. Initial Boer victories at sieges of Ladysmith, Kimberley and Mafeking lead to British change of command with Lord Roberts replacing Redvers Buller

1900: Sieges lifted and British troops go on to capture Bloemfontein, Johannesburg and Pretoria. Orange Free State and Transvaal formally annexed to Britain, but guerilla campaigns prolong the war

1902: Treaty of Vereeniging completes formality of transfer of power to Britain, although Boer farmers compensated for their losses during the war

1910: Formal Union of South Africa created, including Boer territories

The Empire in context

When George V came to the throne of the United Kingdom in 1910, he also became ruler of a British Empire which, covering about 11.5 million square miles in every continent, accounted for approximately one-fifth of the land surface of the world. King George eventually became ruler of 410 million people. Much of this territory had been acquired during the eighteenth and earlier nineteenth century. Canada, Australia, New Zealand, South Africa and India were at its heart. Smaller territories, such as Gibraltar and Hong Kong, nevertheless had profound strategic significance for a trading nation, giving access, respectively, to the Mediterranean (and thus to routes into the East) and China and Japan.

KEY TERM:

Imperialism

Imperialism refers to the process of acquiring territory outside the boundaries of a particular state and using the territory and its people either for economic gain (trade and guaranteed markets, for example) or for strategic reasons, or for both. The word did not come into use until the 1890s and it first became associated with the expansion of the British Empire during the period of the so-called 'Scramble for Africa' (see key term on page 259).

This earlier period, though of huge significance, is not normally regarded as the heyday of **imperialism**. The most celebrated period of Britain's imperial acquisitions was the last quarter of the nineteenth century and the first few years of the twentieth, and concentrated in Africa. Figure 26.1 shows how Britain's territory expanded in what historians down to the Second World War were still prone to call 'The Dark Continent'.

British school children in the early twentieth century were taught to measure, memorise and marvel at the scope of the Empire. They were encouraged also to glory in the world's most extensive empire, on which

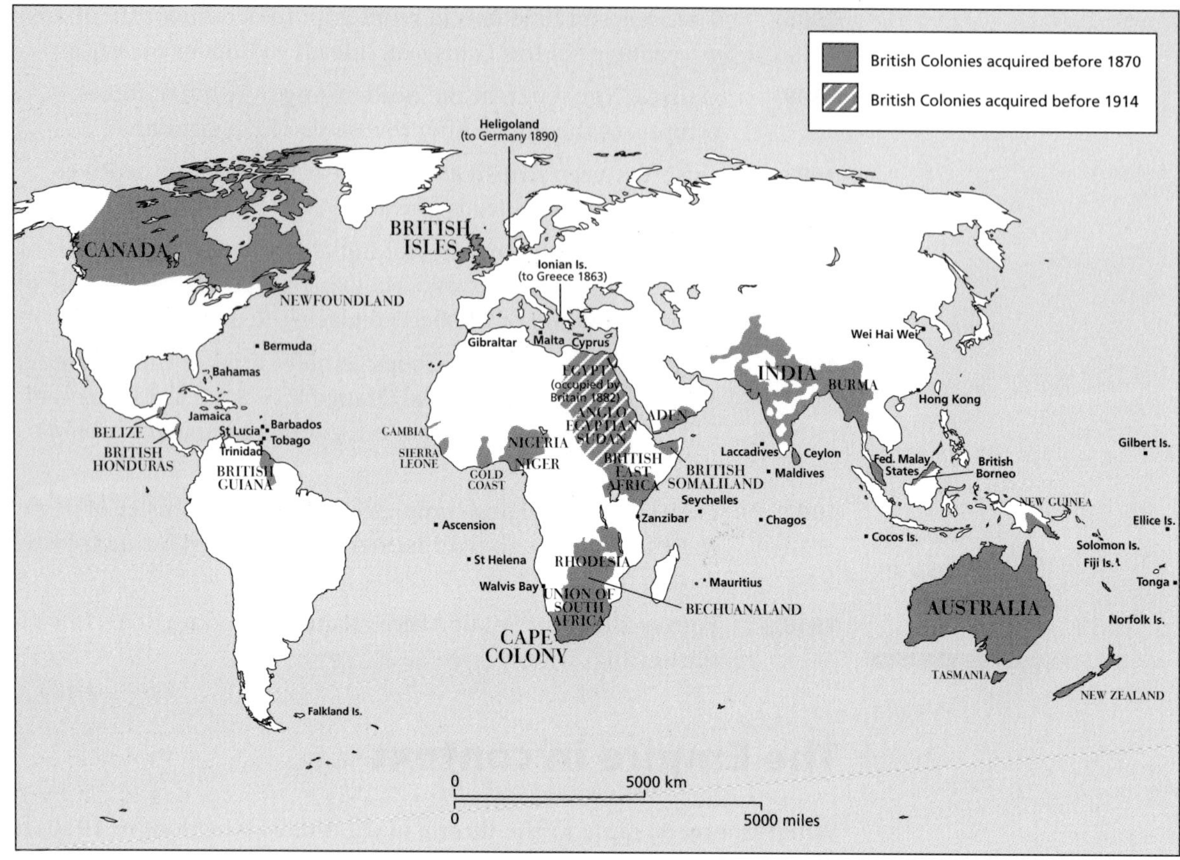

Figure 26.1 *Map of British Empire in 1914*

'the sun never set'. Hymns written to be sung not only in Church but also at Sunday School and school assemblies not infrequently included at least implicit reference to Empire. One of the most beautiful of all simple Victorian tunes was written to accompany 'The Day Thou Gavest, Lord, is ended'. An important part of that hymn's message was that, while the sun might be setting on the heart of the empire, it was rising elsewhere. The message of 'Hills of the North, rejoice' may not have been explicitly imperial but it certainly boxed the compass. Lands, 'north, east, west and south' were equally to be remembered, the strong implication being that lands 'unvisited' and 'unblessed' would soon improve both their economic and their moral status when the British got around to incorporating them in their beneficent Empire. The Christian God was not only a loving God; he smiled equally on the British and on their subject races.

The imperialists' view of Empire

The leading supporters of Empire (imperialists) knew exactly what the Empire was for. Five main objectives may be identified. Individual imperialists would put them in different orders of priority, but all were important:

1 To increase Britain's wealth by making use of colonial raw materials, by developing new markets for manufactured goods and by creating opportunities for favourable investment.

2 To enhance Britain's prestige and international status at a time of challenge by overseas rivals (see chapter 25).

3 To bring to the colonies instruction, enlightenment and improvement. The colonies would benefit if they were taught to understand British attitudes and values. Imperialists had no hang-ups about respect for what is today called ethnic diversity. For them, British was best and it was the colonialist's duty to demonstrate why to the subject races.

4 To bring Christianity to the 'natives'. Christian missionaries played an extremely significant part in the development of most of Britain's African colonies.

5 To use the colonies as a training ground for high-quality administrators, governors and officers in the armed forces. The route ran directly from the English public schools – where duty, respect for discipline, collective effort through team games and self-sacrifice were taught to a generation of privileged adolescents – to the exercise of power and responsibility in the colonies. The British upper classes learned how to lead by example.

Figure 26.2 *Queen Victoria's Diamond Jubilee procession passing the National Gallery, Trafalgar Square, London, 1897*

PROFILE: *Lord Curzon*

George Nathaniel, Lord Curzon, was one of the most prominent Conservative politicians associated with imperialism. Born in 1859 into an established aristocratic family and developing academic as well as political and administrative interests, he travelled widely in Asia before becoming Under-Secretary for India in 1891–2. He was Viceroy for India from 1898 to 1905, during which time he developed his expertise in Indian architecture and culture. He was throughout his career an advocate of using the empire to advance British interests. He served in government during the wartime coalition and narrowly missed becoming prime minister in 1923. He died in 1925.

The combination of duty and pride was almost overwhelming. The historian Bernard Porter has collected some powerful examples to show the links between imperialism and British destiny. Joseph Chamberlain, the Colonial Secretary in 1895, stated that 'the British race is the greatest of governing races the world has ever seen'. **Lord Curzon** was equally certain: 'To me the message is carved in granite, hewn on the rock of doom: that our work is righteous and it shall endure.' In introducing his book *Problems of the Far East*, published in 1894, he asserted that the British Empire was, under God, 'the greatest empire for good that the world has seen'. The leader of the Liberals at that time, the Earl of Rosebery, echoed the same sentiment: 'the greatest secular agency for good the world has seen'. By the turn of the century, he could scarcely contain his enthusiasm: 'How marvellous it all is! Built not by saints and angels but by the work of men's hands ... Human, and not yet wholly human, for the most heedless and most cynical must see the finger of the divine.'

Ruling over the largest empire the world had ever seen was an enormous privilege, of course, but it implied duty as well. Here is Lord Curzon again, seeking in 1907 to elevate people both at home and in the colonies:

> *'Empire can only be achieved with satisfaction or maintained with advantage, provided it has a moral basis. To the people of the mother state it must be a discipline, an inspiration, a faith. To the people of the circumference, it must be more than a flag or a name, it must give them what they cannot otherwise or elsewhere enjoy: not merely justice or order or material prosperity; but the sense of participating in a great idea, the consecrating influence of a lofty purpose.'*

KEY TERM:

Scramble for Africa

The so-called **Scramble for Africa** is the term associated with the division of much of the territory of Africa among the major European powers – the United Kingdom, France, Germany and Belgium. It began in the 1870s when France and Belgium began to challenge what Britain had always regarded as its unchallenged sphere of influence in Africa. The threat of war between the European powers was averted by two conferences on imperial matters, held in Berlin in 1884 and Brussels in 1890, where they effectively agreed upon their respective spheres of influence. The main period of colonisation was between the mid-1880s and the early 1890s.

PROFILE: *Cecil Rhodes*

Cecil Rhodes, who gave his name to the colony of Rhodesia, was born in 1853 into a clerical family and spent most of his life in Africa. His early years there were taken up in making a fortune out of diamonds in south Africa. He founded the de Beers diamond company in 1880 before making more money from gold. From the mid-1880s he became more interested in gaining territory for Britain as part of the **Scramble for Africa**. He was involved in the acquisition of Bechuanaland for the Cape Colony in 1884. The British South Africa Company, one of many which he founded, received a royal charter in 1889 and moved into territory above the Limpopo River which became part of Rhodesia and recognised as a British colony in 1890. In 1891 the boundaries of this new colony were extended north of the Zambezi. Rhodesia became a major supplier of copper to the Empire. Rhodes became Prime Minister of Cape Colony in 1890, resigning over the Jameson raid in 1896 (see case study). His controversial career involved both philanthropy (his will endowed a number of educational scholarships) and deceit (the means by which he acquired territory from African kings and chieftains has been widely criticised by African historians).

And yet, before all of these benefits could be bestowed, lands had to be conquered. None was a more ardent advocate of conquest, or a more successful practitioner of it, than **Cecil Rhodes**. He envisaged Britain conquering and settling . . .

> *'the entire Continent of Africa, the Holy Land, the valley of the Euphrates, the Islands of Cyprus and Canada, the whole of South America, the islands of the Pacific not heretofore possessed by Great Britain, the whole of the Malay Archipelago, the seaboard of China and Japan.'*

This accomplished, Britain's manifest destiny could encompass 'the ultimate recovery of the United States of America as an integral part of the British Empire'. Only then, according to Rhodes, would Britain be free from the threat of war!

KEY TERMS:

Informal empire

Informal empire is the term given to territory which was not formally taken over by a country but in which it exercised dominant trading and other rights. Partly because of cost and partly because of the importance of the economic policy of free trade (some historians talk about 'an informal empire of free trade'), it was the preferred means by which Britain exerted worldwide commercial influence until the mid-1870s. From then the threat from European competitors forced a reappraisal, followed by more formal annexations of territory, especially in Africa.

Imperial preference

Imperial preference was the policy associated with Joseph Chamberlain in the early years of the twentieth century. It represented an important move away from free trade. In 1903 Chamberlain formed a 'Tariff Reform League' with the objective of making the British Empire into a formal trading bloc. The idea was based on continuing free trade only within the empire and imposing tariffs on those outside. Chamberlain saw it as a policy which would both halt Britain's relative economic decline and also provide more cash for a range of necessary social reforms. The idea split the Conservative Party and was almost certainly the most important reason for its massive defeat in the general election of 1906. A form of imperial preference was eventually adopted, but not until 1931 and by a coalition government during the worldwide depression which followed the Wall Street Crash.

Imperialism in context

Imperialist views of Empire were controversial at the time and have become more so since the Second World War when all European nations have shed their empires. Many will read the views of Chamberlain, Curzon and Rhodes nowadays with a mixture of embarrassment and anger. There is no doubt that, in Europe at least, anti-imperial sentiment is at least as prevalent at the end of the twentieth century as imperialist sentiment was at the end of the nineteenth. Historians, however, should not be overly swayed by the values and assumptions of the world in which they happen to live. Their primary task is to *understand* the attitudes and values of people in the past. They may also wish to *pass judgement* on them but historians should always do so from a clear understanding of the world which they are evaluating. Far too much judgement about imperialism is made from present-minded assumptions without a proper understanding of the historical context.

The following points about imperialism are intended to provide that context. Use them to see whether, and how effectively, the pro-Empire arguments given in the previous section, stand up.

1 Britain had no developed policy of imperial acquisition until the last quarter of the nineteenth century. It had acquired substantial territory in the eighteenth and early nineteenth centuries, but usually for commercial reasons. It was easier, and certainly much cheaper, to exercise *influence* over territories which were profitable markets for British manufactured goods or suppliers of cheap raw materials than actually to *rule* them. Thus had developed an **informal empire**, increasingly based on free trade. George Canning had known all about this in respect of South America in the 1820s. His views represented dominant British thinking for about a half century after his death in 1827.

2 When this policy changed it was for defensive reasons. As Bernard Porter has said: 'Popular imperialism is usually associated with national self-confidence. In the 1880s it could equally well be associated with national self-doubt.' The so-called Great Depression (see chapter 25) induced much gloom. Britain's share of the world's overseas trade was shrinking with every passing year. The Empire was promoted as a means of winning back the pre-eminence which free trade could no longer secure. Joseph Chamberlain was only the most famous of many to argue that Empire could be used as a central element in economic policy. **Imperial preference** was the policy, and it did enormous political damage to the Conservative Party.

3 The Empire was at least as much about finding a home for a surplus population as it was about glory and flag-waving. Since the British population was continuing to increase (albeit at a slower rate than in the first half of the century), emigration to the colonies by some of the mother country's 30 million people might be of benefit all round. Imperialists frequently talked about a 'surplus population'. It is often forgotten that migration out of the United Kingdom was not all connected with the Irish Potato Famine. Between 1900 and 1914 about 5 per cent of UK population emigrated – overwhelmingly to the colonies.

4 The Empire was very costly. Many researchers have argued that Britain's high defence costs reflected the need to defend a far-flung empire. Without an empire, British taxation might have been as much as 20 per cent lower.

5 Were the benefits of Empire enjoyed by British society as a whole? Without doubt, certain well-defined sections of it did extremely well. Finance capitalists, for example, got high rates of return for investment in the colonies. Probably wealthy colonials benefited as well. They got high-quality administration, security and protection from the British on the cheap. Cheap colonial raw materials also found their way into British market places. They lowered the cost of living of those in work during the so-called Great Depression. During the First World War (1914–18) willing colonial recruits (more than 2 million of them) and available supplies of food from the colonies (notably Canadian wheat) helped to stave off real crises both on the Western and Home Fronts. Britain's success in the war owes more to the colonies – particularly Australia, New Zealand, Canada and India – than is usually recognised.

6 Imperial propaganda in the 1880s and 1890s was immensely powerful. Although it conveys the impression of a united nation pulling together in support of a great objective, the Empire was always a controversial and divisive force. There were few anti-imperialists in the Conservative Party and they kept a very low profile anyway, but the Empire split the Liberals. The years of division which Gladstone's leadership had begun (see chapters 22 and 24) were continued by splits between imperialists (Rosebery, Grey, Haldane, Asquith) and anti-imperialists (Bright, Morley and Lloyd George). It was also far from certain that the majority of working people marched to the beat of the imperialist drum. Some clearly saw it as a showy but wasteful extravagance when government could be spending money more usefully on a range of social causes at home.

Case study in imperialism: southern Africa, 1890–1902

Few aspects of imperial history illustrate the importance of economic factors better than the story of Britain's extension of political authority over southern Africa at the end of the century. The British already controlled Cape Colony (established in 1795) and Natal (1843) but settlers of Dutch origin had established control and secured semi-independent status in the republics of Orange Free State and Transvaal after moving north in a 'Great Trek' to escape British rule.

For much of the century the British saw no need to extend formal control. As late as 1881, Gladstone was not prepared to commit forces to reverse defeats in the first Anglo-Boer War (see time chart). The discovery of gold in the Transvaal in 1886 transformed the situation. Miners and traders, many of them British, poured into the Transvaal. Soon complaints were being heard that British subjects (called 'Uitlanders' – outsiders – by the Boers) were being denied political rights. The Transvaal government, headed by Dr Paul Kruger, continued to assert its independence as it attempted to exploit its new wealth.

British traders and colonialists, led by Cecil Rhodes, were determined to bring the Boers to heel and to annex increasingly profitable Boer territories for the British Empire. A pre-emptive strike, led by Dr L. S. Jameson, aimed at provoking revolt in the Transvaal was a miserable failure and led to Rhodes's dismissal from office (see time chart). It did, however, convince the Conservative government, and especially its Colonial Secretary Joseph Chamberlain, that matters could not be left to trading companies and aggressive freebooters. Chamberlain's ally **Alfred Milner** was sent out to South Africa. British interests must be maintained in an area of great economic significance. Though it was the Boers who declared war on Britain in October 1899, the British had been building up their military strength in the area and would almost certainly have forced the issue. As it was, the government could use the Boer declaration as an opportunity to mobilise public opinion in Britain behind a 'just' war.

Both the justice of the war – and also the depth of feeling in Britain in support of it – can be disputed. It is true that many working-class men volunteered for service in South Africa and that noisy demonstrations were held to celebrate the turning of the tide in the war during 1900 after initial Boer successes (see time chart). The lower middle classes, in particular, seem to have been enthusiastic. One of the first successful mass press campaigns, by the strongly imperialist *Daily Mail*, focused attention on Britain's glorious struggle and on the need for victory to ensure

PROFILE: *Alfred Milner*

The British Empire in the late nineteenth century depended to a large extent upon the quality of its professional administrators. Probably the most celebrated of these (though his later career was in politics) was **Alfred Milner**, who was born in 1854. Like Curzon, he was educated at Oxford and made his name in the Empire – in his case as High Commissioner in South Africa (1897–1905), Governor of Cape Colony (1897–1901) and Governor of the Transvaal and Orange River Companies administering Boer territories (1901–5). Unlike Curzon, however, he was of German descent, coming from Hesse-Darmstadt and going to Tübingen University before coming to Britain. His early career in Britain in the 1880s was as a barrister, a journalist supporting the Liberal Party and a civil servant. His first experience of colonial administration was in Egypt (1889–92). He was created a viscount in 1902, in recognition of his service in the Boer War. He opposed Irish Home Rule and was a vigorous critic of Lloyd George's 'People's Budget' (see chapter 31), but later served in his war cabinet and, from 1919 to 1921, as Colonial Secretary. He died in 1925.

Figure 26.3 *The Boer War, 1899–1902*

continued pre-eminence against competitor nations. A general election, called two years early by the Conservatives in 1900 in part to capitalise on pro-war sentiment, produced a satisfyingly large majority over the Liberals.

Much of the enthusiasm for an imperialist war proved both skin-deep and brief. The later stages of the war were not glorious at all but involved brutal methods used against Boer forces who refused to accept open military defeat and took up guerilla tactics. It was the British, under General Kitchener, who laid waste large stretches of Boer land to deprive fighters of cover and support and herded many families into concentration camps where almost 30,000 died. The war had become an expensive slog to victory. Over 22,000 British troops died, more than in the Crimean War half a century earlier. Most died from disease. Though eventual victory was assured it lowered Britain's reputation in the international community. The country was too easily criticised as bullying and showing none of that famous sense of 'fair play' which was supposed to be bred into Christian English gentlemen.

Within Britain, also, criticism mounted in the later stages of the war. Some argued that the British army was incompetent in the face of brave but relatively untrained and ill-equipped opponents. Why did it take so long, and cost so much, to win? Why did so many British troops die? Why, also, were so many troops recruited from the heart of the empire only marginally fit while large numbers of others were rejected as unfit for military service? How could an imperialistic nation tolerate gross inadequacies in the imperial stock at home? Almost 40 years earlier, Benjamin Disraeli was already pointing out the obvious message: poor health could fatally hamper a nation striving for greatness:

> *'The question [of health] is becoming both in town and country one of paramount interest. The greatness of the country depends on the race that fills it, and, whatever our ancestors may have done to make the country great or famous, whatever liberty they may have acquired, whatever wealth they may have accumulated, if the race becomes inferior you lose all these results and all these blessings.'*
>
> Speech to the Buckinghamshire Agricultural Association, 22 September 1864. Quoted in P. R. Ghosh, 'Style and Substance in Victorian Social Reform, 1860–80' in P. J. Waller (ed.), *Politics and Social Change in Modern Britain* (1987).

We shall look further at the important connections between imperialism and social reform in chapter 30.

Other critics concentrated on the brutality of British methods in South Africa. The new Liberal leader Henry Campbell-Bannerman – not a supporter of imperialism anyway – polarised opinion both in his own party and in the country at large when he asked his rhetorical question, 'When is a war not a war? When it is carried on by methods of barbarism.'

Perhaps the most thoughtful analysis came from anti-imperialist critics who looked beyond South Africa to argue that Britain should not have allowed itself to be sucked into imperial adventures to please financiers. In the year the Boer War ended the Liberal anti-imperialist J. A. Hobson published his famous book *Imperialism: A Study*. It is a complex and theoretical book but its basic purpose was simple enough. Hobson sought to show that imperialism was an unsound policy promoted to benefit a few at the expense of the many. Far from increasing the national wealth, imperial acquisitions must eventually decrease it. The main planks in the argument were these:

1 Imperialism had an economic cause: industrial nations were now producing too much to be consumed either at home or within the existing industrial world. Therefore, capitalists had to search for new markets to consume their products. Colonies fitted the bill.

2 Governments had helped traders to create empires, but the main benefits were enjoyed not by the nation as a whole but by the industrial and commercial middle classes. In Hobson's view 'the public purse' was being used 'for the purposes of private profit-making'.

3 The creation of empires does not help world trade in the long run. Colonies are very expensive to run and administering them makes colonial nations more inward looking. Free trade (which for so many Liberals was the foundation of all wealth and prosperity) was fatally compromised in an imperialist world.

4 National prosperity does not depend so much on overseas as on domestic trade. Imperialism deflects attention away from the more stable and profitable home markets towards more risky and expensive overseas ones.

5 Much investment in the Empire came from what Hobson called 'the well-to-do classes' in the south-east of England who had 'excessive purchasing power'. This distorted national economic performance. Too much emphasis was placed on financial manipulators and brokers, not enough on the real creators of national wealth – the industrialists and manufacturers who were mostly situated in the north of England, south Wales and central Scotland.

Tasks

Hobson's answer to the question which forms the title of the chapter was simple. The Empire was for the benefit of finance capitalists. As you have seen, the imperialists' answer was quite different. This chapter has given some evidence on which to base your own judgement about imperialism.

1 Use that evidence to draw up a balance sheet on which you identify the advantages and disadvantages of British imperial expansion at this time. Remember to put in subheadings because people supported, and opposed, imperialism for different reasons. You might like to set up a debate between 'imperialists' and 'anti-imperialists'.

2 The first paragraph of the section 'Imperialism in context' offers the author's own view about how historians should approach controversial issues. Do you think the author is right in what he says? If you wanted to argue against him, what points of your own would you make?

Further reading

B. Porter, *The Lion's Share: A Short History of British Imperialism, 1850–1970* (Addison Wesley Longman, second edition, 1984) – a very lucid and witty survey of the role of the British Empire.

P. J. Cain and A. G. Hopkins, *British Imperialism: Innovation and Expansion, 1688–1914* (Addison Wesley Longman, 1993) – an important new interpretation which stresses the worldwide economic and commercial dimension.

D. K. Fieldhouse, *Economics and Empire, 1830–1914* (Macmillan, 1984).

D. C. M. Platt, *Finance, Trade and Politics in British Foreign Policy, 1815–1914* (Clarendon Press, 1968).

B. Porter, *Britain, Europe and the World: Delusions of Grandeur, 1850–1986* (Allen and Unwin, 1987).

A. Offer, 'The British Empire, 1870–1914: a waste of money?', *Economic History Review* (1993).

THEMATIC AND EVALUATION OF EVIDENCE

27 Women's work and women's role, 1867–1914

Time chart

1857: Matrimonial Causes Act makes divorce possible without need for a private Act of Parliament. Both divorces and separations increase in second half of the nineteenth century

1867: London Society for Women's Suffrage founded to press the case for women to vote in parliamentary elections

1869: Girton College became the first university college for women students. It transferred to Cambridge in 1872, one year after Newnham College was founded there. (Lady Margaret Hall became the first women's Oxford college in 1878.) Municipal Corporations Act enables unmarried women to vote in municipal elections

1870: Married Women's Property Act gives women the right to keep their own earnings from employment after marriage and also to keep separate savings accounts. Elementary Education Act permits women ratepayers to vote for, and serve on, the new school boards

1875: Women able to be elected as Poor Law Guardians (women ratepayers had been entitled to vote in guardian elections since the Poor Law Amendment Act was passed in 1834)

1878: Judicial separation between a husband and wife is formally permitted for the first time

1882: Women allowed to keep separate property which they had acquired before marriage

1888: Local Government Act permits women to vote for new county and county borough councils

1891: Legal judgement confirms that a man cannot compel his wife to live in the matrimonial home

1894: Parish Councils Act permits women to serve on urban and district councils

1897: Non-militant National Union of Women's Suffrage Societies (NUWSS) formed

1903: Militant Women's Social and Political Union (WSPU) founded

1905: Suffragettes imprisoned after disrupting a Liberal rally in Manchester

1910: Violence between suffragettes and police after a proposal to give women householders the vote is defeated in Parliament

1911: First Conciliation Bill, which would have given the vote to single women with property, introduced. Pankhursts suspend militancy while the bill was discussed. Despite support in principle, the bill was put to one side

1912: After a further Suffrage Bill defeated, suffragettes riot in London. Main period of militancy begins

1913: Further violence with Women's Suffrage and Political Union mounting arson and bombing campaigns. 'Cat and Mouse Act' passed, whereby women hunger strikers were to be released from prison but re-arrested when fit enough to continue their sentence. **Emily Davison** died after throwing herself under the King's horse at the Derby

1914: With the outbreak of war suffragettes announce suspension of their political campaign

A changing topic

Until recently, if students did any work at all on that majority of Britain's population which happened to be women it was in the context of 'the suffrage question'. It is obviously important to understand the way in which campaigns to achieve votes for women developed after 1870. However, modern scholarship is concerned about much more than women's votes. Much is now understood about the work women did, about their aspirations and their changing role in the family. This chapter gives you the opportunity to investigate the findings of this research.

PROFILE: *Emily Davison*

Emily Davison, who was born in 1872, is now best remembered as the suffragette 'martyr' who threw herself under the King's horse during the Derby of 1913. By this time, however, she was already a committed militant suffragette. After joining the WSPU in 1906 she was frequently arrested for assault and setting fire to pillar boxes. She responded to frequent prison sentences by going on hunger strike, and the WSPU made much propaganda out of the forced feeding to which the authorities resorted in response.

Women and work

Women did many paid jobs in industrial Britain. Unfortunately, it is difficult to be certain about their range because the censuses (which were taken every 10 years in Britain throughout our period) under-record women's economic activity. Those who took the census ('census enumerators') had no difficulty in recording full-time paid work in obvious places of employment. We can be reasonably certain from census evidence that there were about 519,000 women textile workers in Britain in 1871 and that a large proportion of them worked in factories. By 1911 the overall number had increased to about 604,000. Though women workers as a whole earned less than men, the differentials were narrower in textiles than in any other occupations.

The real problems associated with deciding on the range and extent of women's paid work are that:

1 much of it was not full time. Part-time work is often not recorded in the census.

Figure 27.1 *Cotton workers in a Manchester mill, late nineteenth century*

KEY TERM:

Separate spheres

The term **separate spheres** refers to the dominant view in respectable Victorian society that men and women had separate talents and that their development should be kept separate. According to the stereotype, women were emotional, self-sacrificing and tied up with home and family; men were rational, more political and career-orientated. The poet Coventry Patmore wrote 'The Angel in House' in praise of the domestic virtues of women. 'Separate spheres' ideas meant that women who wished to work or have careers after marriage had to contend with strong prejudice and, frequently, ridicule.

2 work done in the home (which remained extensive throughout the nineteenth century) frequently went unrecorded, especially when done under the supervision of the (male) head of the household.

3 much work was short term and supplementary. Working-class women would frequently do menial tasks, such as extra cleaning or taking in neighbours' washing, to tide the family over a financial crisis.

4 a strong prejudice existed against 'respectable' women doing paid work. According to the 'domestic ideal', which most middle-class and upper working-class families accepted, it was the responsibility of the male head of household to provide for the material needs of the family. According to **separate spheres**, the woman's role was to manage that household and to bring up children. Thus periods when women *did* work often went concealed and unrecorded in the hope that the family could 'keep up appearances'.

We can be sure that women were much more involved in the world of work than official records suggest. Girls and young women were extensively involved in the labour force. Textile work was carried on not only in factories but also in small workshops where thousands of women worked as seamstresses. Women were also found doing jobs not usually considered as 'women's work'. Scottish fishergirls were employed to deal with the catch on the Norfolk coast at Great Yarmouth, for example. Much the fastest growing occupational category for young women, however, was that of domestic servant. Middle-class households were not considered properly respectable unless they employed servants to help with domestic drudgery. By the 1870s, many upper working-class families would also employ a servant or two. As you can see from Figure 27.3,

Figure 27.2 Scottish fishergirls working at Great Yarmouth, late nineteenth century

at the peak in 1871, about one woman in eight was working as a domestic servant. The great majority were young, unmarried and very poorly paid doing a variety of menial tasks. As new opportunities for work as shop assistants and clerks grew from the 1880s and 1890s, so domestic service began to lose its attractions. Landowners' and middle-class households were beginning to complain about the difficulty of recruiting, and keeping, good servants.

Women appear to have been more vulnerable to unemployment during periods of economic depression. At first women were much less likely to be members of trade unions, which until the 1890s were largely the preserve of skilled workers anyway. From the 1890s, however, female trade unionism kept pace with the rise in trade union membership as a whole. Women were numerous, generally young and frequently less skilled and it was easy for employers to lay women off when times were hard. They could as readily be recruited again when conditions improved. In a depressed sector of the economy, like agriculture after the mid-1870s, employment opportunities collapsed. Figure 27.4 shows statistics for female textile workers. They reflect long-term depression, but also the especially serious effects on the female workforce. Some women undoubtedly resented what they saw as discrimination. Others, however, felt that when work was scarce, menfolk (as heads of the family) had priority for any work that was going.

Figure 27.3 *Domestic servants (all ages)*

Date	*Total (England and Wales)*	*% of total female population*	*Total (Scotland)*	*% of total female population*
1851	1,069,865	9.8	154,554	10.2
1871	1,508,888	12.8	155,307	8.9
1891	1,759,555	11.6	190,051	9.1
1911	1,662,511	11.1	159,658	6.5

Figure 27.4 *Female textile workers in different materials*

Date	*Cotton*		*Woollens & worsteds*		*Silk*		*Flax*		*Jute & hemp*	
	E & W	*S*	*E & W*	*S*	*E & W*	*S*	*E & W*	*S*	*E & W*	*S*
1851	247,705	26,675	96,638	6,641	68,342	1,059	13,219	39,579	4,818	1,816
1871	279,870	13,188	117,494	14,117	51,100	1,256	10,629	26,863	1,516	3,677
1891	332,784	11,909	130,094	18,123	31,811	2,615	5,592	19,216	2,333	22,059
1911	374,785	9,360	127,148	15,148	29,643	810	2,930	16,360	995	27,074

E & W = England and Wales
S = Scotland

Marriage

According to the stereotype of 'the woman's role' marriage was the ideal state: the natural prelude to the procreation of children and the fulfilment of a woman's destiny. Marriage was certainly popular. Well over 90 per cent of women were married at some stage in their lives. It was also an economic watershed for many. In all working-class communities, married women were less likely to work than unmarried ones. This generalisation, however, conceals substantial variations. In textile communities more than three unmarried women in four were in full-time paid employment at the time of the 1911 census; this proportion declined to about two in five after marriage. The national average was about 55 per cent before marriage and 14 per cent afterwards. Mining communities offered far fewer opportunities for the working woman. In County Durham, for example, only about 30 per cent of unmarried women and 5 per cent of married women worked.

Marriage in late Victorian Britain, however, was far from the unvarying prelude to a long life of cosy domesticity. Given the strength of the popular image of the Victorian home and family, the following observations may be surprising:

1 About 13 out of every 20 women between the ages of 20 and 25 in 1871 were unmarried; so were about six out of every 20 between the ages of 25 and 34. The trend towards late marriage increased between 1871 and 1911.

2 In late Victorian Britain family sizes were decreasing quite sharply. The higher up the social scale, the smaller the family size. More or less effective forms of contraception were being practised.

3 Partly because families were getting smaller, a larger proportion of children were surviving. Death rates went down after the 1870s, but more so for women than men. The consequence was that women were frequently widowed. Most of these did not remarry. The 'surplus' of women over men increased steadily in the period 1871–1911.

4 Divorce, informal and formal separations were all on the increase, helped by changes in legislation (see time chart). The numbers, however, remained tiny. Death of the male was far and away the main reason for marriages to end. However, what we now call single-parent families were more common in late Victorian Britain than we might suppose.

Education and employment

The period from about 1870 to the outbreak of the First World War was generally one of improved employment opportunities for women. This was especially true of the professions to which strong-minded and determined women were gaining access. Able working-class pupils coming through the elementary schools might move up into the lower middle classes as elementary school teachers. Heavy growth in the number of women teachers, nurses, clerks and secretaries ensured that middle-class occupations grew much more rapidly than working-class ones in the 30 years before the First World War. For a very few by 1914, the gates of medical, legal and academic professions creaked resentfully ajar.

KEY TERMS:

Blue-stocking

The term **blue-stocking** had been used since the late eighteenth century to describe highly educated women. It was not intended to be flattering. Academic or learned women were often pictured as highly unattractive, the 'blue stockings' symbolising lack of dress sense or 'frumpishness'.

Natural selection

Natural selection relates to the evolutionary theories developed by Charles Darwin (1809–82) and Alfred Wallace (1823–1913). They argued that the stronger species survived by a process of constant evolution over a long period of time. The full title of Darwin's famous book is *On the Origin of Species by Means of Natural Selection* (1859). The ideas were dynamite because they challenged the orthodox Christian explanation that God had created not only the universe but all of the creatures within it. By extension, Darwinian ideas became associated with the evolution of more, or less, successful genetic types within the same species. By the early twentieth century 'social Darwinism' was developing policies designed to favour 'fitter' elements within society and even to discourage the 'unfit' from breeding.

Education for women was strongly status-related. Elementary schools, extended as a result of the emergence of rate-supported Board Schools after 1870, had always been open to boys and girls on a more or less equal basis. Not so the secondary schools, whether 'public' or 'grammar'. Here girls had to fight hard to achieve recognition. The tradition that the middle classes and the aristocracy paid large sums of money to have their male children educated for leadership while girls had to make do with 'domestic accomplishments' died hard. Nevertheless, change did come from the later 1860s, particularly in higher education. Between 1869 and 1880, Girton and Newnham (Cambridge) and Somerville and Lady Margaret Hall (Oxford) opened their doors as all-women colleges. The majority of early entrants were between 15 and 25 years of age, and it seems that far more were from middle-class backgrounds (especially daughters of academics, schoolmasters and merchants) than from the aristocracy – where 'good breeding stock' continued to take heavy precedence over the well-stocked mind.

Highly educated middle-class women were widely perceived as a threat to male complacency if nothing else. As so often, newcomers with ambition and drive found themselves satirised for their pretensions. The successful light opera combination of Gilbert and Sullivan devoted a whole piece to the subject in 1884. *Princess Ida* is the story of a thinly disguised **blue-stocking** who teaches the superiority of women over men. One of the lecturers in her 'women's university' scornfully dismisses 'Darwinian man' by comparison with women. Man may have evolved to a reasonable degree of intelligence by a process of **natural selection** but 'Darwinian man, though well-behaved, at best is only a monkey shaved'. Naturally, Gilbert ensured that men had the last laugh. Princess Ida needs men to defend her university from attack and then – ultimate shame – she falls in love with the hero and marries him. The prince captures his princess and the world is placed the right way up again.

Women and the vote

Many students think that women did not receive the vote until 1918. This is only true of elections for Members of Parliament. The time chart shows that, between 1869 and 1894, women were permitted to vote in an increasing range of local elections. They also sat as councillors. Some had by 1900 achieved positions of considerable influence in education administration and local government. By 1914 almost half of the elected local authorities (including poor law) had women representatives sitting on them.

In general, men were happier to have women take a share in political activities concerned with 'caring' (that is, according to the stereotype, 'female') issues like poor law relief and education. Parliament and national government were different. Here women had to fight. Coordinated campaigns for women to vote in parliamentary elections began in the 1860s, strongly linked to the pressure from middle-class women for equality within marriage, access to higher education and the medical profession. In most years during the 1870s and 1880s Parliament debated votes-for-women proposals, though none came near to success.

Within the Liberal Party, in particular, support for female enfranchisement grew steadily. The issue, however, was never a straight left-right division across the established male political spectrum. Significant numbers of Conservatives, from the Marquis of Salisbury downwards, could see the sense of giving women with property the vote, since they believed they would be a force for stability if not outright conservatism. It was also noted that women were more dutiful church attenders than men; many would be keen supporters of the Church of England and that would help the Conservative Party. On the other side of the fence, the masculine culture which suffused many trade unions, especially the miners, made many workers hesitant about extending the vote to women. It was also noted how much the suffrage campaign owed to middle-class women and fear that this would operate against the interests of the working classes. In the 1880s Gladstone expressed concern that giving women the vote might only strengthen the 'one-issue' campaigners who, in his view, were deflecting the energies of the Liberal Party from his great moral causes. Considerations of party political advantage – would women be more likely to vote Conservative or Liberal? – undoubtedly influenced many MPs' views on the suffrage question.

Votes for women: the main arguments in favour

1 Votes are a political right; such rights cannot be the reserved to one sex.

2 Everyone has to obey the law. People should, through their elected representatives, have a say in the laws they have to obey.

3 Some laws – especially those concerning the home and property – apply particularly to women yet women cannot help to make them.

4 Women have specific skills and experience which Parliament should be able to draw upon when it is discussing changes to the law.

5 Women's self-esteem and their wish to participate in political life would increase if they had the vote.

6 Highly educated, well-qualified women are denied a vote while large numbers of unworthy men have one.

Votes for women: the main arguments against

1 Women and men are different. They should fulfil different roles in life (see **separate spheres** – page 270). Men are rational, women emotional. Thus men are better in the world of politics and work, women in the world of the home.

2 Women are the weaker sex. They cannot be asked to bear arms for their country. Therefore, because they are not asked to risk losing their lives in wars, they are not citizens in the fullest sense.

3 The campaign for women's suffrage had been hijacked by a small, articulate but unrepresentative minority of feminists. At bottom, most women did not really care whether they had the vote or not.

4 Middle-class women would use political rights to develop their careers and neglect their domestic duties. Also, if the educated delayed having families, or did not have them at all, a larger proportion of babies would be born to 'socially undesirable' elements (see **natural selection** – page 273). The nation would suffer.

5 To give votes to women would almost certainly lead to a further extension for men and thus enfranchise unskilled, rootless and generally undesirable people.

6 'Votes for women' was the thin end of the wedge. If women could vote and sit in Parliament, would they then demand to be members of male clubs, to be bishops or trade union leaders? Where would it all end?

Figure 27.5 'The Shrieking Sister': a cartoon in Punch, *1906*

THE SHRIEKING SISTER.

THE SENSIBLE WOMAN. "*YOU* HELP OUR CAUSE? WHY, YOU'RE ITS WORST ENEMY!"

It is doubtful whether, despite the enthusiasm and organisation of many predominantly middle-class women, much progress was made towards achieving the vote in the 1880s and early 1890s. The formation of the National Union of Women's Suffrage Societies in 1897 gave the movement more focus but much greater publicity attended the increasingly militant tactics of the **Pankhursts** after the Women's Social and Political Union was founded. In the decade before the outbreak of the First World War the 'woman issue' was rarely out of the headlines. The main outline

KEY TERMS:

Suffragists and suffragettes

The term **suffragette** was coined by the *Daily Mail* newspaper in 1906 to distinguish the radical and militant methods employed by the Women's Social and Political Union (WSPU) (led by Emmeline and Christobel Pankhurst) from the non-violent arguments employed by the National Union of Women's Suffrage Societies (NUWSS) (the **suffragists**), whose president was Millicent Fawcett (1847–1929). The newspaper, though opposed to women's suffrage anyway, made it clear that it preferred argument to arson. Suffragettes took up militancy as a means of drawing constant attention to the cause of votes for women. The NUWSS continued to work through campaigning journalism and parliamentary petition. It had half a million members but, arguably, did less to make 'votes for women' a central political issue than the WSPU.

PROFILE: *Emmeline Pankhurst*

Emmeline Pankhurst was born in 1858 to comfortably-off parents in Manchester. With her husband Richard Pankhurst, a radical barrister, she campaigned for women's suffrage. She used the opportunities for women to participate in local politics, being elected a Poor Law Guardian in Chorlton (Manchester) in 1893, the year she joined the Independent Labour Party (ILP). The ILP was not sympathetic to the cause of women's suffrage and Emmeline Pankhurst left in 1903 to found the Women's Social and Political Union. She was responsible for much militant activity as a means of publicising the suffragette cause. During the First World War she was an enthusiastic advocate of conscription into the armed forces. She died in 1928.

of events between 1903 and 1914 is provided in the time chart. Historians, like contemporaries, have debated ever since whether militancy did more to advance the cause or to retard it. Certainly, distinctions between **suffragists and suffragettes** provoked internal disputes and splits, as Figure 27.5 and this report in the *Daily Graphic* demonstrate.

'"The organ of the Women's Social and Political Union in future" [said Mrs Pankhurst] will be The Suffragette, *which has come into existence since last Monday. Mr and Mrs Pethick-Lawrence disagreed with what we considered the best policy, and we decided it was best that they should take the paper they founded,* Votes for Women, *and run it along their own lines. "This is our policy," continued Mrs Pankhurst slowly. "Short of taking human life we shall stop at no step we consider necessary to take ... Our militant policy is fixed and unalterable."*

Mr and Mrs Pethick-Lawrence, in an interview with a Daily Graphic *representative yesterday, emphatically denied that their withdrawal could be construed as a split in the ranks. "We withdrew," declared Mrs Pethick-Lawrence, "so that there should be no split. If we had remained and the opinions of Mrs and Miss Pankhurst and my husband and myself had not coincided, as they have in the past, it would have meant disruption. That is what we did not desire. We have the cause at heart and we thought it best to work separately. We are ... as militant at heart as anyone. It was on the question of the expediency of a certain militant policy which was discussed a few days ago that we disagreed. That is all."'*

Report in *Daily Graphic*, 18 October 1912.

PROFILE: *Christabel Pankhurst*

Christabel Pankhurst, born in 1880, was the elder daughter of Emmeline. She trained as a lawyer at Manchester University but was refused entry to Lincoln's Inn in 1904 because she was a woman. With her mother, she founded the Women's Social and Political Union. She was imprisoned for militant activity in 1905. She was a noted orator and effective journalist, editing *The Suffragette*. Like her mother, she was a strong supporter of the First World War. After the war, she stood unsuccessfully as a parliamentary candidate of the Women's Party. She emigrated to the United States where her oratorical career was extended as an evangelical preacher. She died in 1958.

Recent studies have attempted to throw the spotlight away from the attention-seeking militancy and aggressive activities of the Pankhursts. More attention has been paid to support for the vote from working-class groups outside London, notably Lancashire textile workers. Non-militant feminism appears to have enjoyed a revival in 1913–14. However, the vote did not come.

Since there was no universal male suffrage before 1914, there was no question of giving the vote to all women. Many Liberal and Labour MPs, however, were also uneasy about a suffrage restricted to elderly single women of independent means. They argued (and subsequent evidence has abundantly justified their fears) that such women would be overwhelmingly Conservative. As with Ireland (see chapter 24), the First World War intervened with a critical constitutional issue frustratingly unresolved.

Further reading

M. Pugh, *State and Society: British Political and Social History, 1870–1992* (Arnold 1994) – integrates social and political themes very skilfully.

E. Roberts, *Women's Work, 1840–1940*, Studies in Economic and Social History (Macmillan, 1988) – Pugh and Roberts together provide very useful student introductions to the main political and economic themes respectively.

J. Lewis, *Women in England, 1870–1950* (Wheatsheaf, 1980).

P. Thane, 'Late Victorian Women' in T. R. Gourvish and A. O'Day (eds), *Later Victorian Britain, 1867–1900* (Macmillan, 1988).

D. Thompson, *British Women in the Nineteenth Century*, New Appreciations in History (Historical Association, 1989).

M. Pugh, *Votes for Women in Britain, 1867–1928*, New Appreciations in History (Historical Association, 1994).

B. Harrison, 'Women's Suffrage at Westminster' in M. Bentley and J. Stevenson (eds), *High and Low Politics in Modern Britain* (Oxford University Press, 1983).

THEMATIC

28 Britons at play: sport and leisure in Victorian Britain

Time chart

1854: Respectable pleasure gardens opened at Crystal Palace

1862: Formation of the Working Men's Club and Institutes Union

1863: Football Association (FA) formed

1866: Marquis of Queensbury's rules governing boxing issued: they prohibit 'spiking, biting, gouging, strangling [and] butting'. Amateur Athletic Association founded

1871: Bank Holidays established in England and Wales. Rugby Union established

1872: First FA Cup competition played

1875: First Gilbert and Sullivan light opera – *Trial by Jury* – produced. Alexandra Palace opened in north London

1877: First Cricket Test Match between Australia and England played; first All-England Lawn Tennis Championships played at Wimbledon

1878: Cyclists' Touring Club founded. By 1899 it had about 60,000 members

1879: Racecourses Act passed to reduce rowdiness at race meetings. It contributed to reducing the number of racecourses during the 1880s

1880: Popular magazine *Tit-bits* founded

1883: Boys' Brigade founded. Its aim was 'the advancement of Christ's Kingdom amongst boys and the promotion of habits of obedience, reverence, discipline, self-respect and all that tends towards true Christian manliness'

1885: Professional Association Football legalised

1888: Football League founded. At first it comprised only northern and midland clubs because southern teams were almost all amateur

1890: Reconstitution of the County Cricket championship in its more or less modern form. Amateurs and professionals play together but strict social segregation is maintained off the field

1895: Rugby Football Union refuses request from players with northern teams for payments to compensate for time lost from work. A separate Northern Union formed which develops into professional Rugby League. National Trust founded to protect Britain's countryside and buildings

1896: Foundation of the *Daily Mail* costing a half-penny. It becomes Britain's first popular mass-produced daily newspaper with a circulation of about 2 million by the end of the century. Capitalising on rising levels of literacy, its success is also based on entertaining articles

1901: Crowd of 100,000 attends FA Cup Final at Crystal Palace

1903: *Daily Mirror* founded, originally as light reading for women

1914: George V becomes the first monarch to present the FA Cup, symbolising the new acceptability and respectability of professional football

Sport: rules and regulations

Look at the time chart and scan it carefully for the words 'first' and 'founded'. Notice how frequently they appear. In the last quarter of the nineteenth century, sport in Britain was codified, regulated and professionalised as never before. This is no accident. As the historian Keith Robbins ironically observed, 'In the late nineteenth century, leisure became a serious business'. The following points help to explain the trend towards both greater availability and regulation:

1 Improvements in transport made it possible for players and spectators to travel long distances to 'away' venues. These improvements also helped iron out regional variations in the way games were played. National competitions could now emerge.

2 Living standards were improving. Working people (predominantly men) could spend money attending high-quality sporting contests. Professional national competitions and leagues came into being. Association Football became truly 'the people's game', though it faced severe competition from rugby in the industrial north and came a very poor second to it in south Wales.

3 Leisure time was both increasing and becoming more clearly identified. Sir John Lubbock's Bank Holidays Act brought agreed public holidays to Britain. The Bank Holiday break on the first Monday in August was particularly important since summer holidays became arranged around it. The British still had far fewer holidays than most

Figure 28.1 The Aston Villa football team in the season 1912–13. Villa, Birmingham's most important football club, had been one of the founder members of the Football League, a competition it had already won five times by the First World War. Like many early football clubs it began life as a church team, in its case a Wesleyan Methodist organisation.

Catholic countries (where 'saints' days' offered a convenient excuse either for rest or a celebration) but Lubbock's Act was a significant step. At the same time, employers were rationalising those customary periods of recreation frequently called 'wakes' and agreeing to shut down their works for the same week or fortnight every year. By 1914 a few, like the North West Railway Company and Levers, the Cheshire soap manufacturers, were providing holidays with pay. Holiday sporting fixtures became particularly popular. Widespread agreement that no work would be done on a Saturday afternoon allowed the early Football League to flourish.

4 Professional sport could not exist unless all competitors agreed to common rules (however much they might try to bend them as they played!). Rules were not introduced for the sake of uniformity alone. No country in the world was so urban as late Victorian Britain had become. Many of the sports which town dwellers brought from a predominantly rural society were unstructured and frequently violent. Rules were a necessary way of curbing violence in aggressive young men. The formulation of rules and the establishment of a hierarchy of competition which allowed talented sportsmen to progress from games between local boys' clubs right up to national and even international competition was a wonderful way of channelling that aggression which is the twin of competitiveness. High population densities and uncontrolled aggression were a

dangerous mixture. Add freely available beer and, some Victorians believed, you had the recipe for revolution. The late Victorians needed sporting competition for more than amusement. Some would say that they needed it as a means of control (see below).

Not all sport was aggressive or competitive. Cycling was introduced into Britain in the 1860s and became the nation's fastest growing sport by the 1890s. Cycling afforded opportunity both for races and for more sociable recreation. It was one of a fairly small number of social activities which gave opportunities for men and women to be seen together as equals.

Figure 28.2 *A woman cyclist at the turn of the century. Cycling did not commend itself to all commentators as a proper recreational activity for women. Here the* Badminton Magazine *offers trenchant views in 1900, not only on cycling but on what it was proper for women to be seen doing: 'For women . . . beauty of face and form is one of the chief essentials, but unlimited indulgence in violent outdoor sports, cricket, bicycling, beagling, otter-hunting, paper-chasing and – most odious of all games for women – hockey, cannot but have an unwomanly effect on a young girl's mind, no less her appearance . . . Let young girls skate, dance and play lawn tennis . . . but let them leave field sports and rough outdoor pastimes to those for whom they are naturally intended – men.'*

Holidays

The other main recreational development of this period was seaside holidays. The seaside itself had been popularised at the end of the eighteenth century by George III, who made frequent visits to Weymouth on the Dorset coast, and his son, George IV, who in 1815 commissioned the celebrated architect John Nash to design an exotic Indian-style pavilion in Brighton. Fashionable society was increasingly to be seen at the seaside in the early nineteenth century. Working people followed later, although steamboats began carrying London's working classes to Gravesend and Margate as early as 1815. It was the railway which consummated the love affair between the urban masses and the sea and sand. Morecambe (which sees little of the sea for most of the day since the tide goes out a long way) was linked to Leeds by railway from the early 1850s. Thus began a long association between West Yorkshire and the north Lancashire coast; both day-trippers and weekly holiday-makers transformed the previously unknown fishing village of Poulton-le-Sands into a flourishing late nineteenth-century resort. A similar relationship existed between the East Midlands town of Nottingham and the Lincolnshire resort of Skegness.

In the 1850s and 1860s it was mostly the middle classes who took seaside holidays, as opposed to day trips and excursions. This situation was transformed from the 1870s. Blackpool became the unofficial seaside capital of Lancashire: brash, titillating, go-ahead and vulgar. It pioneered a 'pleasure beach' on the south shore, which offered a bewildering range of ways of spending sixpence or a shilling ($2\frac{1}{2}$ p or 5p) on tricks, machines and trinket stalls. Fish-and-chip shops provided food which was nutritious, cheap and, of course, popular. The town had soon erected three piers and a tower, which cheekily copied the Eiffel Tower in Paris. Like the popular newspaper proprietors who flourished at the same time, Blackpool businessmen rapidly learned that no one went bankrupt by underestimating popular taste. The town took four times as many visitors

Figure 28.3 Great Yarmouth was the biggest resort on the Norfolk coast, receiving almost 500,000 visitors just before the First World War. Most came by train, but a few, as in this photograph from 1908, arrived by steamboat from London.

in 1873 as 10 years earlier. By 1913 an astonishing 4 million came to what was now the fun centre of Britain if not the world. Visitors were predominantly working class, most of them from the cotton towns of industrial Lancashire between 30 and 50 miles away. To save money, many of the first holiday-makers to Blackpool took their own food which their landladies would cook for them.

All seaside resorts – even Blackpool – were to a degree status-conscious. Some, like Eastbourne (where the Dukes of Devonshire, the town's dominant landowners, kept the railway away for many years) or Torquay, prided themselves on being 'select'. These offered a range of amenities to attract the middle classes. Hotels and golf courses were socially defining. Resorts like Brighton and Scarborough possessed clearly identified middle-class zones or suburbs. In Blackpool, the north shore was more select than the south; Lytham St Anne's, about four miles to the south, more exclusive than either. Lytham developed as both a commuter and a retirement town for Manchester businessmen and solicitors.

Was leisure a form of 'social control'?

Historians of leisure have debated the importance of social control (see key term, page 136) as a factor in explaining changes in the second half of the nineteenth century. Some think it a successful assault on the lifestyles

Figure 28.4 Worthing, on the Sussex coast, marketed itself as a select health resort, especially beneficial to sufferers of chest complaints. This postcard, which shows carts being pulled by goats, rather than the normal donkeys, offers many clues to its upmarket status.

of working people in order to ensure the success of the bourgeoisie in imposing capitalist values on society. Marxist historians have been prominent in social control arguments because they believe that the working and middle classes, having separate economic interests, are in inevitable conflict.

Those who believe in 'social control' have pointed to the pronounced trend in British society towards the provision of what is called 'rational recreation'. Much money was spent both by local authorities and private benefactors in the second half of the nineteenth century on the provision of public parks, where people could walk and enjoy themselves separate from the grime of an industrial city. Here trees, drinking fountains and ornamental shrubberies created an atmosphere of peace, conducive to rest and renewal. Sir Robert Peel donated substantial sums towards the provision of parks and amenities. Whitworth Park was donated to the citizens of Manchester by the successful engineer and philanthropist Sir Joseph Whitworth. Similarly, public libraries, swimming baths and wash houses were means of providing food for the mind and that cleanliness which, the Victorian proverb asserted, was next to godliness.

Local authorities, often under political pressure from religious nonconformists, mounted attacks on forms of leisure which had survived from the pre-industrial era. These included such brutal sports as bull-baiting and cock-fighting, fairs (which could involve nothing more sinister than petty trading and circus acts but which notoriously attracted prostitutes, pickpockets and confidence tricksters) and unlicensed gambling and drinking. Much of the work of the early police forces was directed towards ridding the streets of the petty criminals who invariably attended amusements of this sort and breaking up the frequent violence associated with beer shops and public houses.

It is not difficult to note a greater concern in the middle of the nineteenth century for respectability and the 'improving' use of leisure time. At the same time, criticism of violence, gambling and drink increased. It should not be assumed, however, that these concerns became dominant throughout society or even within the middle classes with whom they are most usually associated. The continued political and social influence of the aristocracy often worked against puritanism and 'rationality'. The spectacular career of John Gully (1783–1863) perhaps deserves to be better known. Born the son of a publican near Bath, Gully's early career did not prosper. He spent some time in prison for debt. However, his prowess as a prize-fighter brought him to the attention of members of the aristocracy, including the Duke of Clarence, later William IV. Capitalising on influential connections, he became first a gambler on horses and later a successful racehorse owner. In 1832 Gully, who owned that year's winners of both the Derby and St Leger, won the enormous sum of £85,000. Investing his winnings in a landed estate, his subsequent career spanned both politics and industry. His landed connections enabled him to be nominated for the then small Yorkshire borough of Pontefract. He was its MP from 1832 to 1837. Later winnings on the turf were invested in collieries in the north-east of England. His investments there prospered

Figure 28.5 *Whitworth Park, Manchester, was opened to the public in 1904. It was part of the vision of improved urban Britain. As the pioneer town planner T.C. Horsfall put it: 'The town of the future . . . must by means of its schools, its museums, its playgrounds, parks and gymnasia, its baths, its wide tree-planted streets and the belt of unspoiled countryside which must surround it, bring all inhabitants in some degree under the* best *influence of all regions and all stages of civilisation.'*

and he ended his life as the sole owner of Trimdon Collieries, living in considerable style at Cocken Hall, near Durham*.

Gully's career is significant because it invites us to challenge stereotypes. Much writing and preaching was directed at revealing the 'evils' of gambling, the cruelty and irrationality of prize-fighting and the unworthiness of those whose lives were bound up in the prospect of quick gains and 'easy' money. Yet the Victorian economy was market-led and many (albeit often silently) utterly rejected what they saw as the suffocating philosophy of high-minded improvement and rational recreation. Gully's career owed its success to physical strength, courage, the willingness to take risks and the shrewdness to see that 'persons of quality' could be of use to an ambitious man. The prosperous County Durham collier who died just as William Gladstone was preaching moral lessons to the respectable working man is an excellent example of how what we might consider an eighteenth-century success story could still be told in the heyday of Queen Victoria.

There is no doubt that, by the last quarter of the nineteenth century, Victorian towns were much better organised and regulated than they had been in, say, the 1830s and 1840s. They were also becoming less insanitary. The question is: was this because of the imposition of 'social control' policies by a dominant bourgeoisie? Like so much else associated with Marxism, the idea is superficially plausible but does not stand up to a detailed scrutiny of the evidence. So much Marxist analysis depends on the polarisation of society into 'have-nots' (workers) and 'haves' (middle classes and landowners). The reality is much more complex. So are the cultural forms which different groups generate. While many nonconformists and middle-class intellectuals sought improvement and enlightenment in work, study and sobriety, others with reasonable resources spent heavily in clubs and the more expensive seats in the new music halls. While some in the aristocracy spent lavishly on art collections (sometimes loaning portions of their collections for public viewing), others wasted fortunes on the turf. In racing, the links between the sporting 'toff' and the gambling working man (whose 'flutter' on the horses occasionally paid off) could be close. The gambling culture, without which horse racing would have no rationale, infuriated puritanically minded middle-class figures but their clear-minded contempt had minimal effect on public preferences.

The working classes were socially diverse anyway. Artisans needed no lessons in improvement from their betters. Many campaigned for public

* I owe much of this information to Raymond Hill, who has investigated the career of John Gully in a Lancaster University undergraduate dissertation, written in 1995.

libraries and, when they got them, were avid consumers of the knowledge and understanding which they advanced. The self-taught working man valued both his independence and the superior status his craft and his knowledge brought with them.

Workers also were able to adapt any high-minded 'gifts' to their own purposes. The Working Men's Club and Institutes Union, for example, was intended as an improving organisation. It did not really catch on until it toned down the lectures and increased the provision of alcohol. As the Conservative Party rapidly discovered after 1867, political clubs (see chapter 23) needed to place the accent firmly on entertainment, excursions and, of course, drink.

Drink was also the essential lubricant of the music halls. Enterprising publicans had been applying to local authorities for licences to have singing and dancing on their premises since the early nineteenth century. The 'singers' were often locals whose inhibitions had been reduced by the effects of alcohol. The potential for good-quality entertainment, however, was not missed by a generation of new businessmen like H. E. Moss, who founded a chain of music hall 'empires' in the second half of the century. Music halls varied greatly in quality but by the 1890s the best had become thoroughly professionalised, attracting variety artistes like Marie Lloyd, George Robey and Vesta Tilley who became household names and icons of popular culture, much as pop stars have become a century later. The music halls attracted mass audiences but by no means all from one class. Rationing was by price but almost all could afford the hard benches upstairs in 'the gods', from where usually good-humoured banter could be directed at 'toffs' sustaining perhaps sexually indiscreet liaisons in the plusher seats below.

The word 'variety' indeed summed it up: variety of clientele, variety of acts or 'turns'. Patrons expected to laugh, to cry and to be amazed all in the course of an evening. They also wanted value for money. So comedians, ballad singers, conjurors and jacks-of-all-trades filled up an always-crowded bill. Political comment and satire were frequently found. The aristocracy and middle classes were just as pleased to see political leaders sent up as were working men. Topical songs helped to educate the nation on big political issues like the Bulgarian Crisis of 1876–8 (see chapter 23).

Of course, more 'respectable' counterparts to the music hall existed. The Hallé Orchestra in Manchester was only the best known of a number of symphony orchestras which flourished in the second half of the nineteenth century. Brass bands were their working-class counterpart. At the end of the nineteenth century few large northern firms lacked a brass band. They helped to foster a spirit of community in the workplace and

Figure 28.6 *Victoria Coffee Palace and Music Hall, London, 1880*

became very popular. National standards were very high and a strong market developed for brass-band transcriptions of leading operatic pieces like the soldiers' chorus from Gounod's *Faust* and the triumphal march from Verdi's *Aida*.

Religious nonconformity helped to spread the fashion for sacred choral works. Neither Easter nor Christmas could pass without performances of oratorios such as Handel's *Messiah* (1742) and Mendelssohn's *Elijah* (1846). These were given by massed choirs and much larger orchestras than their composers (now safely dead) envisaged. Less talented, but contemporary, British composers also made their contribution to this movement. Maunder's *Olivet to Calvary* and Stainer's *The Cruxifixion* were sung with much greater fervour and commitment than most twentieth-century musical taste would say they deserved.

Palm-court concerts of chamber music were less reverential but still serious. Victorian education also laid great stress on musical accomplishment. Respectable ladies were expected to be able to play a musical instrument – usually the piano – at least passably. However, music lessons were widely given even in elementary schools in the last quarter of the nineteenth century.

The picture, therefore, is diverse. If any clear message of sobriety and improvement was intended to be imposed on the working classes by a culturally dominant elite (and this is anyway doubtful), there is little enough evidence that it was heeded. The working classes had their own authentic, rational, improving tradition. This was probably not much weaker than its middle-class counterpart. However, most of the working classes ignored it. Church attendance in the larger cities continued to be low. From the 1890s, large crowds at football matches were already drawing condemnation of 'rowdies' who turned up, it seemed, for the purpose of making trouble. As always, commentators identified the dangerous effects of drink as an important cause of trouble.

We may conclude that many in Victorian Britain wished people to make productive use of their leisure time. However, some historians have been over-impressed by the extensive writings of a literate and persistent

Figure 28.7 *This photograph shows no fewer than 29 young violinists who were receiving lessons at a small rural school, Long Preston, near Settle in north Yorkshire. Musical training was regarded both as a valuable social skill and also as a means of acquiring self-discipline through the rigours of practice. As the Victorian proverb put it 'practice makes perfect'. What we do not know, however, is how far these children progressed, or how quickly they gave the instrument up. Parents often found the sound of a badly played violin excruciating and were not prepared to listen for the long hours necessary for their children to approach 'perfection'.*

'improving' minority. Leisure opportunities in Victorian Britain increased very substantially. These were associated much more with higher disposable income, improved living standards and keen entrepreneurial awareness than with respectability and moral uplift.

Task: working with visual sources

The visual material in this chapter is mostly from photographs. Remember that the captions will give you useful additional evidence. You should consider them as part of the source when working through the following questions.

1 a Which of the pictures (Figures 28.1–7) are obviously 'posed' and which 'natural'?

b In what ways does a posed photograph reduce its value as evidence about the subject matter? How can posed photographs nevertheless be used to give insights into late Victorian society?

2 From the photographic evidence in this chapter:

a List those elements which can be used to support the view that Victorian society was divided between upper and middle classes, on the one hand, and working classes on the other.

b List those elements which suggest that society cannot be easily divided in this way.

c If you find more items in one list than the other, why might you be cautious about concluding from this evidence that late Victorian society was polarised on class lines (or was not)?

3 On the basis of *all* the evidence in this chapter, answer the following question:

'The way Victorians used their sporting and leisure time suggests that Victorian society was polarised on gender, rather than on class, lines.' How far do you agree?

Further reading

F. M. L. Thompson, *The Rise of Respectable Society: A Social History of Britain, 1830–1900* (Fontana, 1988) – good on leisure and social control.

H. Cunningham, *Leisure in the Industrial Revolution* (Croom Helm, 1980).

T. Mason (ed.), *Sport in Britain: A Social History* (Cambridge University Press, 1989) – a collection of informative and authoritative essays.

J. Walvin, *Leisure and Society* (Addison Wesley Longman, 1978).

F. M. L. Thompson, 'Social Control in Victorian Britain', *Economic History Review*, vol. 34 (1981), pp. 189–208 – discusses arguments on the proposition that leisure was manipulated by the ruling classes to keep the masses quiet.

CAUSATION

29 The emergence of Labour in an age of Conservative dominance, 1885–1906

Time chart

1885–6: Liberal split over Irish Home Rule; many quit the party

1886: Conservatives and their 'Unionist' sympathisers from the Liberals win a majority of more than 100 in the general election. The Conservatives return to office under Lord Salisbury

1888: Scottish Labour Party founded

1888–9: Widespread strikes by dockers, match-girls, gas workers and others. New Unionism seeks to recruit large numbers of unskilled male workers and women and to cast off image of respectability

1891: The 'Newcastle Programme' adopted by the Liberals. It proposed heavier taxes on landowners, including death duties. Other policies included disestablishment of the Church in Scotland and Wales, and further electoral reform

1892: Conservatives defeated in general election, though they remain the largest single party; Gladstone forms his last government. Keir Hardie becomes the first working man to be elected as a Labour candidate

1893: Formation of Independent Labour Party (ILP) in Bradford; ILP strength concentrated in West Yorkshire

1894: Gladstone retires and Rosebery briefly succeeds him as Prime Minister

1895: General election sees Conservatives returned to government; Salisbury resumes as Prime Minister. No Independent Labour Party candidates elected and Keir Hardie loses his seat

1896: Hardie fails to get back into Parliament, losing a by-election in Bradford. Legal decision in the case of *Lyons* (a leather-goods manufacturer) *v. Wilkins* (secretary of a small union) declares that even peaceful picketing is illegal. This decision upheld in High Court and Court of Appeal (1897–9)

1899: Outbreak of Boer War causes further division within Liberal Party

1900: Conservatives win the 'Khaki election', with support for the Boer War an important factor: overall majority 268 seats. Formation of the Labour Representation Committee (LRC). Two LRC candidates elected to Parliament

1901: Taff Vale case makes unions liable to actions for damage in consequence of a strike

1902: Salisbury retires as Prime Minister and is succeeded by Balfour

1903: Joseph Chamberlain provokes split in Conservative Party by advocating policy of imperial preference rather than complete free trade. Electoral pact between Liberal chief whip, Herbert Gladstone, and LRC Secretary Ramsay MacDonald. Liberals would not oppose LRC candidates

1905: Conservative government falls and is replaced by Liberal administration headed by Henry Campbell-Bannerman

1906: General election confirms Liberals in power with overall majority of 271 seats. Labour, unopposed by Liberals in most of the seats it fights, wins 29 seats. Labour Representation Committee changes its name to Labour Party

This chapter asks two important 'cause' questions about politics at the end of the nineteenth century:

- Why did these years witness the emergence of a separate Labour Party?
- Why were the Conservatives in power for all but 3 of these 21 years?

The rise of Labour

The Reform Acts of 1867, 1868 (in Scotland) and 1884 substantially increased the number of working men entitled to vote in parliamentary elections. After 1884, upwards of 60 per cent of adult males could vote and working men were in a majority in a large number of constituencies. Yet the national Labour Party did not emerge until 1900. Why not? The answer is not entirely straightforward, but one important reason for the delay is the long-standing alliance between the Liberals and organised working men, an alliance which Gladstone for a time seemed to have strengthened. For many years radical working men, very few of whom had any interest in **socialism**, had few quarrels with Liberal policy.

KEY TERM:

Socialism

Socialism is the doctrine which advocates that the ownership and control of capital, land and property should be held in common and not individually. It was closely linked in the late nineteenth century with Marxist ideas, but socialists were keenly divided over whether necessary changes to the economic system should be brought about by argument and other peaceful means of persuasion, or by revolution. Neither brand of socialism was specially popular among working men. The organisations which stood on both sides of the socialist divide – the revolutionary Social Democratic Federation, led by H. M. Hyndman, and the more moderate and gradualist Fabian Society – had middle-class and intellectual leaderships.

However, as in so much else concerning Liberal fortunes, 1886 proved to be a watershed (see chapters 22 and 24). About a dozen 'Lib-Labs', as working men supporting the Liberal Party were called, had sat in

Figure 29.1 *Gas workers' strike, 1888–9. Police protection for a cart leaving Covent Garden, London.*

Parliament in the early 1880s, but the split of 1886 was a crippling financial burden to the Liberals. Local associations were reluctant to adopt working men as candidates because they had no independent source of income and would be more expensive to support. Another reason for the long delay in the formation of a separate Labour party was the limited size and considerable fragmentation of the trade union movement. Here, too, the 1880s brought change in the form of increased worker militancy and a number of well-publicised strikes (see time chart). These alienated many Liberal politicians and supporters. For a short time, unskilled workers' unions flourished. Counter-offensives by employers' organisations in the 1890s saw many of these new unions collapse. Paradoxically, the long-established skilled workers' unions were the main beneficiaries of the new developments. They became keener in the 1890s to admit the less skilled to membership. In the 12 years between 1888 and 1900 union membership more than doubled, to about 2 million. For the first time trade unionism became a mass movement.

The late 1880s and early 1890s saw the decisive moves towards

PROFILE: *James Keir Hardie*

James Keir Hardie was born in 1856 the son of an unmarried farm servant in Lanarkshire. He became a coal miner at the age of 10. In his twenties he was organising miners' unions and helped to found the Scottish Labour Party in 1888 and was first Chairman of the Independent Labour Party in 1893. He was elected an MP in 1892 and served until defeated in the election of 1895. His 'cloth cap' was rapidly taken up as the image of the independent working man. He spent much of the later 1890s working for a more broadly based Labour organisation than the ILP. He was a leading light in the formation of the Labour Representation Committee in 1900, and returned to Parliament in the same year. He became the first leader of the Labour Party when it was reorganised and adopted its modern title in 1906. He undertook relatively little party organisation in his later years. He resigned the chairmanship of the Labour Party in 1907. His later years were spent in urging labour supporters to work for peace. He was also a strong supporter of the suffragettes. He died in 1915.

independent Labour representation in Parliament. A Scottish independent Labour party was formed in 1888. In the 1892 general election **James Keir Hardie** was elected to Parliament as member for West Ham. His election was a fluke; the Liberal candidate, who would certainly have won, died just before the election and could not be replaced on the ballot paper. Nevertheless, Hardie's presence in Parliament mattered. In 1893 it encouraged working men, especially from the Yorkshire textile districts, to form the Independent Labour Party (ILP). The old alliance with the Liberals was no longer producing benefits. The riskier course of separate development might in the long run also prove the wiser.

The following sources give an interesting insight into the reasons why members joined the ILP. You can detect the idealism and the mounting frustration with a Liberal Party which appeared to have lost its way.

Three members of the ILP try to explain why they joined it

A. R. Orage, a teacher and later a newspaper editor:

'Well, you see, I joined first and found out why afterwards . . . I joined the ILP because I felt it was the right thing for me to do: I continue in the ILP because I know it is. The feeling, however, came first, and the reasons, in plenty, afterwards.'

Arthur Shaw, president of the Leeds Trades Council, and parliamentary candidate for South Leeds:

'My reasons for joining the ILP are the same that have induced thousands of Trades Unionists to cut themselves adrift from the orthodox Political Parties to work out their own social and industrial salvation. Previous to 1890 I worked with ardour and perseverance for the success of the Liberal Party in Leeds, believing them to be the friends of the workers. We had just returned, for the South Ward of Leeds, a Liberal Councillor, a professed friend of Labour, when the gas-workers justly demanded an Eight Hours' Day. To this demand my friends the Liberals opposed a strenuous resistance, as proof of their friendship, and imported into the town the scum of labour from all parts of England.'

D. B. Foster, candidate for Holbeck Ward:

'A better system must be found, wherein we shall all work for each and each for all: and then "we shall arrive" ... Let thy dreams be deeds, and all thy life a never-ceasing effort, till Politics shall be purged, and wise and righteous laws be made the rule of earth whereon shall dwell true peace and universal brotherhood. And so my heart was moved to join a small struggling band whose sole supreme purpose is to give to all an equal chance to live and grow beyond what men have often been, mere slaves to grind, and grind, and grind, while others lived in ease ...'

Reproduced in J. Clayton (ed.), *Why I Joined the Independent Labour Party: Some Plain Statements* (1894) and in K. Laybourn, *The Labour Party, 1881–1951: A Reader in History* (1988).

The ILP was always short of cash and made little progress outside the industrial north of England. The socialist societies thought that it made too many compromises in order to obtain trade union support. Ultimately, though, it was union support which mattered. As the time chart shows, key legal decisions went against the unions in *Lyons v. Wilkins* and at Taff Vale. In 1899 the Trades Union Congress agreed to try to bring together labour and socialist organisations. The purpose was to secure 'united political action' on behalf of working people. The Labour Representation Committee (LRC) was the result. **Ramsay MacDonald** became its first Secretary.

This organisation was the new Labour Party in all but name; the name followed in 1906. From the beginning the party was heavily dependent upon trade union support. Because many of the biggest unions did not pledge that support immediately, the early Labour Party was extremely short of funds. It could field only 15 candidates in the election of 1900; two of them, Hardie in Merthyr Tydfil and Richard Bell in Derby, were elected. It was a very modest start.

PROFILE: *James Ramsay MacDonald*

The most significant part of **Ramsay MacDonald**'s career lies outside the scope of this book, since he was Prime Minister in the first two Labour governments (1924 and 1929–31) and in the National coalition (1931–5). He was, however, an important figure in the early history of the Labour Party. Like Hardie, he was a Scot. He was born in Lossiemouth, in north-east Scotland, in 1866. He joined the Fabian Society in 1886 and the ILP in 1894. He proved himself an effective organiser and a good speaker but had to wait until the general election of 1906 to become an MP, having been defeated in the elections of both 1895 and 1900. He was formally recognised as leader of the Labour Party in 1911. He died in 1937.

The Labour Party was able to establish itself because of increased trade union support and a fateful electoral alliance with the Liberals. The Taff Vale case persuaded many more trade union leaders that supporting Labour, rather than the Liberals, was the only way of putting pressure on the established authorities to change what they saw as firm anti-Union attitudes. More than 100 unions joined, bringing membership of the infant party up to about 850,000. The mine workers, however, stayed loyal to the Liberals.

The electoral alliance negotiated by Herbert Gladstone and James Ramsay MacDonald was born out of a sense of weakness on both sides. The LRC needed to make an impact at a general election. New parties usually need initial help and the first-past-the-post electoral system disadvantages minority parties. For their part, the Liberals were suffering the consequences of having been out of office for most of the previous 20 years. Long periods in opposition often cloud the judgement and it can easily be appreciated with the wisdom of hindsight that giving the new party a genuine chance of election in up to 50 seats was excessively generous. At the time, however, the need to beat the Tories seemed paramount. Ironically, the pact was signed in the very year that the Conservatives were torn asunder by Joseph Chamberlain's proposals for tariff reform. In all probability, the Liberals had no need of a pact which, in the long term, did them so much damage. In 1906 it brought the Labour Party 29 elected MPs and respectable minority representation in the House of Commons. The party was on its way.

Conservative dominance

The Conservatives at this time enjoyed their first period of dominance over politics since, as the Tories, they had emerged as the 'party of order' in the late eighteenth and early nineteenth centuries (see chapters 6 and 9). The ending of Liberal domination is a political issue of huge importance and it is surprising that students seem to make little study of the reasons why the Conservatives established themselves in these years as the main party in the state.

This neglect is undeserved. Perhaps it has something to do with the absence of 'great leaders' in the Conservative Party. The **Marquis of Salisbury**, though a shrewd and effective leader, does not convey a strong 'image' as, in their different ways, Gladstone, Disraeli, Lloyd George and the young Winston Churchill all do. His nephew and successor, **Arthur Balfour**, is much more famed for his high intelligence and for his love of the arts than for his political skills. Neither characteristic usually inspires much enthusiasm, especially perhaps in a Conservative politician, from the population at large. We can dismiss charisma as a reason to explain the change of fortunes which so favoured the Conservative Party in the last years of the nineteenth century.

PROFILE: *Marquis of Salisbury*

Robert Arthur Talbot Gascoyne-Cecil, third **Marquis of Salisbury**, was born in 1830, the second son of the second Marquis of Salisbury, succeeding to the peerage in 1868 because his elder brother had died a little earlier. He was educated at Oxford, and became Conservative MP for Stamford in 1853. He served briefly as Secretary of State for India under Derby (1866–7), but resigned because of disagreements with Disraeli over parliamentary reform. Disraeli brought him back to office in 1874, first as Secretary for India again (1874–8) and then as Foreign Secretary (1878–80). He worked closely with Disraeli over the negotiations at Berlin which settled the Eastern Question (chapter 23). He succeeded Disraeli as leader of the party in 1881 (a role he at first shared with Stafford Northcote). He became Prime Minister on three occasions: 1885–6, 1886–92 and 1895–1902. Each time he also doubled as Foreign Secretary, though he resigned this post finally in 1900 on grounds of ill health. Not surprisingly, he gave relatively little time to domestic affairs, though his shrewdness was always apparent. In foreign affairs, he tried to keep Britain out of close diplomatic entanglements. He died in 1903, soon after resigning office.

PROFILE: *Arthur Balfour*

Arthur Balfour, the nephew of the Marquis of Salisbury, was born in East Lothian in 1848 into an extremely wealthy Scottish family. He was educated at Eton and Cambridge, first entering Parliament as MP for Hertford in 1874. He acted as Salisbury's Private Secretary during the Congress of Berlin in 1878. He became closely allied with Lord Randolph Churchill in the early 1880s and held his first government office as President of the Local Government Board in 1885–6. He was Secretary for Scotland in 1886–7 and then Chief Secretary for Ireland (1887–92), in which post he gained the nickname 'bloody Balfour' for severity against Nationalists. He was, however, anxious to increase Irish landownership as part of a policy he called 'killing home rule by kindness'. He was also Leader of the Commons in 1891–2. In Salisbury's last government he was First Lord of the Treasury and Leader of the Commons (1895–1902) before succeeding his uncle as Prime Minister, a post he held until the end of 1905. He remained leader of the Conservative Party until 1911. He died in 1930.

Why, then, did it happen – and, having happened, set the scene for a century of Conservative dominance? To understand growing Conservative strength in the last two decades of the nineteenth century, it is crucially important to understand the reasons for Liberal weakness.

The usual explanation is that the Liberals split over Home Rule. This is certainly true but it does not tell the whole truth. We have seen that the Whig element in the Liberal Party was becoming increasingly disenchanted with Gladstone's leadership even before 1885–6 (chapters 22 and 24). It was the Whigs who dominated the ranks of 'Liberal Unionists' who supported the Conservatives on vital issues in the late 1880s and, increasingly, joined the Tory Party in the 1890s. Many radicals also left Gladstone in 1886. Since the most famous of them, Joseph Chamberlain, never came back, it is easy to assume that the radicals did not come back either. In fact, most radicals could never find a comfortable home in any Conservative Party, let alone one led with easy superiority by the Marquis of Salisbury.

The real problem for the Liberals was not that so many radicals deserted Gladstone over Home Rule in 1886, but that most of them came back! With most of the old Whigs now supporting the Conservatives, or entirely alienated from politics altogether, the Liberal Party increasingly drew its support from supporters of Mr Gladstone and from those who wanted to use the party to advance the role of the state in taking up social, educational and welfare measures. Many local party activists actually welcomed the defection of the Whigs because they believed it would remove a major stumbling block in the way of their conception of 'progress'. Martin Pugh concludes that the Liberal split 'virtually completed the radicalisation of Liberalism'.

The Conservatives seemed to have benefited from this development. The increasingly influential suburban voter was easily frightened by proposals for spending on social measures which would cost the taxpayer money, particularly when that party was led by a politician whose sole remaining aim seemed to be to weaken the Empire by taking Ireland out of it. The Conservatives seemed the safer alternative, and certainly presented themselves as such. Suburban voters turned to the Tories because they trusted them not to change things very much and they trusted the Liberals not at all. Even religious nonconformists, previously unblinkingly Liberal, began to waver. Their big battles had already been won: no more campaigning was necessary, for example, over Church rates or admittance to universities. They were no longer either outsiders, or much disadvantaged. Many wealthier nonconformists now thought of themselves as part of the social elite. And that elite was increasingly voting Conservative.

The Liberals did win one general election – in 1892 – after promising the electorate radical reform in the Newcastle Programme (see time chart). The victory was, however, a small one and quickly reversed. The Conservatives won 70 more seats in England than the Liberals did and almost 40 more overall. The Liberals depended on Irish nationalist support to secure a majority in the Commons. The price, of course, was another divisive Gladstonian assault on Irish Home Rule (see chapter 24). When it failed, Gladstone resigned. **Rosebery**, his successor, proved weak. Against this one slender Liberal victory, the Conservatives could place three blockbusters – in 1886, 1895 and 1900 – in each of which they won at least 390 of the 670 United Kingdom seats. On each occasion Conservatives and Unionists won at least 200 more seats in England than the Liberals did. The sheer scale of Conservative dominance is easily overlooked. There is absolutely no doubt which of the two major parties English voters considered the more attractive.

Narrower organisational issues also favoured the Conservatives. Before Salisbury came to office, the party had developed its organisation. Lord Randolph Churchill, the leader of an independent-minded and quite radical ginger group of Tories known as 'the fourth Party', had founded the Primrose League in 1883. This was named in memory of Disraeli, whose favourite flower the primrose was said to be. By the 1890s the Primrose League had recruited about half a million members and had extended

PROFILE: *Earl of Rosebery*

Archibald Philip Primrose, fifth **Earl of Rosebery**, was born in London in 1847 and educated at Eton and Oxford. He succeeded to the earldom on the death of his father in 1868 and also inherited large landed estates in Scotland. He never sat in the House of Commons. He first held office as Under-Secretary at the Home Office with responsibility for Scotland (1881–3) before becoming Commissioner of Works (1884–5) and, very briefly, Lord Privy Seal in 1885. His only experience of high office before becoming Prime Minister in 1894 was as Foreign Secretary for five months in 1886 and again for less than two years from 1892 to 1894. He led a divided cabinet and could not resolve its divisions. Not a natural politician, he also resigned office with some relief in 1895. He resigned as Liberal Party leader the following year. He was one of the strongest imperialists in the Liberal Party. Having declared against Home Rule for Ireland in 1905 and Lloyd George's 'People's Budget' in 1909, Rosebery gave less and less time to politics. He devoted himself to the more congenial task of writing historical biographies, including books on the Elder Pitt and Napoleon Bonaparte. He died in 1929.

Tory organisation very substantially. Its female membership was especially significant. The Tories made the most both of the organisational expertise and the considerable free time of middle-class women. It is probably no accident that twentieth-century opinion polls almost always reveal that women support the Conservatives in larger numbers, and more loyally, than men.

The Conservatives sustained Disraeli's emphasis on party organisation. Party leaders and candidates should be highly visible. It is necessary to persuade voters (whatever may be the truth) that they are 'in touch' and understand the issues which concern ordinary people. The Conservatives were willing to do this whatever their private opinions. Here are Salisbury's 'not for publication' views about campaigning at general elections:

> *'The days and weeks of screwed-up smiles and laboured courtesy, the mock geniality, the hearty shake of the filthy hand, the chuckling reply that must be made to the coarse joke, the loathsome, choking compliment that must be paid to the grimy wife and sluttish daughter, the indispensable flattery of the vilest religious prejudices, the wholesale deglutition [swallowing] of hypocritical pledges.'*

The redistribution of parliamentary seats in 1885 favoured the Conservatives. Many of the new single-member constituencies were in the southern suburbs where the middle classes were turning to the Conservatives in large numbers. The suburban middle-class voter's long-standing love affair with the Conservatives was kindled in these years.

The Empire was a big vote winner for the Conservatives by the end of the nineteenth century. We have investigated the growing Empire elsewhere (chapter 26). Its political importance at home should not be under-estimated. Gladstone had been widely criticised during his 1880–85 administration for not being decisive on imperial matters. Many did not forgive his failure to save General Gordon at Khartoum. What Disraeli had begun in imperial matters, Salisbury eagerly continued. He believed in imperial acquisition as part of the wider strategic objective of consolidating British interests overseas. He also saw how effectively the patriotic card could be played in domestic politics. Celebrations of empire and the golden and diamond jubilees of Queen Victoria's accession to the throne (in 1887 and 1897 respectively) were used to reinforce the patriotic message. The lower middle classes seem to have been the most eager patriots of all. They associated the Conservative Party with success overseas and stability at home. The Liberals were a party of divisions, excessive radicalism at home and unsoundness abroad. Salisbury's decision to exploit the

Figure 29.2 *Luxury apartments, Earl's Court, London, 1890*

improved situation in South Africa (chapter 26) by calling a general election two years early (in 1900) reaped the anticipated reward.

Salisbury avoided detailed policy commitments at home. It was enough that the Conservatives were not radical, not for ever planning new initiatives and not divided. The Conservatives were the party of empire and patriotism. The Colonial Secretary, Joseph Chamberlain, took imperialism to its logical economic conclusion by declaring in 1903 that he favoured a policy of imperial preference. Salisbury did not live to see the political consequences. Chamberlain resigned office and devoted the next three years to campaigning for his big issue. The consequences were, in the short term, disastrous for the Conservatives. Not only did the division demonstrate to the electorate that the Liberals had no monopoly on party splits but it was on one of the most sensitive issues of all. Free trade still had enormous political impact. Generations of voters had been led by both parties to believe that it was the only economic policy which offered the prospect of jobs and prosperity. Chamberlain was far-sighted enough to see that this had long since ceased to be true. He could not, however, convince either his party or the electorate. From a position of enormous political strength after the election of 1900 the Conservatives crumbled from 1903 to 1906. Balfour resigned in December 1905 and the general election which followed three months later saw the rejuvenated Liberals sweep the country. They would hold on to power until, and indeed beyond, the outbreak of war in 1914. The advances made by Salisbury and the Conservatives in the 1880s and 1890s, however, proved to be the more durable. It was the Conservatives who would emerge from the war with much the firmer base.

Further reading

J. Belchem, *Class, Party and the Electoral System, 1867–1914* (Blackwell, 1990) – emphasises the importance of the role of Labour and written in a lively style.

G. A. Phillips, *The Rise of the Labour Party 1893–1931*, Lancaster Pamphlet (Routledge, 1993) – a very useful student introduction.

Martin Pugh, *The Making of Modern British Politics, 1867–1939* (Blackwell, second edition, 1993).

Martin Pugh, *The Tories and the People, 1880–1935* (Blackwell, 1985) – explains why so many ordinary people found Conservative ideas politically attractive.

E. H. H. Green, *The Crisis of Conservatism, 1880–1914* (Routledge, 1995) – a major new research sudy which argues that the Tories were actually in trouble during a time when most historians believe that they were putting down the roots of what turned out to be long-term political dominance.

G. R. Searle, *The Liberal Party: Triumph and Disunity, 1886–1929* (Macmillan, 1992).

HISTORICAL CONTROVERSY

30 The Liberals and social reform, 1905–14: the coming of a welfare state?

Time chart

1903–4: Inter-Departmental Committee on Physical Deterioration established to enquire into claims that the health of the nation was getting worse. It found no evidence of actual *deterioration* but much of poor living standards

1905: Conservative government passes Unemployed Workmen Act, which establishes local 'Distress Committees' to help provide employment or assistance

1905: Liberal government comes into office (December)

1906: Education (Provision of Meals) Act gives local authorities powers to arrange school meals to improve the diet of working-class children

1907: Education (Administrative Provisions) Act gives local authorities powers to authorise medical inspections at school

1908: Children Act gives children protection from imprisonment and establishes separate juvenile courts. Parents could be punished for neglecting children

1908: Pensions Act: first old age pensions paid in January 1909

1909: Labour Exchanges Act establishes state labour exchanges, mostly by bringing existing private labour exchanges into a state scheme. By 1914, state exchanges were dealing with almost 2 million workers a year

Trade Boards Act sets minimum wages in certain low-paid industries, including box-making and lace-making. By 1914, 10 industries were covered and wages were increased, especially for many low-paid women

Royal Commission on the Poor Laws produces its 'majority report'. This recommends keeping the poor law of 1834 but transferring its powers to county councils. An influential 'minority report', written by Sidney Webb, proposes abolition of the poor law and establishment of organisations to deal with separate aspects of policy, such as unemployment

1909: Housing and Town Planning Act establishes compulsory slum clearance schemes, but does not provide support to enable new houses to be built to replace slums

1911: National Insurance Act

1912: Board of Education grants support the school medical inspections introduced in 1907

The Liberal government of 1905–14 passed more social legislation than any before it. The time chart gives you the main headings and you will find further details about old age pensions and national insurance (the two most important innovations) below. Much of this legislation was built upon and developed by later governments. Some historians have seen an unbroken chain of legislation leading on to the establishment of a National Health Service and a 'welfare state' by the Labour government of 1945–50. The fact that **William Beveridge**, the active civil servant who analysed the causes of unemployment in 1909, would also produce in his famous Report of 1942 the blueprint for Labour's welfare state only seems to add to the impression of continuity in welfare legislation. Beveridge was a lifelong Liberal supporter and many leading Liberals have claimed that it was their party, and not Labour, which laid the foundations of the welfare state.

This book ends in 1914 so we cannot follow the story to its conclusion. If you wish to do so, however, Robert Pearce's book in this series

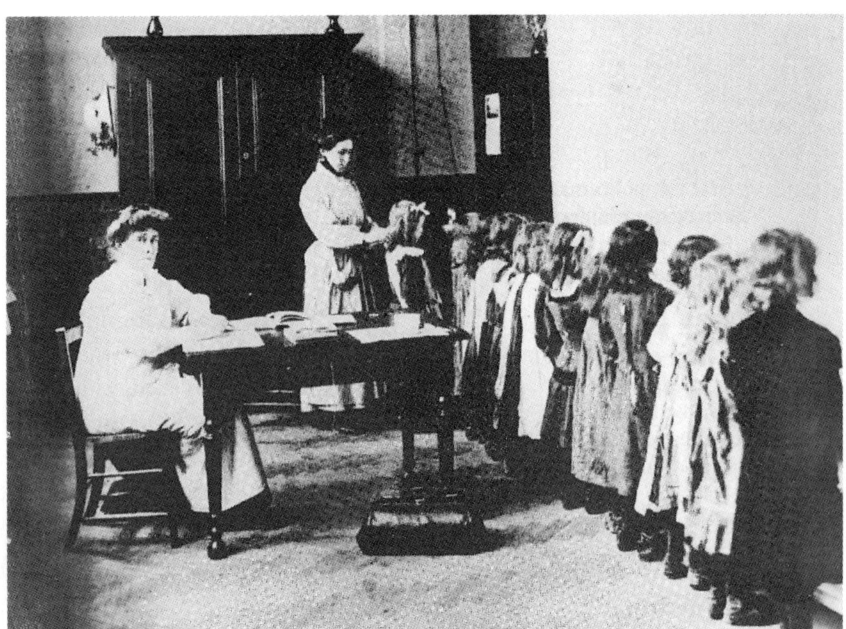

Figure 30.1 *A school nurse conducting medical examinations in London, 1911*

PROFILE: *William Beveridge*

William Beveridge was born in 1879 and made his reputation through an economic analysis of the causes of unemployment, published in 1909 as *Unemployment: a Problem of Industry*. This argued that the main problem in the existing market was under-employment. Unemployment was largely caused by the way industry operated and so was not primarily the fault of the individual. Beveridge quickly established himself as a supporter of 'new Liberalism' which advocated an increasing role for the state in social problems. Churchill appointed him into a senior position in the civil service and from 1909 to 1916 he was Director of Labour Exchanges. Much of his later career, before the publication of his famous Report in 1942, was spent in academic life. He was Director of the London School of Economics from 1919 to 1937. In 1937, he became Master of University College, Oxford, a post he held until 1944 when he briefly became a Liberal MP. He died in 1963.

(*Contemporary Britain, 1914–79*) is valuable. However, you have already had sufficient warnings from the earlier chapters in this book against assuming the inevitability of certain developments which appear to follow logically from one to another. Keep the following questions in mind as you read through the chapter. Both the text and the sources provide evidence on them:

a Did the Liberals have any 'master plan' to create a new, caring, welfare-based society in Edwardian Britain?

b How far did the Liberal reforms threaten *laissez-faire*? What was the balance between compulsory and 'voluntary' legislation?

c Were the reforms introduced primarily for social or for political reasons?

Three points are worth making to put the reforms in context:

1 They did not emerge out of nothing in 1906. Both major political parties at the end of the nineteenth century contained leading figures who believed that the state had an important role to play in social questions, especially in the provision of pensions for the elderly and in providing opportunities for the unemployed to find work. On the Tory side, Lord Randolph Churchill in the 1880s had advocated social reform as part of his 'trust the people' campaigns. Joseph Chamberlain took his reformist social policies into the Conservative Party after quitting the

Liberals over Ireland in 1886. After 1903, he clearly linked payment for more social services to the success of his policy of 'imperial preference' (see chapter 29). It was a Conservative government, also, which passed an Education Act in 1902. This put administration of state education in the hands of local authorities. Liberals criticised the Act because it required local authorities to subsidise Church of England schools. However, under the direction of gifted administrators like Robert Morant, opportunities for more extensive education became available for local authorities to exploit. It was also a Conservative government which introduced the Unemployment Workmen Act on which later Liberal legislation built.

The Liberal Party at the turn of the century contained an increasingly influential '**progressive**' wing. **David Lloyd George** was to prove himself much the most effective political operator within this group but Liberal thinkers such as J. A. Hobson and L. T. Hobhouse were prominent in justifying an increased role for the state. In *The Crisis of Liberalism*, published in 1909, Hobson asserted that the debate between old Liberal 'individualists' and progressives must come to an end. 'Individualists' mistrusted the state and thought that state help made people less responsible for their own efforts.

'Liberalism is now formally committed to a task which clearly involves a new conception of the State in its relation to the individual life and to private enterprise. On all sides we find the State making active provision for the poorer classes, and not by any means for the destitute alone. We find it educating the children, providing medical inspection, authorising the feeding of the necessitous at the expense of the ratepayers, helping them to obtain employment through free Labour Exchanges ... and providing old age pensions for all whose incomes fall below thirteen shillings [65p] a week, without exacting any contribution [from the pensioner] ...

The function of the State is to secure conditions upon which its citizens are able to win by their own efforts all that is necessary to a full civic efficiency. It is not for the State to feed, house, or clothe them. It is for the State to take care that the economic conditions are such that the normal man who is not defective in mind or body ... can by useful labour, feed, house, and clothe himself and his family ... [This] is owning partly to an enhanced sense of common responsibility, and partly to the teaching of experience.'

L. T. Hobhouse, *Liberalism* (1911).

KEY TERM:

Progressive

This term was applied particularly to those within the Liberal Party who advocated using state powers to reduce social inequality and to give greater opportunities for the underprivileged to fulfil their potential. Progressives are often contrasted with 'individualist Liberals' who continued to believe in those principles of individual self-reliance which had dominated the age of Palmerston and Gladstone. Progressive ideas were also held by others, including Fabian socialists and trade union leaders, who called for a range of reformist social legislation on pensions, unemployment and insurance etc.

PROFILE: *David Lloyd George*

David Lloyd George was one of the cleverest of all Liberal leaders and almost certainly the most unscrupulous and two-faced. All political colleagues admired his political skills; few trusted him an inch – and with reason. This politician, who played greatly on his reputation as a Nonconformist Welshman, was in fact born in Manchester in 1863, though his family moved to Llanystumdwy in north Wales when he was one year old. He trained as a solicitor and was elected MP for Caernarvon Boroughs at a by-election in 1890. His early career was characterised by what might be termed 'aggressive Welshness'. He hated hereditary privilege, especially that enjoyed by English landowners. He naturally gravitated to the radical wing of the Liberal Party, supported all anti-Anglican causes and soon became interested in educational and social reforms. He was appointed President of the Board of Trade in Campbell-Bannerman's government of 1905–8 and succeeded Asquith as Chancellor of the Exchequer in 1908, a post he held continuously until 1915. In addition to piloting pensions and National Insurance legislation through Parliament, he took on the Lords with relish when they rejected his 'People's Budget' in 1909 (see chapter 31). He was a notorious womaniser and also enjoyed a 30-year extra-marital relationship with his secretary, Frances Stevenson, whom he finally married 18 months before his death. He was a strong supporter of votes for women. He was involved in 'insider dealing' when he bought shares in the Marconi company and narrowly avoided public disgrace when the matter was investigated by a House of Commons select committee. He became Minister for Munitions in 1915 and supplanted Asquith as Prime Minister at the head of a new wartime coalition in 1916. He remained Prime Minister until 1922 when the Conservatives, who had joined him in a post-war coalition, threw him out. Lloyd George died in 1945.

2 Working-class leaders were clamouring for social reform. The Trades Union Congress and the infant Labour Party called for action on unemployment, pensions, free education for all, scholarships to allow the brightest working-class children to compete on equal terms with those who were receiving expensive schooling, and the abolition of the hated poor law. After the electoral changes of 1867 and 1884, furthermore, many parliamentary constituencies had working-class majorities. Could the two main parties afford to ignore 'pressure from below' for social change? Some historians have claimed that the political and social elite was frightened into conceding reform for fear of being turned out by a working-class electorate if they did not.

3 The climate affecting social reform changed in the late nineteenth and early twentieth centuries because of three linked factors:

a The so-called 'Great Depression' (see chapter 25) challenged old assumptions about the virtues of free trade and individual self-reliance. If families could not make ends meet as a result of effective foreign competition, could it be seriously maintained that it was their own fault?

b Social investigations on broadly scientific principles carried out by Charles Booth in London and Seebohm Rowntree in York revealed poverty on a much more extensive scale than had previously been realised. Booth showed in his monumental 12-volume *Life and Labour of the People in London* (1892) that not only were what he called 'occasional labourers, loafers and semi-criminals' and the 'very poor' subject to a continuous struggle to make ends meet but those with 'small regular earnings' were frequently in poverty. He calculated that 35 per cent of London's population was vulnerable. Rowntree's *Poverty: A Study of Town Life* (1901) challenged the complacent assumption that London's problems were unique. He calculated that 'the minimum weekly income upon which physical efficiency can be maintained in York is 21s 8d [£1.08½]'. Almost 28 per cent of York's population lived in poverty on this criterion.

c Recruitment for the Boer War showed how physically unfit many of those who volunteered for military service were. Since most volunteers presumably thought themselves reasonably fit, they may have represented only the tip of the iceberg. Some thought the problem would worsen as the unfit bred and produced unhealthy children. As Major-General Frederick Maurice concluded in 1903 'neither the unskilled labourer who has been tempted into the towns, nor the hereditary townsman who, after two or three generations, has deteriorated in physical vigour, will be able to rear a healthy family'.

It is perhaps not surprising, therefore, that even a sceptical prime minister like **Henry Campbell-Bannerman**, who continued to believe in the old Liberal philosophy of 'freedom in all things that affect the life of the people', should not stand in the way of important new initiatives. A range of legislation affecting the health of children was passed while he was Prime Minister. Its scope significantly broadened after **Herbert Asquith**, who was more receptive to progressive ideas, became Prime Minister in 1908.

PROFILE: *Henry Campbell-Bannerman*

Henry Campbell-Bannerman was a Scot, born into a middle-class commercial family in Glasgow in 1836. He was educated at Cambridge. He became MP for Stirling in 1868. He was frequently criticised for taking politics less seriously than his colleagues did, eschewing major speeches and taking long European holidays. He supported Gladstone's Home Rule policy as Secretary for Ireland (1882–6). His wit and easy manner made him popular, aiding his rapid advance during the 1890s. He was Secretary for War from 1892 to 1895 but an error occasioned his resignation from Rosebery's government in January 1895 after the Commons passed a vote of censure on him for not ensuring that the army had sufficient cordite. After both Rosebery and Harcourt quickly resigned the leadership, Campbell-Bannerman was elected in 1898. He did much to bring the warring factions in the Liberal Party together, despite taking a firm anti-government line during the Boer War. He became Prime Minister on Balfour's resignation in December 1905, leading the party to its famous election victory in March 1906. He supported payment for MPs and also laid some of the foundations for later curbs on the power of the Lords. He died in office in 1908.

PROFILE: *Herbert Henry Asquith*

Herbert Asquith was born in Yorkshire in 1852, educated at Oxford and early in his career served with distinction both as a politician and a barrister. He served both Gladstone and Rosebery as Home Secretary in the years 1892–5. Concerned to advance his legal career, he refused the party leadership after Harcourt's resignation in 1898 but attacked the new leader, Campbell-Bannerman, over the Boer War. He enhanced his reputation by elegant and popular defences of free trade against Chamberlain's tariff reform campaigns and returned to government as Chancellor of the Exchequer in 1905. His succession to Campbell-Bannerman in 1908 was not seriously challenged. He drafted the pensions legislation which Lloyd George later piloted through the Commons and supported Churchill and Lloyd George's campaigns to extend the role of the State. He was not, however, a supporter of female suffrage. His ministry faced many crises after the loss of its majority in 1910, but Asquith survived and continued as Prime Minister in the early stages of the First World War until ousted by Lloyd George in a coup in December 1916. He was created Earl of Oxford and Asquith in 1925 and died in 1928.

Figure 30.2 The first drawing of old age pensions, January 1909

Old age pensions, first collected in 1909

1 Pensions restricted to those over 70 years of age.

2 Single person to receive 5s (25p) a week; married couples 7s 6d (37½p) – later increased to 10s (50p).

3 Full pensions only payable to those with incomes below £21 a year; no pension at all to those whose income exceeded £31 10s (£31.50).

4 To qualify, pensioners needed to have been British citizens resident in the country for at least 20 years and not to have been in prison during the previous 10 years.

5 Pensions were not to be paid to those who had 'habitually failed to work according to . . . ability, opportunity and need'.

National Insurance, 1911

1. *Part I: against sickness* – employees contribute 4d (1½p), employers 3d (1p) and the state 2d (1p). Lloyd George said that workers were getting 'ninepence for fourpence'.
2. Sickness benefit for insured people of 10s (50p) a week for up to 13 weeks, then 5s (25p) a week for a further 13 weeks in any one year. Medical treatment and professional maternity care provided.
3. Scheme extended to all manual workers and others on small incomes (less than £160) a year. Initially, it covered about 10 million men and 4 million women.
4. To reduce opposition from existing voluntary societies, insurance companies and friendly societies were designated as 'approved societies' and they helped to administer the scheme.
5. Government provides £1.5 million to help cover costs of sanatoria for treatment of tuberculosis.
6. Scheme did not cover dependants of contributors.
7. *Part II: against unemployment* – employers, employees and government each contribute 2½d (1p) a week.
8. Workers qualify for unemployment benefit of 7s 6d (37½p) a week for up to 15 weeks in a year.
9. Scheme restricted only to trades where seasonal unemployment was common – including building, shipbuilding and engineering. About 2.25 million workers were insured, most of them skilled men.

The range of social initiatives undertaken by the Liberals is impressive. However, it should not be assumed that, taken together, they represented an initial investment in a fund which would grow over the next 40 years into a full-blown 'welfare state'. Some have undoubtedly claimed too much for them; others have been too anxious to understand them using their knowledge of what came later. Some historians have used the phrase 'the social service state' to describe the Liberal achievement in these years. This phrase emphasises the *availability* of services. It also avoids any confusion about 'universal provision' or 'state control' both of which are implied by the use of the term 'welfare state'. Judged by the standards of the time, the balance between change and continuity is perhaps a finer one than appears at first sight. Consider the following points as you judge the overall significance of the reforms.

1 Much of the legislation, especially that concerning children, placed the burden of implementation on local services. Central government 'facilitated' rather than 'insisted'. The extent to which efficient medical inspection operated, for example, depended much more on the priorities of local government. Giving local authorities powers was hardly an innovation. It had been the guiding principle of governments since the 1830s and had been extensively used by Gladstone's famous Liberal government of 1868–74.

2 When introducing new schemes, the Liberals were careful to make use of expertise which had been built up in the private sector. This was so in the case of unemployment legislation. Friendly societies were used in the administration of National Insurance. Here, then, we can also see continuity as well as change. There was no danger, either, that doctors would be seen as mere employees of the state. The President of the British Medical Association, Sir James Barr, feared in 1911 that National Insurance represented a 'long step in the downward path towards socialism'. He, and his colleagues, required, and received, reassurance and financial reward for their reluctant cooperation with new ideas.

KEY TERM:

Redistributive taxation

This refers to taxation which takes money disproportionately from the better-off in order to provide services or other forms of relief or benefit to the poor. In Edwardian Britain, its critics considered redistributive taxation both a form of robbery and an illegitimate use of state power. The Lloyd George Budget of 1909 (see chapter 31) was heavily criticised for its redistributive nature.

3 Only old age pensions were designed to be funded exclusively by the taxpayer, and pensions soon proved much more costly than expected. The National Insurance scheme was precisely that; beneficiaries had to contribute to the cost of sickness and unemployment relief. This angered many in the Labour Party, who wanted to use **redistributive taxation** to improve the position of the working classes.

4 The Liberal proposals did not offer universal provision. Look at the details of the old age pensions scheme (page 310) to see who did *not* qualify. Look also at the National Insurance scheme (page 311) to see who was left out. The insurance net could have been cast much wider than it actually was.

> The ways of the Bill are dark and devious and, though it meddles in every home, so often has it been altered that it is difficult to say what the householder will have to pay. But he is required every week to stick a certain number of stamps, varying in value from 2½d [1p] to 4d [1½p] according to numerous obscure rules, on each of his servants' cards, at his own expense ... The money is taken from the servants and their employers to swell the reserves of other classes. The Bill adds a new terror to domestic life, and, if only for this reason, its application in this manner to servants is to be condemned.

Daily Mail, 4 November 1911.

5 Very frequently, progressives had to be content with second best. Despite fierce criticism from Fabian socialists like Sidney and Beatrice Webb, the old poor law was not abolished in 1909. The majority report of the Royal Commission on the Poor Laws firmly upheld old values: 'The causes of distress are not only economic and industrial; in their origin and character they are largely moral. Government by itself cannot correct or remove such influences.' The Report looked to old systems to work better, rather than seeking to replace them with new state-controlled structures. Similarly, although the Liberal government, like its predecessors, continued to favour slum-clearance programmes, it did not make funds available to build new houses and thus reduce one of the major causes of social deprivation in Edwardian Britain.

Questions on historical interpretation

Read the sources below, all of which comment on the reforms introduced by the Liberals in this period, and then answer the questions which follow.

View 1

'The extension of the power of the state at the beginning of this century, which is generally regarded as having laid the foundations of the Welfare State, was by no means welcomed by members of the working class, was indeed undertaken over the critical hostility of many of them, perhaps most of them.'

Henry Pelling, *Popular Politics and Society in Late Victorian Britain* (1969).

View 2

'... in several respects the Edwardian innovations ... broke with the localist and permissive principles of the Victorian era, they took the state into areas of its citizens' lives hitherto avoided, and they involved a major increase in the central bureaucracy. During the twenty years before 1906, the accumulating evidence about the extent and causes of urban poverty had gradually increased the pressure on governments to involve themselves more closely. None of this, however, had produced any startling changes in the methods of dealing with poverty ... The alternative options became clearer but the political will had not yet been found ... The New Liberals were not yet entrenched in the local organisations, and while they became influential at national level, their party remained out of office ...

By the time of the 1906 election expectations were clearly high, both among politicians and in the working-class community. Though the Liberals returned to office without a formal programme of social reform, their MPs were undoubtedly committed to a number of innovations ... The emergence of a substantial Labour Party in the House of Commons simply strengthened the pressure.'

Martin Pugh, *State and Society: British Political and Social History, 1870–1992* (1994).

View 3

'Even if the suggestion of a changed atmosphere for discussion [about social reform] seems persuasive, its effects within the half-closed society at Westminster requires demonstration and often receives none: politicians are viewed as members of a wider community and expected to reflect its concerns and preoccupations . . . An astute selection of individuals and documents will bring social theory leaping from the archives. At the beginning of successive Liberal governments in 1906 and 1908 the mood seems especially exuberant as a young idealist like Herbert Samuel tried to convince Sidney Webb that Campbell-Bannerman's new administration "was to be a Government of Social Reform", or Churchill urges Asquith to lead his new cabinet in 1908 towards "a tremendous policy in Social Organisation" . . . Once stand back from these exhortations, however, and their significance soon diminishes. Neither Samuel nor Churchill held senior posts at the time of their remarks; and as Churchill rose, so did his preoccupations move away from social radicalism towards defence and the maintenance of a large army . . . Among cabinet ministers who remained quietly agnostic over such issues, their perspective often turned not on the doctrinal desirability of state intervention, but rather on the crisis in state finance which left governments with little choice but to intervene.'

Michael Bentley, *Politics Without Democracy, 1815–1914* (1984).

View 4

'National health insurance represented the balance of ideological forces. To the industrialists it meant fitter workers returning faster to work . . . To the workers, despite the protests of some of their representatives, it meant, for the first time for many of them, professional medical treatment and a medical income during illness. To the medical profession it meant an expanded occupation at increased remuneration for the "panel doctors". And to the central and local civil servants who operated the scheme it meant more employment, higher prestige and an opportunity to practise **social engineering***. As Morant himself put it in 1913, "we can make work at the Government Department the most marvellous means for true social reform that the world has ever seen".'*

Harold Perkin, *The Rise of Professional Society: England since 1880* (1989).

a What benefits, according to Harold Perkin (view 4), did the National Insurance scheme bring to different groups? *5 marks*

b What evidence in this chapter might Martin Pugh (view 2) use in support of his statement that there was 'accumulating evidence about the extent and causes of urban poverty'? *6 marks*

c Does Michael Bentley (view 3) believe that politicians at Westminster in the early years of the twentieth century were strongly influenced by new ideas in 'social theory'? Explain your answer by reference to this source. *6 marks*

KEY TERM:

Social engineering

Social engineering is a useful, and recently coined, term. Engineers often change structures, so that they can bear greater loads or endure greater stresses. Sociologists study how society functions. We can bring two apparently different fields of activity together by using a phrase which describes the application of sociological principles to bring about change in society. The purpose of the change is to 'improve' society. Critics of 'social engineering' believe that it is not possible to improve social attitudes or to increase social harmony by passing legislation which gives 'experts' a greater say over people's lives.

d Are Henry Pelling (view 1) and Martin Pugh (view 2) in agreement about the eagerness of the working-class community for programmes of 'social reform'? Explain your answer by reference to the views of both historians, as given here. *8 marks*

e To what extent is the interpretation given by Martin Pugh (view 2) about 'Edwardian innovations' in the role of 'the state' in 'citizens' lives' challenged by the evidence in the remainder of this chapter? *10 marks*

f Henry Pelling (view 1) says that 'the extension of the power of the state at the beginning of this century . . . is generally regarded as having laid the foundations of the Welfare State'. In the light of all the evidence in this chapter, how far do you agree with Pelling's interpretation of the social reforms passed by the Liberals in the period 1906–14? *15 marks*

Total: 50 marks

Tips for answering interpretation questions

- Read all of the 'views' first. This will give you a general understanding. The views have been arranged to make it easier for you to follow the arguments. Don't worry that the first question isn't concerned with view 1 but with view 4. Examiners often ask you to deal with sources apparently out of sequence; you should be prepared for this.
- The mark allocations should be a general guide to the length of your answers – the fewer the marks the shorter the answers. Thus, question **a** should be answerable in a paragraph, while you should consider **e** and **f** as requiring more extended writing – short essays in fact.
- Examiners always have a primary 'focus' in mind when they set questions. This focus is sometimes called a 'target'. The intended 'target' for each question is given below. Use the targets to help shape your answers.

  a *Target: comprehension* – use only view 4 and answer by showing that you understand. Don't quote; use your own words.

  b *Target: relating information from one source to its wider context* – here you are asked to relate one specific statement to a section in the chapter. You should hunt through the chapter for information on how much poverty there was, and what caused it.

c *Target: judgement based on comprehension of source* – first, you need to show that you understand the point Bentley is trying to get across. This done, you will be able to judge what he thought about the extent to which politicians at the time were influenced by social theory. This question should be answered from view 3 only.

d *Target: judgement based on understanding of viewpoints from two sources* – the starting-point here is again comprehension, but now about the views of two historians. Once you understand what Pelling and Pugh are saying about working-class attitudes to social reform, you should quickly be able to reach a judgement. The question does not require you to go beyond these two sources.

e *Target: evaluation of validity of a viewpoint in the light of wider evidence* – this higher tariff question requires you first to understand Pugh's point of view about innovation in social policy. You should relate this to your wider understanding of the points made in the chapter. Here you get an opportunity to express your own view (and make your own interpretation) based on evidence.

f *Target: critical analysis of a given interpretation* – the 'given interpretation' here is that the Liberal reforms 'laid the foundations of the Welfare State'. You will find some discussion of this in the chapter. Use it, and information from elsewhere if you have it, to reach your own conclusion. You don't have to agree with either Pelling or with the author of this book. The examiner will assess your ability to reach a reasoned conclusion about this interpretation. It will be 'reasoned' because it will be based on careful and logical consideration of the evidence, rather than just asserting that you do, or do not, agree with the interpretation.

Further reading

J. R. Hay, *The Origins of the Liberal Welfare Reform,* Studies in Economic and Social History (Macmillan, 1975) – looks briefly at a range of factors influencing state intervention.

D. Read, *Edwardian England* (Addison Wesley Longman, 1972) – a good illustrated survey.

J. Harris, *Private Lives, public spirit: a social history of Britain, 1870–1914* (Oxford University Press, 1993) – authoritative general text which explains why collectivist ideas increasingly took hold.

P. Thane, 'The Working Class and State Welfare in Britain 1880–1914', *Historical Journal,* 1984 – a very useful research article.

J. R. Hay, 'Employers and Social Policy: The Evolution of Welfare Legislation, 1905–14', *Social History,* 1977 – brings a sometimes under-studied aspect of welfare legislation into effective focus.

EVALUATION OF EVIDENCE

31 Political and social conflict, 1909–14

Time chart

1905: Balfour's Conservative government, hopelessly divided over Chamberlain's tariff reform proposals, resigns and Henry Campbell-Bannerman forms a Liberal government

1906: General election, largely fought on the issue of free trade, brings huge victory for Liberals (399 seats) over the Conservatives (156). Election of more than 200 new Liberal MPs brings prospect of changed policies

1908: Asquith succeeds Campbell-Bannerman as Prime Minister; Lloyd George succeeds Asquith as Chancellor of the Exchequer

A legal judgement supports the case brought by a Liberal trade unionist, W. V. Osborne, that unions should not be permitted to use their funds for political purposes. This decision hampered the Labour Party

1909: Lloyd George introduces the People's Budget, which initiates a constitutional crisis when the House of Lords refuse to pass it

1910: Two general elections held (in January and December). In the first the Conservatives win back more than 100 seats and leave Liberals dependent on Irish and on Labour Party support for a majority. The second election does not alter the pattern significantly

King Edward VII dies and is succeeded by George V

1911: Parliament Act resolves the constitutional crisis. The previously permanent House of Lords veto on legislation passed in the Commons is reduced to two years. The maximum length of Parliament is reduced to five years (from seven). For the first time, salaries (£400 a year) paid to MPs

Andrew Bonar Law replaces Arthur Balfour as leader of the Conservative Party

1911–14: Three years of intensive strike activity, involving dockers, railwaymen, miners and cotton workers

1912: 40 million working days lost to strikes – the largest number of the period. Government passes minimum wage legislation for miners

1913: 1,459 separate strikes took place – the largest number of strikes in the period
Trade Union Act permits unions to maintain a fund for political purposes, though individual unionists may opt out of contributing to such a fund

1914: Plans made by the three biggest unions (the so-called Triple Alliance – railwaymen, other transport workers and miners) for a concerted national strike

'The old ordered world in which one was brought up seems to be passing away.' This judgement was made three months before war broke out in 1914 by John Bailey, an obscure Conservative politician, and it was widely shared among the political and intellectual classes. Quite apart from the tempest which was brewing in the Balkans (see chapter 32), the outlook for those brought up in comfort and in a world of civilised certainties seemed stormy enough. Conflict between nationalists and unionists in Ireland (see chapter 24) seemed likely to erupt into civil war in that country with the Liberal government powerless to prevent it. Suffragettes were using various forms of direct action, including violence, to urge their demands for women to have the vote (see chapter 27). Unknown to most citizens, the Liberal government had created a most illiberal counter-espionage agency in 1909 to deal with threats from 'enemies within'. It later became known as MI5.

This chapter concentrates on the two other crises which directly threatened John Bailey's 'old ordered world': the constitutional conflict of 1909–11 and the bitter industrial strife which frequently paralysed Britain in the four years before the outbreak of war. It is worth noting at the outset, however, that Ireland, votes for women, peers versus people and strikes all evinced similar elements which were deeply unsettling for the old elites:

a a preparedness to use violence and coercion to advance the cause

b a direct challenge to existing authority

c a reluctance to compromise – mediation did not figure highly on the agendas of those who wanted change.

The imagery of force, coercion and violence is reinforced by much of the visual material of this era. Lloyd George is famously depicted in *Punch* cartoons either as a highwayman demanding money with menaces (Figure 31.1) or as a giant aiming to club his opponents into submission. Policemen sit on guard on top of a delivery cart during one of London's many strikes. Suffragettes chain themselves to railings; a famous photo-

Figure 31.1 *Punch cartoon showing Lloyd George as a highwayman*

THE PHILANTHROPIC HIGHWAYMAN.

MR. LLOYD-GEORGE. "*I'LL* MAKE 'EM PITY THE AGED POOR!"

graph exists of Emily Davison throwing herself under the King's horse at the 1913 Derby. Even the advertisers of proprietary medicines got in on the act. 'Beecham's Pills', the 'national medicine', are promoted as a remedy to save the constitution (Figure 31.2). The normally jolly jack-tar (a familiar symbol of national defence) has no smile now, but fixes his opponents with a menacing stare. In his left hand he holds a pistol, in his right a sword.

Figure 31.2 *Advertisement for Beecham's pills*

All of this is a far cry from the opulent, expansionist imagery of empire, symbolised by the appearance of the new King, George V, at the Delhi Durbar (royal ceremonial) of December 1911. Here the King (who was also, of course, Emperor of India) announced a massive expenditure programme on public buildings for Delhi, which was to be India's new capital. The Durbar was widely publicised in a British press anxious, perhaps, to take the nation's collective mind off serious trouble at home. Edward Elgar (1857–1934), now firmly installed as the nation's premier composer and perhaps Britain's greatest ever, published a bombastic 'Crown of India Suite' to mark the occasion, just as he had composed a Coronation March a year or so before. Elgar is often, and quite wrongly, considered an unthinking imperialist. The trite, ethnocentric insensitivity of E. F. Benson's words 'Land of Hope and Glory', which has become indelibly attached to Elgar's Pomp and Circumstance March No. 1, does Elgar no service. Alongside the splendid, stirring tunes which Elgar turned out both for profit and to earn that public adulation which a basically insecure man craved all his life, was much deeper music. In the years 1907–11, Elgar composed two symphonies of the highest quality and a violin concerto which, though its last movement meanders, is not far behind them. All three works perfectly capture the schizophrenic national mood of superficial optimism set against deeper insecurity and introspection. Elgar's art truly mirrored the ambiguities of the age.

Constitutional conflict

Most progressives considered the powers of the House of Lords an indefensible anachronism. The constitutional position on passing legislation was clear. New laws had to be acceptable to the King (or Queen) and the House of Lords as well as to the Commons. Monarchy, though immensely rich, privileged and – in the bloatedly self-indulgent person of Edward VII – morally compromised, at least knew its constitutional place. No monarch had refused the royal assent to parliamentary legislation since 1708. The House of Lords was a different matter. Dominated by hereditary aristocrats, it had a large in-built Conservative majority and no qualms about voting down major legislation passed through the Commons. It had done for Gladstone's Home Rule proposals in 1893 and it set to work again with a will after the large Liberal majority of 1906 had given the House of Commons what the new government considered a strong mandate for change. A Liberal Education Bill, which would have reduced Anglican influence, was voted down in 1906. The brewers lobbied their Tory friends in the Lords against a new Licensing Bill passed by the Commons in 1908 and got the answer they wanted. Proposals to end the dubious practice of plural voting in elections by those who held appropriate property qualifications were also vetoed.

Until 1909, however, the Lords had carefully avoided using their powers to block financial legislation. It is often thought that what became known as Lloyd George's 'People's Budget' was framed precisely to provoke a conflict. This is not so. Lloyd George, perhaps against his own better judgement (he hated landed privilege), acted on cabinet advice. He framed a budget which, although it needed to raise millions in order to pay for the new pensions and for increased naval expenditure as well as to replace funds lost to the exchequer during an economic recession, was designed not to antagonise the Lords. Nevertheless, the budget proposals for an extra tax ('super tax') on the very rich, for a new land tax and for an increase on the hated death duties caught their lordships on the raw. Since they were among the tiny minority who then could afford cars, they might also have been aggrieved at the first example of a tax on petrol and a compulsory motor car licence. In November 1909, they rejected the whole budget. This meant a general election since, without funds, a government cannot govern.

Both Asquith and Lloyd George looked forward to making this election into a contest between peers and people. Lloyd George's taste for biting, negative rhetoric was given free rein. In a famous speech, he asked whether 'five hundred men, ordinary men chosen accidentally from among the unemployed should override the judgement … of millions of people who are engaged in the industry which makes the wealth of the country'. At a speech in Newcastle, he turned up the heat: 'They are forcing a revolution, and they will get it. The Lords may decree a revolution, but the people will direct it. If they begin, issues will be raised they little dream of.'

'Given that the money had to be raised, unless both National Defence and Social Reform were to be crippled and starved, it is difficult to see in the means actually proposed, any adequate ground for the outcry with which the country resounded for the best part of two years against Spoliation, Socialism and breaches of the Decalogue [the Ten Commandments]. Apart from the land taxes … there was nothing that, in principle, could not be abundantly justified by financial precedent.

It was the Land Tax, and perhaps still more the proposed valuation of land, which 'set the heather on fire'. Their immediate yield was estimated to be very small, but the alarmists saw in them a potential instrument for almost unlimited confiscation …

Whatever judgement a dispassionate observer may now pronounce upon the merits of the case, there can be no doubt as to the genuineness of the alarm which the Budget excited, or of the enthusiasm with which it was greeted and defended by the bulk of the Liberal Party.'

From *Fifty Years of Parliament*, the autobiography of Herbert Asquith, 2 vols (1926).

> *'10 Downing Street, Whitehall, SW – 15 December 1909. Lord Knollys [Private Secretary to King Edward VII] asked me to see him today and he began by saying that the King had come to the conclusion that he would not be justified in creating new peers (say 300) until after a second general election ... The King regards the policy of the Government as tantamount to the destruction of the House of Lords and he thinks that before a large creation of Peers is embarked upon or threatened the country should be acquainted with the particular project for accomplishing such destruction ...*
>
> *Before coming away I thought I had better ask Lord Knollys whether the King realised that at the next General Election the whole question of the Lords would be fully before the country, and that the electors would know that they were being invited to pronounce, not indeed upon the details, but on the broad principles which were involved in the Government's policy.'*
>
> From a Memorandum by Asquith's Private Secretary, Vaughan Nash, 1909.

The first general election of 1910, held in January, did not produce the outcome the Liberals wanted. The Liberals faced the country after an economic depression resulting in several by-election defeats. The Conservatives won back much of the ground which had been so disastrously conceded in 1906. Their candidates' condemnation of the budget as 'socialistic' seems to have struck a chord, particularly in rural England where the Tories resumed their normal dominance. The industrial North stayed mostly Liberal but the Conservatives won 46.9 per cent of the popular vote to only 43.1 per cent by the Liberals. Only the quirks of an electoral system not based on proportional representation gave the Liberals two more seats than the Conservatives, and even this tiny advantage was conceded at the second election of the year, held in December, when the Conservatives maintained their advantage in the popular vote.

> *'There is immense interest in the election everywhere – I don't think the country has ever been so excited. The issues are tremendous: first, the constitutional question – the power of the House of Lords is to be either immensely increased or almost destroyed; second, Free Trade and Protection, which alone made the last election [of 1906] the most important I could remember; third, the Land Taxes, embodying a principle I have cared for every since I began to know economics and capable, I believe, of transforming the lives of working people; fourth,*

Home Rule, which convulsed the country for 10 years, but is now almost unnoticed. The power of the brewers, which is the worst influence in our politics, is also involved; and I think [women's] Suffrage stands a chance if the Liberals are returned, whereas it certainly has no chance from the Tories.

Every part of the country blazes with Tory posters representing men out of work owing to foreign competition, with wife and children weeping. Unemployment is the other chief basis of the Tory appeal to the working man; their other support is beer. Our strong cards, besides cheap food, are Old Age Pensions and the popularity of the proposed Land Taxes; also the idiocy of the Peers, who are on the stump, and make fools of themselves everywhere. All the brains and all the oratory are on our side; all the money is on theirs. Almost everybody who is neither a nonconformist nor a working man is going to vote Tory, even those who voted Liberal last time. But the Liberal enthusiasm is much greater than four years ago. Lloyd George is worshipped as Gladstone was, and Winston [Churchill] has shown himself capable of speeches which put close economic reasoning in a form that anybody can understand ... The Liberal appeal has been very full of argument and solid instruction, and so far as I can discover that is what people are wanting – they seem to resent appeals to their emotions. It is all very interesting, and I can think of nothing else.'

A private letter from the philosopher and mathematician Bertrand Russell to a friend, Lucy Donnelly, 2 January 1910, in N. Griffin (ed.), *The Selected Letters of Bertrand Russell*, vol. I (1992).

The Conservatives were kept out of office by just over 80 Irish nationalists and just over 40 Labour MPs. Since both groups felt that they had much more to gain from a Liberal than a Conservative government, their own course was plain. So was the price they exacted. Labour would expect (and get) favourable trade union legislation (see time chart). The Nationalists demanded another Home Rule Bill. The Conservative and Unionist Party (to give it its full, and significant, title) hated both developments. The Tories were no nearer office than they had been in 1906 and many of their leaders were wondering by 1914, despite winning 14 by-elections since 1910, whether dangerous left-wing electoral pacts would keep them out of office for ever.

In the short term, of course, the return of the Liberals guaranteed action against the Lords. Asquith knew that, at need, George V would create sufficient peers to force a Parliament Bill through the Lords but (as with a similar crisis in 1832 – see Chapter 11) it never came to that. The Conservative leader of the Lords, Lord Lansdowne, proposed an alternative scheme whereby the membership of the Upper House would be radically reformed, although the Conservative majority would remain. It got nowhere. The opponents of constitutional change were split on how far to push their opposition. They knew that the alternative to a second rejection of the budget was the creation of hundreds of peers who would fatally 'dilute' the blue blood of landed aristocrats. Abstentions on the crucial vote were numerous enough to give the Liberals a small, but sufficient, majority of 17.

The Parliament Act which resulted was a lost opportunity for the Liberals.

PUTTING A GOOD FACE ON IT.

LORD LANSDOWNE. "SAY THIS HOUSE IS BADLY CONDUCTED, DO THEY? AND MEAN TO STOP THE LICENCE? AH, BUT THEY HAVEN'T SEEN MY COAT OF WHITEWASH YET. THAT OUGHT TO MAKE 'EM THINK TWICE."

Figure 31.3 *A* Punch *cartoon*

Although the Lords' veto was abolished, the Upper House retained the right to delay the passing of legislation for two years. This could be vital during a time of high political crisis, as for example, over Irish Home Rule. The Lords soon gave notice that they would use their remaining powers to block this measure for as long as they were able.

Perhaps more importantly for Britain, Asquith did not attempt to reduce the immense dominance of hereditary peers in the Lords, settling rather for more frequent general elections (which were irrelevant to the Lords anyway) and the payment of MPs (which Labour members wanted). It is not clear that either of these changes had dramatic results. A permanent Conservative majority in the Lords remained and the Lords also retained important powers. The House of Lords discovered that it could live with the Parliament Act well enough.

Industrial conflict

Figure 31.4 *Trade union membership, 1888–1914*

Year	*No.of members*
1888 (est.)	750,000
1892	1,576,000
1901	2,513,000
1910	2,565,000
1911	3,139,000
1912	3,416,000
1913	4,135,000
1914	4,145,000

Figure 31.4 makes an important point about the growing importance of trade unions in British society. Most students know about the rise of so-called 'new unionism' in the late 1880s, and the outbreak of strikes with which it was linked (see chapter 29, time chart). The story after the early 1890s is much less well known, though in fact much more important. During the 1890s, skilled unionism survived counter-attacks by employers much better than unskilled unionism did. Trade union membership grew steadily, as it did during the first decade of the twentieth century. In the 29 years from 1892 to 1910 union membership grew by about 62 per cent. What is far less frequently noted is the crucial point that in the five years immediately preceding the First World War membership grew by an almost identical amount (61 per cent). Much of this growth came from unskilled and semi-skilled workers and reflected the changing nature of work in many industries, particularly engineering, where a previously small and influential elite was coming under increasing pressure. In these years, too, a combination of declining real wages with reasonably good employment opportunities provided ideal conditions for industrial militancy because workers had many genuine grievances and also the leverage to put pressure on their employers. Trade unions are never powerful at times of mass unemployment.

Two conclusions follow from this brief analysis:

1 Trade unions developed a truly mass membership during the Edwardian period, not earlier. Growth was especially pronounced in the years immediately before the First World War.

KEY TERM:

Syndicalism

Syndicalism was more important in the history of European socialism but was also of significance in British trade unionism in the period 1910–14. Syndicalists believed in the power of organised labour to promote political change by militant action. A favoured weapon was the general strike. Tom Mann, who had been a member of the socialist Social Democratic Federation in the 1880s, was Britain's leading syndicalist, tirelessly advocating worker militancy and denouncing Labour members of Parliament as traitors to their class who made cosy deals with the political establishment.

2 Mass membership was of great significance for the infant Labour Party. You can see why trade unionists were so anxious to get the Osborne judgement reversed (see time chart). With membership rising so rapidly, the political levy was crucial to Labour's ability to organise extensively and to present itself as a genuinely national party. This was especially important after the miners, the most extensively unionised group and previously staunch Liberal supporters, threw in their lot with the Labour Party in 1909.

Industrial militancy was often accompanied by violence and casualties. The best-publicised strike was that by the miners in South Wales. It lasted 10 months, beginning in November 1910. During it, the Home Secretary, Winston Churchill, called out the troops to suppress disorder in the town of Tonypandy; two miners were killed. The Welsh never took Churchill to their hearts. In England, the **syndicalist** union leader Tom Mann was especially active. After one of his speeches in Liverpool in 1911 an enraged crowd attacked troops with stones and led an assault on the police and prison vans. When the troops responded, two demonstrators were killed.

In the years before the war, numerous plans existed to bring industry to its knees. *The Miners' Next Step*, published in 1912, advocated centralising all miners in one union and using this as a base to link with workers in other industries to gain permanent control of the workplace, probably after a general strike. It was clear that, spurred by agitation from the grassroots, union leadership had passed in many cases to men of socialist beliefs who were anxious to use industrial weapons as a means of weakening 'capitalist' government. From Russia, the Bolshevik leader Vladimir Lenin looked on approvingly: 'Since the miners' strike the British

Figure 31.5 *Blackpool Central Station paralysed by a railwaymen's strike, 1911*

proletariat *is no longer the same*. The workers have learned to fight. They have come to see the *path* that will lead them to victory.'

Many of the middle classes took the threat very seriously. *The Times* newspaper feared in 1913 that the unions were turning their backs on agreements they had once favoured. Instead, socialists were making 'collective bargaining a waste of time', wanting 'to secure for industrial anarchy and warfare a new lease of life'. Robert Baden-Powell was more concerned about the growing powers of the state but also took a bilious view of developments in working-class culture. He compared Britain's situation to that of the Roman Empire in rampant decline.

'Another cause of the downfall of Rome was that the people, being fed by the State to the extent of three-quarters of the population, ceased to have any thought or any responsibility for themselves and their children, and consequently became a nation of unemployed wasters. They frequented the circuses, where paid performers appeared before them in the arena, much as we see the crowds now flocking to look on at paid players playing football.'

Robert Baden-Powell, *Scouting for Boys: A Handbook for Instruction in Good Citizenship* (1908). [Baden-Powell founded the Boy Scout movement in 1908. The author is assured that the ambiguity of the journal's title is entirely unintentional.]

How justified were such fears? Was Britain on the verge of collapse? It seems unlikely. Working-class socialists were frustrated at the lack of revolutionary fervour shown by Labour MPs. As historians such as Kenneth O. Morgan have shown, the leaders of the party were trying to forge an effective alliance with the Liberals and considered themselves very much junior partners. The electorate anyway seems to have disapproved of industrial militancy. The Labour Party did very badly in by-elections after 1910. Its rise was a far from unstoppable process. In 1914, it was very difficult to envisage circumstances in which it could take over from the Liberals as the main challenger to the Conservative Party. In this, as in much else, the advent of war changed everything.

If we look to elements of stability, we might stress the new services which the Liberals provided in the years before the First World War (see chapter 30). These might not have been overwhelmingly popular but few ordinary citizens wanted them torn up. Rather, they wanted them extended. Educational provision should be further developed; national insurance should cover more people, including dependants. The administration of the new services required more civil servants. Middle-class jobs both grew and became more important. The number of professional and administrative occupations for men increased by 41 per cent between the censuses of 1891 and 1911 and for women by 42 per cent. Just short of a quarter of Britain's 20 million employed people in 1911 were in middle-class occupations and the proportion undoubtedly increased from then until 1914. The middle classes had a vested interest in the security of the state. We may conclude that, outside Ireland, while the United Kingdom endured crisis, the fundamental structure of the state was considerably more stable than its defenders feared and its opponents hoped.

Task: evaluation of sources and interpretation

In 1935, George Dangerfield published a very influential book entitled *The Strange Death of Liberal England.* It concentrated on the period 1910–14 and argued that in these years the old values of liberal England – freedom, tolerance, peaceful resolution of problems etc. – were pulled down by dangerous new forces. Increased hostility between social classes was exploited by militant trade unionism and the new Labour Party. These forces destroyed not only the Liberal Party but 'liberalism' as a viable political philosophy.

How divided *were* British politics and society in the years before 1914 and how much was the old order under threat?

Divide into two groups: one to consider the conflict created by 'Peers versus People', the other to discuss the Labour Party and industrial militancy. When you have had separate discussions, the groups should come together, pool their resources and write a brief report on the validity of 'the Dangerfield thesis'.

Though you will be working to answer a big question, the following more specific questions might help you towards your conclusion:

a Can you work out from Asquith's autobiography (page 321) how big a threat *he* thought the budget posed to the old order?

b What can you work out from the evidence of Asquith's Private Secretary (page 322) about the attitude of the King towards the House of Lords and the Liberal policy towards it?

c How useful, and how informed, is Bertrand Russell's account of the political climate at the time of the first general election in 1910 (pages 322–3)? What can you learn about Russell himself from his letter?

d How much light does the visual material in this chapter shed on the nature and extent of conflict at this time?

e How much support did the Labour Party have at this time? Was this support growing?

f Did industrial militancy do more to advance the cause of Labour, or to hinder it?

Further reading

A. O'Day (ed.), *The Edwardian Age: Conflict and Stability, 1900–14* (Macmillan, 1979) – a useful collection of essays.

D. Read, *The Age of Urban Democracy: England 1868–1914* (Addison Wesley Longman, second edition, 1994) – an impressive textbook which covers a range of political, economic and social history themes with aplomb.

S. Constantine, *Lloyd George*, Lancaster Pamphlet (Routledge, 1992).

M. Pugh, *Lloyd George* (Addison Wesley Longman, 1988) – a fairly brief, lively biography.

P. Thompson, *The Edwardians: The Remaking of British Society* (Routledge, second edition, 1977) – a valuable study which makes use of interviews of people who remembered.

G. R. Searle, *The Liberal Party: Triumph and Disintegration, 1886–1922* (Macmillan, 1992) – a major new study based on wide original research.

P. Clarke, *Lancashire and the New Liberalism* (Cambridge University Press, 1972) – an influential study which examines how important new 'progressive' ideas actually were.

CHANGE AND CONTINUITY

32 Taking sides: the system of alliances and the origins of The First World War

Time chart

1902: After Boer War, British policy-makers increasingly recognise dangers of isolation. An alliance with Japan is signed
Germany begins building up its navy; Admiralty formulates plans for the navy to respond to any German aggression

1904: Diplomatic understanding based on common interests (entente) between Britain and France signed. It settles long-standing colonial disputes in North Africa, recognising on both sides British dominance in Egypt and French dominance in Morocco. Britain also surrenders claims to Madagascar

1906: Anglo-French alliance tested when Germany tries to weaken French position in Morocco. Britain supports France; Germany backs down

1907: Entente with Russia signed. This agreement settles differences of territory in Asia, particularly Persia, Afghanistan and Tibet. Russia acquires influence in northern Persia, including Tehran; Britain assumes influence on the Indian frontier and also the Persian Gulf coast, thus safeguarding the route to India

1908: Crises in the Balkans: Austria-Hungary annexes Bosnia; Bulgaria declares itself independent of Turkish rule; Crete revolts against Turkey and proclaims its union with Greece. Events in Balkans strengthen links between Germany and Austria against Russia since Austria needs German support for its policies. Britain fails to persuade Austria to submit territorial claims to an international conference. Relations between Britain and Austria become cool

1909: Serbia, independent since 1882, reluctantly accepts Austria-Hungary's takeover of Bosnia

1910: Kaiser Wilhelm II attends Edward VII's funeral, suggesting improved relations between Britain and Germany. Negotiations for mutual limitation of arms expenditure

1911: A further crisis begins over the future of Morocco when Germany sends the gunboat *Panther* to Agadir. Britain's support for France goes so far as to threaten war and ensures German withdrawal

1912: Naval agreement signed between Britain and France to check German expansion. Britain concentrates its fleet in the Channel and North Sea: France takes responsibility in the Mediterranean
Formation of Balkan League of Serbia, Greece, Bulgaria and Montenegro. The League successfully attacks remaining Ottoman territories in southern Europe, driving the Turks out. Austria feels threatened

1913: Disputes within the Balkan League. Other Balkan states defeat Bulgaria. Despite the instability, Austria-Hungary and Russia avoid being drawn into conflict

1914: Assassination of Archduke Franz Ferdinand, heir to the throne of Austria-Hungary, on 28 June by Serbian terrorists during a visit to the Bosnian capital of Sarajevo. The assassination provokes immediate anti-Serbian response by Austria-Hungary. During the next five weeks, troop mobilisations take place, then declarations of war are made by all of the great European powers
Britain declares war on Germany (4 August) when Germany violates Belgian neutrality, guaranteed under 1839 treaty

This chapter looks at the reasons why *Britain* went to war in 1914. To do this, it is necessary to have some knowledge also of *European* history. If you are also studying this period of European history, you should consult Christopher Culpin and Ruth Henig's companion volume, *Modern Europe 1870–1945*.

The eighteenth century, which conventionally stretches down to 1815, had been a century of European wars. Nineteenth-century Europe had been comparatively peaceful, though there had been conflicts in central and southern Europe concerning nationalism. Only once between 1815 and 1914 – during the Crimean War of 1854–6 (see chapter 18) – had Britain become involved in war in Europe. Some believed in the late 1860s and early 1870s that Britain's industrial and economic strength, buttressed by its all-conquering navy, was proof against major challenge. Britain could afford to leave squabbles on the Continent to other, lesser, nations. Disraeli's apparent ability to settle the peace of Europe at Berlin in 1878 (see chapter 23) polished the image of Britain as the 'world's umpire', descending from a great height to arrange peace in everyone's best interests. Underpinning this olympian detachment was hard-headed economic reality. The prevailing belief in *laissez-faire* (see chapters 13 and 23) required conditions of peace for free trade to flourish and increase national prosperity. Britain needed peace as much as certain other European nations felt that they needed conflict in order to advance their interests.

The complacency and arrogance about Britain's superior position was rudely shattered in the last two decades of the nineteenth century and the first decade of the twentieth. Important forces were building up which threatened Britain's interests. The most important were:

1 *colonial rivalry*. The British Empire was the world's largest (see chapter 26) but its expansion led to frequent conflict with other European powers, especially France and Germany. In the 1880s and 1890s, France and Britain came close to war in Africa more than once.

2 *the growing strength of Germany*. Germany had been united as an empire in 1871. Over the next 40 years it set about making itself into a great power, fit to rank alongside, or even to supersede, Britain, France and Russia. It was Germany's growing industrial might which first alarmed Britain (see chapter 25) but early in the twentieth century the Kaiser's decision to build up the German navy threatened Britain even more directly.

3 *the weakness of the Turkish (Ottoman) Empire*. This presented an international threat because growing nationalist aspirations in the Balkans and North Africa gave opportunities for the great powers with interests in the Mediterranean to advance them and, thereby, to come into conflict. The most important powers to profit from Ottoman weakness were the empires of Austria-Hungary and Russia. Instability in the Mediterranean not only jeopardised the balance of power; it also threatened Britain's trade routes to the East and its vital imperial link with India.

At the turn of the twentieth century, three main power blocs could be identified:

- **a** *the British Empire* – dominant on the seas and in most places outside Europe
- **b** *an alliance between France and Russia* – forged to ensure that powerful central European neighbours would have to contend with challenge from both east and west if they went to war
- **c** *the so-called Triple Alliance of Germany, Austria and newly independent Italy* – an increasingly powerful alliance in central Europe which was nevertheless fearful of 'encirclement' from France and Russia and perhaps from Britain as well.

It is significant that the two main treaties which Britain signed with European powers – those with France in 1904 and Russia in 1907 – were called 'ententes', rather than alliances. Britain was anxious not to commit itself to the kind of arrangement which ran the risk of dragging it into

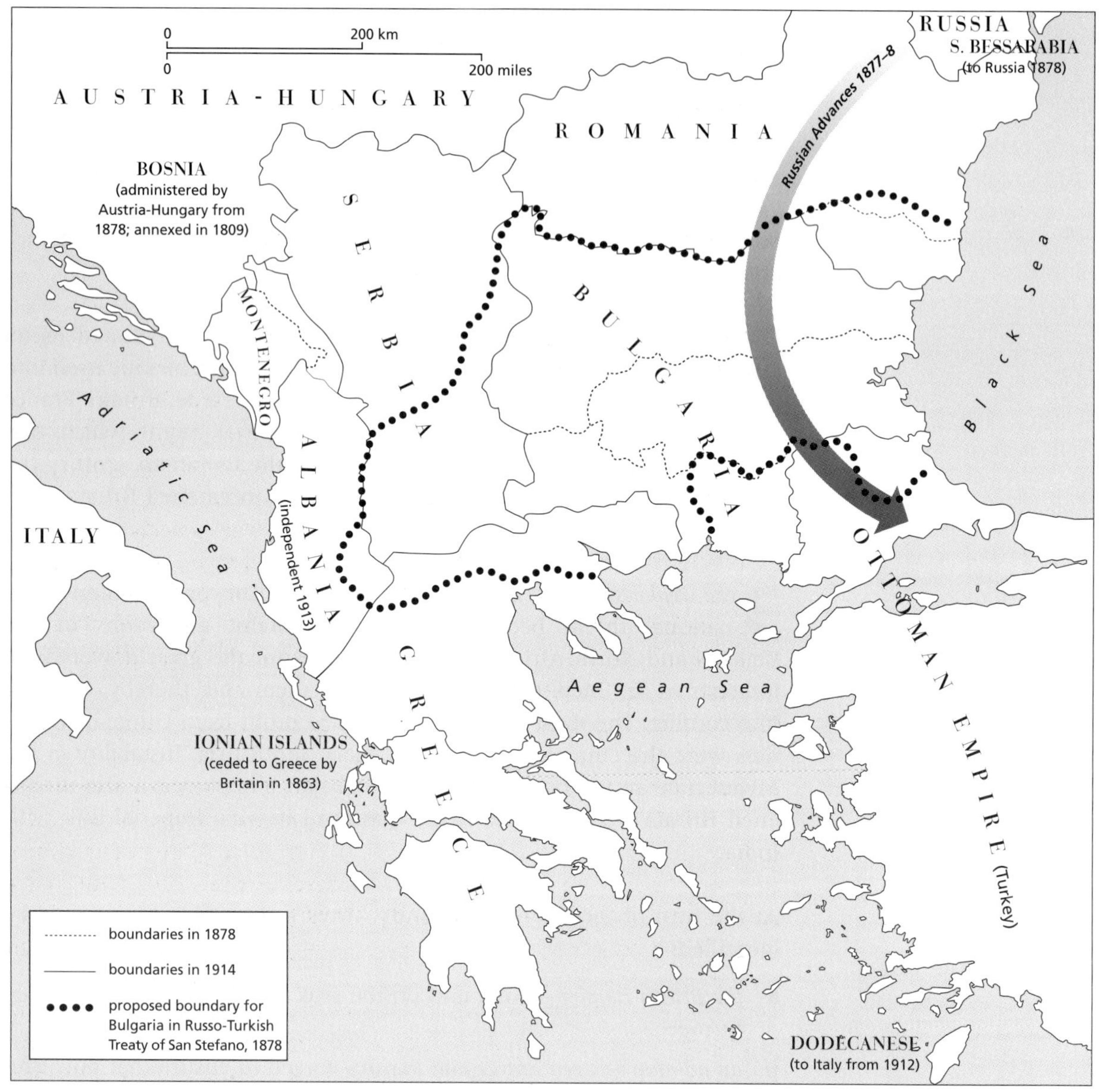

Figure 32.1 *Map of the Balkans, 1877–1914*

war on behalf of another power. It did not escape notice, however, that the understandings of 1904 and 1907 represented something of a diplomatic revolution. Most of Britain's diplomacy in the eighteenth and nineteenth centuries had been with the central European powers to curb the expansionist policies of France and Russia. During the eighteenth century, France had been the natural enemy; in the nineteenth, fear of Russian expansion into the Mediterranean had been the mainspring of policy.

The change was brought about by the growing strength of Germany and particularly by its naval build-up. As Britain's Foreign Secretary, **Sir**

PROFILE: *Sir Edward Grey*

Edward Grey, who was born in 1862 into one of the leading Whig families, was educated at Winchester and Oxford, which university sent him down for being too idle. He enjoys two distinctions: he was the youngest MP in the House of Commons when elected for Berwick-upon-Tweed at the age of 23 in 1885; he was also the longest-serving Foreign Secretary, holding the office without a break for eleven years from 1905 to 1916. All of his governmental expertise lay in foreign affairs. His first ministerial post was as parliamentary Under-Secretary at the Foreign Office under first Gladstone and then Rosebery in 1892–5. He was a strong pro-imperialist and supporter of the Boer War. As Foreign Secretary, he worked hard to rebuild close relations with France and frequently spoke about the growing danger from Germany. He offered staunch support to France in the two Moroccan crises of 1906 and 1911. His statement the day before Britain declared war on Germany in 1914 has survived as the epiphany of a dying age: 'The lamps are going out all over Europe; we shall not see them lit again in our lifetime.' Grey was created a viscount in 1915 and resigned office a few months later. He accepted office as the President of the League of Nations in 1918. Grey died in 1933.

Edward Grey, explained: 'If the German navy ever becomes superior to ours, the German army can conquer this country. There is no corresponding risk of this kind to Germany: for however superior our Fleet was, no Naval victory would bring us nearer Berlin.' The result was a naval arms race: between 1900 and 1914 Britain increased expenditure on its navy by 62 per cent; Germany's naval expenditure more than tripled. The balance of naval advantage, however, remained substantially with Britain. Only 20 per cent of Germany's total military expenditure just before the First World War was on its navy; 62 per cent of Britain's was. This is the true measure of the different priorities of a continental and an island power.

Evidence also mounted that Germany was encouraging its southern neighbour, Austria-Hungary, to aggressive behaviour in the Balkans (see time chart). Many in the Foreign Office began to see Germany as a threat to the balance of power. The War Secretary, R. B. Haldane, formed a new force to be sent to France if Britain intervened in any subsequent war between France and Germany. This British Expeditionary Force represented a significant shift away from total reliance on the navy for national defence.

Over Agadir in 1911 (see time chart), Lloyd George made explicit for the first time Britain's preparedness to risk war. Alongside patriotic assertions which sound faintly embarrassing to modern readers but which meant much to his audience of city magnates at the Mansion House in London, the Chancellor of the Exchequer revealed the iron fist lurking within the velvet glove: if 'peace could only be preserved by the surrender of the great and beneficent position Britain has won by centuries of heroism and achievement, by allowing herself to be treated, where her interests were vitally affected, as if she were of no account in the Cabinet of nations, then ... peace at that price would be a humiliation for a great country like ours'. Although the Germans did not press their claims in Morocco, the British military staff resumed discussions with their French colleagues. Agreement on naval spheres of influence resulted (see time chart).

It is possible to present Anglo-German relations as steadily deteriorating in this period. On this interpretation, Britain's declaration of war in August 1914 appears the logical culmination of a decade of worsening relations. The truth is not so simple. Attempts to improve harmony between Britain and Germany were periodically made. As late as early 1914, relations between the powers seemed to have been improved when Britain and Germany came to an agreement over Portuguese African colonies and Britain withdrew its objection to the strategically important Berlin–Baghdad railway. Although Anglo-French relations grew much closer in the decade before 1914, the French were never confident that Britain would enter a war on its side if Germany attacked. And with good reason. As late as 31 July 1914, the French ambassador to Britain, Jules Cambon, was placidly informed by Grey that Britain remained 'free from engagements'. The Germans probably believed that, if push came to shove, Britain would not involve itself in a European war in which its interests did not seem directly threatened. It is even possible that such a calculation was significant in the approval of the fateful Schlieffen Plan, Germany's famous strategy for quick victory, which involved launching with devastating force a surprise attack on France through Belgium.

So why did Britain declare war on Germany on 4 August 1914? This is a surprisingly difficult question to answer. The *casus belli* (declared reason for waging war) was that Germany had invaded Belgium, to which Britain was committed by a treaty made when Belgian independence was confirmed in 1839. But Britain could easily have finessed this apparent 'obligation' if the political will to avoid war had existed. Clever minds in the Foreign Office were practised at fashioning elegant argument on the lines of 'When is a commitment not a commitment?' It could have argued, for example, as was perfectly true, that the obligation to defend

Belgium was a *collective* rather than an individual one – involving Germany, Russia, Austria and France. Why should Britain make a unilateral declaration of support? In any case, a precedent for not invoking the treaty already existed since Germany had technically been in breach of it during the Franco-Prussian war in 1870. Whatever the press may have wanted the British public to believe (see Figure 32.2), 'gallant little Belgium' might well have been left to twist in the wind.

One can produce a number of cogent reasons why Britain might have been expected to stand aside in 1914:

1 Long-standing policy: Britain's territorial interests had lain outside Europe for almost three centuries. Furthermore, the immediate crisis which led to war had only erupted five weeks earlier with the assassination of Archduke Franz Ferdinand. Stalling for time would have been possible.

2 The specific crisis was a Balkan one. Especially since Britain's recent accord with Russia, it was harder even than usual to say that British interests were affected.

3 On the face of it, the two continental European power blocs – Franco-Russian and Austro-German – seemed well enough matched. No immediate threat to the balance of power existed.

4 The British government had since the end of 1905 been a Liberal one. Liberal governments in the nineteenth century had usually been much more ideologically committed to peace than their Conservative opponents. Moreover, the Liberal Party in 1914 contained a significant number of pacifists. Going to war threatened party unity and both John Morley and John Burns resigned when war was declared. The Labour Party, which normally supported the Liberals, had an even larger proportion of pacifists.

5 Britain had more than enough domestic problems to address without wishing to commit itself to potentially limitless expenditure on a European war.

Some historians have used this final point in precisely the opposite direction. Asquith and Grey committed Britain to war as a cynical diversionary manoeuvre to quieten the suffragettes and, particularly, to stop civil war in Ireland. Furthermore, Britain, if not a full democracy, had a representative government. Liberal social reforms had not proved specially popular while the government's inability to control industrial militancy both infuriated and frightened the middle classes (see chapter 31). Lloyd

BRAVO, BELGIUM!

Figure 32.2 *Cartoon in* Punch, *1914, designed to show Germany as the aggressor and Belgium in need of Britain's help*

George's new plans for land reform, his strategy for recovering electoral popularity, were proving a damp squib. Many thought them punitive. They anyway directly affected only rural society; about 80 per cent of the electorate was urban. A general election was necessary in 1915 and might well be lost. A government at war would not need to fight an election.

This explanation might have been attractive in a more squalid age where professional politicians are less widely educated, more manipulative and vastly more cynical. Lloyd George, whose quick intelligence and deviousness alike persuaded him of the virtues of banging the patriotic drum, was in no way typical of his party. A war is often electorally popular, at least in its early stages or if speedily won. In 1914, much evidence existed that war was popular. Imperialist idealism remained a potent theme. Whereas serious newspapers were more or less evenly divided on the merits of declaring war on Germany, the popular press was unashamedly jingoistic. The Germans were installed as the national enemy and coarse stereotypes about the violent, vulgar Hun abounded. The British royal family would soon find it expedient to abandon its Germanic family name of Saxe-Coburg-Gotha and transmute itself into the entirely synthetic 'House of Windsor'.

The Liberal government was not hustled into war in 1914 either by cynical political calculation or by xenophobic public opinion. The imperial ethic, however, was not irrelevant to Asquith and Grey's decision to take Britain to war. Both, it should be remembered, had been on the 'imperialist' wing of the Liberal Party during the Boer War (see chapter 26). With imperialism went a strong sense of duty and an aversion to shirking difficult decisions. The public-school ethic, in which both men were steeped, also stressed duty and the need for self-sacrifice in pursuit of noble ideals. Although Britain's own interests were not directly threatened in 1914, if Britain remained the only great European power not to go to war, this might be interpreted almost as cowardly – even an abrogation of responsibility. War was a noble endeavour and upheld national pride.

Some more practical considerations also had weight. Germany might not be an immediate threat but outright German victory would eventually threaten the balance of power to which traditional politicians remained committed. The thought of the French and Belgian Channel ports being home to a triumphant German navy was truly alarming. The eagerness of Germany's response to the crisis over Serbia during July also convinced Grey that here was a militarist nation spoiling for a fight. While the crisis was precipitated in the far-away Balkans, therefore, it had Europe-wide implications. Interestingly, Grey's perception about German war aims has been strongly supported by recent historians, who are much keener than their predecessors to lay the main blame for the outbreak of world war at Germany's door.

One further problem remains to be resolved. Why did a Liberal government, with its strong ideological commitment to peace and prosperity through a policy of free trade not raise more objection to Grey's policy? The simple answer is that it was hardly consulted about the matter until the decision was all but unstoppable. Until Grey put the Serbian crisis on the cabinet agenda 10 days before Britain declared war, the cabinet had not considered foreign policy at all for a month. The implications of the assassination at Sarajevo as the crisis unfolded had not merited consideration by busy ministers grappling with Irish Home Rule and other pressing domestic issues. What was almost certainly a pacifist majority in cabinet, therefore, was not so much watching from the side-lines as participating in an entirely different, home, fixture. In the late nineteenth and early twentieth centuries the Foreign Office operated as a semi-independent branch of government, formulating policy in consultation with the armed services and Chiefs of Staff. Civil servants in the Foreign Office took a much more jaundiced view of Germany's rising military strength; most, like the Chiefs of Staff, wanted to put a stop to it and considered war a rational policy to achieve this objective.

Neither Asquith, Grey nor any of the top military brass who took the crucial decisions knew what they were letting the nation in for. No one in Britain in 1914 had any experience of fighting long wars. Only the oldest of men could still recall the Crimean War which anyway lasted only two years and in which the major engagements after the first three months were few. Talk about this new war being over by Christmas – with victory safely and easily accomplished – was common. We should not be too hasty in our condemnation of the policy-makers. They knew not what they did. But their decision was fateful all the same. Before Grey's lamps went out all over Europe, they lit a flame which would consume the old order – empires, kings and infant democracies alike. Nothing in politics, society, culture or the economy would ever be the same again.

Writing an essay under examination conditions

'Britain stumbled into war in 1914, unplanned and under-prepared.' To what extent do you agree with this assessment?

Essay writing under pressure of time is central to all examinations. It is a skill which needs to be acquired and examiners frequently report that too many students go into their examinations uncertain about how to plan and write essays. The following ideas are designed to help you develop essay-writing skills. They relate to the specific question given above, but the points have a wider value.

Choosing an essay title

Remember that examiners are more interested in finding out how well you can direct your answer to the specific question you have been asked than in weighing the amount of knowledge you might have. Only decide on a question when you are absolutely sure that you understand its focus. Sometimes an essay on a topic about which you know a little less may offer you a better focus than one on a topic which you may know well but whose specific focus may be unfamiliar.

Identifying the focus

This involves checking where the question is taking you. To do this you have to identify a question's key words. In the example above, you obviously need to be familiar with the content. Beyond that, however, you should pick out the following *key words*:

- *stumbled*
- *unplanned*
- *under-prepared.*

These three words have been deliberately chosen by your examiner to provide you with a focus. Unless you can say something about each of them, you should probably be looking for another question.

Notice that the question derives from a quotation. This quotation will probably have been made up by the examiner for the purpose of giving you something to argue about. It is very unlikely to be a quotation which gives you no scope to agree or disagree. When you see a quotation, look out for the points of argument.

The other thing to look out for is the conceptual focus. Is your question about causes or consequences or change or general evaluation? This question is not about the causes of the First World War, but it might offer a link to causation. If you decide that Britain did not *stumble* into war but prepared for the possibility, then that relates to cause. However, the main focus here is evaluation of a slanted or biased statement.

Planning an answer

Whether or not you write it out on the examination paper – and most well-prepared candidates will – you should certainly *plan* every essay you write. What is the point of a plan? Simply, to help you to clarify the focus of an essay and then to carry it through. A well-planned essay will have the benefits of proper organisation: it will be coherent, logical and will argue a case. It won't be as long as what follows here (which attempts to investigate a variety of ideas) but it *will* help you to control your answer.

Most essays will have three identifiable elements. Each has a separate function. A useful plan might comprise:

1 An *introduction*: the purpose of this is to not to offer general opening comments or to off-load a lot of information you think you might forget later on. It should have a precise function. It's not a bad idea to use the introduction to convince the examiner that you have grasped the main point of the question. Thus, in the example above, it would be useful to show your understanding

that the question is about the state in which Britain went to war. You might also want to offer a specific comment on one of the key words. For example, you could say that 'stumbled' implies that Britain almost blundered into war without realising what it was doing. If you don't agree that this *was* the case, then say so.

The introduction should not be too long. A couple of paragraphs is usually ample.

2 A *main section*: this should be the longest of the three, comprising perhaps 70–80 per cent of the essay's length. Here you develop the main points you want to make. Remember to back each point up with specific evidence. A historical argument is only valid if it is supported by specific information or evidence. Otherwise, it is mere assertion. Don't rely too much on generalisation.

You might want to make some of the following points, though these are only suggestions:

'stumbled' – implies lack of preparation and clear objective. Britain took the decision to go to war quite late, but the Serbian crisis itself was short-lived and everything happened very quickly. Was Britain any less prepared than any other power? Was Britain pushed into war?

'unplanned' – Britain was not preparing for war for a long period, so it was not 'planned' as part of a long-term strategy. However, Grey had developed quite clear ideas about why Britain should go into war – his views about Germany and the threat it posed. This suggests some degree of foresight. Those in charge of foreign policy seem to have realised that, given the overall situation, war was at least possible. Whether ordinary people realised this is a different matter. For many the outbreak of war was a great shock.

'under-prepared' – again, the specific crisis blew up quickly, so Britain was necessarily 'under-prepared' to deal with the fall-out from the assassination. But was Britain less prepared than anyone else? It is relevant to mention increased expenditure on the navy and the development of the British Expeditionary Force. You might make use of a quotation here: 'Britain was better prepared for the First World War than for almost any war in her modern history' (Martin Pugh) (which directly challenges the premise of the question). Notice how this section says something specific about *each* of the key words and thus attempts to meet the full demands of the question.

3 A *conclusion*: here you draw the threads together. Don't repeat yourself; there isn't time. However, it *is* useful to show how the specific points made in the middle section lead to an overall conclusion. For this question, you might conclude that there was an element of 'stumbling' into war. Perhaps Germany prepared more extensively. However, in military terms, the nation was well enough prepared. You might find space to mention that psychologically, it may have been less well prepared. The conclusion should not be long. It might be a bit longer than the introduction, but three paragraphs will usually be plenty.

Some common questions about essays answered

- *How long?* Since essays normally have to be written in time varying between 45 minutes and an hour, they are not expected to be too long. Examination essays are not speed-writing exercises. You will be judged on quality, not length. Remember, though, that it is difficult to sustain a logical structure throughout a very long essay. Three or four sides of average-length writing is usually enough.
- *Should I spend the same amount of time on each essay?* Broadly, yes. Examiners will be instructed not to make any allowance for a much weaker, or shorter, final answer on a paper. To do so would be unfair to other candidates who have taken the trouble to organise their time properly. Don't think that because you have three good answers you can coast through the final one. If the questions have equal marks, you should give them equal weight.
- *Do I use quotes from historians?* Yes, *if* you can.
  - **a** Remember them accurately – examiners may know them, and if they don't may check!
  - **b** Identify who produced them – attributing a quotation to the wrong historian creates a worse impression than not using it.
  - **c** Use them appropriately – too many candidates drag quotations in for no better reason than that they have remembered them. There's no special merit in using a quotation which everyone else in your school or college will be using. Some hackneyed quotations like Gladstone's 'My mission is to pacify Ireland' are best avoided.

  Overall, students perhaps lay too much emphasis on quotations. Remember that quotations might make an already good essay a bit better; they won't make a weak one good.
- *Should I write the question out before I start?* No; time is short and this is a waste of a precious commodity. The examiner will have the question paper.
- *If the examiner doesn't agree with me, will I lose marks?* No. Examiners are instructed not to let their personal views affect

their judgement. If you offer a plausible argument backed up with well-selected evidence, you will be given high credit. History essays are all about presenting a good argument; there are no *right* answers at this level! So don't try to second-guess the examiner.

- *None of my essays seems to come out right. What should I do?* Keep trying. Essay writing is a specialist skill and it improves with practice. You should practise writing essays to time (45 minutes or an hour) regularly in the last few months before the examination. Don't be tempted only to write timed essays in the 'mocks' and then not again until the examination itself. You should know almost without thinking about it, how quickly 45 minutes goes by. One other tip: *reading* is one of the best preparations for writing. Communication is a vital skill. Don't neglect it. Notice how good writers express themselves. At A level, short sentences are usually better than long, complicated ones. Paragraphs should be used to separate clear sections in your argument.

Further reading

C. Nicolson, 'Edwardian England and the Coming of the First World War' in A. O'Day (ed.), *The Edwardian Age: Conflict and Stability 1900–1914* (Macmillan, 1979) – a useful chapter which, together with Chamberlain below, provides most of the detail needed.

M. E. Chamberlain, *'Pax Britannica': British Foreign Policy, 1789–1914* (Addison Wesley Longman, 1988). Chapter 11 surveys British diplomacy immediately before the First World War.

R. Henig, *The Origins of the First World War*, Lancaster Pamphlet (Routledge, 2nd edition, 1993) – a brief and accessible study, conerned mostly with European diplomacy but very useful in showing how Britain's concerns fitted into the growing international crisis.

P. Kennedy (ed.), *The War Plans of the Great Powers, 1880–1914* (Allen and Unwin, 1979) – a set of well-argued case studies.

P. Kennedy, *The Rise of Anglo-German Antagonism, 1860–1914* (Allen and Unwin, 1980) – a research study in some depth.

Z. Steiner, *Britain and the Origins of the First World War* (Macmillan, 1977).

K. M. Wilson, *The Policy of Entente: the Determination of Foreign Policy, 1904–14* (Cambridge University Press, 1985).

K. M. Wilson, (ed.) *Decisions for War, 1914* (University College London Press, 1995) – a stimulating new collection of essays which explain strategy.

K. G. Robbins, *Sir Edward Grey* (Cassell, 1971) – a good biography of one of Britain's best known foreign secretaries.

P. Kennedy, 'Idealists and Realists: British Views of Germany, 1864–1939', *Transactions of the Royal Historical Society*, 1975.

Index

KEY TERMS

PROFILES

MAIN INDEX

Index